PARADOXES OF RATIONALITY AND COOPERATION

PARADOXES OF RATIONALITY AND COOPERATION

Prisoner's Dilemma and Newcomb's Problem

Edited by
Richmond Campbell and Lanning Sowden

THE UNIVERSITY OF BRITISH COLUMBIA PRESS
VANCOUVER 1985

PARADOXES OF RATIONALITY AND COOPERATION
PRISONER'S DILEMMA AND NEWCOMB'S PROBLEM

BC
185
P37
1985

Canadian Cataloguing in Publication Data

Main entry under title:
Paradoxes of rationality and cooperation

Bibliography: p. 358
ISBN 0-7748-0215-4

1. Dilemma.   2. Prisoner's dilemma
game.   3. Newcomb, William A.   4. Choice
(Psychology)   5. Cooperativeness.
I. Campbell, Richmond.   II. Sowden, Lanning, 1952–
BC185.P37 1985   166   C85-091216-4

International Standard Book Number 0-7748-0215-4
Printed in Canada

13644811

8-24-90
Av

This book is dedicated to David Braybrooke whose life and work reflect an abiding conviction that the human enterprise is a cooperative venture.

Contents

Preface

The papers of this volume concern issues of enduring philosophical interest: What is it for an individual to make a rational decision? What is the relationship between morality and rationality? How is cooperative action for mutual benefit possible? Among philosophers (and others) these issues have received a fillip in recent years, at least in part because attempts have been made to view the issues from a decision theoretic and game theoretic standpoint – a standpoint which puts these issues in a different and new light, making possible original and important answers to those issues. From these derive the focus of attention in these collected papers on Newcomb's Problem and the Prisoner's Dilemma.

We have tried in this volume to get a good mix of classic papers and new papers and of the technical and more readily accessible. Our idea is to provide a collection of papers which gives a statement of the original positions and some idea of how the debate has developed and what new directions it might pursue. We trust that the volume will be of interest to those who are already steeped in the literature and that it will also be a help to those who are not so well-informed. It was particularly with these latter people in mind that we planned the Introduction. It certainly does not cover all the issues involved; nor do we believe that it offers a definitive treatment of the issues it *does* discuss. Nonetheless, it should provide sufficient background for understanding the papers in this volume and appreciating the nature of the dialectic that exists between them.

We owe thanks to our contributors for permission to reprint previously published papers and/or for contributing new papers to this volume. By their willingness to cooperate in the meeting of rather severe deadlines, they made our task very much easier. We also thank the various original publishers who are individually acknowledged on the first page of each reprinted essay. A grant from Dalhousie University enabled us to embark on the project. We were also greatly aided by the Council for Philosophical Studies, Public Choice Institute at Dalhousie University, in providing us with the opportunity to hold discussions with various of our contributors. In this regard we are very grateful for the encouragement and cooperation received from the Chairperson of the Planning Committee for the Institute, Professor Edward F. McClennen. Finally, we thank Judith Fox, Margaret Odell, and Ted Zenzinger for their expert secretarial assistance.

R.C. Halifax, Canada
L.S. Melbourne, Australia

I

INTRODUCTION

1

Background for the Uninitiated

RICHMOND CAMPBELL

Paradoxes are intrinsically fascinating. They are also distinctively philo-sophical because they arise from problems implicit in the general presuppo-sitions of thought and action. Although the problems there may prove ultimately to be insoluble, insight into the origin of paradox can be valued as part of the Socratic ideal of self-knowledge. But this motivation only partly explains the deep attraction of the Prisoner's Dilemma and New-comb's Problem. Their significance lies in the profound problems that they uncover. Quite simply, these paradoxes cast in doubt our understanding of rationality and, in the case of the Prisoner's Dilemma, suggest that it is im-possible for rational creatures to cooperate. Thus, they bear directly on fun-damental issues in ethics and political philosophy and threaten the founda-tions of the social sciences. It is the scope of these consequences that ex-plains why these paradoxes have drawn so much attention and why they command a central place in philosophical discussion.

The interdisciplinary character of the Prisoner's Dilemma has been evi-dent from the beginning. The problem was first formulated about 1950 by a social psychologist, Merrill M. Flood, and an economist, Melvin Dresher. They were devising an experiment to test a theorem in the theory of games, a mathematical theory developed in the early forties by John von Neumann and Oskar Morgenstern to study economic behavior. Later formalized by a game theorist, Albert W. Tucker, the dilemma has been intensively studied outside of philosophy, for example, by psychologists (Rapoport and Chammah, 1965; Rapoport, 1974), political scientists (Taylor, 1976; Hardin, 1982a; Axelrod, 1984), and evolutionary theorists (Trivers, 1973; Dawkins, 1976; Axelrod and Hamilton, 1981a). The response has been different for Newcomb's Problem. This paradox has concerned philosophers primarily. In fact, although it was invented in the early sixties by a physicist, William Newcomb, it was first published by a philosopher, Robert Nozick, in 1969. The explanation of the asymmetry is probably that in its standard form the paradox presents a purely hypothetical dilemma whose practical relevance is not immediately apparent. But this difference is misleading. The literature reflects a growing consensus that the Prisoner's Dilemma is, in one of its basic forms, a special case of Newcomb's Problem. If that is so, the deep problems for decision theory that are posed by Newcomb's Problem must be implicit in the Prisoner's Dilemma as well, and the interdisciplinary significance of the latter should extend to the former.

The essays that follow are organized around a number of basic theoretical issues. The primary goal in this introduction is to explain what these issues are and to provide enough background information so that the previously uninitiated reader can pick up the discussion at almost any point. To this end the paradoxes are introduced in their elementary versions in some detail, without presupposing previous acquaintance with game theory or decision theory. In the course of this exposition the early moves in the discussion of the paradoxes are analyzed as well as the general structure of the ensuing debate. Against this background the reader will be able to place the present papers in perspective and to understand the order in which they are presented.

WHAT IS THE PRISONER'S DILEMMA?

Tucker's example explains the origin of the name. Imagine that you and an accomplice have been charged with having committed a crime and are now prisoners, sitting in separate cells, unable to communicate, and awaiting trial. The prosecutor offers a deal to persuade you to confess: "There is enough circumstantial evidence to convict both of you, so even if you both remain silent you both will be convicted and locked up for a year. But if *you* admit your guilt and help to convict your silent partner, you will go free and he will be put away for ten years. The reverse happens, of course, if he confesses and you remain silent; and if you both confess, then unfortunately you both will get nine years." *Your* dilemma, thus far, can be summarized in the following matrix:

	The other prisoner does *not* confess	The other prisoner *does* confess
You *don't* confess	One year	Ten years
You *do* confess	None	Nine years

FIGURE 1

There are several additional features that form part of the dilemma. First, your only goal in this situation is to get as few years in jail as possible. You are completely indifferent about the fate of your accomplice; you do not care what happens to him one way or the other. You have no moral qualms or any fears about possible revenge. All that matters is reducing *your* sentence. Second, you believe that the prosecutor is telling the truth. Imagine that there are witnesses present who will keep him honest. Third—this is a key assumption for the discussion to follow—you know (from the prosecutor and witnesses present) that the other prisoner faces the very *same* dilemma. Your situations are exactly symmetrical, with respect to information and desires. Finally, each of you knows that you both know all of this; your awareness of your separate dilemmas is fully mutual.

To many persons the solution to the dilemma seems completely obvious, and their reasoning may appear flawless. Either the other fellow is going to confess or he is not. Logically, those are the only possible alternatives. But either way you would do better, that is, get fewer years in jail, choosing to confess rather than choosing not to confess. Hence, if you are rational, you will confess. The same reasoning would seem to apply with equal validity to the other prisoner. If rational, he will also confess. In short, if you both are rational, you will both confess *and both spend nine years in jail!*

Can this conclusion be correct? You could have gotten off with only one year—each of you could have—and you both knew this beforehand. If only you had both kept silent! Preferring one year in jail to nine and knowing that mutual confession would get you nine years instead of one, you both *chose* to confess. How can this choice have been rational?

The reasoning leading to mutual confession may be represented as a deductive argument:

(1) Either the other prisoner will confess or he will not.

(2) If he will confess, then confessing is better for you than not confessing.

(3) If he will not, then (again) confessing is better for you than not confessing.

Therefore: confessing is better for you than not confessing.

Is the conclusion really true? If it is not, then either it is not logically implied by the premises or there is a false premise (or both). But which premise could possibly be false? The content of each premise appears to be built into the terms of the dilemma. Consider premise (2), for example. According to the matrix in Figure 1, if the other prisoner confesses, there are only two possible outcomes: either you get nine years or ten, depending on whether you confess or do not confess, respectively. So in this case confessing is better for you than not confessing. Similar reasoning applies to (3), and (1) appears self-evident. Moreover, the logical form of the argument seems to be impeccable.

(1) *P* or *Q*

(2) If *P,* then *R*

(3) If *Q,* then *R*

Therefore: *R*

How could any argument with this form have true premises and a false conclusion?

Before we consider attempts to answer these questions, it should be noted that the difficulty of the dilemma arises from features of the choice situation that could arise in many other circumstances. Notice first of all that the number of years in jail assigned to each possible outcome does not matter so long as the prisoner's preferences have the same order. Imagine that instead of zero, one, nine, and ten years the jail terms are none, one day, forty years, and forty-five years respectively. The same reasoning proves that each prisoner, if rational, should confess so that both spend forty years in jail instead of a single day. Or, to make the contrast even more bizarre, suppose that the first two possibilities are freedom plus $10,000 and freedom plus $1,000 while the second two are a quick, but painful, death and slow death by torture.

	The other prisoner does *not* confess	The other prisoner *does* confess
You *don't* confess	freedom + $1,000	slow death by torture
You *do* confess	freedom + $10,000	quick but painful death

FIGURE 2

Again, logic seems to compel the conclusion that you should confess. Since the other prisoner faces exactly the same dilemma, the same conclusion would hold for him. If rational, you should both—it seems—choose a quick but painful death rather than go scot-free with $1,000 apiece in your pockets.

At this point it may appear that the dilemma, however tantalizing as a logical puzzle, is too fantastic to have any practical relevance. The prisoner's dilemma story was odd enough in the first version! But is that so? Consider an analogy. Two superpowers sign a nuclear disarmament pact on the shared belief that failure to disarm will result sooner or later in a nuclear holocaust in which each side will be quickly and painfully destroyed, while mutual disarmament will avoid this dreaded outcome. There is a catch..Although the disarmament pact incorporates inspection safeguards, these are far from foolproof. Each side realizes that either could probably secretly rearm, at least to the point where the unarmed nation would be at its mercy and could be forced to make drastic concessions politically and economically. Now, each side regards this vulnerability as a fate worse than mutual destruction, while it regards a position of complete nuclear superiority as ideal. (Each would say that its having complete nuclear superiority is a better guarantee of peace on earth than mutual nuclear disarmament, and each would explain its breaking the agreement as a purely defensive maneuver.) The dilemma, of course, is whether to try to rearm secretly in violation of the disarmament pact.

	The other *adheres* to the agreement	The other *violates* the agreement
You *adhere*	No mutual destruction	A fate worse than mutual destruction
You *violate*	The ideal upshot	Mutual destruction

FIGURE 3

This version of the Prisoner's Dilemma is not much removed from political reality, yet according to the previous reasoning the superpowers ought to violate any such agreement. If the choice situation has this structure, they ought to destroy themselves.

The Prisoner's Dilemma can be exemplified in many familiar contexts. It is not necessary to invoke international politics to feel its force. Immeasurably less important, but poignant nevertheless, would be a power struggle between husband and wife in a deteriorating marriage. The basic ingredients for a Prisoner's Dilemma are simple. The parties to the choice situation must have partly overlapping and partly divergent preferences regarding the possible outcomes. Specifically, both must agree in preferring one of the four possibilities to another but disagree about which is best and which is worst. Moreover, neither can force the other to make one choice rather than the other. So achieving the next best outcome for each, rather than the next worst, demands cooperation and trust. It is hard to imagine a marriage break-up which would not meet these minimum constraints, perhaps in more than one way. And so it is for countless other situations in which parties to a dispute must cooperate at some risk in order to take advantage of the common ground between them.

There are basically two ways in which one might respond to the apparent paradox. One could accept the conclusion (that both prisoners should confess, and so forth) but argue that this is only surprising, not genuinely paradoxical. Or one could deny the conclusion and try to show that its supporting argument is unsound. The following four attempts at a resolution fall into the first category. Later, we will consider the alternative.

(1) *Think of realistic situations.* Despite the claims of the previous section, there remains something very special about the value assumptions built into examples of the Prisoner's Dilemma. It is assumed, for instance, that the prisoners do not care at all about each other, that they are not worried about possible future recriminations, that they place no value on cooperation and trust as such, that no ethical considerations enter into their deliberation at all—in short, that they care *only* about the length of their own jail term and that in this respect their values are precisely *identical*. But surely these assumptions are unrealistic. The conclusion that both prisoners, if rational, will confess is surprising only because we forget how fantastically restrictive these assumptions are.

The charge correctly observes that these standard assumptions are restrictive. But it is not telling, for the paradox remains in force when these restrictions are relaxed. All that we need to assume regarding the preferences of the parties is that they have a certain order. It does not matter what accounts for the order; the factors that determine the order can be as diverse and subtle as you please. Moreover, the degree of value assigned to each outcome need not be regarded as having a certain size relative to the value of the other outcomes (for example, nine years in jail being nine times worse than one year); nor need the degree of value be comparable between persons (for example, your nine years in jail being as bad for you as nine years would be for the other prisoner). Even the choices can be different. These points are worth emphasizing.

	The Other Person Does:	
	Y	*Not-y*
X	B	D
You do: *Not-x*	A	C

FIGURE 4

Actions *X* and *Y* may be entirely different. The value of outcome *B* to you may be in no way comparable to the value of *B* to the other person. One could even suppose that the question of comparing values between persons is not intelligible. It may also be impossible to say how much better *B* is for the other person than *C* is. All that we need to assume is that you *rank* the outcomes from best to worst *A - B - C - D* and the other person ranks them *D - B - C - A*. Such a minimum restriction is hardly unrealistic.

Consider an economic transaction in which you agree to provide money in exchange for a car. Suppose, however, that the delivery of each takes time. The present owner will not know that he is getting his money until after he has shipped the car; you will not know that you are getting the car until the money is sent. But you need the car more than the money, and he needs the money more than the car. Will the transaction take place?

	He *sends* the car	He *keeps* the car
You *send* the money	B	D
You keep the money	A	C

FIGURE 5

Although both of you prefer outcome *B* to *C,* you will, by the previous reasoning, produce outcome *C*. There will be no transaction! Notice that this reasoning makes no assumptions about your relative interests in cars or money. He may like cars less than you do and like money more. The paradox depends only on how each of you ranks the value of the outcomes for yourselves.

(2) *Communicate first, then cooperate.* The original story contains another kind of restriction—that the prisoners are unable to communicate with each other. Everyone knows that cooperation is the outcome of mutual agreement or understanding, not dumb luck. Why should it be surprising, let alone paradoxical, that the prisoners fail to promote their mutual preferences through cooperation when they have no opportunity to communicate their intentions?

Again the objection makes a correct observation without dissolving the paradox. Normally, cooperation does require communication. The reason for denying the prisoners the opportunity to communicate is to emphasize that their choices are causally independent. Obviously one prisoner's intending to remain silent cannot possibly cause the other to have a similar intention if the other is ignorant of this intention. The assumption of non-communication is not, however, essential to the Prisoner's Dilemma. Communication can be added, but it will not make any difference provided that the preference ordering over the possible outcomes remains the same for each person and that each is free to choose contrary to the other's intention. Each may say to the other, "I will remain silent if you say that you will too," but the dilemma remains unchanged so long as each is free to do otherwise and their preferences among the outcomes are from best to worst *A - B - C - D* for one and *D - B - C - A* for the other (see Figure 4). Each would have what appears to be a logically decisive reason to act contrary to the intention that was communicated.

One might suppose that there could be provisions for enforcing agreements, say, special penalties attached to violating an agreement and that these would change the prisoners' preferences. But that supposition would alter the structure of the decision problem. We are assuming that each party is interested only in bringing about the most preferable outcome that he can possibly manage and that his preferences are exactly as given. Under this assumption no "agreement" to cooperate would appear to make any difference.

(3) *Do not be an egoist.* Clearly the preference orderings are crucial, but by the same token neither prisoner is expected to act on the basis of their joint preferences. Instead, each is expected to act as an egoist. It should not be too surprising then that they are led to make choices that defeat their ends in a situation which demands cooperation. The problem is with egoism, not rationality.

This response, at least in its present formulation, founders on a misunderstanding. The most natural interpretation of "egoist" in this context is that it refers to someone who is primarily, if not exclusively, concerned with personal benefit. Thus, the prisoner who cares only about how long he will be in jail is an egoist. But it is clear that Prisoner's Dilemmas need not be confined to egoists in this sense. It is possible to construct examples in which each person in the choice situation is very altruistic. All that is required of each person's preferences among the outcomes, it will be recalled, is that a certain ordering obtains. The motivation behind the ordering can be selfish or unselfish or a mixture of both. For you, the ordering from best to worst may be *A - B - C - D* in Figure 4 because *A* is, you may believe, in the best interest of everyone affected by the outcome. *B* is everyone's second best interest, and so on. The other person, however, may believe that *D* is best for everyone and *A* worst for everyone, while agreeing with you about *B* and *C*. Think of the disarmament example this way with preferences ordered according to political ideals. The Prisoner's Dilemma presupposes a *divergence in preferences* but not selfishness or indifference towards others.

(4) *Blame Rationality.* A strong temptation may arise to conclude that there is no unique rational solution to the dilemma. Rather, rationality can pull us in either direction: toward the cooperative solution or toward the non-cooperative. The surprise lies in the discovery that rationality is not univocal in the circumstances of the Prisoner's Dilemma. Understanding

this fact does not contradict the conclusion of the original argument; it only removes our sense of confusion.

This response will not be convincing without an account of how our conception of rationality can generate conflicting points of view. This is one of the issues addressed in the essays to follow. David Gauthier, for example, compares two conflicting views of rationality as "utility maximization" and argues that "constrained maximization" is superior to its alternative. But can we assume from the start that there is no unique rational solution? To assume that there is none simply to avoid the paradoxical consequence would be *ad hoc* and hence would not constitute a resolution of the problem. Moreover, Lawrence H. Davis gives an argument that implies the existence of a unique rational solution. Suppose that none exists. Then, on the assumption that both prisoners know that they are rational, neither would have any reason to expect that they will choose the same option, despite the fact that the structure of the choice situation is the same for both. But then it would be rational to confess and not rational not to confess! This implication contradicts the original supposition. Therefore, there is a unique solution. (See Davis's first essay, pp. 45-59.) The advice to blame rationality may prove in the end to be a fruitful suggestion, but it does not itself dissolve the paradox.

MORAL REASONS AND COLLECTIVE ACTION

Before pursuing the analysis further let us stand back and look at the paradox from a different perspective. We have noted that the parties to the dilemma can communicate with each other. Suppose then that they have *promised* to cooperate with each other. Take the example of purchasing a car (Figure 5) and imagine that each party has agreed to fulfill his end of the bargain (send the money, send the car). In those circumstances each person has a *moral* obligation to do what he has agreed to do. To do otherwise would be morally wrong—unless the example has some special exonerating feature that was not mentioned. Suppose it does not. Now let us ask: Which is the rational course of action? The previous reasoning implies that the rational choice is to break the agreement. It appears that the rational choice and the moral choice conflict.

This example raises an issue basic to moral philosophy: How rational are the demands of morality? The disarmament pact (Figure 3) is another example that invites the same question; others are easy to construct. It may be objected, however, that the examples fail to allow for the effect that promising would have on the agents' preferences among the outcomes. Normally, people do not want to break promises. Why suppose then that the choice situation would remain a Prisoner's Dilemma once the parties have agreed to cooperate? Some philosophers have thought that a rational person has an intrinsic interest in doing what is morally right. Preferring outcomes in which their promises are kept, such people will not face a Prisoner's Dilemma when they have agreed to cooperate.

There can be no doubt that people's preferences are affected by their moral beliefs, and thus they would sometimes not be in a Prisoner's Dilemma. But the objection is not to the point. What is at issue is whether rational people would have any extrinsic motivation to be moral when they *are* in a Prisoner's Dilemma. We can imagine that in the auto transaction example pictured in Figure 5, the preference orderings form the structure of a Prisoner's Dilemma, even though the parties have agreed to cooperate. (Imagine that making this agreement has made the cooperative outcome more attractive but has not, on balance, changed the *order* of their preferences.) Presumably each still might acknowledge that he has a moral obligation to keep his agreement. The question is whether it is rational for either to do so given his preferences. Apparently not; for each individual, as a rational individual, seems to have a compelling reason to break the agreement given his preferences.

But let us consider another characterization of moral choice. It has sometimes been claimed that moral choice essentially consists of an individual choosing rationally under certain constraints. These constraints are meant to ensure that the individual's choice should have features which satisfy the minimal requirements for a choice to be properly regarded as a moral choice (as opposed to an immoral choice). Plausibly, a minimal requirement is that an individual choice should be *impartial.* And this requirement seems to be met by insisting that an individual choose as if he had an equal probability of being any individual, so in the Prisoner's Dilemma the individual would choose supposing he had an equal chance of being either "prisoner." So, obviously, choosing under this constraint, an individual would consider the average payoff for each outcome and choose to cooperate. (One could say that the individual chooses as an "average" utilitarian.) But the problem still remains since no independent reason why individuals should choose impartially in the Prisoner's Dilemma has been provided. To repeat, each individual seems to have an excellent reason *not* to choose impartially given his preferences.

It is possible to state the conflict between morality and rationality more generally. Let us consider not just the obligation to keep promises but moral obligations of all kinds, and let us construe "personal preference" to mean any preference that is not morally motivated. Most people would concede that there is some degree of conflict between moral demands and those of personal preference. At the same time, most would not deny that there is a profound connection between morality and the satisfaction of personal preferences. It is obvious that virtually everyone is better off from the standpoint of their personal preferences living in a society in which moral demands are generally respected than they would be living in an amoral society in which moral motivation has no role to play in social interactions. From this standpoint virtually everyone would be rational to choose to live in a society in which moral motives constrained everyone's choices rather than in a society in which no one's choices were constrained, although, of course, everyone would prefer a society in which everyone else's choices were so constrained but his were not.

We now have all the ingredients of a Prisoner's Dilemma except that instead of merely two people involved in the decision-making there are as many people as there are members of society. We have what is called an *n-person* or *large scale* Prisoner's Dilemma. As might be expected, this form of the paradox involves further complications. Here an elementary version is presented that highlights the structural similarities to the previous examples. We begin with several analogies. Imagine a number of people undertaking a cooperative enterprise, such as citizens voting for a certain candidate in an election, union members walking off the job, or people generally cutting back in consumption in order to conserve certain dwindling sources of energy. Let us label the cooperative act *C* and its opposite, defecting from the cooperative plan, *D*. We shall assume that 100 percent cooperation is not needed in order to effect the desired result, electing the favored candidate, achieving an effective strike, or avoiding an energy shortage. This assumption permits the existence of "free riders," those who share the benefits of cooperation without sharing the burdens. Suppose, finally, that the number of people involved is so large that the probability is very small that any given person's choice will make a difference between achieving the cooperative effect or not achieving it. The choice matrix would look like this:

	Enough others do *C*	*Not* enough others do *C*
Cooperate *C*	I	K
Defect *D*	H	J

FIGURE 6

Since each person's preference ordering from best to worst is presumably *H-I-J-K* and their actions are (for the most part) causally independent of each other, they should, by our previous reasoning again, choose *D*. But, of course, if every person involved in the cooperative effort reasoned in this way the outcome would be *J*. Not enough people would cooperate to achieve the desired result. Paradoxically the would-be cooperators, by acting rationally, would in fact defeat their common end.

Extending this reasoning to the case of moral motivation is not completely straightforward. For one thing, it is hard to point to any single desired end that people want when they act for moral reasons, unless it is simply to do what is morally right. To construct a parallel situation, we have to think of choosing not a single action but a general pattern of behavior. Suppose that it were possible to choose the moral quality of one's character so that by choosing a certain way one would be determining how one would act in a great variety of situations. Most of these situations one could not anticipate in any detail. One would be choosing the extent to which moral motivation would play a role in one's life, without knowing exactly what the consequences would be. It would be reasonably clear, however, that the outcome of collective cooperation in this case would be a significant improvement in everyone's quality of life over what it would be if no one were ever morally motivated. Such an outcome would be preferable, in other words, from everyone's personal perspective, even allowing for the burdens of cooperation. We can assume, moreover, that in order for the mutually preferred collective effect to obtain it is necessary only that enough people are morally motivated to a high enough degree and that one's own contribution in this respect is very unlikely to make the difference. The choice of whether to be morally motivated now assumes the structure of an *n-person* Prisoner's Dilemma.

	Enough others are moral	*Not* enough are moral
To be *moral C*	*I*	*K*
Not to be moral *D*	*H*	*J*

FIGURE 7

Again the problem of rational cooperation presents itself. Reason would appear to tell us not to be moral and thus to sacrifice the benefits of collective cooperation.

THE ARGUMENT FROM SYMMETRY

It is time to consider whether the original argument leading to this paradoxical conclusion is unsound. As a first step let us look at an argument for the opposite conclusion based on the symmetry of the decision problem in the Prisoner's Dilemma. (A careful presentation and defense of this reasoning will be found in Davis's essays below.) For simplicity we shall apply the reasoning to the original two-person dilemma in which both parties know that their situations are symmetrical. We shall assume, moreover, that they know that they are rational. Since each knows that the ordering of preferences for each person is precisely symmetrical and that both are completely rational, each can expect that the other will do whatever he does. If he confesses, the other would too; if he does not, neither would the other. This conclusion would not follow if there were not a unique rational solution to the decision problem, but we have already observed how one could plausibly argue that there is. In effect, then, there are only two real possibilities: either both will confess or both will not. From each person's standpoint the latter is preferable to the former. Hence, each (if truly rational) will choose *not* to confess. For completely rational agents mutual cooperation is the solution to the Prisoner's Dilemma.

Is the apparent paradox dissolved? It is not enough, of course, to provide an argument that rational persons will cooperate—even a very good argument—for we also have a very good argument for exactly the opposite conclusion. Without an understanding of why one or the other of these arguments is defective, we are left with contradictory conclusions. Hardly a resolution of the paradox!

Recall the original argument for mutual defection:

(1) Either the other prisoner will confess or he will not.

(2) If he will, confessing is better than not confessing.

(3) If he will not, confessing is better than not confessing.

Therefore: confessing is better than not confessing.

The conclusion can have no possible practical relevance unless confessing is a possible option. This point is so obvious that it may seem not worth mentioning. Naturally, we assume that confessing is a real possibility for each prisoner. At the risk of pedantry we might write this presupposition into the conclusion:

Therefore: confessing is possible and is better than not confessing.

In order that the argument be valid, we need to interpret the consequent clauses of premises (2) and (3) similarly. For example, (3) becomes:

(3*) If the other prisoner will not confess, confessing is (still) possible (for you) and is better than not confessing.

Notice, however, that this premise is false if the argument just made for mutual cooperation is sound. By that argument there are just two possibilities—mutual confession and mutual non-confession. If that is correct, then if the other prisoner will not confess, it will not be possible for you to do something different. The third premise, stated explicitly, would be false, and the argument for mutual non-cooperation would prove unsound.

DOMINANCE AND INDEPENDENCE

Unfortunately, there are some serious objections to the argument from symmetry — at least as it has been presented here. One problem is the assumption that both agents are completely rational. Realistically, how could any person in a Prisoner's Dilemma ever be *sure* that this assumption is true? It may seem that one could be sure only if one knew that the "other" party was oneself. (On this point see: Hardin, 1982a, p. 151ff; Lewis's essay, and Davis's second essay.) But even granting that assumption, one could raise other difficult questions. We have already alluded to the issue of whether there is a unique rational solution to the dilemma. Positions on this issue are developed in the essays to follow. In this section we shall introduce another line of objection, one that will lead us eventually to Newcomb's Problem.

In order to explain this objection it will be helpful to introduce the notion of dominance. In the Prisoner's Dilemma there are four possible outcomes, one pair of outcomes corresponding to each possible choice that "the other prisoner" might make. These pairs form columns in the choice matrix. Thus in Figure 4 the pairs are *A, B* and *C, D.*

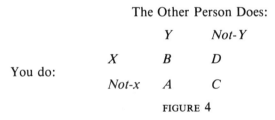

FIGURE 4

Since the first prisoner's preferences are *A* over *B* and *C* over *D,* the non-cooperative choice (confessing in the original story) is said to *dominate* its alternative. In other words, the outcome corresponding to non-cooperation by the first prisoner is superior (according to that prisoner) to the outcome corresponding to cooperation, for each column, or pair of possible outcomes, corresponding to the other party's choice.

Weak dominance may be distinguished from strong dominance. If the outcome of a certain choice is never inferior to the outcome of the other choice for all the possible pairs of outcomes (in these examples there are only two) and in at least one case, though not in all, the outcome of that choice is superior, then that choice weakly dominates its alternative; if it is always superior, it strongly dominates. In every Prisoner's Dilemma non-cooperation strongly dominates cooperation. This result holds, of course, for both prisoners, though the relevant pairs of outcomes would form rows in the choice matrix when viewed from the standpoint of the other prisoner.

Let us suppose, for the sake of argument, that the choice of the other prisoner is completely beyond your control. He will decide whatever he will decide, whether or not you choose to confess. Given this independence between your choice and his, you would be deciding (in effect) between outcomes in a *single* column in the choice matrix, corresponding to his decision. In that circumstance, surely it would be rational to take the dominant action, to confess, since a better outcome would result whichever column of possibilities was determined by the other person's choice. This reasoning, in essence, is the basis of the original argument for non-cooperation. We have simply made explicit the assumption of independence.

Suppose, on the other hand, that the choices are not independent but that his decision depends on yours. Then you would be deciding (in effect) between two outcomes in two distinct columns. In that circumstance it would be absurd to choose the dominant action just because it is dominant. An example (from Bar-Hillel and Margalit, 1972) makes this clear. Suppose that Israel must decide whether to withdraw from its occupied territories and Egypt must decide whether to declare war on Israel.

		Egypt	
		Peace	*War*
	Withdraw	second	fourth
Israel			
	Remain	first	third
		Column 1	Column 2

FIGURE 8

Assume that Israel's preferences regarding the possible outcomes are as indicated, so that remaining in the occupied territories strongly dominates withdrawing from them. If Egypt's decision were entirely beyond Israel's influence, then Israel would be, in effect, either deciding between the first and second outcomes in Column 1 or deciding between the third and fourth outcomes in Column 2. Obviously, it should choose the dominant course of action and remain in the occupied territories. But if, more realistically, we assume that to withdraw is likely to be conducive to peace, whereas to remain is likely to cause war, then the relevant comparison is across the columns between the second and third outcomes which are in different columns. In that case the rational choice would be to withdraw. The dominant action would *not* be rational because choosing it would likely cause an outcome worse than the alternative would cause.

We are now in a position to state the objection to the argument from symmetry. According to that argument the agents' choices are so interdependent that there are only two possible outcomes: mutual cooperation and mutual non-cooperation. If that were so, the choice situation would be analogous to the decision problem facing Israel, and dominance reasoning would be inappropriate. But Prisoner's Dilemmas are, by definition, choice situations in which the choices of the respective parties are *independent*. Neither agent can causally influence the choice of the other. Thus dominance reasoning would be appropriate, and non-cooperation would be the only rational action. Moreover, since there would be four possible outcomes (not two), premise (3*) cited in the previous section would be *justified*.

MAXIMIZING EXPECTED UTILITY

The objection is not conclusive. It assumes that the only relevant kind of dependence is causal, but that assumption can be questioned. Consider the following example. Suppose that you are testing the responses of rats and you find that when tested *separately* the animals invariably respond the same way (say, take the same path to food when given the same options). It is *not* reasonable to suppose in these circumstances that the response of one rat has any causal influence on the response of another rat, even though it would be reasonable to expect that the next rat will respond in the same way. In other words, although a certain response in one rat obviously does not cause the same response in another, the probability that the second rat will respond similarly, given the response of the first rat, is very high. We can assume, moreover, that the unconditional probability that the second rat will respond in just the way it does is not very high; it would be very low.

Let us express this *probabilistic* dependence in general terms. We shall say that the truth of proposition p is probabilistically dependent on the truth of proposition q just in case the probability of the truth of p, conditional on the assumption that q is true, is *not* equal to the probability of the truth of p unconditionally. We shall say that the truth of p is completely dependent on the truth of q just in case the probability that p is true, conditional on the assumption that q is true, is one and is different from the unconditional probability of p. In symbols:

$$pr(p/q) = 1 \qquad pr(p/q) \neq pr(p)$$

(The term "complete" is misleading, since properly speaking the *difference* between $pr(p/q)$ and $pr(p)$ measures the degree of dependence of p on q. We shall ignore this nicety for ease of exposition.) As earlier, we can let "*C*" and "*D*" stand for cooperation and non-cooperation (defection), respectively, using lower case letters to represent the choices of the second agent. Thus "$pr(c/C)$" reads: the probability that the other agent cooperates conditional on the assumption that the first cooperates. The probabilistic dependence of c on C would be expressed:

$$pr(c/C) \neq pr(c)$$

or equivalently:

$$pr(c/C) \neq pr(c/D)$$

and vice versa for the dependence of C on c. In the argument from symmetry, the assumption of *complete* dependence would be represented by the following equations:

$$pr(c/C) = pr(d/D) = pr(C/c) = pr(D/d) = 1$$
$$pr(c/D) = pr(d/C) = pr(C/d) = pr(D/c) = 0$$

These equations do not imply any direct causal relation between the agents' choices. Instead, they state a complete probabilistic dependence, and that is all the argument from symmetry apparently requires. There may be *less* than complete dependence. In that case, the conditional probabilities in the top equations would be less than one and those in the bottom equations would be greater than zero.

Let us now consider how a rational agent might use these equations to arrive at a decision in the Prisoner's Dilemma. It is often suggested that a rational agent will choose that action which has the highest conditional expected utility or, more briefly, that a rational agent will *maximize expected utility*. The conditional expected utility of an action is a weighted average of the values of the outcomes that could result if the action were chosen. The weights are conditional probabilities of the kind just considered. (For a comprehensive introduction to this approach, see Jeffrey, 1983.) Let us look carefully at the application of this approach in the present case.

Although previously we have assumed only that the preferences of each agent have a certain ordering, we must now assume that the agents can assign *numerical* values to the outcomes of their actions to indicate the relative strength of the desirability of each outcome for each of them. In symbols, $V(D,c)$ would be a number reflecting how much the first agent values the outcome in which he defects and the other agent cooperates; $v(D,c)$ would be the numerical value of that outcome for the other agent. (We need not assume that these values are comparable between persons, but we are assuming that a cardinal measure can be assigned to the desirability of outcomes for a single person.) The values of the outcomes are represented in Figure 9 with the values of the agent whose actions are on the left printed to the left of the other agent's values.

	c	d
C	$V(C,c), v(C,c)$	$V(C,d), v(C,d)$
D	$V(D,c), v(D,c)$	$V(D,d), v(D,d)$

FIGURE 9

On the assumption that these values can be assigned, the conditional expected utilities for the four actions would be as follows:

$$E(C) = V(C,c)\,pr(c/C) + V(C,d)\,pr(d/C)$$
$$E(D) = V(D,c)\,pr(c/D) + V(D,d)\,pr(d/D)$$
$$E(c) = v(C,c)\,pr(C/c) + v(D,c)\,pr(D/c)$$
$$E(d) = v(C,d)\,pr(C/d) + v(D,d)\,pr(D/d)$$

Now consider the special case where there is *complete* probabilistic dependence;

$$pr(c/C) = pr(d/D) = pr(C/c) = pr(D/d) = 1$$
$$pr(c/D) = pr(d/C) = pr(C/d) = pr(D/c) = 0$$

If we substitute these probability numbers, these expected utilities become:

$$E(C) = V(C,c) \qquad E(c) = v(C,c)$$
$$E(D) = V(D,d) \qquad E(d) = v(D,d)$$

But we already know from the agents' preference orderings that $V(C,c) > V(D,d)$ and $v(C,c) > v(D,d)$. Hence, on the assumption that the probability numbers are as given, $E(C) > E(D)$ and $E(c) > E(d)$, and the cooperative choice maximizes conditional expected utility for each agent. If rational, both agents would cooperate according to this criterion of rationality.

The similarity of *this* argument to the argument from *symmetry* should be clear. The assumption of complete dependence that is captured in the above set of probability equations implies that a comparison of conditional expected utilities reduces to a comparison of the values of the second and third best outcomes. The dependence assumption implies, in short, that *only* these outcomes are expected and thus their value alone determines which choice is rational.

A word of caution is in order. It is possible to construct a symmetry argument without any reference to probability or maximizing expected utility. Davis does in his essay. Though step (4) in his version is analogous to the assumption of complete dependence, one should not assume that they are identical.

Suppose, however, that the dependence is *less than complete* so that the conditional probabilities equal, say, 0.9 instead of one.

$$pr(c/C) = pr(d/D) = pr(C/c) = pr(D/d) = 0.9$$
$$pr(c/D) = pr(d/C) = pr(C/d) = pr(D/c) = 0.1$$

For the purposes of illustration, imagine that the numerical values of the outcomes are equal to minus the number of years in jail in the original story. Then the expected utilities would be:

$$E(C) = (-1)(0.9) + (-10)(0.1) = -1.9$$
$$E(D) = (0)(0.1) + (-9)(0.9) = -8.1$$
$$E(c) = (-1)(0.9) + (-10)(0.1) = -1.9$$
$$E(d) = (0)(0.1) + (-9)(0.9) = -8.1$$

Cooperation remains the choice that maximizes expected utility. That would be so in this example even if the degree of dependence were a good deal less. So, even if there is less than complete dependence (contrary to the presupposition of the argument from symmetry), we can have a fully problematic instance of the Prisoner's Dilemma. Here we seem to have a good argument that employs the idea that one should maximize expected utility, which will recommend a choice *proscribed* by what looks like another perfectly good argument which employs the idea that one should choose the dominant alternative.

NEWCOMB'S PROBLEM

We now have two methods of reasoning which lead to opposite conclusions. Dominance reasoning recommends non-cooperation as the only rational choice in the circumstances. Maximizing expected utility recommends cooperation. How can we explain this conflict? Consider first some preliminary points. It is generally agreed that if there is causal dependence, then dominance reasoning is not appropriate. If, on the other hand, the actions of the agents are probabilistically independent, both methods of reasoning would lead to the same result: non-cooperation.

A brief digression should make this last point clear. To claim that the agent's actions are probabilistically independent is to say that the probability of the other agent's action would be the same whether we take this probability to be conditional on the first agent's cooperation or on his non-cooperation. Thus, we have the following identities:

$$pr(c/C) = pr(c/D) = x$$
$$pr(d/C) = pr(d/D) = 1-x$$
$$pr(C/c) = pr(C/d) = y$$
$$pr(D/c) = pr(D/d) = 1-y$$

Entering these quantities into the calculation of expected utility (using the equations given just below Figure 9) yields:

$$E(C) = V(C,c)x + V(C,d)(1-x)$$
$$E(D) = V(D,c)x + V(D,d)(1-x)$$
$$E(c) = v(C,c)y + v(D,c)(1-y)$$
$$E(d) = v(C,d)y + v(D,d)(1-y)$$

Now, D strongly dominates C and d strongly dominates c if, and only if, the following inequalities obtain:

$$V(D,c) > V(C,c) \qquad\qquad V(D,d) > V(C,d)$$
$$v(C,d) > v(C,c) \qquad\qquad v(D,d) > v(D,c)$$

But it is obvious that if these inequalities hold, then $E(D) > E(C)$ and $E(d) > E(c)$. In sum, if the choices in the Prisoner's Dilemma are assumed to be probabilistically independent, the dominant action and the action which maximizes expected utility will be the same: namely, the non-cooperative action.

Conflict arises when the actions are considered to be *causally independent* but *probabilistically dependent*. Then dominance reasoning and utility maximization pull in opposite directions. An example invented by William Newcomb dramatizes the difference. Suppose that you have two options: (*C*) to take the contents of an opaque box in front of you or (*D*) to take the contents of the opaque box *plus* the contents of another box which is transparent and obviously contains $1,000 in cash. Since you cannot see the contents of the opaque box, choosing it alone may result in getting nothing. (You might think of "*C*" as short for "chancy choice" and "*D*" for "double box choice.") In the opaque box is either one million or nothing, depending on whether a certain being, called the Predictor, has or has not placed $1,000,000 there *prior* to the time at which you are to make your decision. You know that the Predictor will have placed $1,000,000 there if, and only if, the Predictor has predicted that you will choose the opaque box alone. (The circumstance of its predicting *C* is labelled *c;* that of its predicting *D* is labelled *d*.) You know, moreover, that the Predictor is almost 100 per cent reliable. Imagine that evidence to confirm this reliability is enormous, and the Predictor has done a detailed study of your personality and past behavior. You are practically certain that the Predictor will be right this time. If you choose *C,* then almost certainly the Predictor will have predicted this, that is, *c* will obtain; likewise for *D* and *d*. Which option is it rational for you to choose?

	c	d
C	$1M	$0
D	$1M + $1,000	$1,000

FIGURE 10

The pull in the direction of dominance reasoning is virtually irresistible for many people. A natural explanation for the attraction is that the example intensifies any intuitive connection that might be felt to exist between causal independence and dominance. At the moment of choice the million dollars is *already* contained in the opaque box, or else nothing is there and nothing will be there when the box is opened. Your choosing C will not make it pop into existence if it is not there already; your choosing D will not make it disappear if it is already there. Which is the case is entirely beyond your present control, assuming it does not extend to altering the past, so you might as well take both boxes. To ignore dominance in this context would be like thinking that at the moment of choice circumstances c and d were now in your control, as if you could change the past.

So where is the opposite pull? Suppose that we take seriously the stipulation that the relevant conditional probabilities are high. For the purposes of illustration, let the probabilities be:

$$pr(c/C) = pr(d/D) = .99$$
$$pr(c/D) = pr(d/C) = .01$$

This means that we can expect that people who *do not* choose the dominant action will (almost always) get rich. And getting rich, we have been assuming, is what everybody wants. Imagine two large groups of people individually facing the Predictor. Assume that for everyone in both groups the values of the outcomes in Newcomb's Problem are proportional to the amounts of money that would be received. The two-boxers are people who invariably choose the dominant action when causal independence obtains. They think that it is rational to do so. The one-boxers, who think that they are rational, always maximize expected utility. For the problem at hand their calculations would be:

$$E(C) = (1,000,000)(.99) + (0)(.01) = 999,000$$
$$E(D) = (1,001,000)(.01) + (1,000)(.99) = 11,000$$

If we take the conditional probabilities seriously enough to let them form our expectations, we would have to expect that the one-boxers are going to be much, much better off on average. Do we really want to say that they are mixed-up about what makes an action rational?

In sum, Newcomb's Problem presents a conflict between dominance reasoning and expected utility reasoning, both of which seem to have great intuitive appeal. Newcomb's Problem exemplifies this conflict since the Predictor's choice is probabilistically dependent upon the agent's choice but at the same time causally independent of it. A parallel situation obtains in the Prisoner's Dilemma when there is sufficient probabilistic dependence between the agent's choices. We need to be careful here. Although causal independence is always assumed, Sobel argues (in his first essay in this volume) that the agents' choices need not be probabilistically dependent in *all* forms of the Prisoner's Dilemma. Nonetheless, in Prisoner's Dilemmas where there *is* sufficient probabilistic dependence, the two paradoxes present essentially the same conflict between these two methods of reasoning.

NO-BOXERS

In one form of the Prisoner's Dilemma, the dependence is complete, corresponding to an assumption that the Predictor is infallible; in another, the dependence is less than complete, corresponding to those forms of Newcomb's Problem in which the Predictor is fallible but nearly always right. A number of philosophers have argued that in one or both forms Newcomb's Problem is ill-formed, either because it is incoherent or because its solution is underdetermined. These *no-boxers,* as we might call them, conclude that for the form(s) in question it would be a mistake to prefer either choice over the other. In this category are: Schlesinger (1974); Levi (1974, 1982, 1983); Cargile (1975); Mackie (1977); and Hubin and Ross (forthcoming). We shall introduce in this section the problem of underdetermination and in the next turn to the charge of incoherence.

To say that the Predictor is nearly always right and that its predictions are a highly reliable indication of how the agent will choose is to say that certain conditional probabilities are very nearly equal to unity:

$$pr(C/c) \approx 1 \approx pr(D/d)$$

But it does not follow, as Isaac Levi has pointed out (1975), that both *converse* conditional probabilities are high. That is, we cannot directly infer:

$$pr(c/C) \approx 1 \approx pr(d/D)$$

Levi illustrates the fallacy by imagining statistics concerning the past performance of the Predictor in three possible cases:

TABLE 1

Cases	Choices	Predictions	
		c	d
I	C	900,000	10
	D	100,000	90
II	C	495,045	55,005
	D	55,005	495,045
III	C	90	100,000
	D	10	900,000

If probabilities can be assigned according to these relative frequencies, the following values are obtained:

TABLE 2

	$pr(C/c)$	$pr(D/d)$	$pr(c/C)$	$pr(d/D)$	$pr(C)$
Case I	0.9	0.9	0.9999888	0.0008991	0.9999000
Case II	0.9	0.9	0.9000000	0.9000000	0.5000000
Case III	0.9	0.9	0.0008991	0.9999888	0.0000999

The figures in Table 2 represent ratios drawn from the tabulation of frequencies in Table 1. Take Case I in Table 2. The conditional probability $pr(C/c)$ is defined as the ratio: $pr(C$ and $c)/pr(c)$. This ratio gives the fraction of instances where both C and c obtain among all the instances where c obtains, that is, 900,000 / (900,000 + 100,000) or 0.9. Conversely, $pr(c/C)$ is the ratio $pr(c$ and $C)/pr(C)$, the fraction of instances where both c and C obtain among the instances where C obtains, that is, 900,000 / (900,000 + 10) or 0.9999888. The unconditional probability $pr(C)$ is the fraction of instances where C obtains among all the instances: 900,010 / 1,000,100 or 0.9999000.

It is clear from Table 2 that only in Case II do the converse conditional probabilities remain high. In the other cases, although one conditional probability is high, its converse is not. Yet, in the standard calculations of expected utility maximization, it is assumed that both sets of conditional probabilities are nearly equal to unity. This assumption, as Levi has emphasized, is not guaranteed in the standard formulation of the problem. Moreover, if we assume as before that the value of an outcome is proportional to the amount of money obtained, in Cases I and III it would be choice D which would maximize expected utility, and there would be no discrepancy between maximizing and dominance reasoning; only in Case II does expected utility reasoning favor choosing C.

Levi's results bear directly on the question whether *every* Prisoner's Dilemma has the structure of Newcomb's Problem. This question is addressed by Lewis and Sobel. The heart of Sobel's argument may be seen in Case III. Table 2 shows that in this case the unconditional probability of C is very low. Hence, the unconditional probability of D would be high as would be the unconditional probability of the disjunction (C and c) or (D and d). Thinking of C as cooperation and D as defection in a Prisoner's Dilemma, we have a case where one can be nearly certain that the agents will act alike, either both cooperate or both defect. (If, for example, in the argument from symmetry we grant that it is nearly certain that both agents are rational and that there is a unique rational solution, then one can be quite sure that the disjunction (C and c) or (D and d) is true.) But, as Case III in Table 2 makes clear, it does not follow that $pr(c/C)$ is high. Therefore, it does not *follow* that the person choosing between C and D is facing a Newcomb problem, that is, a problem that has the essential elements of Newcomb's original dilemma. On this basis, it can be argued that it is possible to meet all the requirements for being in a Prisoner's Dilemma (even when the agents are nearly certain that they are both rational and hence because of symmetrical information must arrive at the same solution) but fail to meet a necessary condition for being in a Newcomb problem.

But now suppose that someone simply stipulates that the relevant conditional probabilities, $pr(c/C)$ and $pr(d/C)$, are both high (as Horgan does in his second essay). Such a case is logically possible. An example would be Case II in Levi's tables. What would Levi say to this move? He would say that in this situation one ought to take just the opaque box. But he would add that the problem of underdetermination has been suppressed, not eliminated, for now the decision problem has become so specific in its structure that we cannot trust our intuitive feel for the nature of the problem but must fall back on some general principle. An immediate consequence is that we cannot use the problem to *test* the principle, since to do so would be question begging. The original underdetermination problem presents, in effect, a dilemma. Either one begins by assuming only that $pr(C/c)$ and $pr(D/d)$ are high—which is the most that a natural reading of the story implies—and then the problem is too indeterminate to argue definitely for either of the principles in question, or else one has to impose so much structure on the problem that it cannot be used as an intuitive confirmation of the principle one favors.

Another source of underdetermination that needs to be noted is the interpretation of the conditional probabilities. The above tables show relative frequencies, and we have taken these to justify certain probability statements. For the purpose of illustrating a probabilistic fallacy, this assumption is legitimate. Still, there is the general issue of how probability statements are to be justified, and this question bears directly on our understanding of Newcomb's Problem. How, in particular, would we justify assigning a high probability value to any of the relevant conditional probabilities? How would we explain the Predictor's amazing success?

J. L. Mackie (1977) suggests many possibilities, too many indeed to canvass here, but in each case he argues that the suggestion perverts the intended structure of the original problem. Suppose, for example, the Predictor works by hypnotizing the agent to choose as the Predictor predicts. That would explain the success rate and even the fallibility of the Predictor. (Some people hypnotize better than others.) But it also destroys the decision problem in those cases where the hypnosis determines the choice, since then the agents would have no real option. The question "What is it reasonable for the decision maker to do? would be idle. If, on the other hand, one believes that hypnosis is not really effective in this way, one is again without an explanation of the Predictor's success. The same kind of problem arises when we imagine that the Predictor is a brilliant psychologist who has properly discerned that part of the agent's character which rigidly determines how the agent will act at the time of choice, whether or not that choice is reasonable. Again the question of the arriving at the reasonable choice will be idle. In still other examples, the agent would have a genuine choice (say, if the agent can change the past through backwards causation or if the Predictor has just been plain lucky in the past), but then another aspect of the natural and intended interpretation of the problem would be lost. Mackie concludes that there can be no satisfactory explanation of the probabilities — one that will preserve all the elements that are supposed to be included in Newcomb's Problem.

The problem of finding a realistic interpretation of the probabilities in Newcomb-like situations is addressed by Eells, Jackson and Pargetter, and Levi.

INFALLIBILITY AND SYMMETRY

Mackie's complaint is especially troublesome since it suggests that Newcomb's Problem may not be so much underdetermined as it is overdetermined and incoherent in its deep structure. In this section we shall look at the problem of incoherence as it arises for the case where the Predictor is assumed to be infallible, so that $pr(C/c) = pr(D/d) = 1$.

Notice that in this form of the puzzle the converse probabilities will be unity automatically. This may be seen on inspection by substituting a zero frequency for the outcomes (C,d) and (D,c) in the tables of the previous section. One could reason as follows. The conditional probability $pr(p/q)$ is defined as $pr(p \text{ and } q) / pr(q)$ for any p and q. Since $pr(C/c) = pr(D/d) = 1$, from the definition of conditional probability we have:

$$pr(C \text{ and } c)/pr(c) = pr(D \text{ and } d)/pr(d) = 1$$

and hence:

$$pr(C \text{ and } c) = pr(c)$$
$$pr(D \text{ and } d) = pr(d).$$

Now, since C and D are both mutually exclusive and jointly exhaustive, we know:

$$pr(c) = pr(C \text{ and } c) + pr(D \text{ and } c)$$
$$pr(d) = pr(D \text{ and } d) + pr(C \text{ and } d)$$

and therefore:

$$pr(D \text{ and } c) = pr(C \text{ and } d) = 0.$$

But c and d are similarly mutually exclusive and exhaustive. So,

$$pr(C) = pr(C \text{ and } c) + pr(C \text{ and } d)$$
$$pr(D) = pr(D \text{ and } d) + pr(D \text{ and } c)$$

and hence:

$$pr(C) = pr(C \text{ and } c)$$
$$pr(D) = pr(D \text{ and } d)$$

Therefore, from the definition of conditional probability, it follows:
$$pr(c/C) = pr(d/D) = 1.$$
Maximizing and dominance reasoning appear to diverge, if anything, more clearly than before.

For some philosophers, like Horgan or Lewis, the form of the problem makes no difference. Horgan is an invariant one-boxer and Lewis an invariant two-boxer. Others (and Nozick has been interpreted this way) are one-boxers for the case of an infallible Predictor and two-boxers otherwise. Levi (1975) has argued that this position is incoherent. He interprets the position to imply that dominance reasoning should be appropriate whenever there is causal independence. Since the assumption of causal independence remains even when the Predictor is infallible, dominance reasoning should apply here too if the position is to be consistent. Levi believes, however, that dominance should apply in neither case, since in both there is probabilistic dependence. For him whether one should be a one-boxer or a two-boxer will depend on the exact nature of the probabilities, which may vary when the Predictor is fallible, as shown in the previous section. If the probabilities are unknown, he argues (1975) for the maximin choice, two boxes. For these reasons Levi has been labelled as a no-boxer for the general case. In the specific case of Predictor infallibility, he is a one-boxer.

But is the case of the infallible Predictor coherent? The notion of an infallible Predictor is open to interpretation. It might be a being who could make a mistake but in fact never will. Or it might be a being for whom a mistaken prediction is impossible. Hubin and Ross (forthcoming) have argued that the second interpretation is appropriate when correctness of prediction is stipulated as part of the decision problem and that the problem then becomes incoherent. If we set aside the question of why the second interpretation is appropriate, a simplified version of their reasoning might run as follows. Suppose that the Predictor cannot make a mistake. Then if the agent were to choose the one box, the Predictor would have predicted it; and if the agent were to choose both boxes, again the Predictor would have predicted it. These conditional statements are called "counterfactual conditionals" or simply "counterfactuals" since their truth (or falsity) does not depend on whether the supposition contained in the if-clause is contrary to fact. (For relevant background, see Lewis, 1973a.) Using conventional notation, we can express the Predictor's infallibility by a conjunction of counterfactuals:

(1) $C \boxright c$ and $D \boxright d$

This represents the conjunction of counterfactuals expressed in English four sentences above. The difficulty is that it is also part of the specification of the decision problem that c and d are causally independent of C and D. Expressed in counterfactuals, this requirement would entail:

(2) $(C \boxright c$ and $D \boxright c)$ or $(C \boxright d$ and $D \boxright d)$

This statement says, in effect, the Predictor's prediction, whichever it happens to be, is "fixed" independently of the agent's choice. In other words, either c would be the case regardless of whether the choice were C or D; or d would be the case, regardless of whether the choice were C or D. Together the constraints (1) and (2) rule out the possibility that the agent has any real choice, for they imply that either C or D is impossible. Notice the similarity to Mackie's conclusion.

The implication may be proved by considering in turn each half of the disjunction in (2). Beginning with the left half of (2), we suppose:

(3) $C \boxright c$ and $D \boxright c$

Together with (1), (3) implies:

(4) $D \boxright d$ and $D \boxright c$

which implies:

(5) $D \,\square\!\!\!\rightarrow (d$ and $c)$

But it is impossible for (d and c) to be true, since the possibilities c and d are mutually exclusive. Therefore, given (5), D is not possible. Parallel reasoning from the other half of (2) leads to the impossibility of C. Either way, one of the choices is not open to the agent. If we insist that each choice be possible, as we must (otherwise there is no decision problem), the assumptions that define the problem now become self-contradictory.

This result bears on the argument from symmetry. A first step of that argument was to establish that rational agents with symmetrical information would act alike in a Prisoner's Dilemma since there is a unique rational solution. Suppose that we grant this step. Allowing the box symbol to mean "is true in all possible circumstances" and restricting the class of possibilities to those in which both agents are rational, we can express this symmetry assumption as follows:

(6) $\square (C$ and $c)$ or $\square (D$ and $d)$

We have assumed that the box can be placed on both sides of the disjunction, for presumably the unique rational solution would be the same in all possible circumstances. Given that C, D and c, d are mutually exclusive pairs, the infallibility constraint (1) immediately follows from (6). (Any possible circumstance in which C (or D) is true is one in which D (or C) is false; hence, by (6), c (or d) is true in that circumstance.) Do we now have an argument for choosing cooperation based on symmetry? Or do we have assumptions that rule out the possibility of choice?

We need to remind ourselves that "not possible" in this context means "not rationally possible" or, in other words, "not in the set of possible circumstances specified in this paragraph"—it does not mean "not causally possible." Hence, the result that either C or D is not possible is not *itself* a difficulty; it does not mean that the agent cannot (causally) make a choice between C and D. It means only that one of these (causally possible) alternatives is not rational. This we know directly from (6).

There may remain a difficulty, however. If " $\square$ " and " $\square\!\!\!\rightarrow$ " do *not* convey causal necessity, then some philosophers will find it hard to understand just how the infallibility constraint expressed in (1) provides a basis for choosing C in order that the outcome be C and c instead of D and d. Given (1), an agent *can* choose C only if it is rational for both to do so, but that it is rational to choose C is precisely what is at issue.

Must a defender of the argument from symmetry rely on (1)? And how is (1) to be understood? Are there only these two interpretations? To answer these questions, the reader should examine closely the essays of Davis and

Horgan where various analogues of the counterfactuals in (1) are explicitly examined. For an illuminating earlier discussion of the relation of these counterfactuals to dominance reasoning the reader may wish to consult Olin (1976 and 1978).

CAUSAL DECISION THEORY

Philosophers who are invariant two-boxers believe that dominance reasoning is appropriate under the assumption of causal independence regardless of whether the Predictor is fallible or infallible. For them Newcomb's Problem and similar examples represent counterexamples to expected utility reasoning of the kind described above. They face the problem of developing a general theory of rational decision that is consistent with this judgment. The definition of expected utility we have considered is one which simply involves conditional probabilities. An alternative conception, however, has recently emerged (Stalnaker, 1972/1981; Levi, 1975; Sobel, 1978; Gibbard and Harper, 1978; Cartwright, 1979; Skyrms, 1980b, 1982; Jeffrey, 1981b; Lewis, 1981). It has come to be known as causal decision theory, and a consequence of this theory is that one will be an invariant two-boxer.

There are several variations of this theory. One is presented by Gibbard and Harper; other variations are described by Eells in his first essay. Basic to all variations is the idea that the rationality of a decision depends on the comparative value of the effects that this decision would *cause* to occur if it were taken. It is understood, of course, that an agent may not be certain about what would be caused by the various alternative courses of action. The agent must consider, therefore, the *probable* truth of the relevant causal hypotheses. In the Gibbard-Harper version this means considering the probable truth of the counterfactual conditionals that express what would (be caused to) happen if a certain choice were made. Broadly and loosely speaking, the rational choice is the one that maximizes *causal* expected utility. In other words, like its rival which bids the agent to maximize *conditional* expected utility, this approach considers the average expected value of each feasible action, but the average is to be weighted according to the probable causal connection between the action and each possible state of the world. The difference lies in the weighting factor. In the previous approach, which we shall call evidential decision theory, this factor is (in its simplest form) the probability of the state conditional on the action. In causal decision theory the weighting factor is something more complicated, designed to make the probability reflect causal rather than evidential dependence or independence.

According to causal decision theory, when causal independence obtains, the probability weighting amounts to the *unconditional* probability of each alternative state. Using this weighting factor to average the values of the outcomes is equivalent to maximizing *conditional* expected utility under the assumption that the states are *probabilistically* independent of the actions, though causal independence may in fact come without probabilistic independence. We have already seen how in the case of probabilistic independence the dominant action is identified with the rational action according to evidential decision theory. Thus, causal decision theory entails that the dominant action is rational when the states are causally independent. In Newcomb's Problem the two-box choice is therefore rational, be the Predictor fallible or not. A lucid demonstration of this result for several different forms of causal decision theory is given in the essay by Eells.

The case where there is a dominant action is, of course, not very common. And that is also true for the assumption of complete causal independence. Causal decision theory, however, purports to provide a general account of rational choice for all cases in the manner outlined above. When the relevant conditional probabilities reflect causal dependence or probabilistic and causal independence, the two general approaches are designed to deliver the same result. The controversy over their relative merit centers naturally on the range of cases where there is probabilistic dependence and causal independence — as in Newcomb's Problem — or where probabilistic independence masks an underlying causal dependence, as in the case of Reoboam, described in the essay by Gibbard and Harper.

Some of the criticism of causal decision theory has focused on Newcomb's Problem itself. Levi has charged that the implication that the two-box choice is rational when there is *certainty* that it will produce an inferior outcome is "absurd" (Levi, 1982, 1983, 1985a). Moreover, Levi has argued in the same articles that the theory leads to a contradiction when applied to such cases. The issue there concerns how the relevant outcomes are to be described. The claim made by Levi and by Eells in his first essay is that evidential decision theory yields decisions which are stable under various descriptions of outcomes, while its rival does not. See Levi (1982, 1983, 1985a), Lewis (1983), and Eells (1985d).

REASONS AND COMMON CAUSES

The term "Newcomb problem" is also used to refer to decision problems which are like Newcomb's in their basic structure but in which the probabilistic dependence is explained by the existence of a common cause. A much discussed example is Fisher's smoking hypothesis. According to this hypothesis, a certain genetic predisposition is causally responsible for both smoking and lung cancer. (For a critical discussion of the use of R. A. Fisher's hypothesis in this connection, see Levi's essay.) Suppose that we think of the decision problem as a choice between smoking (S) and not smoking ($-S$), given that the agent either has the genetic predisposition (G) or does not ($-G$). To simplify, suppose we also imagine that lung cancer is only caused by G, so that all the difference in value between having and not having lung cancer is contained in the difference between G and $-G$. Since S is pleasurable, we suppose that it has some value in itself, so that $V(S,G) > V(-S,G)$ and $V(S,-G) > V(-S,-G)$. In other words, S dominates $-S$. But since $V(-S,G)$ is very low compared to $V(S,-G)$, we also have the payoff structure of Newcomb's Problem. Moreover, since S does not in any way cause G, the condition of causal independence is met; and, finally, since we have imagined that all cases of S are caused by G, the condition of probabilistic dependence is met as well:

$$pr(G/S) > pr(G/-S)$$

We have, in sum, a Newcomb problem decision problem.

The relevance of causal decision theory should be obvious. The agent cannot change his genetic predisposition for cancer if he already has G. So it would be absurd to forgo the pleasure of smoking in order to avoid lung cancer. If he already has G, he probably will get lung cancer anyway; he might as well enjoy smoking. If he does not, then he will not get lung cancer and again smoking is better than not smoking. The dominant choice, smoking, is *intuitively* the rational choice on the assumptions given, and this is the choice that would be selected by any version of causal decision theory. But, given the probabilistic dependence noted (and assuming the relevant inequalities in probability and value are large enough), we can infer that $-S$ would maximize conditional expected utility. The upshot is that this Newcomb problem provides an apparent counterexample to evidential decision theory as much as it confirms its rival.

It is possible, however, to argue that the appearance of counterexample is an illusion. Eells has argued (1981, 1982, 1983, 1984a) that if the agent is fully rational and aware of his reasons for acting, then he will choose *smoking* according to evidential theory. (Here we follow the summary of the argument in Eells and Sober, 1983, p. 56.) According to that theory, a rational act is a function of three variables: how probable the agent considers various events to be, how desirable he finds them, and his decision rule. Presumably the decision rule will remain constant if the agent is fully rational, and the relative desirability of the possible outcomes will be as indicated. That leaves the conditional probabilities. Eells reasons as follows: if R is the combination of variables at work in the rational agent (that is, his beliefs and desires, that is, his reasons), then we can expect R to "screen off" the dependence of S on G.

$$(1) \quad pr(S/R \text{ and } G) = pr(S/R \text{ and } -G)$$

In other words, the probability that the agent assigns to S should be the same whether it is conditional on R and G or R and $-G$. Why? Because the agent believes that he is rational and that in a rational agent, if what the agent does is genuinely an action of his, then it was done for a reason. His having these reasons is state R. Hence, he believes that G can influence S only through the causally intermediate state R. But since the agent is fully aware of his reasons and thus aware that R obtains, he also assigns R the unconditional probability of one:

$$(2) \quad pr(R) = 1$$

From (1) and (2) it follows:

$$(3) \quad pr(S/G) = pr(S/-G)$$

or, equivalently:

$$(4) \quad pr(G/S) = pr(G/-S)$$

Finally, on the basis of (4), the rational agent will believe that the dominant choice, smoking, maximizes conditional expected utility. The appearance of counterexample has vanished! We invite the reader to examine the details of this defense in Eells's first essay and in his book (1982). Criticism is provided in the essay by Jackson and Pargetter and in Davis's second essay (note 10).

ITERATED PRISONER'S DILEMMAS

So far we have confined our attention to versions of the Prisoner's Dilemma and Newcomb's Problem in which an agent chooses just once. It is possible, however, to think of agents making a *series* of choices in situations with the same structure. This type of decision problem is more complex, and for this reason discussion has been postponed until now.

Iterated Prisoner's Dilemmas were, in fact, the first to be studied and are often perceived to be more like decision problems in real life than the "single-shot" case which has preoccupied philosophers. A leader in the experimental research on this subject has been the psychologist Anatol Rapoport (see Rapoport and Chammah, 1965, and Rapoport, 1974). Such research is usually designed to determine which variable factors might control the number of cooperative outcomes in a long series of interactions. The experimenter could vary, for instance, the size of the payoffs, the kinds of communication allowed, or even the personality types of the agents. Although the nature and results of these tests have considerable intrinsic and indeed practical interest, we shall continue to focus in this volume on the purely philosophical question of what *rational* agents should choose when they are fully informed about the structure of their choice situation.

Most philosophers believe that if rational agents know ahead of time just how many interactions there will be, they will always defect. (An exception is Hardin, 1982a, p. 146.) The reason for this conclusion is the so-called "roll-back" argument. Suppose there will be n moves in the series. Then after n-1 plays, both agents know that they should choose the dominant action and defect on the last play. (The argument assumes at this point that the symmetry argument, studied above, is invalid, contrary to Davis.) But, then, after n-2 plays, they know, for the same reason as before, that they should defect on the penultimate play. There is, after all, no reason at this point in the game to convince the other party that one has a cooperative disposition. Both know that they will defect on the very last play, so the one before that becomes, in effect, "the last." Again, the same argument can now be applied after n-3 plays, and so on. In brief, cooperation will never be rational in the iterated case.

David Braybrooke accepts this reasoning but argues that a convincing case for cooperation can be made if there is no definite end point in the series. Suppose one assumes that there is only a certain probability that the series will continue for another play and the agents know that. Then they have reason to demonstrate their cooperative disposition in order to encourage cooperative responses in the future. Both would prefer, of course, a series of cooperative moves to a series of defections. Sobel argues in his second essay that the fact of no definite end point will make no difference to completely rational agents. Given their mutual understanding of their rationality and their circumstances, they will defect just as surely as they would in the previous case.

In the penultimate essay, Axelrod studies the decision problem from a somewhat different perspective. Suppose that there is a large group of agents, each committed separately to some rule or other for generating the choice between C and D at each play, and suppose that each has an opportunity to interact with every other agent in a series of indefinite length. What will happen then? This question is enormously complex. If the probability for interacting with the same individual another time is set at .99654 (the number Axelrod uses), the average number of moves will be 200, and therefore the number of possible combinatons of C and D that are available on average for each individual is 2^{200}. Then, if there are n different individuals, the number of different possible interactions for an average number of moves per series is 2^{200n} where $n \geq 2$. One may wonder how Axelrod could hope to analyze the staggering number of possibilities that are implicit in these multiple decision problems.

What Axelrod did is to devise a round robin tournament to be run on a computer where the rules that would generate the series of C and D for each player in each series of interactions would be determined by entries submitted by experts in the field. A given rule could, of course, generate more than one combination of *C* and *D,* for the rule could be formulated as a function of what the other player in the interaction had done in the past. Two tournaments were run, one with fourteen rules entered plus a rule for choosing randomly between *C* and *D,* the other with sixty-two rules submitted by experts from six countries. In both tournaments the same rule received the highest score. This rule, called "Tit for Tat," tells that agent to cooperate on the first move with any given player and afterwards to do whatever the other did on the previous move. This extremely simple rule was submitted by Rapoport, the psychologist mentioned at the beginning of this section.

The result may seem perplexing, since it is obvious after a little reflection that Tit for Tat cannot possibly do better than any other strategy. Its best score comes from interacting with a player who always cooperates, but then both do well; Tit for Tat does not do better. If the player defects against Tit for Tat after cooperating, Tit for Tat does worse on that play and never recoups the loss as long as the other player continues to defect. If the other later decides to cooperate, then the loss is reversed to even the score, but Tit for Tat is still not doing better in total score relative to *that* player. The success of Tit for Tat, which has been described as perfect reciprocity, comes from the relative lack of success displayed by the non-reciprocating rules in their interactions *among themselves,* as illustrated in the next section.

This important insight is a direct result of considering iterated Prisoner's Dilemmas in the context of multiple players. Hardin argues, however, that a further step needs to be taken in the direction of involving more players. In Axelrod's set-up, the agents interact two-by-two rather than in the fashion described above as a "large-scale" Prisoner's Dilemma involving many individuals interacting simultaneously. In these cases, there can be free riders who refuse to cooperate with the majority but who nevertheless enjoy the fruits of cooperation. Hardin argues that the rationality of collective action remains unsolved in these instances.

Braybrooke makes a similar point in his essay on the traditional problem of the social contract. In particular, Braybrooke would agree with Hardin that the conclusions that hold for dyadic interactions among members of large groups cannot easily be generalized to a "collective" interaction of the group as a whole. Many of the most important interactions in modern society are of this kind and seem not to be amenable to the dyadic analysis. On Braybrooke's view the problem of collective choice must be redefined to allow the agents to have certain social motivations which could not be assumed in the traditional formulation of the problem. He argues that otherwise it is impossible to explain the collective cooperation of rational individuals. When the problem is redefined, however, new questions can be raised. For example, should rational persons seek to acquire the relevant social motivations? An evaluation of Braybrooke's answer is provided in So-bel's second essay.

But how exactly is it that cooperation can evolve even in *two*-person iterated dilemmas? Given the technical nature of some of Axelrod's discussion, it may prove helpful by way of introduction to characterize his findings in a little more detail and to comment on their philosophical significance.

One might want to know what kind of decision rules formed the "social environment" in which Tit for Tat was played. Clearly a tournament with sixty-two rules is small compared to the astronomical number of possible rules from which one might choose. Some possible rules are very simple, such as, "Always Defect," "Always Cooperate," or "Always Choose Randomly." Tit for Tat is almost that simple. Most of the rules actually used, however, were much more complicated. A rule called Downing, named after Leslie L. Downing (see Axelrod, 1984, p. 34), was designed to test whether other rules were responsive to it. Accordingly, it estimates the relevant conditional probabilities, $pr(c/C)$ and $pr(c/D)$, then calculates the conditional expected utility of each option and finally chooses the option which maximizes this value. After each move of a given player, it updates its estimate of the relevant probabilities, beginning with the assumption that these probabilities are each 0.5 and dropping this assumption after the first move.

This is obviously a fairly sophisticated decision rule, yet it fared badly in the tournament. The reason that it did was that it would automatically defect on the first two moves, no matter how cooperative the other player is initially. Consequently, in playing with rules that are cooperative in the beginning but designed to retaliate unmercifully in the face of defection, it suffers very badly for its non-cooperative posture in the first two moves.

This example illustrates a general point that Axelrod emphasizes (for example, 1984, pp. 39–40) and that has profound philosophical significance. How successful a rule is depends not just on its own characteristics but also on the properties of the other rules which interact with each other. In fact, had the Downing rule been initially cooperative in the first tournament (and thus based on a more optimistic view of the responsiveness of the other strategies), it would have been more successful than Tit for Tat by a wide margin. Another strategy that would have scored higher than Tit for Tat is Tit for Two Tats: "Only defect when the other player has defected twice in a row." There is, in short, no best rule. How good any rule is is relative to the environment in which it functions. (The proof is to be found under

Theorem 1 in Axelrod's essay.) A relatively uncompetitive rule may succeed in a field of mutually defeating strong competitors.

One may ask, nevertheless, whether there is any rule which is relatively successful over a wide range of "environments." This is the empirical question of *robustness*. Tit for Tat has been demonstrated to be extremely robust on the basis of these tournaments and computer reruns that vary the proportion of other rules in the field. It continues to score high even after it is set against rules designed to probe its possible weaknesses and to imitate its best features.

What is it about this rule that explains its robustness? Axelrod attempted to answer this question through a statistical analysis and arrived at four key features. First, the rule is "nice" in the sense that anyone following it is *never the first to defect*. Almost without exception nice rules scored better than others. Second, it is *quick to return defection for defection,* but, third, it is also *quick to return cooperation for cooperation*. Rules that were slow to retaliate or slow to forgive tended to provoke more defection than more responsive rules. Finally, its pattern of response is very *easy to recognize*. Other rules, though potentially very responsive, lacked sufficient clarity to elicit appropriate responses. Thus, a rule that inserts a defection at random intervals to test the responsiveness of a cooperator may trigger excessive retaliation from a player programmed to respond unforgivingly to gratuitous aggression.

Perhaps the most interesting questions that Axelrod addresses concern *collective stability* and *initial viability*. Suppose a rule does prove to be empirically robust. We have already noted that this does not mean that it is the best strategy possible. But then can we expect that a population of individuals employing a robust strategy like Tit for Tat must be inherently unstable? The answer is no. As demonstrated in the proof for Theorem 2, if the probability of meeting the same individual another time (that is, the probability w that a series of interactions with this individual does not end at that point) is sufficiently high and all the players in a population are following Tit for Tat, then a different ("mutant") strategy that appears on the scene cannot do better than the norm. No mutant rule of behavior can "invade" the population. In this sense, Tit for Tat is collectively stable. What it takes in general for a rule to be collectively stable is explored in Theorems 3, 4, and 5. Other rules can be stable as well, in particular, pure defection (Theorem 6). The question arises: how does a "nice" rule like Tit for Tat ever get started if the total environment is hostile, for example, if it consists of nothing but players who always defect? Does the existence of stability depend entirely on the initial distribution of rules in the population? These questions concern the initial viability of a rule.

Axelrod's answer is given in Theorems 7 and 8 which imply that a rule like Tit for Tat can invade a population of pure defectors under certain conditions although the rule "Always Defect" cannot invade a population of Tit for Tats under similar circumstances. Both rules are collectively stable; so a *single* Tit for Tat player cannot invade. But a small number of such players, arriving on the scene in a "cluster," can. How large would a cluster have to be? Surprisingly small! Suppose that the probability w of another interaction with the same individual is 0.9 and suppose the values of the payoffs in the Prisoner's Dilemma are 5, 3, 1, 0 — five units being the temptation to defect when the other player cooperates. Then if there is only a 5 per cent chance that a Tit for Tat player will meet another Tit for Tat on any given interaction, this rule will do better than the norm of pure defection. Indeed, Axelrod points out that if w is set at .99654, as in the tournament, the probability of meeting another member of the cluster need be only one in a thousand.

Still, as the final theorem demonstrates, the reverse does not hold. Imagine that the evolving scores as players proceed to interact are interpreted from an ecological perspective, so that players whose sums are relatively poor are displaced by the more successful players (see Axelrod, 1980b; Axelrod and Hamilton, 1981a). One then imagines the character of the population changing from almost 100 per cent pure defectors with a tiny cluster of Tit for Tats to a population consisting in nothing but Tit for Tats. In fact, this evolutionary trend has been borne out under computer simulation. Yet it is demonstrably impossible for a small cluster of pure defectors to invade a population of 100 per cent Tit for Tats. Once the nice strategy is fully established, the situation is stable. If w is high enough so that a nice strategy cannot be invaded by an individual, it cannot be invaded by a cluster.

WHAT IS RATIONAL CHOICE?

Much of this volume concerns the issue of how *rational* agents should choose. The reader is urged to keep track of the various conceptions of rational choice that are endorsed or presupposed in the essays to follow. Prominent among them will be conceptions that consist in some form of evidential or causal decision theory. Are any of these conceptions likely to have a place in a successful behavioral science? Or to illuminate the foundations of moral norms? How different are these conceptions from the way people ordinarily think of rational choice? Must rational choice involve conscious reasoning in a unified human personality?

It is worth remarking how little is assumed in Axelrod's discussion regarding the rationality of his players. There is no assumption that they have reasons and intentions or even that they are conscious beings. Not that these additional assumptions would destroy his conclusions. The point is that these extra postulates would be gratuitous. It is possible, therefore, to apply his results to the evolution of cooperation in primitive biological organisms (as shown in Axelrod and Hamilton, 1981a). If the evolution is conceived to occur through Darwinian natural selection, then the payoffs would be interpreted as levels of fitness and the results concerning initial viability, robustness, and stability would be understood in these terms. The issue of rationality expressed in the language in which this question is often discussed, involving reference to conscious desires, conscious calculations, and a unified personality, simply would not arise in that context. One might wonder, however, whether a successful human player must have at least the cognitive capacity to apply evidential or causal decision theory. Apparently not. A player following Tit for Tat, for example, need have only the capacity to distinguish one player from another and to remember the last move in any given case. Nothing more is required for success.

But we must not forget the contention of Braybrooke and Hardin that a dyadic analysis may not be plausibly generalized to large-scale Prisoner's Dilemmas. Moreover, a satisfactory solution to the iterated dyadic Prisoner's Dilemma need not be applicable to the "one-shot" Prisoner's Dilemma addressed in Part I by Davis, Watkins, Gauthier, and McClennen. It would not be surprising if complex cognitive operations were needed to achieve a cooperative solution in a non-repeated, large-scale Prisoner's Dilemma. And indeed the authors who deal with this case in the essays to follow suppose that their views on rational choice apply to sophisticated decision-makers who can understand the structure of the decision problem: the relevant payoffs, probabilities, causal connections, and so on.

How are we to understand rational choice in a non-repeated, large-scale Prisoner's Dilemma? The aim of rational choice seems straightforward: to maximize the number of units of payoff received in the outcome of the choice. There are, of course, serious complications here. Causal decision theorists will remind us that payoffs are to be gained as the result of choice, not accidentally. Others (see, for example, Allais and Hagen, 1979, and Sowden, 1984) may question the outcome-oriented perspective in which the decision problems are posed. But let us press on. Even granting that the maximization of utility is the aim of rational choice, there can remain profound differences regarding the nature of this aim. These are differences about what rational choice is. A clear instance of this contrast may be found in Gauthier's comparison of two ways to try to maximize: "straightforward" versus "constrained." Though the ultimate aim of rational choice is in each case to maximize utility, the behavior exemplifying this aim, and the results that follow, can differ significantly in the two cases. In particular, constrained maximization can do better in certain non-repeated, large-scale Prisoner's Dilemmas. In view of this possibility, Gauthier argues that constrained maximization is better able to achieve its aim and therefore represents a superior conception of rational choice. McClennen's essay provides yet another perspective. For McClennen part of what is at issue is how the aim of rational choice is to be defined with respect to the agents' possibly changing preferences. There McClennen defends a conception of rationality as "resolute choice." Like Davis and Gauthier, McClennen argues that rational cooperation is possible in the non-repeated Prisoner's Dilemma.

The question of what is rational choice, though fundamental, is obviously difficult. The answers proposed in the essays to follow are complex and controversial, and their ramifications myriad. The answers are collected here in the belief that they are among the best that are now available. The reader is invited to examine them first hand.*

*I am indebted to Lanning Sowden for help in planning this essay and for detailed criticism and advice at every stage of its preparation. Extensive suggestions for improvement from David Braybrooke, David Copp, Lawrence H. Davis, and Howard Sobel are gratefully acknowledged.

II

MORALITY AND THE POSSIBILITY OF
RATIONAL COOPERATION

2

Prisoners, Paradox, and Rationality

LAWRENCE H. DAVIS

A typical statement of what is called the "Prisoner's Dilemma" runs as follows:

> Two men suspected of committing a crime together are arrested and placed in separate cells by the police. Each suspect may either confess or remain silent, and each one knows the possible consequences of his action. These are: (1) If one suspect confesses and his partner does not, the one who confessed turns state's evidence and goes free and the other one goes to jail for twenty years. (2) If both suspects confess, they both go to jail for five years. (3) If both suspects remain silent, they both go to jail for a year for carrying concealed weapons—a lesser charge. We will suppose that there is no "honor among thieves" and each suspect's sole concern is his own self-interest. Under these conditions, what should the criminals do?[1]

This case and others like it contain an element of paradox. There is a compelling *basic argument for confessing,* even though *if neither confessed, the outcome would be better for each.* In this version, if both confess they each go to prison for five years, but if they are both silent, they each go to prison for only one year. Rationality, represented by the basic argument for con-

From *American Philosophical Quarterly* 14, no. 4 (October 1977): 319–27. Reprinted by permission.

fessing, leads them to an outcome less attractive in the self-interested view of each than another outcome which lies in their grasp, so to speak. Apparently in these situations, "rational pursuit of self-interest generates an outcome detrimental to sheer self-interest," as Max Black has recently put it.[2] Closer examination shows, however, that the matter is quite complex. In particular, it seems there is no genuine paradox, and the basic argument for confessing may be inapplicable to a theoretically important class of cases. An implication of this would be that cooperation between individuals with clashing interests may be more rationally defensible than has been widely thought; but this implication will not be explored here.

1. To begin with the basic argument for confessing; in a sentence it is that each prisoner is better off confessing than maintaining silence, no matter what the other does. Let us represent the four pairs of alternatives and the associated outcomes in the standard way, abstracting from details of the example which shall not concern us.

		Column	
		do not do A	do A
Row	do not do A	(b,b)	(d,a)
	do A	(a,d)	(c,c)

Here the two individuals are named "Row" and "Column," and the choice each faces is whether to do A (in the example, "maintain silence") or not to do A (in the example, "confess"). The outcome for each pair of alternatives is represented in the matrix by an ordered pair whose members indicate how the four outcomes are ranked in the judgment of Row and Column, respectively. The outcome (d, a), for example is rated "best" by Row and "worst" by Column; the outcome (c, c) is rated "second best" by each.

Now consider from Row's point of view what happens if Column does not do A. If Row also refrains from doing A, the outcome is (b, b), Row's third best. But if Row does A, the outcome is (a, d), his worst. If Column does not do A, then, Row does better if he follows suit.

If Column does A, then if Row does not do A, the outcome is the one he rates best, and if Row does A, the outcome is only his second best. Again, he does better if he does not do A. In the standard phrase, not doing A *dominates* doing A from Row's point of view. The conclusion seems inescapable that Row should not do A (in the example: he should confess).

Since the positions of Row and Column are exactly symmetrical, parallel reasoning yields the conclusion that not doing A is the rationally prescribed alternative for Column also. If both are rational enough to see and accept this argument, the outcome is the one each ranks "third best," even though if each does A, the outcome is the one each ranks "second best."

2. Why, exactly, is this result supposed to be paradoxical? Luce and Raiffa find it "slightly uncomfortable that two so-called irrational players [i.e., individuals in this sort of situation] will both fare much better than two so-called rational ones," and others have shared this discomfort.[3] But rationality has never been supposed to be a *guarantee* of the best possible outcome; at least it would be a mistake to suppose that it is. An agent forced to choose between an hour alone with a rattlesnake or a lion, who may be hungry or sleeping, may be best advised to choose the snake. If the snake bites him, he can still get medical attention later; but the lion can kill him easily within an hour. For all that, it may be that the lion is asleep on a full stomach and the agent suffers snakebite "needlessly."

If there is a paradox here, it arises from the fact that each agent faces neither a lion nor a snake, but another rational agent like himself. And although they rank the outcomes differently, they do agree in rating the outcome of their both doing *A* above the outcome of their both not doing *A,* to which their rationality apparently condemns them.

Even so there would be only tragedy but not paradox if neither agent *knew* whether he faced a rational agent or a dangerous animal, or simply an *ir*rational agent. And now we notice a curious omission in some presentations of the prisoner's dilemma and the theory of games in which it is discussed. The version quoted specifies that "each one knows the possible consequences of his action," but only that "we" suppose there is no "honor among thieves." Now, it is natural enough to suppose that each has this information about the other's motivation. Or, as Luce and Raiffa (p. 54ff; cf. pp. 47–50) make conveniently explicit for game theory in general,

> Each player is assumed to know the rules of the game in full detail [and] also the payoff functions of the other players.
>   Each player is assumed to be "rational" in the sense that, given two alternatives, he will always choose the one he prefers, i.e., the one with the larger utility.

This still does not quite say that each knows the *others* have this knowledge; nor does it say that each knows the others are "rational" in the indicated sense. Taking this silence as an indication of the contrary, it appears that in Luce and Raiffa's view, we do *not* assume the players have this knowledge about one another, in which case the "discomfort" they feel about the prisoner's dilemma does not arise from any genuine paradox.[4]

Other writers feel differently. Harsanyi speaks of "mutually expected rationality" and the "mutual perception of each other's rationality"; Rapoport refers to Harsanyi and goes on to assert that "the fundamental assumption of game theory is that everything there is to know about a situation is known at the start by 'rational players.'"[5] Davis (p. 101ff) also cites Rapoport's view that arguments like the basic argument for confessing given in section 2 depend on the assumption "that one's opponent will act rationally" and does not disagree. For writers making assumptions like these, there may indeed be something paradoxical about the basic argument for confessing. In fact, explicitly making a strong assumption about the players' knowledge of one another's rationality and knowledge enables an apparently valid argument for *not* confessing! To this argument we now turn.

3. The basic argument for confessing was that "each prisoner is better off confessing than maintaining silence, no matter what the other does." Whatever Column does, the outcome is better as Row ranks outcomes if he does not do A than it is if he does A; not doing A is a dominant strategy for Row. Now phrases such as "*whatever* Column does" suggest that Row is uncertain what Column will do, and it may be that applicability of the argument — relevance of dominance considerations — sometimes depends crucially on there being this uncertainty.[6]

If we assume that *each prisoner knows that each knows that* each is rational, as well as knowing the information represented in the matrix in section 1, it appears that Row is *not* uncertain what Column will do. More precisely, he can and will determine what Column and he himself *should,* and so by assumption *will,* do. He knows that Column is a rational agent and that he himself is. He knows further that their situations and information are symmetric: whatever considerations would lead Row himself to choose one way would lead Column to choose *exactly the same way.* The information Row has, then, implies that *the outcomes (d, a) and (a, d) are not in fact possible.* Of the two outcomes remaining, (c, c) is rated higher by both Row and Column. The rationally prescribed alternative for each, then, is to do A — maintain silence. And, by assumption, each will take this alternative, secure in the knowledge that the other will take it also.

This may be called the *basic argument for cooperating;* a somewhat more formal version is presented in section 5, below. It will emerge that the only part of this argument open to serious question is the emphasized clause to the effect that two of the outcomes are not "possible"; in section 6 I try to clarify and defend the relevant sense of "possibility." Other questions about the argument are dealt with in the next section.

Before starting on these questions, however, it is worth noting that the principle of maximizing expected utility may seem to yield the same conclusion where the assumption is made that each prisoner knows that each knows that each is "rational" in this strong sense, which entails that each will take the alternative rationally prescribed for him. For we have from Row's point of view:

$$\text{E.U. (confessing)} = (u(b,b) \times pr((b,b)/\text{Row confesses}))$$
$$+ (u(d,a) \times pr((d,a)/\text{Row confesses})).$$

The utilities of (*b, b*) and (*d, a*) from Row's point of view are *b* and *d*, respectively. It may be thought that *pr*((*b, b*)/Row confesses) is equal to one, since by assumption Row and Column each take the rationally prescribed alternative: if Row confesses, then confessing must be rationally prescribed, in which case Column also confesses, and the outcome is (*b, b*). If this is correct, then we also have *pr*((*d, a*)/Row confesses) = 0, and the expected utility of confessing is precisely *b*. Similarly, the expected utility of maintaining silence is *c*, and so Row will maintain silence.

A problem with this is that there is another, perhaps equally plausible, way of interpreting the probabilities here. Perhaps "(*pr*((*b, b*)/Row confesses))" should be read as the probability that the outcome would be (*b, b*) if Row *were* to confess, where it is allowed that the antecedent of the conditional may be contrary to fact. If a "fact" to which "Row confesses" may be contrary is the assumed fact that he takes the rationally prescribed alternative, we cannot reason as above that the probability is one. There may be other problems with using the principle of expected utility in this way, so we shall not consider it further.[7]

4.1 In his *Two-Person Game Theory,* Rapoport presents an argument the final portion of which is virtually identical with the basic argument for cooperating. It will pay to quote it in full, adjusting the notation to coincide with ours:

> The best outcome for both of us is (*c, c*). However, if Column assumes that I shall do *A*, he may well not do *A* to win the largest payoff. To protect myself I will also refrain from doing *A*. But this makes for a loss for both of us. Two rational players certainly deserve the outcome (*c, c*). I am rational and by the fundamental postulate of game theory, I must assume that Column is also rational. If I have come to the conclusion that doing *A* is the rational choice, he too must have come to the same conclusion. Now knowing that he will do *A*, what shall I do? Shall *I* not refrain from doing *A* to get the greatest payoff? But if I have come to this conclusion, he has also probably done so. Again we end up with (*b, b*). To insure that he does not come to the conclusion that he should refrain from doing *A*, I better avoid it also. For if I avoid it and am rational, he too will avoid it if he is rational. On the other hand, if rationality prescribes not doing *A*, then it must also prescribe not doing *A* for him. At any rate because of the symmetry of the game, rationality must prescribe *the same choice to both*. But if both choose the same, then (*c, c*) is clearly the better. Therefore I should choose to do *A*.[8]

Prior to the sentence beginning "On the other hand," Row argues back and forth, from the wisdom of doing *A* to the need to protect himself against Column's *not* doing A to the realization of the folly of their *both* not doing A and so on — a process that threatens to be endless. The chain of reasoning in the final four sentences is not a continuation of what precedes, but an entirely fresh approach, which leads to a definite conclusion. But the key assumption, that each knows (or assumes) that each is rational and has precisely the same relevant information as the other, plays an explicit role in both chains of reasoning.

J. W. N. Watkins, acknowledging Rapoport, has made use of an argument essentially the same as that of the *first* part of Rapoport's, and his use of the "key assumption" is criticized by A. K. Sen:

> Furthermore, the type of egoistic reasoning outlined by Watkins essentially makes each prisoner assume — at least temporarily — that the other prisoner's action will be a *function* of his own action and will in fact coincide with it. . . . It is precisely because [Column's] choice cannot be assumed by [Row] to be a mirror-reflection of his own choice that the dilemma of the prisoners is supposed to arise.[9]

But Sen does not here defend the alleged impossibility of Row's assuming Column's choice to be a "mirror-reflection" of his own. To the contrary, it seems an obvious entailment of the assumption that each knows that each knows that each is rational, together with the symmetry of the situation. And I have argued in Section 2 that the Prisoner's Dilemma is paradoxical only if we make this assumption.

The assumption licenses each to assume the other will act precisely as he himself will act only if "being rational" is understood in a very strong way. Occasionally Luce and Raiffa seem to imply that a "rational" agent *does not make mistakes,* and although they should not be held to this implication, anything weaker would dissolve all element of paradox.[10] Assume for the moment that the basic argument for cooperating is valid. If Row thinks of the argument and has no worries about Column's "rationality," then it is indeed rational for him to go ahead and do A. But if he has the slightest doubt — even if his doubt is that Column might *fail to think* of the argument, or might *make some mistake* in assessing it — then it is by no means so obvious what he should do. Well, *if* he is really limited to the information represented in the matrix, then the basic argument for confessing (not doing A) presumably applies. If he knows what the outcomes are, as well as their rank ordering, then, depending on the details, it may be "rational" for him to gamble. Either way, his situation is unfortunate and perhaps difficult — and in this sense a "dilemma" — but there is no *paradox.* Our interest then is only in cases where each knows (or is willing to act on the assumption) that each is "rational" in the *quite* strong sense of not making mistakes *and* not failing to think of relevant arguments. This may remove the discussion from reality, but should not remove its theoretical interest.

4.2. The basic argument for cooperating may seem to *abuse* the assumption about their rationality and knowledge, by having each agent think his (free?) choice *determines* what *is* rational and thereby determines what the other agent chooses. This impression is fostered by Rapoport's having his agent say "two rational players *deserve* the outcome (*c, c*)" and "to *insure* that he does not come to the conclusion . . . I better avoid it also." Watkins also has his agents say:

> But dammit, we *don't* have to resign ourselves to (*b, b*). We have been offered the chance of (*c, c*). Let us grab it.[11]

This suggestion of a *causal* or other *determining* relation between the two choices may be part of what Sen finds objectionable in each agent's assuming that the other's action "will be a *function* of his own." But the choices and actions of each may be a function of what is rationally prescribed for each, rather than of each other. (Cf. two clocks known to work perfectly and to have been synchronized at an earlier time. By looking at one we can know what time the other indicates, which is not to say we can *make* the other one indicate an arbitrarily selected time by setting the first to that time.) The misleading passages do not occur in the second part of Rapoport's argument or in the argument of section 3, above, and nothing like them is presupposed.

4.3. If valid, the basic argument for cooperating overcomes the following apparent circularity. "To conclude that the outcome of doing *A* is better than the outcome of not doing *A*, Row must know what these outcomes are. This depends on what Column does, which by assumption depends on what is rationally prescribed for him (and Row also). But *this* depends on which action has the better outcome. Row must know the answer in order to arrive at the answer!" The way in which the argument purports to overcome this circularity may be clarified by listing its premises:

(1) An alternative *X* is rationally prescribed for an agent *y* if *y* knows that there are just two possible outcomes *m* and *n*, such that if *y* takes *X* then the outcome is *m*, if *y* does not take *X* then the outcome is *n*, and *m* is better (in *y*'s judgment) than *n*.

(2) Each prisoner knows that each knows that each will take the rationally prescribed alternative.

From the background information supplied by the matrix and the fact that (2) assigns the same information and rationality to each, it can be inferred that an alternative is rationally prescribed for one just in case it is for the other. From (2), it can then be inferred that each *does* just what the other does. What the two possible outcomes are can now be determined first on the assumption that doing *A* is rationally prescribed and then on the assumption that not doing A is rationally prescribed, and so it can be determined that A satisfies the sufficient condition given in (1) for being rationally prescribed, for each.

The "trick," then, is to reason about "the rationally prescribed alternative" before it is known which it is. But this presupposes *that* there is one. Worse, (2) presupposes further that each agent *knows* there is one. What may be called the "cyclic aspect" of the reasoning in the first part of Rapoport's argument, repeated in Watkins's version, suggests the conclusion Watkins in fact draws, that the agents *"are* in a dilemma; there is no determinate solution to their optimization-problem."[12] If this is correct, (2) cannot be true. And even if it is not correct, (2) can be true only if the agents can *know* there is a unique rationally prescribed alternative before they reach the conclusion of an argument based on (2).

But it is easy to show there exists a unique rationally prescribed alternative. Assume there is none. Then all our strong assumptions about the rationality of the agents and their knowledge of their rationality leaves each still unable to determine what the other will do. (This is the situation portrayed in the first part of Rapoport's argument.) But if Row, say, cannot determine what Column will do, then the basic argument for confessing applies, and the rationally prescribed alternative for him is to confess. (In this situation, "confessing" satisfies a sufficient condition for being rationally prescribed other than the one given in (1).)

But then there *is* a rationally prescribed alternative for him, contradicting the assumption that there is none. Row and Column can know, then, that there is a rationally prescribed alternative and be confident they will each take it before they have figured out what it is; (2) can be true, at least so far as this issue is concerned.

4.4. The question remains, what is wrong with the "cyclic aspect" of the reasoning in the first part of Rapoport's argument (and in Watkins')? For unless there is some error, we may expect that the second part of Rapoport's argument, our basic argument for cooperating, is itself but the first link in another endless chain, in which case (as just argued) the rationally prescribed alternative is after all to confess.

One subsidiary point is that the word "cyclic" is really inappropriate, since the reasoning would *not* continue indefinitely as both Rapoport and Watkins seem to think. The "cyclic aspect" would at best simply be a *reductio* of the assumption or any attempted argument that the rationally prescribed alternative is to maintain silence. (See steps (9) to (12) of the more formal presentation below.)

The main point however is that what is rationally prescribed for an agent is *relative to the relevant information he has,* and this means *all* the relevant information. If all that Row knows is that Column will do A (maintain silence), then it is certainly rational for him *not* to do A, yielding the outcome (*d, a*) which he rates as optimal. But Row is never in the situation of knowing or thinking *merely* that Column will do *A*. "Column will do *A*" occurs in his reasoning only as an inference from premises including or implying the premise that it is rational for *both* of them to do *A*. Thus we quoted Rapoport's agent as saying:

> If I have come to the conclusion that doing *A* is the rational choice, he too must have come to the same conclusion. Now knowing that he will do *A*, what shall I do?

But Row "knows" this only if he also "knows" that doing *A* is the rational choice, and in fact the one that he will make. His question "What shall I do?" has already been answered, understood as "What is rationally prescribed for me relative to all the relevant information I have?" Understood as "What is rationally prescribed for me relative *simply* to my knowledge that he will do *A*?" the question is irrelevant.

5. This discussion of the "cyclic aspect" may be better appreciated if we attempt a more formal statement of the basic argument for cooperating and the attempted *reductio* of its conclusion. We begin with the premises listed above but will not attempt to include all the steps and background assumptions.

(1) An alternative *X* is rationally prescribed for an agent *y* if *y* knows that there are just two possible outcomes *m* and *n*, such that if *y* takes *X* then the outcome is *m*, if *y* does not take *X* then the outcome is *n*, and *m* is better (in *y*'s judgment) than *n*.

(2) Each prisoner knows that each knows that each will take the rationally prescribed alternative (recall the independent argument that there *is* just one rationally prescribed alternative).

(3) Each knows that an alternative is rationally prescribed for one of them just in case it is also rationally prescribed for the other of them.

(4) Each knows that he will maintain silence just in case the other does and that he will confess just in case the other does.

(5) Each knows that if silence is rationally prescribed and he maintains silence, then the outcome will be (*c, c*); and that if confessing is rationally prescribed and he confesses, then the outcome will be (*b, b*).

(6) Each knows that (*c, c*) and (*b, b*) are the only possible outcomes.

(7) Each knows that he judges (*c, c*) to be better than (*b, b*).

(8) Therefore, maintaining silence is rationally prescribed for each.

Rapoport and Watkins would presumably have the argument continue as follows:

(9) Each prisoner knows that maintaining silence is rationally prescribed for each.

(10) Each knows that the other will maintain silence.

(11) Each knows that if he were to confess, the outcome would be one he judges better than (c, c).

(12) Therefore, confessing is rationally prescribed for each.

This result contradicts (8), showing there must be a flaw somewhere in the argument. But it is not clear that the flaw occurs prior to (8); to the contrary, the step from (11) to (12) is invalid, if it is supposed to be based on (1). For (1) would be applicable only if the outcome judged better than (c, c) — either (d, a) or (a, d), depending on the agent — were known to be "possible," along with (c, c). But this is not known, and is in fact contradicted by (6), according to which (c, c) and (b, b) are the *only* possible outcomes. The argument leading to (6) makes use of (2), whereas a claim that (d, a) or (a, d) is "possible" seems to require averting one's gaze from (2). The prisoners themselves could think that (a, d) or (d, a) was "possible" only if they ignored the information which (2) asserts they possess; but surely it is out of place for agents to ignore relevant information in the course of deliberating. This is the point made at the end of the preceding section.

One response is to deny that the step to (12) is based on (1). It may be claimed that:

(1') An alternative X is rationally prescribed for y if y knows that the outcome that would result if he took X is one he judges better than the outcome that would result if he did not take that alternative

is at least as plausible as (1), and warrants the move from (11) to (12).[13] But if (1) is satisfactory as it stands, with its notion of "possible outcomes," then it seems clearly superior to (1'). For in terms of this notion of "possible outcomes," (1') would have to be understood in something like the following sense:

(1'') X is rationally prescribed for y if y knows that there are outcomes m and n such that if y were to take X, then m would be possible and in fact would be the outcome; if y were not to take X, then n would be possible and in fact would be the outcome; and m is better (in y's judgment) than n.

Thus (11) should be understood as saying that each prisoner knows that if he *were* to confess — contrary to the facts as described in (10) — then one of the outcomes ruled out by (6) *would be* both possible and actual. But why should consideration of what "*would* be possible *if*" be relevant to determining what *is* rationally prescribed for an agent in the actual world?

The claim must be then that (1') is superior to (1) because the latter is wholly *un*satisfactory, employing a notion of "possible outcomes" which *cannot* be clarified. This, rather than any of the other objections considered in section 4, is the challenge facing the basic argument for cooperating.

6. At first blush, the relevant notion of "possible outcomes" may seem perfectly clear. Each prisoner is assumed to know that each will take the ra-

tionally prescribed alternative, and to know that their situations are symmetrical in all relevant respects. "Obviously" it cannot happen that they do different things, so only two outcomes are "possible": that which would result from their both confessing and that which would result from their both maintaining silence. Perhaps nothing *need* be said to defend the notion and hence the basic argument for cooperating; the problem is the difficulty of finding much more which *can* be said.

Perhaps every coherently describable outcome is "possible" in some sense; for example, it may be *logically* possible that the prison walls dissolve before the prisoners announce their decisions. But this is not the desired sense. Assuming each prisoner has the *ability* to confess and the ability to remain silent, there is a sense in which each outcome represented in the matrix is "possible." For we naturally move from "*y* has the ability to take alternative *X*" to "*y*'s taking *X* is possible," and so from "*y* has the ability to take *X* and *z* has the ability to take *W*" to "*y*'s taking *X* and *z*'s taking *W* are (jointly) possible." But this also is not the desired sense. In the desired sense, there are two and only two "possible" outcomes, not as many as there are entries in the matrix, and not as many as there are coherently describable ones.

The desired sense is *epistemic,* and *relative:* the outcomes (*b, b*) and (*c, c*) are said to be alone possible *relative to each agent's relevant information.* The word "relevant" is necessary here, for example, in case they already know how they will act. (A reliable oracle told them, or they have gone through this argument before; I assume this sort of knowledge is possible and would not block deliberation.) If they know how they will act, they know what the outcome *will* be, and relative to *this* bit of information, no *other* outcome can be considered "possible." Exactly what is to be included in and excluded from the body of "relevant" information may be a troublesome problem in its own right, but we shall assume it solved and focus on another.

The desired sense of "possible" is *epistemic.* Roughly, if on the basis of his relevant information, a rational agent will realize that a certain one of the outcomes represented in the matrix will not be the actual outcome, then that outcome is *im*possible relative to that information. Let '*p*' stand for a sentence conjoining all the relevant information of one of the agents. If we assume that an ideally rational agent knows everything entailed by everything he knows, we might try defining "possible outcome relative to *p*" by:

(D) (*x*) (*x* is a possible outcome relative to *p* if and only if
   (i) *x* is an outcome; and
   (ii) *p* does *not* entail that the outcome is *not x*.)

We can understand (i) as "*x* is represented in the matrix." Ordinarily, an agent's information is not enough to rule out any of these outcomes, so all remain "possible." But as noted in the preceding paragraph, if the agent knows how each will act, then only one outcome is possible relative to this information.

Unfortunately, if the argument from (1) to (8) (supplemented by the unstated background assumptions) is deductively valid, then if (D) is accepted it again follows that only one outcome is possible relative to p. For (8) and (2) entail that each will remain silent, and together with (5) this yields the conclusion that the outcome will be (c, c). This means that the argument is *not* deductively valid, since it requires (at step (6), needed for the applicability of (1)) that (b, b) also be "possible." To avoid this result, (D) must be abandoned or altered.

Now actual agents do *not* know everything entailed by everything they know, and it is a mistake to attribute this knowledge to the "ideally rational" agents of our example and of game theory in general. (Alternatively, certain of the things entailed could be excluded from the agent's "relevant" information.) Clause (ii) of (D), then, is too strong. Perhaps an ideally rational agent could *come* to know any given thing entailed by some proposition he knows, if he reasoned "in the right direction," so to speak. This suggests replacing (ii) with

(ii′) an ideally rational agent could *not* infer from p that the outcome is *not* x.

This will not do, for essentially the same reason as before. If the basic argument for confessing is valid, then an ideally rational agent *could* infer (8), hence that the outcome is not (b, b), from p.

What we must note is that a reasoning process takes *time* and involves *steps*. We have no comprehensive and convincing theory of the nature and individuation of the objects of thought and belief. Let us imagine that an agent reasons from one *sentence* to another. In our example, we suppose the agent starts with p (which incorporates (1) and (2)) and ends up with (8); along the way, he reasons to (6). And the point is that he reaches (6) *before* he reaches (8) or an equivalent in his reasoning. This suggests:

(ii″) an ideally rational agent could *not* infer from p, before inferring for some w that w is the rationally prescribed alternative for him, that the outcome is *not* x.

as a substitute for (ii) in (D). After he reaches (8), the agent may realize that (b, b) also cannot be the outcome. That is, there may perfectly well be a sense in which his relevant information entails that there is only one "possible outcome," namely the one which will be actual. But since he cannot rule out (b, b) until after he concludes that maintaining silence is rationally prescribed, there is a sense in which he can correctly label it "possible" while engaged in the reasoning which finally leads him to that conclusion. This is the sense in which (6) declares that (b, b) as well as (c, c) is a "possible outcome."

But is it really *true* that an agent "cannot" rule out (b, b) until after he reaches (8) or an equivalent? If it is possible at all for him to validly infer (8) from the relevant information he starts with, hence also to validly infer that (*b, b*) will not be the outcome, it may be that the latter can be validly inferred, reached by a chain of valid reasoning, without using (8) or any obvious equivalent as a "steppingstone." I have not devised a precise substitute for (*D*) which guards against this possibility, and it may be doubted that one can be devised that would do this. The problem of clarifying the notion of "possible outcome" employed in (6) remains unsolved, and the basic argument for cooperating remains neither refuted nor conclusively established.

Finally, I summarize the main conclusions of the preceding sections and suggest a few applications and directions for further inquiry.

1. The "Prisoner's Dilemma" may be a dilemma, but presents no strict *paradox* unless (2) is assumed; and if the basic argument for cooperating is valid, there is no paradox even if (2) is assumed.

2. Some standard discussions of the "Prisoner's Dilemma" have left it unclear whether or not (2) was to be assumed, but some would apparently insist on (2). Yet (2) is implausible in the extreme for any real-life analogues of the Prisoner's Dilemma. To know or assume that an agent is "rational" in a sense that he *will* without fail take the alternative rationally prescribed for him is to know or assume that he already knows which alternative that is or can be relied upon to figure it out in the finite time available for deliberating, even if there is no known algorithm for doing so. There must also be no "slip-up" between his awareness of the rationally prescribed alternative and his taking it — no "weakness of the will" or sudden physiological malfunction. But (2) requires that both agents know or assume that they are both "rational" in this super-strong sense.

3. Despite the implausibility of (2), there is some point to considering its implications in Prisoner's Dilemma and other contexts. It is needed for speculation à la Hobbes or Rawls as to what ideally rational agents would do in a "state of nature" or other "original position." Hobbes in particular would seem to be vindicated if the basic argument for cooperating is valid.[14] Similarly, the argument bears on discussions of the rationality of voting: if valid, it shows that it is rational for ideally rational citizens to vote if they believe that enough others are equally rational.[15] True, none of us are in such a situation, and so *in practice* it may often be irrational to vote (ignoring secondary reasons agents usually have). But mere knowledge of the theoretical result should soothe the misgivings of some over the rationality of participation in democratic institutions. More generally, the argument, if valid, shows that cooperation is rational from a self-interested point of view in some contexts in which it was thought not to be. As both cooperativeness

and egoistic rationality have been touted as virtues, it cannot help but be beneficial to know that they are not *so* irreconcilable.

4. But *is* the basic argument for cooperating valid? So far as the matter has been pursued here, the answer depends on a notion of "possible outcome" which resists formal definition. This may show the argument invalid. Alternatively, it may show that there is something about the idealized notion of a rational agent which just cannot be captured by a formal theory. The latter would have significant implications for the whole enterprise of formal decision theory, and it is to be hoped that the correct verdict is neither of these two extremes.[16]

NOTES

1. Morton Davis (1970), p. 93.
2. Black (1978). I am indebted to this paper and numerous discussions with Professor Black for the inspiration of this study and many details along the way, but he should not be held responsible for my conclusions.
3. Luce and Raiffa (1957), p. 96.
4. On p. 5 they speak of the need to make explicit all "assumptions about [each player's] ability to perceive the game situation."
5. Harsanyi (1961) and (1962). Rapoport (1966), pp. 139–41; cf. also p. 54ff., 60, 70, 103f.
6. More than this certainly needs to be said about the force of dominance considerations and their limitations, but I will not try to do so here. One reason is that a full treatment would require examination of such other topics as Newcomb's paradox. See Nozick (1969) reprinted in this volume. I will only assert dogmatically my belief that the "dominance principle" which bids one to employ a dominant strategy if available is *not* a fundamental principle of choice such as the principle of maximizing expected utility may be. Its applicability apparently depends on assumptions about the choice situation normally taken for granted in the usual matrix representations of these situations, assumptions which Newcomb's paradox and the class of cases discussed here call into question. Perhaps this discussion will make this claim somewhat plausible.
7. The contrary-to-fact conditional re-enters the discussion briefly in a different context, at the end of section 5.
8. Rapoport (1966), p. 141ff. I learned of Rapoport's argument, and the variant presented by Watkins (see next note), several days after developing the argument of section 3.
9. Sen (1974b), p. 80. Sen is here responding to Watkins (1974) which is itself a set of comments on Sen (1974a).
10. In the passage quoted above, they say a rational agent "*will* always choose the [alternative] with the larger utility," but earlier they say merely that a player "will *attempt* to maximize expected utility." (Emphasis added. See also pp. 50 and 80.)
11. Watkins (1974), p. 73. In his earlier presentation, however, Watkins merely has his agent say "I should choose (*A*), confident that he, by similar reasoning, will choose (*A*)" (1970), p. 205.
12. Watkins (1974), p. 73. Rapoport also seems unwilling to say definitely that the

rationally prescribed alternative for each is cooperation. Shortly after the passage quoted, he writes, "Either the concept of rationality is not well defined in the context of the nonnegotiable nonzero-sum game; or if the definition of rationality in the context of the zero-sum game is applied to the 'solution' of some nonzero-sum games, the results are paradoxical." His conclusion seems to be that the concept of rationality is not well defined in these contexts. See his remarks on p. 142ff.

13. This is essentially a suggestion made by Robert Stalnaker. I am indebted to him for several helpful discussions and illuminating criticisms of the argument of this paper; again, responsibility for my conclusions is solely my own.
14. Watkins (1970) argues that rational agents in a Hobbesian state of nature could never get out of it, in accordance with his view that there is no rationally prescribed alternative for agents in these situations.
15. More exactly, the others must not only be "equally rational," but also convinced of one another's rationality and convictions. The argument is then that all will behave alike; the only "possible outcomes" are that in which all vote who can and that in which none vote. Of these two, the first is presumably judged better by each, so is rationally prescribed for each.
16. This paper was written while I was a fellow in the Humanities, Science, and Technology Unit of the Cornell University Program on Science, Technology, and Society.

3

Second Thoughts on Self-Interest and Morality

JOHN WATKINS

An agent A has a strategy a_1 that strictly dominates strategy a_0 if it invariably gives him a better payoff than would a_0, whatever the other agents do. And a social state (a_1b_1) is strictly Pareto-inferior to social state (a_0b_0) if all agents are better off in (a_0b_0). As everyone knows, in the Prisoner's Dilemma each agent has a strictly dominant strategy, and if they all use it, they achieve a strictly Pareto-inferior state. They are led, in a way that might have startled Adam Smith, by a malevolent invisible hand to promote an end which was no part of their intention and which none of them wants.

If that is where rational pursuit of pure self-interest leads people in situations of this type, it is natural to conclude that a dose of morality will help them to do better. But what sort of morality, and how much will it help?

These were questions that Amartya Sen addressed (1974a) and on which I have commented (1974). The present contribution, written in the light of Sen's reply (1974b), consists of: (i) a somewhat abridged and tidied up version of the first section of my comment, in which, however, I leave the wording of the main argument intact, even where I now consider it defective; (ii) a new second section in which I relate Sen's ideas about moral orderings of the outcomes of the Prisoner's Dilemma game to what was said in the first section; (iii) a new third section, in which I review the main argument in the light of various criticisms and objections that have been raised against it, most of which I consider valid; and a concluding section. My 1974 argument, which was intended to take moralism down a peg, involved the following three theses: (a) two rational egoists in a Prisoner's Dilemma situation are in a genuine *dilemma;* (b) two rational moralists in such a situation may very well be in a genuine dilemma; (c) an injection of moralism into it sometimes improves, but sometimes worsens, the situation; moralism here has no clearcut advantage over egoism. I will retain (b), but (a) will have to go, and (c) will be weakened. But I will again reach a rather discouraging conclusion.

1. To simplify the discussion I will operate exclusively with two pure types of actor. I will call them the Egoist and the Moralist. They are equally intelligent and rational, and they have similar personal preferences. There is just one big difference between them: the Egoist in all his actions is trying to satisfy optimally just his preferences, whereas the Moralist gives equal weight to the preferences of people who would be significantly affected by his action.

In a society where some people have power over others, it seems rather likely that someone in a position of power would act differently if he were a Moralist than if he were a Egoist. But game theory, in which the Prisoner's Dilemma arises, assumes that the players are essentially equal. No player exercises any *control* over another player. The police set the conditions of the Prisoner's Dilemma game, but they are a part of "Nature"; only the prisoners play it, and *they* are equals. (I suggested in (1970) that, except that there are only two of them, the situation confronting the prisoners is formally analogous to that confronting the individuals in a Hobbesian state of nature, which is a paradigm of a human condition where no one is in any way beholden to anyone.) Given conditions of non-coercion and equality, it is no longer so obvious that a Moralist will act differently, other things being equal, than an Egoist would. After all, the Egoist, in trying to do as well as he can for himself, has to take very careful account of the people with whom he is competing, cooperating, or otherwise interacting. True, he takes other people's preferences into account in a very different spirit from that in which a Moralist takes them into account. Still, he does attend to them (if he is rational, as game theory assumes) very closely.

In the Prisoner's Dilemma game let the prisoners be A and B, let a_1 stand for "A confesses" and a_0 for "A does not confess," and similarly for b_1 and b_0. And let the payoffs be as follows:

> $(a_0\ b_0)$: A and B both get two years;
> $(a_1\ b_1)$: A and B both get ten years;
> $(a_0\ b_1)$: A gets twenty years and B goes free;
> $(a_1\ b_0)$: A goes free and B gets twenty years.

Just how A would rank these four outcomes if he were a Moralist we will consider in a moment. That he would rank them differently than he would if he were an Egoist is not in dispute. The question is whether his different, and moral, ranking of them would lead him to *act* differently. I will now investigate this question. The results will turn out to be rather counterintuitive. Various assumptions are possible about the amount of information one prisoner has about the other. It will turn out that, under most of these assumptions, even if *both* prisoners were Moralists, they would be in a dilemma about how to act, analogous to the dilemma of two Egoists. Under one limiting assumption the dilemma gets resolved in the right way. But under an alternative assumption it gets resolved in the *wrong* way. It will turn out that, judged by a criterion of collective utility, Moralism has no clear-cut advantage over Egoism.

Now to the details. Let prisoner A be a Moralist. (How he came to be involved in a serious crime need not concern us.) How he will rank the outcomes is, I think, clear enough. He will regard both $(a_1\ b_0)$ and $(a_0\ b_1)$ as bad because they are so grossly *unfair*. Since they are equally unfair, he is free to discriminate between them on extra-moral grounds. He therefore ranks $(a_0\ b_1)$ (which gives him twenty years in prison) last and $(a_1\ b_0)$ next to last. As to the two equally fair outcomes, he obviously prefers $(a_0\ b_0)$ as Pareto-superior to $(a_1\ b_1)$. Thus his ranking (in descending order) will be: $(a_0\ b_0)$, $(a_1\ b_1)$, $(a_1\ b_0)$, $(a_0\ b_1)$.

But does he act differently from the way he would if he were acting out of self-interest? Let us consider the problem that faces A under various assumptions about his knowledge about B.

(1) Suppose that A does not know whether B is an Egoist or a Moralist. (In this imaginary society everyone *is* either an Egoist or a Moralist.) Then the fact that A regards $(a_0\ b_0)$ as the best outcome by no means dictates that he should choose a_0. In this case, A faces a painful dilemma: a_0 will lead either to the *best* or (if B chooses b_1) to the *worst* outcome. Choosing a_0 in-

volves a major gamble. Choosing a_1 involves a lesser gamble, but guarantees that the morally best outcome will *not* be achieved. I will call this horrid choice a type-(1) dilemma.

(2) Suppose that A knows that B is a fellow Moralist who, however, does not know that A is a Moralist. Then A knows that B is facing a type-(1) dilemma: there is a serious risk that B will play safe with b_1, and A may still prefer to defend against that risk with a_1. I will call A's dilemma here a type-(2) dilemma.

(3) Suppose that A knows that B is a Moralist who knows that he, A, is a Moralist; but A also knows that B does not know that A knows him, B, to be a Moralist. Then A knows that B is facing a type-(2) dilemma and hence that he, B, may prefer to play defensively with b_1. Then A's dilemma is still unresolved (though his temptation to gamble on a_0 has no doubt grown stronger as we proceeded from case (1) to case (3)).

(4) Suppose that A and B are both Moralists who know that the other is a Moralist *and* that the other knows him to be a Moralist. Now at last the dilemma is resolved, and in the right way: A can choose a_0 knowing that B will choose b_0.

Case (4) constitutes a clear success for Moralism. But now consider a different case which, however, is like (4) in not being infected by uncertainty owing to lack of information about the other player:

(5) Suppose that A is a Moralist who knows that B is an Egoist. Now the orthodox game-theoretical view is that a rational agent acting from pure self-interest is bound to choose a dominant strategy, if one is available to him, as it is here. (I will shortly question this view; but the result we are about to obtain will not be disturbed.) This means that B is bound to choose b_1. Suppose that A accepts the orthodox view and hence regards b_1 as certain. Then A must choose a_1 to secure the second best and avoid the worst outcome. In this case, the $(a_1 \ b_1)$ outcome seems inevitable. Here, the Moralist's dilemma *is* resolved, but in the wrong way.

Let us now make A an Egoist, like B. Is it true that two Egoist prisoners are likewise condemned to the $(a_1 \ b_1)$ outcome? The orthodox view implies that the so-called Prisoner's Dilemma is not really a *dilemma* at all (for self-interested prisoners). Against this I have argued (1970, pp. 202-6), with acknowledgments to Rapoport, that the Prisoner's Dilemma does confront (Egoist) prisoners with a genuine dilemma, that it represents one kind of situation (there are others) where the idea of acting rationally (in the sense of acting in an optimizing way according to the logic of the situation) breaks down. Since this argument is relevant to the present discussion, I will reproduce it here.

The argument gains plausibility as the $(a_1 \ b_1)$ outcome is worsened and the $(a_0 \ b_0)$ outcome improved relative to $(a_1 \ b_0)$ and $(a_0 \ b_1)$. (The criterion of identity for this "game" is just the *order* of the payoffs; so long as this is preserved, changes in the amounts of the payoffs do not alter the game from a game-theoretical point of view.) So as a preliminary step I will revise the outcomes as follows: if one prisoner confesses and the other does not, the first gets one year in prison, the second twenty years; if both confess, both get eighteen years; if neither confesses, both get two years. As before, a_1 dominates a_0 and b_1 dominates b_0.

(6) Suppose now that A and B are both rational Egoists. Prisoner A begins by reasoning as follows: "If B chooses b_0, I do better with a_1 than with a_0; and if B chooses b_1, I again do better with a_1. So I must obviously choose a_1."

At this early stage A is still looking at (a_1 b_0) as a hopeful possibility. But now he reflects that B, likewise, will obviously choose b_1. The immediate effect of this realization is simply to reinforce A's previous conclusion: "If B is sure to choose b_1 I must certainly *not* choose a_0, for that would give me the worst payoff of all."

So far, so good; or rather, so bad: for it now seems to A that they are heading inevitably for eighteen years; although eighteen years is not so bad as twenty years, it is nearly as bad. Presumably B too is bleakly resigned to a similar fate.

"But dammit," A exclaims to himself, "we *do not* have to resign ourselves to eighteen years. We have been offered the chance of two years. Let us grab it. We have only to swerve from our present collision courses. B must surely see this too."

So A veers towards a_0. But now he has second thoughts. "What if B outsmarts me with b_1? Twenty years! And suppose he does not: then I can outsmart him with a_1. One year!"

So A veers back towards a_1. But not for long. He sees all too well that if B is likewise veering towards b_1, they are back at square one, heading for eighteen years. "But dammit," A exclaims. . . .

I am claiming, not that rational self-interest does dictate a_0 for A and b_0 for B, but only that it does not dictate a_1 and b_1: the prisoners *are* in a dilemma; there is no determinate solution to their optimization-problem.

I will round off this part of the discussion by reconsidering the mixed case of an Egoist up against a Moralist.

(7) Suppose that B is an Egoist who knows that A is a Moralist who knows that B is an Egoist. Then B might reason as follows: "For A the best outcome is (a_0 b_0). So A would dearly like to choose a_0. Good. I will choose b_1 and stand a good chance of getting (a_0 b_1), my best outcome. But wait: A will presumably anticipate this choice of mine, since he knows that I am an Egoist; and this will oblige him to choose a_1, since (a_1, b_1) is his second-best outcome, while a_0 b_1 is his worst outcome. But this only makes it all the more essential for me to stick to b_1: it would be disastrous for me to choose b_0 against his a_1."

Case (7) is case (5) again, but considered now from the Egoist's point of view. If B's reasoning here is correct, as it seems to me to be, that supports the conclusion provisionally reached under (5), namely that our Moralist A would be obliged to choose a_1 if he knew that he was up against an Egoist B.

Thus we arrive at the remarkable, and rather disconcerting, conclusion that the prospect of the happy $(a_0\ b_0)$ solution of the Prisoner's Dilemma is even less hopeful when one of the prisoners is a Moralist than when both are Egoists. How can this be?

I think that the answer lies in the equality and symmetry of the prisoners' situation when both are Egoists. Just because both can depend on the other instinctively plumping for his dominant strategy, each can see very well where they are heading (eighteen years) and each can see that if both swerve on to the opposite course they will serve their interests much better (two years). (True, each can also see that if only *he* swerves, he will get twenty years; yet if neither of them swerves. . . . This is the dilemma.) In the other case there is no such symmetry: the Egoist knows that his thinking is not being duplicated by the other prisoner. Now he is up against someone who rates eighteen years for both as the *second-best* outcome.

The results of our survey seem to me to be rather interesting, in a discouraging sort of way. The orthodox game-theoretical view that two rational Egoist prisoners are bound to end up in $(a_1\ b_1)$ is certainly plausible; and given this view, it is again plausible to attribute this poor collective performance to their egoism: if only A had not selfishly preferred $(a_1\ b_0)$ and B had not preferred $(a_0\ b_1)$ to $(a_0\ b_0)$, if only each had tried to satisfy the other's interest equally with his own, then, presumably, they would have achieved $(a_0\ b_0)$?

Instead, it has turned out that the honors, with regard to collective benefit, are pretty even between Egoism and Moralism. In those cases, namely (1) to (3), where a Moralist lacks a relevant piece of information about the other prisoner, he is faced by a dilemma which he may resolve in either way. In those cases, namely (4) to (7), where both prisoners know all they need to know about each other, Moralism scores one success: if both prisoners are Moralists, then their dilemma is resolved in the right way and $(a_0\ b_0)$ is assured. Egoism cannot match this result: if both prisoners are Egoists, there is only the *possibility* that each will emerge from his dilemma in a way that achieves $(a_0\ b_0)$. The outcome of their situation is indeterminate. But this Moralist success is offset by a failure. Replacing one of two Egoist prisoners by a Moralist *worsens* their situation: its outcome is now determinate, but in the wrong way: $(a_1\ b_1)$ is now assured.

2. The above was written over ten years ago, and there is much in it that I now regard as unsatisfactory. For one thing, my characterization of the Moralist was rather hasty and dogmatic. He actually relies on the following three criteria, in descending order of priority. (1) An unfair outcome is al-

ways worse than a fair one, irrespective of utility considerations. (2) If two outcomes are equally fair, or unfair, they should be ranked by utility considerations. (3) If two outcomes are equal with respect both to fairness and to utility, the Moralist may rank them by considerations of self-interest. Taking the utilities of $(a_1\ b_0)$ and of $(a_0\ b_1)$ to be equal, all this means that two such Moralists order the Prisoner's Dilemma outcomes in descending order, as follows:

$$A: (a_0\ b_0),\ (a_1\ b_1),\ (a_1\ b_0),\ (a_0\ b_1);$$
$$B: (a_0\ b_0),\ (a_1\ b_1),\ (a_0\ b_1),\ (a_1\ b_0).$$

Sen pointed out that a purely utilitarian Moralist might rank $(a_1\ b_1)$ below the two unfair outcomes, especially in cases, such as the one I considered, where both players are nearly as badly off in it as just one of them would be in his very worst outcome.

Anyway, it is clearly possible that there are ways, other than the above, in which a more or less morally minded person might order the four outcomes. I take it for granted that any such ordering must give first place to $(a_0\ b_0)$; and six out of all the twenty-four possible orderings do this. Of these six, at least three can be dismissed at once as involving something absurd. But that still leaves two alternatives to what I have called the Moralist ordering, and both of these were considered, more or less approvingly, by Sen (1974a). One of these, which he called Assurance Game preferences, given in descending order, is as follows:

$$A: (a_0\ b_0),\ (a_1\ b_0),\ (a_1\ b_1),\ (a_0\ b_1);$$
$$B: (a_0\ b_0),\ (a_0\ b_1),\ (a_1\ b_1),\ (a_1\ b_0).$$

We might call this a quasi-Moralist ordering. A quasi-Moralist is less self-abnegating than our Moralist, in that he puts the unfair outcome, where he comes out top and the other fellow bottom, above the second-best fair outcome, but more self-abnegating than our Egoist since he puts the best fair outcome above the one where he comes out top.

It is of interest to compare the performance of two quasi-Moralists, in a Prisoner's Dilemma game, with that of our Moralists. A two-person game has an equilibrium-point if, given that one player is known by the other to be using a particular strategy, there is just one strategy that is rational for the other player to use in reply. And Sen pointed out that if both prisoners have this Assurance Game ordering, or are quasi-Moralists, the game has two equilibrium points; if B is using b_0, then A must use a_0, and if b_1 then a_1. And if both Prisoners are Moralists, the game likewise has these two equilibrium points. Suppose that, in analogy with our case (1), A is a quasi-Moralist who does not know what B is. Then a_0 will give him, just as it gave the Moralist, either the best or the worst outcome. He too faces a type-(1) dilemma; and from this, type-(2) and type-(3) dilemmas can be generated as before. (I will be reformulating this last dilemma later, in response to an objection by Segerberg.)

Before considering the case analogous to case (4), let us first consider one, analogous to case (5), where a quasi-Moralist A is up against B, whom he knows to be an Egoist. So A has every reason to fear that B will play b_1. Now were A to reply to b_1 with a_0, his least preferred outcome would result. So he must play a_1. Again, the quasi-Moralist acts just as a Moralist would.

Suppose, finally, that two quasi-Moralists are in a situation analogous to case (4), where both know all they need to know about each other. Now Segerberg (1979, p. 368ff) has questioned whether even two Moralists are bound to play cooperatively here, adding: "Watkins has provided no argument that settles the issue" (p. 372). Let me try to plug this gap now, for the reasoning that shows that two Moralists will play cooperatively will also show that two quasi-Moralists will.

Whether he is a Moralist or a quasi-Moralist, A is always *hoping* that he is free to play a_0, just because it alone can give him his most preferred outcome. If fear that B will play b_1 drives A to play a_1 (as it does in case (5) and may do in cases (1) to (3)), he resorts to it reluctantly, knowing that it will give him only the second- or third-best outcome. So A has an initial bias in favor of a_0. And he reflects that, because of the symmetry of their situations, B likewise has an initial bias in favor of b_0. And this reflection strengthens his own bias in favor of a_0 by diminishing any fear he might have had that B would play b_1. And then he further reflects that B's bias in favor of b_0 will likewise have been strengthened by a similar reflection on B's part; and A's own bias is again strengthened . . . until eventually he is fully committed to a_0 as is B to b_0.

So it turns out, rather interestingly, that the performance of two of Sen's quasi-Moralists in a Prisoner's Dilemma situation is identical with that of two of my Moralists. The latters' more equalitarian and self-abnegating attitude did not bring them any collective benefit. A less severe attitude suffices. It is enough if they say: "Best of all I prefer the fair outcome that is best for all; but if I cannot have that, then I put self first."

So in cases analogous to (1), (2), and (3), both a Moralist and a quasi-Moralist are in a dilemma and *may* play defensively, while in case (5) they *will* play defensively. Is there an ordering of the outcomes that would eliminate all dilemmas and ensure that someone who acted according to this ordering will always play cooperatively? To secure this, it would be necessary for A's a_0 to dominate his a_1; and this would mean that A must prefer $(a_0\ b_1)$ to both $(a_1\ b_0)$ and $(a_1\ b_1)$. The other ordering considered by Sen, which he called an OR (other regarding) one, has just this feature. It is as follows:

A: $(a_0 \ b_0)$, $(a_0 \ b_1)$, $(a_1 \ b_0)$, $(a_1 \ b_1)$;
B: $(a_0 \ b_0)$, $(a_1 \ b_0)$, $(a_0 \ b_1)$, $(a_1 \ b_1)$.

On this he commented, rather cautiously, that one can say, "if one wishes to," that it is morally superior to the previous quasi-Moralist ordering which, in turn, is morally superior to the Egoist ordering (p. 63). We might perhaps call this an ultra-Moralist ordering. As Sen pointed out, if all people were in a moral tradition that constrains them to act as if this were their ordering, then all practical problems posed by Prisoners' Dilemma situations would melt away. An ultra-Moralist A might suspect that B is an Egoist or perhaps a Moralist or quasi-Moralist in a type-(1) dilemma; no matter, A would persist with a_0; and if B were in fact a fellow ultra-Moralist, they would of course achieve $a_0 b_0$.

Yes, but what an extraordinary ordering this is. It is at once more self-abnegating and less Kantian than the Moralist ordering since A puts the grossly unfair outcome where he comes out bottom and B comes out top *above* its mirror image where A comes out top and B bottom and also above the fair but suboptimal $(a_1 \ b_1)$. Nor is there, on Sen's presentation, any obvious utilitarian justification for any of this. (He had $(a_1 \ b_1)$ yield a total of 2×10 years in prison, and $(a_0 \ b_1)$ and $(a_1 \ b_0)$ yield 1×20 years.) One is inclined to conclude that if *this* is what would be needed to make the problem go away, then the problem will remain.

3. I begin my review of the argument in the first section above by reporting an inconsistency in it that was exposed by Segerberg (1979). It afflicts my case (3). In this case, A is supposed to know that B is facing a type-(2) dilemma, which places A in a type-(3) dilemma. But B is placed in a type-(2) dilemma if he knows that he is facing an agent in a type-(1) dilemma. Segerberg pointed out that if A knows that B knows that p, then by the canons of epistemic logic A himself knows that p and, moreover, p is true. But in the present case, A is supposed to know that B knows that B is facing someone, namely A, who is in a type-(1) dilemma. But if A is in a type-(1) dilemma, he cannot be in a type-(3) dilemma; for in the former, he does *not* know whether B is an Egoist or a Moralist, whereas in the latter he *does* know that B is a Moralist. So there is a contradiction.

Segerberg pointed out that this inconsistency would disappear if, wherever I had said that one player *knows* something about the other player, I had been content to say that he *believes* or *assumes* it. Now I do not in fact hold that it is possible for one player actually to *know* matters of this sort about another player, and it would have been more in keeping with my epistemological outlook if I had used the non-committal *assumes*. My reason for not doing so was that I wished to pinpoint the consequences of certain specific bits of ignorance in the players' situational appraisals without blurring matters by shrouding them in a general uncertainty. In order both to maintain this policy and to eliminate the contradiction I now reformulate case (3) as follows:

(3') Suppose that A knows that B is a Moralist who knows that A is a Moralist; but A also knows that B does not know that A knows B to be a Moralist. Then A knows that *it is as if B* were facing a type-(2) dilemma and hence that B may prefer to play defensively with b_1; which places A in a type-(3) dilemma.

In the remainder of this section I will concentrate on the following two questions. Was I unfair to Moralism in the first section? And how valid is my 1974 contention that two Egoist Prisoners, if fully rational, find themselves in a genuine *dilemma?* The two questions are connected; for my claim "that the honors, with regard to collective benefit, are pretty even between Egoism and Moralism" relied essentially on that contention. In answering the first question, I will begin by assuming the correctness of that contention. It will be rejected later.

My justification for the "honors are even" judgment was this. If we replace one of two Egoist players by a Moralist and assume that both know all they need to about each other, as in case (5), that actually *worsens* the situation, since $(a_1\ b_1)$ is now assured. If we replace both Egoists by Moralists and assume that both know all they need to about each other, as in case (4), that improves the situation, since $(a_0\ b_0)$ is now assured. But if we replace two Egoists by two Moralists who do not know all they need to about each other, that does not improve the situation, since they will be in a genuine dilemma. (I conceded that as we progress from case (1) to case (3), or now to case (3'), the temptation to gamble on the cooperative strategy grows stronger, becoming absolute in case (4).)

Let us now try to devise a fair scoring system by which to assess Egoism and Moralism, from the standpoint of collective benefit, in Prisoner's Dilemma situations. Consider the following three situational levels:

      level-(i): the players face no dilemma, and the $(a_0\ b_0)$ outcome is assured;

    level-(ii): the players face a real dilemma, and no outcome is assured;

    level-(iii): the players face no dilemma, and the $(a_1\ b_1)$ outcome is assured.

I will treat level-(ii) as midway between level-(i) and level-(iii) in point of desirability. (I agree that this is questionable; it might justly be objected that a situation from which *any* outcome may emerge is simply incomparable with one where a good, or a bad, outcome *will* emerge. I will revert to this point later.) Then we may lay down that a shift, in one or both players, from one way of ordering the outcomes to another scores one if it raises them either from level-(iii) to level-(ii) or from level-(ii) to level-(i); minus one if it lowers them either from level-(i) to level-(ii) or from level-(ii) to level-(iii); plus two if it raises them from level-(iii) to level-(i); minus two if it lowers them from level-(i) to level-(iii); and zero if it leaves them at the same level. Then if we take as our starting point case (6), where both players know each other to be Egoists, and if, for the moment, we stick to my 1974 contention that they will be at level-(ii), then Moralism scores zero in cases (1) to (3′), plus one in case (4), and minus one in case (5). (I omit case (7) because it replicates case (5).) The overall score is zero, and it may therefore seem that the honors are even.

But there is an unfairness here, as Sen pointed out:

> The responsibility for the failure in the case with one Egoist and one Moralist is put on the shoulders of moralism. Why so? It is, of course, true that we can arrive at this case by "replacing one of the two Egoist prisoners by a Moralist," but we can equally easily arrive at it by replacing one of the two Moralist prisoners by an Egoist! (1974b, p. 79)

To rectify the unfairness we need to supplement the above scoring, in which case (6) was taken as the starting point and there was then some shift towards Moralism, with the scores obtained when case (4) is taken as the starting point and there is then some shift towards Egoism. Here, Egoism scores minus two in case (5), and minus one in case (6). The overall score is minus three. The honors are not even.

And, of course, the balance tilts dramatically in favor of Moralism if we replace my 1974 contention that two rational Egoists face a dilemma and are at level-(ii) by the orthodox view that they face no dilemma and are at level-(iii). For then, taking case (6) as the starting point, Moralism scores one in cases (1) to (3′), two in case (4), and zero in case (5); and taking case (4) as the starting point, Egoism scores minus two in cases (5) and (6). Moralism would then be well ahead of Egoism.

Should we reject the above contention? There is no doubt that the majority view is that we should, and I have come to respect the majority view. As a way of entry into this question, I will begin by considering an argument, not for my previous contention that two rational Egoists would be at the intermediate level-(ii), but for the even more optimistic conclusion that they would attain level-(i). This argument, which relies very much on symmetry considerations, may be summarized thus: since the players recognize each other's rationality and know that they order the outcomes in similar ways, they know that they are going to reach similar decisions; but this means that they know in advance that $(a_0\ b_1)$ and $(a_1\ b_0)$ are excluded; and of the remaining outcomes, both players prefer $(a_0\ b_0)$ to $(a_1\ b_1)$; and so they play cooperatively.

The defect in this reasoning is, I think, clear enough. Just suppose that A finds himself dithering between a_0 and a_1 and then *arbitrarily* opts for a_0. In that case he obviously could not argue: "I have chosen a_0 and I am rational;

B's situation is exactly like mine, and he too is rational; therefore, he will choose b_0." As Lawrence H. Davis put it, *A* can predict, from considerations of symmetry, that *B*'s decision will mirror *A*'s, only if "there is a unique rationally prescribed alternative" for *A* himself (1977, p.52 in this volume). To put it another way, *A*'s prediction concerning *B* should fall out as a consequence (if indeed it *is* a consequence) of his analysis of what anyone should do in *A*'s situation and hence what anyone should do in *B*'s analogous situation. The prediction that *B* will act similarly should not figure as a *premise* in *A*'s calculations as to what he should do. Yet it obviously does so figure in the above argument, where *A* *begins* by excluding the $(a_0\ b_1)$ and $(a_1\ b_0)$ outcomes from his consideration merely on symmetry grounds.

Even more serious misuse has been made of the symmetry argument. Suppose that *A* is painfully dithering between a_0 and a_1, having as yet found no convincing reason to prefer one to other. He then argues: "Whichever I opt for, *B* will do likewise; so by opting for a_0 I can ensure the $(a_0\ b_0)$ outcome." This suggests that *A*'s private reasoning can have a Svengali-like control over *B*'s.

Davis rightly took Rapoport to task for misusing the symmetry argument in this sort of way. At one point Rapoport had Prisoner *A* say (I have adjusted his notation to ours):

> To insure that *B* does not come to the conclusion that he should play b_1, I better avoid a_1 also. For if I avoid it and am rational, he too will avoid it if he is rational (1966, p. 141).

Yet Davis himself seems to use the symmetry argument as a main premise in *A*'s calculations as to what his best alternative is. (I say "seemed" because he subsequently expressed certain misgivings about this.) He wrote:

> *A* knows that *B* is a rational agent and that he himself is. He knows further that their situation and information are symmetric: whatever considerations would lead *A* himself to choose one way would lead *B* to choose *exactly the same* way. The information *A* has, then, implies that *the outcomes* $(a_0\ b_1)$ *and* $(a_1\ b_0)$ *are not in fact possible* (p. 48 in this volume, his italics).

Of course, *if A* could be quite sure that $(a_0\ b_0)$ and $(a_1\ b_1)$ are the only outcomes that are "in fact possible," then knowing that both he and *B* prefer the former, he should choose a_0, confident that *B* will choose b_0. The snag is, though, that there may be the following asymmetry between them: *B* may be a player who rightly refrains from using the symmetry argument in calculating his best move and who uses a dominant strategy when he has one; in that case the "impossible" outcome (a_0 b_1) results, and A is heavily punished for his misuse of the symmetry argument.

Let us now consider how far the above strictures against misuse of the symmetry argument apply to the reasoning with which I supported my previous contention that two rational Egoists are at level-(ii) and face a genuine dilemma. I may begin by mentioning that, when I wrote the first section, the game-theoretician who had most influenced me was Rapoport. Moreover, on Sen's reading of it, that reasoning is wide open to such strictures:

> The possibility of the emergence of the "right" solution ... is demonstrated by Watkins by an argument that crucially involves the symmetry of the two prisoners' situations ...
>
> Furthermore, the type of egoistic reasoning outlined by Watkins essentially makes each prisoner assume — at least temporarily — that the other prisoner's action will be a *function* of his own action and will in fact coincide with it. (1974b, pp. 79–80).

As I said, the symmetry argument is not being misused if A first independently reaches the conclusion that he must act in a certain way and then proceeds to the conclusion that B, being in an exactly analogous situation and being equally rational, will decide similarly. In the reasoning imputed in section 1 to A in case (6), he begins by doing just that. His conclusion is that they must choose a_1 and b_1 respectively and bleakly resign themselves to eighteen years in prison. Then he looks longingly at the prospect of only two years, and assumes that B is likewise looking longingly at it. His monologue continues: "We have been offered the chance of two years. Let us grab it. We have only to swerve from our present collision courses. B must surely see this too." And here, I now think, I was misusing the symmetry argument. B must indeed see that they are, in all likelihood, heading for eighteen years; but this does not mean that he too will want to swerve to the other course. He may be saying to himself: "With luck, A will swerve from a_1 in the naive expectation that I will swerve from b_1. But I won't." As Sen duly commented:

> It is precisely because B's choice cannot be assumed by A to be a mirror-reflection of his own choice that the dilemma of the prisoners is supposed to arise. "Let us grab it" is a hollow slogan in this non-cooperative game. (Ibid., p. 80)

I agree. I now wonder whom A supposed himself to be addressing when he exclaimed "Let *us* grab it." He is not on the telephone to B (and if he were, it would not help, given that agreements are unenforceable). He is talking to himself. And it would have been silly if he had said to himself "Let *me* grab it." The whole point here is, of course, that it can be grabbed only if *both* use their cooperative but dominated strategies.

However, as I portrayed him, A does not come to rest with the conclusion that he must switch to a_0 and that B will surely do likewise. He sees the dangers and sees that B will see them too. And he glumly recognizes that they should both defend themselves against them by using their dominant but non-cooperative strategies. Back to square one.

But instead of letting things finally come to rest at this point, I had A start up all over again, looking in dismay at the prospect of eighteen years and longingly towards the prospect of two. My conclusion was "not that rational self-interest does dictate a_0 for A and b_0 for B, but only that it does not dictate a_1 and b_1: the prisoners *are* in a dilemma." But I now see that this is open to a *reductio*. Suppose it to be true: A and B are, and know each other to be, in a genuine dilemma. Now consider this from A's point of view. B is dithering between b_0 and b_1, and may opt for either. Then it is quite clear what A should do; he should (i) hope to take advantage of b_0 with a_1, and (ii) guard against the danger of b_1 with a_1. So A is in no dilemma; and similarly for B. If they were in a dilemma, they would not be in a dilemma.

And so, a chastened Johnny-come-lately, I now turn orthodox: the Prisoner's "Dilemma" presents rational Egoists with no dilemma: their strictly dominant strategies drive them infallibly, provided they act rationally, to a strictly Pareto-inferior state.

4. Then what, if anything, survives from my earlier attempt to *épater les moralistes,* given that the honors are not even between Egoism and Moralism? The editors of this volume suggested that I consider the implications of the revised results for what incentive, if any, they give an individual to prefer Moralism to Egoism. This I will now do, and my conclusion will be rather discouraging. I start by asking whether a switch by an Egoist to Moralism can ever have harmful results from a moral point of view. I will not cling to my 1974 contention that an $(a_1 \ b_1)$ outcome, which at least has the merit of being fair, is always morally preferable to the unfair outcomes $(a_0 \ b_1)$ and $(a_1 \ b_0)$, irrespective of the utilities involved; but surely it sometimes is. (Consider the case where $(a_1 \ b_1)$ gives two equally nefarious prisoners five years each, while $(a_0 \ b_1)$ gives one of them twenty years and lets the other go scot free.) Now a Moralist or quasi-Moralist A, who faces one of the dilemmas generated by one of the kinds of epistemic uncertainty mentioned earlier, *may* turn what would have been $(a_1 \ b_1)$, had A been an Egoist, into $(a_0 \ b_1)$, by opting hopefully but vulnerably for a_0; and this *may* be a case where $(a_0 \ b_1)$ surely is morally inferior to $(a_1 \ b_1)$. So there remains some possibility of some moral damage being caused by an injection of Moralism. As to Moralism doing neither harm nor good: this would happen in the

above case if A had opted defensively for a_1; and it would also happen in cases where he assumes, correctly, that he faces an Egoist and is therefore obliged to opt for a_1.

It is natural to hope that reflection upon the baleful consequences of the rational pursuit of self-interest in Prisoner's Dilemma situations should encourage a shift away from Egoism toward Moralism or quasi-Moralism; surely a rational Egoist A must come to see that everyone, himself included, will be better off if the (a_0 b_0) outcome is regarded as superior to (a_1 b_0). Yes, but in the absence of a *Volkgeist* or group mind that could switch to Moralism, carrying individual Egoists along in its wake, everyone will become a Moralist only if each individual Egoist decides to switch (and no individual Moralist decides to switch to Egoism). And when we consider what incentive an individual Egoist A has to switch, the foregoing results yield a pretty discouraging answer.

To keep matters simple, suppose once more that everyone in a certain society is either a rational Egoist or a rational Moralist and that Prisoner's Dilemma situations arise quite often in this society. And suppose, to begin with, that there is a fifty:fifty division into Moralists and Egoists. Now there is one case where A, as an ex-Egoist turned Moralist, would unhesitatingly choose a_0, where previously he would have chosen a_1, namely case (4), where everyone involved knows, and knows that the others know, that they are all Moralists. But if we allow that someone who is now an Egoist may switch to Moralism, we must surely allow the converse possibility that a Moralist may become disillusioned with Moralism and switch to Egoism. But if we allow *that,* then the conditions for case (4) can never be satisfied; it will always be possible that the other fellow is a renegade. It just is not possible for A and B to *know* all they would need to know about each other for them to be in a case (4) situation. Moralists and Egoists *look* alike. The former do not have haloes or other infallible signs of their Moralism. An apparent case (4) is really a case (1) plus a strong presumption that the other fellow B is a Moralist. How will A, if he turns Moralist, resolve type-(1) dilemmas? Suppose first that he is in the dark about whether B is a Moralist or an Egoist. Then for A the probability that B will choose b_1 is *greater than a half;* for half the people in this society are Egoists, and if B is a rational Egoist he *will* use b_1; and if B is a Moralist he *may* use b_1, for just the reasons that will now incline A, himself now a Moralist, to guard against b_1 with a_1.

But if A were always going to resolve such dilemmas in this defensive way, a switch to Moralism would be ineffectual and pointless, since he would continue acting just as though he were still an Egoist. So, assume that he would sometimes choose a_0 in cases where he believes B to be a fellow Moralist. In these cases his switch to Moralism *may* do good. So A has some incentive to switch. But he also has some *dis*incentive; for it may, also, do moral *harm,* even if we optimistically assume that A never makes a mistake when he judges the other fellow B to be a Moralist. Perhaps B is in the dark as to A's Moralism; or perhaps B is familiar with A's Egoist track record and has not heard about his switch to Moralism; or perhaps he has heard about this alleged switch but suspects that it is a feint to tempt Moralists like B into b_0 to be met with a_1. In all these cases, B is likely to guard against a_1 with b_1; and in choosing a_0, A may not merely go against his self-interest but help to bring about an outcome, namely $(a_0\ b_1)$, that is morally inferior to the $(a_1\ b_1)$, outcome that would have resulted had he acted as a pure Egoist. For A, when he reflects on all this, the incentive may be balanced, or even outweighed, by the disincentive. Of course, these negative considerations would be strengthened if Moralists were in a minority in this society.

Suppose, now, that Moralists are in a big majority, say 95 per cent or more. Then the incentive for A to switch to Moralism would now be rather strong. Except in rare cases where he has reason to suspect that B is an Egoist, he could regularly risk choosing a_0, pretty confident that B is a fellow Moralist who will risk using b_0. This policy might miscarry occasionally, but the good that A would now be doing should far outweigh any harm. There would be a kind of bandwagon effect: if Moralism had already spread very far within this society, it could be expected to spread still further.

The discouraging feature of this analysis is that, on any estimate of the ratio of truly moral people in any actual society that is not wildly optimistic, the bandwagon would never start rolling.

4

Maximization Constrained: The Rationality of Cooperation

DAVID GAUTHIER

1. What follows these introductory remarks is part of chapter six of my forth-coming book, *Morals by Agreement*.[1] In the first section of the chapter, not included here, I discuss the problem posed by Hobbes's Foole, who "hath sayd in his heart, there is no such thing as Justice ... seriously alleaging, that every mans conservation, and contentment, being committed to his own care, there could be no reason, why every man might not do what he thought conduced thereunto: and therefore also to make, or not make; keep, or not keep Covenants, was not against Reason, when it conduced to one's benefit."[2]

Think of the state of nature as a condition in which each person seeks straightforwardly to maximize her individual utility. In interaction with her fellows, then, each chooses what she believes to be a utility-maximizing re-sponse to the choices she expects the others to make. Is it always possible for each person to be successful — that is, for each to act in a way that is utility-maximizing given the actions of the others? No — not if we take "action" in its ordinary sense. If you and I must choose between going to Toronto and going to Pittsburgh, and I want to go where you go, and you want to go where I do not go, then one of us will act in a way that is not utility-maximizing, given what the other does. But if we replace "action" by "strategy," where a strategy is a probability distribution over possible actions, then it is always possible for each person to be successful — for each person's strategy to be utility-maximizing given the others' strategies.[3] (There are some qualifications here; there must be only finitely many persons each with only finitely many actions. But they are not important.)

Suppose then that everyone is successful. We say that the outcome is in equilibrium – no one could do better for herself, given what the others do. No one could benefit from a unilateral change of strategy. But all may not be well. For although each is doing her best for herself, given what the others do, it may be possible for all to do better. The outcome may not be optimal (in the Pareto sense); some alternative might afford some persons greater utility and no person lesser utility.

In every (finite) situation, there is at least one outcome in equilibrium and at least one optimal outcome, but in some situations, no outcome is both in equilibrium and optimal. The Prisoner's Dilemma is the most familiar example of a situation with a unique equilibrium (mutual confession) which is not optimal (since mutual non-confession is better for both prisoners). If each person maximizes her utility given the strategies of others, then at least some person receives less utility than she might given each other person's utility. And if each person receives as much utility as she can, given each other person's utility, then at least some person does not maximize her utility given the strategies of others.

In the state of nature, each seeks to maximize her own utility. And so in some situations the outcome is not optimal. This provides a basis for society, considered (in Rawlsian terms) as "a cooperative venture for mutual advantage."[4] Think of a cooperative venture as implementing a joint choice, without requiring each person's strategy to be utility-maximizing given the others. And think of mutual advantage as affording each person greater utility than she would expect otherwise – greater, then, than she would expect were each to maximize her utility given the others' choices.

The Foole then says, "Agree to a cooperative venture, but only if you expect agreement to pay." This is sound advice. But the Foole goes on to say, "And adhere to a cooperative venture, but only if you expect adherence to pay." This is not sound advice. In effect, the Foole advises you to adhere only if it proves utility-maximizing. But then no one does better than if each were to maximize her utility given the others' choices. The venture does not improve on the state of nature.

On the Foole's view, reason stands in the way of cooperation. What follows seeks to refute the Foole – to exhibit the rational basis, not merely for entering, but for adhering to, cooperative ventures.

In my discussion I refer to the preceding chapter five of the book, in which I argue that rational cooperation satisfies the principle of minimax relative concession. When straightforwardly maximizing behavior yields a sub-optimal outcome, there may be many different possible joint choices or cooperative ventures, each of which would afford mutual advantage. Not every such venture will be rationally acceptable to all concerned. Think of persons bargaining over possible cooperative ventures.[5] Each considers her share of the benefits from cooperation, as compared with others' shares. Each begins by claiming as large a share as possible – the greatest utility for herself compatible with no one doing worse than in the absence of cooperation. To reach agreement on a particular venture from these claims, each must concede a part of her claim, but no one can be rationally expected to concede more, proportionately, than she recognizes some person must concede to reach agreement. Thus rational bargainers agree on that cooperative venture for which the maximum proportionate or relative concession made by any person is a minimum.

I refer also to condition A' for strategic rationality. The underlying condition A is that each person's choice must be a rational response to the choices he expects the others to make. The usual interpretation of this treats a rational response as a utility-maximizing response. But this leaves everyone in the state of nature. Condition A' states that each person's choice must be a fair optimizing response (where fairness is captured by the requirements of minimax concession) to the choices he expects the others to make, provided such a response is available to him; otherwise, his choice must be a utility-maximizing response. I defend condition A'.

2.1 The Foole, and those who share his conception of practical reason, must suppose that there are potentialities for cooperation to which each person would rationally agree, were he to expect the agreement to be carried out, but that remain unactualized, since each rationally expects that someone, perhaps himself, perhaps another, would not adhere to the agreement. In chapter five we argued that cooperation is rational if each cooperator may expect a utility nearly equal to what he would be assigned by the principle of minimax relative concession. The Foole does not dispute the necessity of this condition but denies its sufficiency. He insists that for it to be rational to comply with an agreement to cooperate, the utility an individual may expect from cooperation must also be no less than what he would expect were he to violate his agreement. And he then argues that for it to be rational to agree to cooperate, then, although one need not consider it rational to comply oneself, one must believe it rational for the others to comply. Given that everyone is rational, fully informed, and correct in his expectations, the Foole supposes that cooperation is actualized only if each person expects a utility from cooperation no less than his non-compliance utility. The benefits that could be realized through cooperative arrangements that do not afford each person at least his non-compliance utility remain forever beyond the reach of rational humans beings—forever denied us because our very rationality would lead us to violate the agreements necessary to realize these benefits. Such agreements will not be made.

The Foole rejects what would seem to be the ordinary view that given neither unforeseen circumstances nor misrepresentation of terms, it is rational to comply with an agreement if it is rational to make it. He insists that holders of this view have failed to think out the full implications of the maximizing conception of practical rationality. In choosing, one takes one's stand in the present and looks to the expected utility that will result from each possible action. What has happened may affect this utility; that one has agreed may affect the utility one expects from doing, or not doing, what would keep the agreement. But what has happened provides in itself no reason for choice. That one had reason for making agreement can give one reason for keeping it only by affecting the utility of compliance. To think otherwise is to reject utility-maximization.

Let us begin our answer to the Foole with the distinction between an individual strategy and a joint strategy.[6] An individual strategy is a lottery over the possible actions of a single actor. A joint strategy is a lottery over possible outcomes. Cooperators have joint strategies available to them.

We may think of participation in a cooperative activity, such as a hunt, in which each huntsman has his particular role coordinated with that of the others, as the implementation of a single joint strategy. We may also extend the notion to include participation in a practice, such as the making and keeping of promises, where each person's behavior is predicated on the conformity of others to the practice.

An individual is not able to ensure that he acts on a joint strategy since whether he does depends, not only on what he intends, but on what those with whom he interacts intend. But we may say that an individual bases his action on a joint strategy insofar as he intentionally chooses what the strategy requires of him. Normally, of course, one bases one's action on a joint strategy only if one expects those with whom one interacts to do so as well, so that one expects actually to act on that strategy. But we need not import such an expectation into the conception of basing one's action on a joint strategy.

A person cooperates with his fellows only if he bases his actions on a joint strategy; to agree to cooperate is to agree to employ a joint rather than an individual strategy. The Foole insists that it is rational to cooperate only if the utility one expects from acting on the cooperative joint strategy is at least equal to the utility one would expect were one to act instead on one's best individual strategy. This defeats the end of cooperation, which is in effect to substitute a joint strategy for individual strategies in situations in which this substitution is to everyone's benefit.

A joint strategy is fully rational only if it yields an optimal outcome or, in other words, only if it affords each person who acts on it the maximum utility compatible in the situation with the utility afforded each other person who acts on the strategy. Thus we may say that a person acting on a rational joint strategy maximizes his utility, subject to the constraint set by the utilities it affords to every other person. An individual strategy is rational if, and only if, it maximizes one's utility given the *strategies* adopted by the other persons; a joint strategy is rational only if (but not if, and only if) it maximizes one's utility given the *utilities* afforded to the other persons.

Let us say that a *straightforward* maximizer is a person who seeks to maximize his utility given the strategies of those with whom he interacts. A *constrained* maximizer, on the other hand, is a person who seeks in some situations to maximize her utility, given not the strategies but the utilities of those with whom she interacts. The Foole accepts the rationality of straightforward maximization. We, in defending condition A' for strategic rationality, accept the rationality of constrained maximization.

A constrained maximizer has a conditional disposition to base her actions on a joint strategy, without considering whether some individual strategy would yield her greater expected utility. But not all constraint could be rational; we must specify the characteristics of the conditional disposition. We shall therefore identify a constrained maximizer as someone (i) who is conditionally disposed to base her actions on a joint strateg, or practice should the utility she expects were everyone so to base his action (a) be no less than what she would expect were everyone to employ individual strategies, and (b) approach what she would expect from the cooperative outcome determined by minimax relative concession, and (ii) who actually acts on this conditional disposition should her expected utility be greater than what she would expect were everyone to employ individual strategies. Or, in other words, a constrained maximizer is ready to cooperate in ways that, if followed by all, would yield outcomes that she would find beneficial and not unfair, and she does cooperate should she expect an actual practice or activity to be beneficial. In determining the latter, she must take into account the possibility that some persons will fail, or refuse, to act cooperatively. Henceforth, unless we specifically state otherwise, we shall understand by a constrained maximizer one with this particular disposition.

There are three points in our characterization of constrained maximization that should be noted. The first is that a constrained maximizer is conditionally disposed to act not only on the unique joint strategy that would be prescribed by a rational bargain, but on any joint strategy that affords her a utility approaching what she would expect from fully rational cooperation. The range of acceptable joint strategies is, and must be left, unspecified. The idea is that in real interaction it is reasonable to accept cooperative arrangements that fall short of the ideal of full rationality and fairness provided they do not fall too far short. At some point, of course, one decides to ignore a joint strategy, even if acting on it would afford one an expected utility greater than one would expect were everyone to employ an individual strategy, because one hopes thereby to obtain agreement on, or acquiescence in, another joint strategy which in being fairer is also more favorable to oneself. At precisely what point one decides this we make no attempt to say. We simply defend a conception of constrained maximization that does not require that all acceptable joint strategies be ideal.

The second point is that a constrained maximizer does not base her actions on a joint strategy whenever a nearly fair and optimal outcome would result were everyone to do likewise. Her disposition to cooperate is conditional on her expectation that she will benefit in comparison with the utility she could expect were no one to cooperate. Thus she must estimate the likelihood that others involved in the prospective practice or interaction will act cooperatively and calculate not the utility she would expect were all to cooperate, but the utility she would expect if she cooperates, given her estimate of the degree to which others will cooperate. Only if this exceeds what she would expect from universal non-cooperation does her conditional disposition to constraint actually manifest itself in a decision to base her actions on the cooperative joint strategy.

Thus, faced with persons whom she believes to be straightforward maximizers, a constrained maximizer does not play into their hands by basing her actions on the joint strategy she would like everyone to accept, but rather, to avoid being exploited, she behaves as a straightforward maximizer, acting on that individual strategy that maximizes her utility given the strategies she expects the others to employ. A constrained maximizer makes reasonably certain that she is among like-disposed persons before she actually constrains her direct pursuit of maximum utility.

But note that a constrained maximizer may find herself required to act in such a way that she would have been better off had she not entered into cooporation. She may be engaged in a cooperative activity that, given the willingness of her fellows to do their part, she expects to be fair and beneficial, but that, should chance so befall, requires her to act so that she incurs some loss greater than had she never engaged herself in the endeavor. Here she would still be disposed to comply, acting in a way that results in real disadvantage to herself, because given her *ex ante* beliefs about the dispositions of her fellows and the prospects of benefit, participation in the activity affords her greater expected utility than non-participation.

And this brings us to the third point, that constrained maximization is not straightforward maximization in its most effective disguise. The constrained maximizer is not merely the person who, taking a larger view than her fellows, serves her overall interest by sacrificing the immediate benefits of ignoring joint strategies and violating cooperative arrangements in order to obtain the long-term benefits of being trusted by others.[7] Such a person exhibits no real constraint. The constrained maximizer does not reason more effectively about how to maximize her utility, but reasons in a different way. We may see this most clearly by considering how each faces the decision whether to base her action on a joint strategy. The constrained maximizer considers (i) whether the outcome, should everyone do so, be nearly fair and optimal, and (ii) whether the outcome she realistically expects should she do so affords her greater utility than universal non-cooperation. If both of these conditions are satisfied, she bases her action on the joint strategy. The straightforward maximizer considers simply whether the outcome he realistically expects, should he base his action on the joint strategy, affords him greater utility than the outcome he would expect were he to act on any alternative strategy — taking into account, of course, long-term as well as short-term effects. Only if this condition is satisfied, does he base his action on the joint strategy.

Consider a purely isolated interaction in which both parties know that how each chooses will have no bearing on how each fares in other interactions. Suppose that the situation has the familiar Prisoner's Dilemma structure; each benefits from mutual cooperation but each benefits from non-cooperation whatever the other does. In such a situation, a straightforward maximizer chooses not to cooperate. A constrained maximizer chooses to cooperate if, given her estimate of whether or not her partner will choose to cooperate, her own expected utility is greater than the utility she would expect from the non-cooperative outcome.

Constrained maximizers can thus obtain cooperative benefits that are unavailable to straightforward maximizers, however farsighted the latter may be. But straightforward maximizers can, on occasion, exploit unwary constrained maximizers. Each supposes her disposition to be rational. But who is right?

2.2 To demonstrate the rationality of suitably constrained maximization we solve a problem of rational choice. We consider what a rational individual would choose, given the alternatives of adopting straightforward maximization and of adopting constrained maximization, as his disposition for strategic behavior. Although this choice is about interaction, to make it is not to engage in interaction. Taking others' dispositions as fixed, the individual reasons parametrically to his own best disposition. Thus he compares the expected utility of disposing himself to maximize utility given others' expected strategy choices with the utility of disposing himself to cooperate with others in bringing about nearly fair and optimal outcomes.

To choose between these dispositions, a person needs to consider only those situations in which they would yield different behavior. If both would be expressed in a maximizing individual strategy or if both would lead one to base action on the joint strategy one expects from others, then their utility expectations are identical. But if the disposition to constraint would be expressed in basing action on a joint strategy whereas the disposition to maximize straightforwardly would be expressed in defecting from the joint strategy, then their utility expectations differ. Only situations giving rise to such differences need be considered. These situations must satisfy two conditions. First, they must afford the prospect of mutually beneficial and fair cooperation, since otherwise constraint would be pointless. And second, they must afford some prospect for individually beneficial defection, since otherwise no constraint would be needed to realize the mutual benefits.

We suppose, then, an individual, considering what disposition to adopt, for situations in which his expected utility is u should each person act on an individual strategy, u' should all act on a cooperative joint strategy, and u'' should he act on an individual strategy and the others base their actions on a cooperative joint strategy, and u is less than u' (so that he benefits from cooperation as required by the first condition) and u' in turn is less than u'' (so that he benefits from defection as required by the second condition).

Consider these two arguments which this person might put to himself:

Argument (1): Suppose I adopt straightforward maximization. Then if I expect the others to base their actions on a joint strategy, I defect to my best individual strategy and expect a utility, u''. If I expect the others to act on individual strategies, then so do I, and expect a utility, u. If the probability that others will base their actions on a joint strategy is p, then my overall expected utility is $(pu'' + (1-p)u)$.

Suppose I adopt constrained maximization. Then if I expect the others to base their actions on a joint strategy, so do I, and expect a utility u'. If I expect the others to act on individual strategies, then so do I, and expect a utility, u. Thus my overall expected utility is $(pu' + (1-p)u)$.

Since u'' is greater than u', $(pu'' + (1-p)u)$ is greater than $(pu' + (1-p)u)$, for any value of p other than 0 (and for $p = 0$, the two are equal). Therefore, to maximize my overall expectation of utility, I should adopt straightforward maximization.

Argument (2): Suppose I adopt straightforward maximization. Then I must expect the others to employ maximizing individual strategies in interacting with me; so do I, and expect a utility, u.

Suppose I adopt constrained maximization. Then if the others are conditionally disposed to constrained maximization, I may expect them to base their actions on a cooperative joint strategy in interacting with me; so do I, and expect a utility u'. If they are not so disposed, I employ a maximizing strategy and expect u as before. If the probability that others are disposed to constrained maximization is p, then my overall expected utility is $(pu' + (1-p)u)$.

Since u' is greater than u, $(pu' + (1-p)u)$ is greater than u for any value of p other than 0 (and for $p = 0$, the two are equal). Therefore, to maximize my overall expectation of utility, I should adopt constrained maximization.

Since these arguments yield opposed conclusions, they cannot both be sound. The first has the form of a dominance argument. In any situation in which others act non-cooperatively, one may expect the same utility whether one is disposed to straightforward or to constrained maximization. In any situation in which others act cooperatively, one may expect a greater utility if one is disposed to straightforward maximization. Therefore, one should adopt straightforward maximization. But this argument would be valid only if the probability of others acting cooperatively were, as the argument assumes, independent of one's own disposition. And this is not the case. Since persons disposed to cooperation only act cooperatively with those whom they suppose to be similarly disposed, a straightforward maximizer does not have the opportunities to benefit which present themselves to the constrained maximizer. Thus argument (1) fails.

Argument (2) takes into account what argument (1) ignores — the difference between the way in which constrained maximizers interact with those similarly disposed and the way in which they interact with straightforward maximizers. Only those disposed to keep their agreements are rationally acceptable as parties to agreements. Constrained maximizers are able to make beneficial agreements with their fellows that the straightforward cannot, not because the latter would be unwilling to agree, but because they would not be admitted as parties to agreement given their disposition to violation. Straightforward maximizers are disposed to take advantage of their fellows should the opportunity arise; knowing this, their fellows would prevent such opportunity arising. With the same opportunities, straightforward maximizers would necessarily obtain greater benefits. A dominance argument establishes this. But because they differ in their dispositions, straightforward and constrained maximizers differ also in their opportunities, to the benefit of the latter.

But argument (2) unfortunately contains an undefended assumption. A person's expectations about how others will interact with him depend strictly on his own choice of disposition only if that choice is known by the others. What we have shown is that if the straightforward maximizer and the constrained maximizer appear in their true colors, then the constrained maximizer must do better. But need each so appear? The Foole may agree, under the pressure of our argument and its parallel in the second argument we ascribed to Hobbes, that the question to be asked is not whether it is or is not rational to keep (particular) covenants, but whether it is or is not rational to be (generally) disposed to the keeping of covenants, and he may recognize that he cannot win by pleading the cause of straightforward maximization in a direct way. But may he not win by linking straightforward maximization to the appearance of constraint? Is not the Foole's ultimate argument that the truly prudent person, the fully rational utility-maximizer, must seek to appear trustworthy, an upholder of his agreements? For then he will not be excluded from the cooperative arrangements of his fellows, but will be welcomed as a partner, while he awaits opportunities to benefit at their expense — and, preferably, without their knowledge, so that he may retain the guise of constraint and trustworthiness.

There is a short way to defeat this maneuver. Since our argument is to be applied to ideally rational persons, we may simply add another idealizing assumption and take our persons to be *transparent*.[8] Each is directly aware of the dispositions of his fellows and so aware whether he is interacting with straightforward or constrained maximizers. Deception is impossible; the Foole must appear as he is.

But to assume transparency may seem to rob our argument of much of its interest. We want to relate our idealizing assumptions to the real world. If constrained maximization defeats straightforward maximization only if all persons are transparent, then we shall have failed to show that under actual, or realistically possible, conditions, moral constraints are rational. We shall have refuted the Foole but at the price of robbing our refutation of all practical import.

However, transparency proves to be a stronger assumption than our argument requires. We may appeal instead to a more realistic *translucency,* supposing that persons are neither transparent nor opaque, so that their disposition to cooperate or not may be ascertained by others, not with certainty, but as more than mere guesswork. Opaque beings would be condemned to seek political solutions for those problems of natural interaction that could not be met by the market. But we shall show that for beings as translucent as we may reasonably consider ourselves to be, moral solutions are rationally available.

2.3 If persons are translucent, then constrained maximizers (CMs) will sometimes fail to recognize each other and will then interact non-cooperatively even if cooperation would have been mutually beneficial. CMs will sometimes fail to identify straightforward maximizers (SMs) and will then act cooperatively; if the SMs correctly identify the CMs, they will be able to take advantage of them. Translucent CMs must expect to do less well in interaction than would transparent CMs; translucent SMs must expect to do better than would transparent SMs. Although it would be rational to choose to be a CM were one transparent, it need not be rational if one is only translucent. Let us examine the conditions under which the decision to dispose oneself to constrained maximization is rational for translucent persons and ask if these are (or may be) the conditions in which we find ourselves.

As in the preceding subsection, we need consider only situations in which CMs and SMs may fare differently. These are situations that afford both the prospect of mutually beneficial cooperation (in relation to non-cooperation) and individually beneficial defection (in relation to cooperation). Let us simplify by supposing that the non-cooperative outcome results unless (1) those interacting are CMs who achieve mutual recognition, in which case the cooperative outcome results, or (2) those interacting include CMs who fail to recognize SMs but are themselves recognized, in which case the outcome affords the SMs the benefits of individual defection and the CMs the costs of having advantage taken of mistakenly basing their actions on a cooperative strategy. We ignore the inadvertent taking of advantage when CMs mistake their fellows for SMs.

There are then four possible payoffs: non-cooperation, cooperation, defection, and exploitation (as we may call the outcome for the person whose supposed partner defects from the joint strategy on which he bases his action). For the typical situation, we assign defection the value one, cooperation u'' (less than one), non-cooperation u' (less than u''), and exploitation zero (less than u'). We now introduce three probabilities. The first, p, is the probability that CMs will achieve mutual recognition and so successfully cooperate. The second, q, is the probability that CMs will fail to recognize SMs but will themselves be recognized, so that defection and exploitation will result. The third, r, is the probability that a randomly selected member of the population is a CM. (We assume that everyone is a CM or a SM, so the probability that a randomly selected person is a SM is $(1-r)$.) The values of p, q, and r must, of course, fall between zero and one.

Let us now calculate expected utilities for CMs and SMs in situations affording both the prospect of mutually beneficial cooperation and individually beneficial defection. A CM expects the utility u' unless (1) she succeeds in cooperating with other CMs or (2) she is exploited by a SM. The probability of (1) is the combined probability that she interacts with a CM, r, and that they achieve mutual recognition, p, or rp. In this case, she gains $(u'' - u')$ over her non-cooperative expectation u'. Thus the effect of (1) is to increase her utility expectation by a value $(rp(u'' - u'))$. The probability of (2) is the combined probability that she interacts with a SM, $1 - r$, and that she fails to recognize him but is recognized, q, or $(1 - r)q$. In this case she received zero, so she loses her non-cooperative expectation u'. Thus the effect of (2) is to reduce her utility expectation by a value $((1 - r)qu')$. Taking both (1) and (2) into account, a CM expects the utility $(u' + (rp(u'' - u')) - (1 - r)qu')$.

A SM expects the utility u' unless he exploits a CM. The probability of this is the combined probability that he interacts with a CM, r, and that he recognizes her but is not recognized by her, q, or rq. In this case he gains $(1 - u')$ over his non-cooperative expectation u'. Thus the effect is to increase his utility expectation by a value $(rq(1 - u'))$. A SM thus expects the utility $(u' + (rq(1 - u')))$.

It is rational to dispose oneself to constrained maximization if, and only if, the utility expected by a CM is greater than the utility expected by a SM, which obtains if, and only if, p/q is greater than $((1 - u')/(u'' - u') + ((1-r)u')/(r(u'' - u')))$.

The first term of this expression, $((1 - u')/(u'' - u'))$, relates the gain from defection to the gain through cooperation. The value of defection is of course greater than that of cooperation, so this term is greater than one. The second term, $(((1-r)u')/(r(u'' - u')))$, depends for its value on r. If $r = 0$ (that is, if there are no CMs in the population), then its value is infinite. As r increases, the value of the expression decreases, until if $r = 1$ (that is, if there are only CMs in the population) its value is zero.

We may now draw two important conclusions. First, it is rational to dispose oneself to constrained maximization only if the ratio of p to q, that is, the ratio between the probability that an interaction involving CMs will result in cooperation and the probability that an interaction involving CMs and SMs will involve exploitation and defection, is greater than the ratio between the gain from defection and the gain through cooperation. If everyone in the population is a CM, then we may replace 'only if' by 'if, and only, if' in this statement, but in general it is only a necessary condition of the rationality of the disposition to constrained maximization.

Second, as the proportion of CMs in the population increases (so that the value of r increases), the value of the ratio of p to q that is required for it to be rational to dispose oneself to constrained maximization decreases. The more constrained maximizers there are, the greater the risks a constrained maximizer may rationally accept of failing to achieve mutual recognition for cooperation with other CMs and failing to recognize SMs and so being exploited by them. However, these risks, and particularly the latter, must remain relatively small.

We may illustrate these conclusions by introducing typical numerical values for cooperation and non-cooperation and then considering different values for r. One may suppose that, on the whole, there is no reason that the typical gain from defection over cooperation would be either greater or smaller than the typical gain from cooperation over non-cooperation and, in turn, no reason that the latter gain would be greater or smaller than the typical loss from non-cooperation to exploitation. And so, since defection has the value one and exploitation zero, let us assign cooperation the value two-thirds and non-cooperation one-third.

The gain from defection, $(1 - u')$, thus is two-thirds; the gain through cooperation, $(u'' - u')$, is one-third. Since p/q must exceed $((1 - u')/(u'' - u') + ((1-r)u')/(r(u'' - u')))$ for constrained maximization to be rational, in our typical case the probability p that CMs successfully cooperate must be more than twice the probability q that CMs are exploited by SMs, however great the probability r that a randomly selected person is a CM. In general, p/q must be greater than $(2 + (1-r)/r)$ or, equivalently, greater than $(r+1)/r$. If three persons out of four are CMs, so that $r = 3/4$, then p/q must be greater than 7/3; if one person out of two is a CM, then p/q must be greater than three; if one person in four is a CM, then p/q must be greater than five.

Suppose a population evenly divided between constrained and straightforward maximizers. If the constrained maximizers are able to cooperate successfully in two-thirds of their encounters and to avoid being exploited by straightforward maximizers in four-fifths of their encounters, then constrained maximizers may expect to do better than their fellows. Of course, the even distribution will not be stable; it will be rational for the straightforward maximizers to change their disposition. These persons are sufficiently translucent for them to find morality rational.

2.4 A constrained maximizer is conditionally disposed to cooperate in ways that, followed by all, would yield nearly optimal and fair outcomes and does cooperate in such ways when she may actually expect to benefit. In the two preceding sub-sections, we have argued that one is rationally so disposed if persons are transparent or persons are sufficiently translucent and enough are like-minded. But our argument has not appealed explicitly to the particular requirement that cooperative practices and activities be nearly optimal and fair. We have insisted that the cooperative outcome afford one a utility greater than non-cooperation, but this is much weaker than the insistence that it approach the outcome required by minimax relative concession.

But note that the larger the gain from cooperation, $(u'' - u')$, the smaller the minimum value of p/q that makes the disposition to constrained maximization rational. We may take p/q to be a measure of translucency; the more translucent constrained maximizers are, the better they are at achieving cooperation among themselves (increasing p) and avoiding exploitation by straightforward maximizers (decreasing q). Thus, as practices and activities fall short of optimality, the expected value of cooperation, u'', decreases, and so the degree of translucency required to make cooperation rational increases. And as practices and activities fall short of fairness, the expected value of cooperation for those with less than fair shares decreases, and so the degree of translucency required to make cooperation rational for them increases. Thus our argument does appeal implicitly to the requirement that cooperation yield nearly fair and optimal outcomes.

But there is a further argument in support of our insistence that the conditional disposition to cooperate be restricted to practices and activities yielding nearly optimal and fair outcomes. And this argument turns, as does our general argument for constraint, on how one's dispositions affect the characteristics of the situations in which one may reasonably expect to find oneself. Let us call a person who is disposed to cooperate in ways that, followed by all, yield nearly optimal and fair outcomes, *narrowly compliant*. And let us call a person who is disposed to cooperate in ways that, followed by all, merely yield her some benefit in relation to universal non-cooperation, *broadly compliant*. We need not deny that a broadly compliant person would expect to benefit in some situations in which a narrowly compliant person would not. But in many other situations a broadly compliant person must expect to lose by her disposition. For insofar as she is known to be broadly compliant, others will have every reason to maximize their utilities at her expense, by offering "cooperation" on terms that offer her but little more than she could expect from non-cooperation. Since a broadly compliant person is disposed to seize whatever benefit a joint strategy may afford her, she finds herself with opportunities for but little benefit.

Since the narrowly compliant person is always prepared to accept cooperative arrangements based on the principle of minimax relative concession, she is prepared to cooperate whenever cooperation can be mutually beneficial on terms equally rational and fair to all. In refusing other terms, she does not diminish her prospects for cooperation with other rational persons, and she ensures that those not disposed to fair cooperation do not enjoy the benefits of any cooperation, thus making their unfairness costly to themselves, and so irrational.

2.5   We should not suppose it is rational to dispose oneself to constrained maximization if one does not also dispose oneself to exclude straightforward maximizers from the benefits realizable by cooperation. Hobbes notes that those who think they may with reason violate their covenants may not be received into society except by the error of their fellows. If their fellows fall into that error, then they will soon find that it pays no one to keep covenants. Failing to exclude straightforward maximizers from the benefits of cooperative arrangements does not, and cannot, enable them to share in the long-run benefits of cooperation; instead, it ensures that the arrangements will prove ineffective, so that there are no benefits to share. And then there is nothing to be gained by constrained maximization; one might as well join the straightforward maximizers in their descent to the natural condition of humankind.

Nor should we suppose it rational to dispose oneself to constrained maximization if one does not cultivate the ability to detect the dispositions of others. Consider once again the probabilities p and q, the probability that CMs will achieve mutual recognition and cooperate, and the probability that CMs will fail to recognize SMs but will be recognized by them and so be exploited. It is obvious that CMs benefit from increasing p and decreasing q. And this is reflected in our calculation of expected utility for CMs; the value of $(u' + (rp(u'' - u'))) - (1 - r)qu')$ increases as p increases and as q decreases.

What determines the values of p and q? p depends on the ability of CMs to detect the sincerity of other CMs and to reveal their own sincerity to them. q depends on the ability of CMs to detect the insincerity of SMs and to conceal their own sincerity from them and the ability of SMs to detect the sincerity of CMs and conceal their own insincerity from them. Since any increase in the ability to reveal one's sincerity to other CMs is apt to be offset by a decrease in the ability to conceal one's sincerity from SMs, a CM is likely to rely primarily on her ability to detect the dispositions of others, rather than on her ability to reveal or conceal her own.

The ability to detect the dispositions of others must be well developed in a rational CM. Failure to develop this ability, or neglect of its exercise, will preclude one from benefitting from constrained maximization. And it can then appear that constraint is irrational. But what is actually irrational is the failure to cultivate or exercise the ability to detect others' sincerity or insincerity.

Both CMs and SMs must expect to benefit from increasing their ability to detect the dispositions of others. But if both endeavor to maximize their abilities (or the expected utility, net of costs, of so doing), then CMs may expect to improve their position in relation to SMs. The benefits gained by SMs, by being better able to detect their potential victims, must be on the whole offset by the losses they suffer as the CMs become better able to detect them as potential exploiters. On the other hand, although the CMs may not enjoy any net gain in their interactions with SMs, the benefits they gain by being better able to detect other CMs as potential cooperators are not offset by corresponding losses, but rather increased as other CMs become better able to detect them in return.

Thus, as persons rationally improve their ability to detect the dispositions of those with whom they interact, the value of p may be expected to increase, while the value of q remains relatively constant. But then p/q increases, and the greater it is, the less favorable need be other circumstances for it to be rational to dispose oneself to constrained maximization.

3.1 In defending constrained maximization we have implicitly reinterpreted the utility-maximizing conception of practical rationality. The received interpretation, commonly accepted by economists and elaborated in Bayesian decision theory and the Von Neumann-Morgenstern theory of games, identifies rationality with utility maximization at the level of particular choices. A choice is rational if, and only if, it maximizes the actor's expected utility. We identify rationality with utility maximization at the level of dispositions to choose. A disposition is rational if, and only if, an actor holding it can expect his choices to yield no less utility than the choices he would make were he to hold any alternative disposition. We shall consider whether particular choices are rational if, and only if, they express a rational disposition to choose.

It might seem that a maximizing disposition to choose would express itself in maximizing choices. But we have shown that this is not so. The essential point in our argument is that one's disposition to choose affects the situations in which one may expect to find oneself. A straightforward maximizer, who is disposed to make maximizing choices, must expect to be excluded from cooperative arrangements which he would find advantageous. A constrained maximizer may expect to be included in such arrangements. She benefits from her disposition, not in the choices she makes, but in her opportunities to choose.

We have defended the rationality of constrained maximization as a disposition to choose by showing that it would be rationally chosen. Now this argument is not circular; constrained maximization is a disposition for strategic choice that would be parametrically chosen. But the idea of a choice among dispositions to choose is a heuristic device to express the underlying requirement that a rational disposition to choose be utility-maximizing. In parametric contexts, the disposition to make straightforwardly maximizing choices is uncontroversially utility-maximizing. We may therefore employ the device of a parametric choice among dispositions to choose to show that in strategic contexts, the disposition to make constrained choices, rather than straightforwardly maximizing choices, is utility-maximizing. We must however emphasize that it is not the choice itself, but the maximizing character of the disposition in virtue of which it is choiceworthy, that is the key to our argument.

But there is a further significance in our appeal to a choice among dispositions to choose for we suppose that the capacity to make such choices is itself an essential part of human rationality. We could imagine beings so wired that only straightforward maximization would be a psychologically possible mode of choice in strategic contexts. Hobbes may have thought that human beings were so wired, that we were straightforwardly maximizing machines. But if he thought this, then he was surely mistaken. At the core of our rational capacity is the ability to engage in self-critical reflection. The fully rational being is able to reflect on his standard of deliberation and to change that standard in the light of reflection. Thus we suppose it possible for persons who may initially assume that it is rational to extend straightforward maximization from parametric to strategic contexts to reflect on the implications of this extension and to reject it in favor of constrained maximization. Such persons would be making the very choice, of a disposition to choose, that we have been discussing.

And in making that choice, they would be expressing their nature not only as rational beings, but also as moral beings. If the disposition to make straightforwardly maximizing choices were wired into us, we could not constrain our actions in the way required for morality. Moral philosophers have rightly been unwilling to accept the received interpretation of the relation between practical rationality and utility-maximization because they have recognized that it left no place for a rational constraint on directly utility-maximizing behavior, and so no place for morality as ordinarily understood. But they have then turned to a neo-Kantian account of rationality which has led them to dismiss the idea that those considerations that constitute a person's reasons for acting must bear some particular relationship to the person.[12] They have failed to relate our nature as moral beings to our everyday concern with the fulfilment of our individual preferences. But we have shown how morality issues from that concern. When we correctly understand how utility-maximization is identified with practical rationality, we see that morality is an essential part of maximization.

3.2 An objector might grant that it may be rational to dispose oneself to constrained maximizations but deny that the choices one is then disposed to make are rational.[13] The objector claims that we have merely exhibited another instance of the rationality of not behaving rationally. And before we can accuse the objector of paradox, he brings further instances before us.

Consider, he says, the costs of decision-making. Maximizing may be the most reliable procedure, but it need not be the most cost-effective. In many circumstances, the rational person will not maximize but satisfice—set a threshold level of fulfilment and choose the first course of action of those coming to mind that one expects to meet this level. Indeed, our objector may suggest, human beings, like other higher animals, are natural satisficers. What distinguishes us is that we are not hard-wired, so that we can choose differently, but the costs are such that it is not generally advantageous to exercise our option, even though we know that most of our choices are not maximizing.

Consider also, he says, the tendency to wishful thinking. If we set ourselves to calculate the best or maximizing course of action, we are likely to confuse true expectations with hopes. Knowing this, we protect ourselves by choosing on the basis of fixed principles, and we adhere to these principles even when it appears to us that we could do better to ignore them for we know that in such matters appearances often deceive. Indeed, our objector may suggest, much of morality may be understood not as constraints on maximization to ensure fair mutual benefit, but as constraints on wish-fulfilling behavior to ensure a closer approximation to maximization.

Consider again, he says, the benefits of threat behavior. I may induce you to perform an action advantageous to me if I can convince you that, should you not do so, I shall then perform an action very costly to you, even though it would not be my utility-maximizing choice. Hijackers seize airplanes and threaten the destruction of everyone aboard, themselves included, if they are not transported to Havana. Nations threaten nuclear retaliation should their enemies attack them. Although carrying out a threat would be costly, if it works, the cost need not be borne and the benefit, not otherwise obtainable, is forthcoming.

But, our objector continues, a threat can be effective only if credible. It may be that to maximize one's credibility and one's prospect of advantage, one must dispose oneself to carry out one's threats if one's demands are not met. And so it may be rational to dispose oneself to threat enforcement. But then, by parity of reasoning with our claims about constrained maximization, we must suppose it to be rational actually to carry out one's threats. Surely we should suppose instead that, although it is clearly irrational to carry out a failed threat, yet it may be rational to dispose oneself to just this sort of irrationality. And so, similarly, we should suppose that although it is clearly irrational to constrain one's maximizing behavior, yet it may be rational to dispose oneself to this irrationality.

We are unmoved. We agree that an actor who is subject to certain weaknesses or imperfections may find it rational to dispose himself to make choices that are not themselves rational. Such dispositions may be the most effective way of compensating for the weakness or imperfection. They constitute a second-best rationality, as it were. But although it may be rational for us to satisfice, it would not be rational for us to perform the action so chosen if, cost-free, the maximizing action were to be revealed to us. And although it may be rational for us to adhere to principles as a guard against wish-fulfilment, it would not be rational for us to do so if, beyond all doubt, the maximizing action were to be revealed to us.

Contrast these with constrained maximization. The rationale for disposing oneself to constraint does not appeal to any weakness or imperfection in the reasoning of the actor; indeed, the rationale is most evident for perfect reasoners who cannot be deceived. The disposition to constrained maximization overcomes externalities; it is directed to the core problem arising from the structure of interaction. And the entire point of disposing oneself to constraint is to adhere to it in the face of one's knowledge that one is not choosing the maximizing action.

Imperfect actors find it rational to dispose themselves to make less than rational choices. No lesson can be drawn from this about the dispositions and choices of the perfect actor. If her dispositions to choose are rational, then surely her choices are also rational.

But what of the threat enforcer? Here we disagree with our objector; it may be rational for a perfect actor to dispose herself to threat enforcement, and if it is, then it is rational for her to carry out a failed threat. Equally, it may be rational for a perfect actor to dispose herself to threat resistance, and if it is, then it is rational for her to resist despite the cost to herself. Deterrence, we have argued elsewhere, may be a rational policy, and non-maximizing deterrent choices are then rational.[14]

In a community of rational persons, however, threat behavior will be proscribed. Unlike cooperation, threat behavior does not promote mutual advantage. A successful threat simply redistributes benefits in favor of the threatener; successful threat resistance maintains the *status quo*. Unsuccessful threat behavior, resulting in costly acts of enforcement or resistance, is necessarily non-optimal; its very *raison d'être* is to make everyone worse off. Any person who is not exceptionally placed must then have the *ex ante* expectation that threat behavior will be disadvantageous overall. Its proscription must be part of a fair and optimal agreement among rational persons; one of the constraints imposed by minimax relative concession is abstinence from the making of threats. Our argument thus shows threat behavior to be both irrational and immoral.

Constrained maximizers will not dispose themselves to enforce or to resist threats among themselves. But there are circumstances, beyond the moral pale, in which a constrained maximizer might find it rational to dispose herself to threat enforcement. If she found herself fallen among straightforward maximizers, and especially if they were too stupid to become threat resisters, disposing herself to threat enforcement might be the best thing she could do. And, for her, carrying out failed threats would be rational, though not utility-maximizing.

Our objector has not made good his case. The dispositions of a fully rational actor issue in rational choices. Our argument identifies practical rationality with utility maximization at the level of dispositions to choose and carries through the implications of that identification in assessing the rationality of particular choices.

NOTES

1. To be published by Oxford University Press, 1985.
2. Hobbes (1651), ch. 15.
3. This is proved by John F. Nash (1951).
4. Rawls (1971), p. 4.
5. The account of bargaining sketched here is developed in several of my papers, beginning with (1974) and culminating in (1985c).
6. This answer to the Foole supersedes my discussion in (1975).
7. Thus constrained maximization is not parallel to such strategies as "Tit-for-Tat" that have been advocated for so-called iterated Prisoner's Dilemmas. Constrained maximizers may cooperate even if neither expects her choice to affect future situations. There is no appeal to the kind of reciprocity needed by Robert Axelrod's account; see Axelrod (1981b), reprinted in this volume, pp. 320–39.
8. That the discussion in my (1975) assumes transparency was pointed out to me by Derek Parfit. See his discussion of "the self-interest theory" in Parfit (1984). See also the discussion of my (1975) in Darwall (1983), especially pp. 197–98.
9. Hume (1751), sec. 3, pt. 1.
10. Ibid., sec. 9, pt. 2.
11. Ibid.
12. See, for example, Nagel (1970), pp. 90–124.
13. The objector might be Derek Parfit; see Parfit (1984), pp. 19–23.
14. See my (1984), appearing also in MacLean (1984).

5

Prisoner's Dilemma and Resolute Choice

EDWARD F. MCCLENNEN

In the last twenty-five years a great many very interesting articles have been written about Prisoner's Dilemma. Yet for all that, one has the sense that the discussion has moved less far than one might have hoped, given the rather counterintuitive conclusion with which the dilemma was originally launched. I refer here to the view that for one-shot situations, with choices to be made simultaneously, with no probabilistic (or alternatively, causal) dependence between choices, and conditions of full information, rational players who know each other to be such must play non-cooperatively, despite the fact that this means that they must forgo benefits that would be available to each if only they could manage to cooperate. In the language of the economist, the rational outcome is suboptimal.

There have been some very important developments. Prisoner's Dilemma has proved a powerful diagnostic device for understanding the function of many moral, legal, social, and political institutions. It has also occasioned a much more sophisticated analysis of epistemic conditions and preference patterns under which rational and cooperative choice might coincide.[1] Virtually all of these various explorations, however, have worked from a fixed point of conceptualization according to which a rational agent is one who, on each occasion calling for decision, chooses so as to maximize with respect to an antecendently and exogenously specified preference function, given (again from the perspective of that same occasion for decision) the expected behavior of the other player. That is, the choice situation is conceived as parametrized with respect to two crucial variables: the agent is to maximize a *given* preference function against the *given* (expected) choice of the other player.[2]

On such a view, it remains possible, of course, that the preferences of the two agents are such that each choosing in accordance with the constraints specified above will result in an outcome that is optimal. Alternatively, it may be that each entertains special beliefs, for example, to the effect that their respective choices are causally or probabilistically connected. But it follows from what I want to term the fixed point of the modern theory of rational choice that some story of this sort will have to be told. That is, on this view a potential Prisoner's Dilemma situation will be resolvable only insofar as we can assume something about the particular objects of the players' preferences or the particular content of their beliefs.[3]

I want to try to make a case for thinking about Prisoner's Dilemma in a somewhat different way. Specifically, I want to argue that what it is rational for a player to choose in such a situation is in part a function of a potential in the structure of the game itself for achieving optimality if only there is coordination and not just a function of what would maximize some antecedently specified preference function. Put in slightly different terms, I want to explore the notion that the very preferences a rational agent has in such a situation need to be understood as shaped by the logic of the situation itself.

To pursue such a line of analysis is to travel over ground that has been most ably broken by David Gauthier.[4] Like him, I have become persuaded that there is a need for a reappraisal of the requirements of rational choice as typically presented, a need for a perspective from which cooperation can be understood as arising from the logic of the interaction situation itself. I understand him to advocate that agents choose in the resolute manner I shall argue for in this paper. However, he makes the argument turn on the idea of maximizing expected utility at the level of dispositions to choose instead of at the level of particular choices. I want to suggest instead that the resolute chooser can be interpreted as maximizing utility at the level of the particular choice, but that this utility is contextually dependent on the nature of the interaction situation. My arguments, then, to the extent they succeed, may provide an alternative way to motivate what I take to be a central feature of his position, and to show how it can be defended against the prevailing conception of rationality. The strategy I shall employ is to show that there is an important connection between Prisoner's Dilemma and another type of choice situation about which the theory of rational choice in question has had some interesting things to say. I intend to try to use what it has to say about this other type of choice situation against what it has to say about the rational solution to Prisoner's Dilemma.

THE STANDARD ACCOUNT OF PRISONER'S DILEMMA

To fix on a simple example, consider the Ring of Gyges story to be found in Plato's *Republic*. Gyges had a ring which, when he turned it on his finger, made him invisible. This gave him great power: with its aid, he was able to seduce the queen, kill the king, and seize the throne for himself.

In the original story, of course, only Gyges had such a ring. Suppose, however, each of a number of persons who interact with one another possesses such a ring. If all use their rings, the result is likely to be mutually disadvantageous. Whatever a given person gains by using her ring will be more than offset by the losses incurred by others using theirs against her. Each, then, will stand to gain from all not using their rings. But, of course, for any given player use dominates non-use: no matter what others do, a given player will do better to use her ring. This situation, simplified to the case of two persons, serves plausibly as an interpretation of the usual Prisoner's Dilemma matrix (with the left-hand and right-hand numbers in each box giving the preference ordering for Row player and Column player respectively – a larger number meaning more preferred):

		Column	
		NO-U	*U*
	NO-U	3, 3	1, 4
Row	*U*	4, 1	2, 2

WHO IS RESPONSIBLE FOR THE PROBLEM HERE?

For diagnostic purposes, the game given above has complicating features. *U* dominates *NO-U*, for each player, and on the assumption that both players are able to correctly anticipate what the other player will do, only the pair of strategies (*U, U*) is such that each member of the pair maximizes the antecedently given preferences of that player, given that the other player chooses the other member of the pair. That is, only (*U, U*) is in equilibrium with respect to the specified preferences of each. But independent arguments can be brought in support of a choice of *U*. *U* is the safest strategy for each: it maximizes a player's security level. Each player, then, can plead a willingness to be cooperative, were it not for the need to secure against non-cooperation by the other player.

We can obtain a version of this game without this complication by changing the payoff matrix and description of strategies in the following fashion:

		Column	
		NO-U	*U*
	NO-D	4, 3	1, 4
Row	*D*	3, 1	2, 2

To give this an interpretation, suppose that only Column has a ring, while Row has but a partial defense that can be marshalled against it. Let *D* be Row's option of providing such a defense and *NO-D* the option of not so providing. As before, let *U* be Column's option of using the ring, with *NO-*

U the option of not using it. The situation is one in which both players would be better off with the outcome of *NO-D/NO-U* than with the outcome of *D/U,* but Column's dominant strategy is *U,* and Row's rational choice might plausibly be taken to be *D.* On the usual account, the outcome of this game, then, when played between completely rational agents who know each other to be such and who are able to correctly anticipate each other's choices, will be *U/D,* to the mutual disadvantage of both.

In this game, Column cannot plead that Row's disposition to non-cooperation requires a security-oriented response of *U.* Row's maximizing response to a choice of *NO-U* by column is *NO-D,* not *D.* Under conditions of full information and correct anticipation by each of what the other will do, it is impossible to rationalize a choice of *D* by Row, except on the hypothesis that Column must choose a dominant over a dominated strategy or, more generally, must choose so as to maximize her antecedently specified preferences, given what she expects the other player to do. Thus, it is Column's own maximizing disposition so characterized that sets the problem for Column.

This point can be driven home even more clearly by considering one more alteration in the game. Let us interpret it as a game in which choices are to be made in sequence, with Row going first and Column choosing subsequently, after being informed what choice Row has made. In standard tree-diagram form:

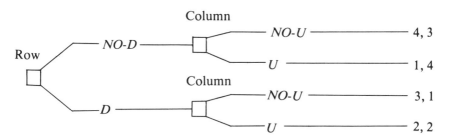

Introducing this particular sequencing of choices changes nothing for a theory that requires rational choices to be in equilibrium with respect to antecedently specified preferences. Column's rational choice,when it comes her turn, will be *U,* regardless of which branch of the tree Row choice places her on, and thus row player must expect column player to select *U* over *NO-U.* But then, the rational choice for row player will be *D.* Consequently, the outcome of rational interaction will be *D/U.* Yet if Row player had reason to suppose that Column player would choose *NO-U,* her best opening move would be *NO-D,* and the outcome would be *NO-D/NO-U.* Once again, then, Column's problem turns upon her own disposition to choose, not the disposition of Row.

There is one condition under which players do not have to forgo the mutual benefits of cooperation that are possible in this game. Let us suppose that prior to making a choice in the game specified above, there is some way Column can precommit to a strategy of *NO-U*. Of course, such a precommitment device will typically require the expenditure of some resources. If this is so, and if the players avail themselves of such a device, the payoffs for each will be somewhat less than those associated with their playing the combination *NO-U* and *NO-D*, say (3.8, 2.8) instead of (4, 3). In tree-diagram form, precommitment (*P*) can be represented as a strategy that Column can choose, prior to Row choosing:

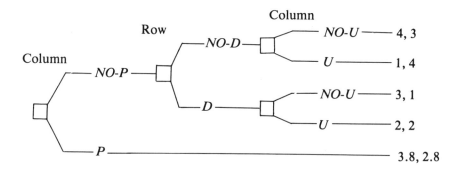

Given the costs of precommitment, Column will prefer the outcome denoted by (4,3) to the outcome of precommitment. But, on the view in question, for the reasons already rehearsed, this outcome is not accessible. And once again, Column cannot blame the problem on the dispositions of Row. Row would be more than willing to play *NO-D*, were it not for the dispositions of Column. Thus, Column's quarrel is with herself. Or should we say, with her own future self? The outcome that Column would most prefer cannot be obtained because, at some subsequent point in time, she herself would prefer to choose *U* over *NO-U*.

ULYSSES AND THE SIRENS

The analysis has led us from one Greek myth to another. The mutual Ring of Gyges problem can be reinterpreted as a version of the problem of Ulysses and the Sirens.[5] As Ulysses approaches the island of the Sirens, he has no desire to be detained by them; but if he acts on his present preferences (to get home as quickly and as inexpensively as possible), he faces a problem. He is informed that once he hears the Sirens, he will want to follow them. Since *here, now* he does not desire to have this happen, he precommits. He buys wax to stop up the ears of his sailors, good strong hemp with which to have himself bound to the mast, and (what is perhaps most costly of all) arranges for his first-mate to act as his agent. In tree-diagram form, Ulysses's problem looks like this:

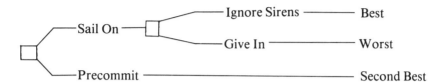

FROM ULYSSES TO ALLAIS

It may be objected that Ulysses faces a very different problem from the one faced by the players in any of the Prisoners' Dilemma games we have explored. The argument is that the latter deal with problems faced by fully rational agents, while the former describes a case in which the self is thought to be temporarily overcome by some irrational (or non-rational) force. But this feature of the story is not essential. We have only to suppose that Ulysses realizes that he is in a situation in which he can predict that his preferences will undergo a specific change.

By way of illustration, consider a sequential version of a paradox that has attracted a great deal of attention in the literature: the Allais paradox. In the original (non-sequential) version, the agent must choose between two gambles, *A* and *B,* and again between two other gambles, *C* and *D,* with the following schedule of payoffs and probabilities:

A	($2,500, 33/34; $0, 1/34)
B	($2,400, 1.0)

C	($2,500, 33/100; $0, 67/100)
D	($2,400, 34/100; $0, 66/100)

Studies have shown that many people prefer *B* to *A,* but prefer *C* to *D.* The reason often given is that *B* is to be preferred to *A* because *B* involves no risk; while *C* is to be preferred to *D,* because, both involving substantial risk, *C* has the larger possible payoff. Such a preference pattern is characterized as "paradoxical" on the grounds that, as natural as it may seem to many decision-makers, it violates a fundamental axiom of rational choice, the independence axiom.[6]

Here is the sequential version of this problem:

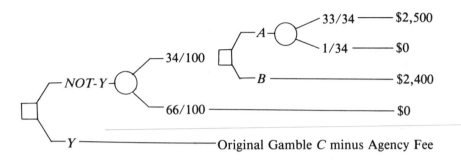

Let Y be the strategy of, say, paying an agent a small fee to execute a choice of A over B in the event the second choice node is reached[7]. Suppose now the player considers the option of *NOT-Y* and contemplates choosing A over B, if the opportunity presents itself. From the perspective of the first choice node, such a plan is equivalent to opting for C, since it offers the prospect of getting \$2,500 with probability $(34/100 \times 33/34) = 33/100$ and \$0 with probability $(66/100 + (34/100 \times 1/34)) = 67/100$. Since C is presumably preferred to Y (it promises the same schedule of payoffs and odds but without the agency fee), one might suppose that the agent will be disposed to reject Y in favor of *NOT-Y* and A. But the agent who has the preference patterns described above must reckon with the following consideration: in the event the second choice node is reached, the choice is between A and B, and by hypothesis, she prefers B to A. On the usual account, then, if she chooses *NOT-Y*, she must expect that, if the opportunity arises, she will choose B rather than A. But given this prediction, a choice of *NOT-Y* is equivalent to D: it offers the prospect of \$2,400 with probability $34/100$, and the prospect of \$0 with probability $66/100$. Since, then, by hypothesis, she prefers Y to D, her rational choice will be Y.

THE POLITICAL ECONOMY OF INTERACTION BETWEEN THE PRESENT AND THE FUTURE SELF

On the view in question, as the above example is designed to illustrate, the present self must assume that its future self will maximize with respect to the antecedently specified preferences it has for the options available to it. Thus, the task confronting the present self is to identify that option presently available to it that will maximize its own antecedently defined preferences, given such maximizing behavior by its future self. The present self who adopts such a stance is characterized as a sophisticated chooser.[8]

Nothing in this account requires of such selves that they coordinate their actions. The present self, to be sure, adjusts its choice in the light of what it expects the future self would choose in response to its own choice — what it would choose from among various possible choice sets (that the present self has the power to make available to the future self). The future self must live with the choice the former self makes, but it has its own agenda of preferences, and when it comes time for it to choose, it maximizes with respect to those preferences. Both, then, are to be understood as maximizers from their own perspective, subject in each case to the constraints that maximizing behavior by the other places on them. If one thinks of the present self as principal, nothing requires the future self to think of itself as an agent, as beholden to some plan of action initiated by the former self.

One must note, of course, that the future self *may* have an interest in coordinating with its past self. Nothing in the analysis so far precludes a preference system for the future self that is responsive to the idea of itself as beholden to the projects of the past self. Rationality, on the view in question, does not rule out such an attitude. But on such a view the attitude must be accounted for *exogenously,* that is, it must be built into the antecedently specified preference of the agent.

The Ulysses-Allais problems of preference change and the various sequential versions of Prisoner's Dilemma are thus seen to be suggestively linked together. In each case, rationality is spelled out in terms of the notion of sophisticated choice. The self's task is simply to adjust its choice in order to maximize (in terms of antecedently specified preferences) against what it takes to be its own future behavior.

Sophisticated choosers do the very best they can, given the constraints imposed by the need to adjust present choice to future given behavior. This is what Ulysses does and what most of us do.[9] But, in the language of the economist, such an approach to choice involves a retreat to second-best. As the various tree-diagrams we have been exploring make clear, sophisticated choosers will typically forgo certain possible gains. If Ulysses manages to save himself from the cursed isle by means of wax, hemp, and agency arrangements, still he could have done even better if he had simply *resolved* to sail right by the island and pay the singing sisters no mind. But so, also, if rational players who know each other to be such do well enough by devising various precommitment schemes or other devices to provide one another with incentives to cooperate, they could do better still by simply resolving to so cooperate.

The connection, however, goes deeper yet. The view that has emerged in the literature on rational dynamic choice is that preference shifts of the Ulysses-Allais type are irrational. Indeed, it has recently been argued that the case for certain of the axioms of utility theory itself rests on the consideration that those whose behavior fails to conform to these axioms will face preference shifts of the type just discussed, shifts that will require resort to second-best strategies, to precommitment and other forms of sophisticated choice.[10] And this, in turn, means that agents whose preferences undergo such shifts will do less well than those whose preferences are not subject to such shifts.

But here the story takes a surprising turn. It is the very theory of rational choice we have been examining that insists that rational agents will be unable to carry through a resolve to act cooperatively in a single-play Prisoner's Dilemma game and that the only recourse will be to various precommitment strategies. But this implies that the preferences of those who act on this theory of rationality are subject to shifts. When faced with Prisoner's Dilemma, each agent wants, *ex ante,* to cooperate, but *ex post,* when called upon to cooperate, each will be disposed to defect. The theory insists, then, upon the reasonableness of preference changes in the one case that are quite analogous to the very preference changes it takes to be irrational in the other case.

RESOLUTE CHOICE AND PRISONER'S DILEMMA

What has gone wrong here? What the theory of rationality in question fails to make room for is the concept of a plan to which the agent might commit herself, not because the plan in question is consonant with some exogenously given set of preferences for various abstractly conceived consequences, but because such a plan resolves a problem posed by the specific interactive logic of the situation confronting the agent. It is a conception of rationality that cannot envision preferences as taking their shape in part from a sense of the limits of strategic interaction because it can only think in terms of what strategy is required by exogenously specified preferences.

Ulysses can solve his problem, I want to suggest, by resolving to sail right by the island and then choosing, when the occasion presents itself, to act on that resolve. Rational agents who know each other to be such can similarly solve the problem they face in sequential versions of Prisoner's Dilemma. The agent who is to choose second has only to resolve to choose in a coordinative fashion and then act on that resolve. If this is the rational approach, the player who is to go first has nothing to fear (at least under conditions of perfect information and a mutual sense of each other's rationality). But given this, and returning to the first two versions of Prisoner's Dilemma, the conclusion is irresistible: rational players who know each other to be such should have no trouble coordinating in these games. Those from whom a resolve is needed (Column in the second version, both players in the original version) have only to so resolve and act accordingly.

Some will argue that this conclusion carries its own measure of paradox. It would seem that what is recommended is that an agent evaluate the situation from some other standpoint than the preferences she has at the time a decision is required, and one is tempted to question whether any sense can be made of that. Moreover, the suggestion that a rational agent will, at a certain point in a decision tree, choose other than what she prefers at that point plays hob with the whole notion of revealed preference: if the agent chooses *A* rather than *B,* then there is a perfectly appropriate sense in which what the agent really prefers (the preference revealed by choice) is A rather than B.

The point is well taken, but it hits wide of the mark. The claim that rationality calls for resolute choice need not be read as a claim that the agent must deny her *ex post* preferences. The agent who resolves to coordinate and then acts on that resolve is to be understood as viewing *ex post* choice differently than one who does not so resolve. The suggestion is that rational agents who have an *ex ante* preference for cooperation will prefer, *ex post,* to act cooperatively. For such agents, the *ex post* situation is different from what it would have been if there had been no *ex ante* resolve. In this respect, then, we can claim that resolute players choose strategies that are in equilibrium with respect to what might be termed their considered preferences, that is, the preferences they have for various options, given their understanding of the logic of the interactive situation they face and the need for coordination if an optimal outcome is to be achieved.

It does not follow, of course, that such an agent conforms to all the canons of the view of rationality in question. Some have recently written as if there is leverage against the rationality of resolute choice to be found in an even more general principle of rational choice. Consider the person who, facing Prisoner's Dilemma, resolves to cooperate and then acts in good faith when the time comes, *ex post,* to choose. Imagine now that this agent also insists that if there had been no mutual sense of a need to coordinate, but the situation was otherwise the same, she would have seized the advantage. The suggestion is that such behavior violates a fundamental standard for normative behavior, a consequentialist principle to the effect that if each of two situations yields precisely the same sets of alternative consequences, then a rational agent must choose the same way in the two situations.[11]

Against this it must be insisted that such a principle, if it is to have the import intended, must construe the concept of consequences in such a narrow way that a failure to act on one's resolve cannot count as a relevant consequence. Such a principle is indeed one that the resolute chooser violates, but so construed the principle is surely doubtful. On the other hand, if consequences are construed broadly enough, then there is no need to suppose that the resolute chooser violates the principle in question.

NOTES

Acknowledgements. Versions of this paper were read to the members of the Philosophy Group at Carnegie-Mellon, The Center for Philosophy and Public Policy at the University of Maryland, the Department of Philosophy at Dalhousie University, the Department of Philosophy at Washington University, and the Council For Philosophical Studies Public Choice Institute, held at Dalhousie University in the Summer of 1984. I am indebted all of these audiences for helpful comments, but in particular to my colleague Teddy Siedenfeld, to Peter Hammond of the Department of Economics, Stanford University, and to Mark Machina of the Department of Economics, University of California, San Diego. Founding support for the project with which this paper is connected was provided by the National Science Foundation, under Grant No. SES-8210730.

1. These developments are well documented in the other papers contained in the present volume, particularly the exploration of epistemic conditions. Barry and Hardin (1982) reprint some of the most important contributions to this literature, particularly those concerned with the relevance of Prisoner's Dilemma to the rationale for various institutions.

2. The *locus classicus* for this is the treatment of Prisoner's Dilemma in Chapter 5, Luce and Raiffa (1957).

3. Traditionally, one such line of exploration is to imagine that the players have moral commitments towards one another. But once these commitments are incorporated into the antecedently specified preferences of each player for the various outcomes, the resultant preference matrix is not necessarily a Prisoner's Dilemma matrix. Alternatively, one can explore various special beliefs the agent might have. Consideration of beliefs about probabilistic dependency between the choices of the two agents leads, of course, by one route, to the framing of epistemic conditions under which coordination is rational and, by a somewhat different route, into the impass of Newcomb's Problem and the whole issue of causal versus probabilistic dependency. See, in particular, the papers in Sections III and IV of the present volume.

4. Of particular relevance here are Gauthier (1975) and "Maximization Constrained: The Rationality of Cooperation," in the present volume, pp. 75–93.

5. I must acknowledge a debt here, of course, to Jon Elster, who has written so perceptively concerning the relevance of the problem of Ulysses and the Sirens to the subject of rational choice. Space limitations preclude my exploring fully the respects in which my analysis relates to his. Very roughly speaking, however, he has been preoccupied somewhat more with the concept of rationality as an explanatory (as distinct from a normative) concept. The particular use to which I have put the analogy between Prisoners' Dilemma and Ulysses and the Sirens is one that, I suspect, he would not accept. See in particular Elster (1979) and (1982).

6. The paradox in question is named after Maurice Allais, who was the first to propose the relevance of this particular type of preference pattern to the foundations of expected utility theory. Allais's contribution, which dates from the early fifties, together with some important papers by others and a very extensive bibliography, is to be found in Allais and Hagen (1979). The suggestion that Allais-type preferences imply preference changes in a dynamic choice context is raised by Raiffa in the course of an extremely lucid and interesting discussion of the Allais Paradox in Raiffa (1968, pp. 80–86). See, however, McClennen (1983), for some second thoughts about the success of Raiffa's argument, an overview of the issue, and a bibliography of the relevant literature.

7. Following in the tradition of the story of Ulysses and the Sirens, one of the tasks, it is alleged, that such an agent will have to perform is refusing to listen to any revised order phoned in by the principal if and when the second choice opportunity occurs. My colleague Teddy Seidenfeld is always eager to offer his services as such an agent, but, of course, he insists upon a fee!

8. There is an extensive literature on changing preferences, sophisticated choice as a strategy for dealing with it, and, more generally, what has come to be known as the problem of "dynamic consistency" posed by such preference changes. For two recent surveys, see Hammond (1976) and Yaari (1977).

9. For a recent survey, see Thaler and Shefrin (1981). See also Schelling (1984), Essays 2, 3, and 4 in particular.

10. See Hammond (1976), in particular, and also his (1982a). A very formal and powerful statement of the potential relevance of preference change and dynamic inconsistency to the foundations of utility theory is to be found in his (1982b).

11. The argument is due to P. Hammond. See the last two papers cited in the previous note.

III

EVIDENTIAL VERSUS CAUSAL
DECISION THEORY

6

Newcomb's Problem and Two Principles of Choice*

ROBERT NOZICK

Both it and its opposite must involve no mere artificial illusion such as at once vanishes upon detection, but a natural and unavoidable illusion, which even after it has ceased to beguile still continues to delude though not to deceive us, and which though thus capable of being rendered harmless can never be eradicated.

IMMANUEL KANT, *Critique of Pure Reason,* A422, B450

Suppose a being in whose power to predict your choices you have enormous confidence. (One might tell a science-fiction story about a being from another planet, with an advanced technology and science, who you know to be friendly, and so on.) You know that this being has often correctly predicted your choices in the past (and has never, so far as you know, made an incorrect prediction about your choices), and furthermore you know that this being has often correctly predicted the choices of other people, many of whom are similar to you, in the particular situation to be described below. One might tell a longer story, but all this leads you to believe that almost certainly this being's prediction about your choice in the situation to be discussed will be correct.

From Nicholas Rescher, *et al,* ed., *Essays in Honor of Carl G. Hempel,* 114–46. All Rights Reserved. Copyright © 1969 by D. Reidel Publishing Company, Dordrecht, Holland. Reprinted with abridgement by permission of author and D. Reidel.

There are two boxes, (*B1*) and (*B2*). (*B1*) contains $1,000. (*B2*) contains either $1,000,000 ($*M*) or nothing. What the content of (*B2*) depends upon will be described in a moment.

$$(B1) \quad \{\$1,000\} \quad (B2) \quad \left\{ \begin{array}{c} \$M \\ \text{or} \\ \$0 \end{array} \right\}$$

You have a choice between two actions:
(1) taking what is in both boxes
(2) taking only what is in the second box.
Furthermore, and you know this, the being knows that you know this, and so on:
(I) If the being predicts you will take what is in both boxes, he does not put the $*M* in the second box.
(II) If the being predicts you will take only what is in the second box, he does put the $*M* in the second box.[1]
The situation is as follows. First, the being makes its prediction. Then it puts the $*M* in the second box, or does not, depending upon what it has predicted. Then you make your choice. What do you do?
There are two plausible looking and highly intuitive arguments which require different decisions. The problem is to explain why one of them is not legitimately applied to this choice situation. You might reason as follows:
First Argument: If I take what is in both boxes, the being, almost certainly, will have predicted this and will not have put the $*M* in the second box, and so I will, almost certainly, get only $1,000. If I take only what is in the second box, the being, almost certainly, will have predicted this and will have put the $*M* in the second box, and so I will, almost certainly, get $*M*. Thus, if I take what is in both boxes, I, almost certainly, will get $1,000. If I take only what is in the second box, I, almost certainly, will get $*M*. Therefore I should take only what is in the second box.
Second Argument: The being has already made his prediction and has already either put the $*M* in the second box or has not. The $*M* is either already sitting in the second box, or it is not, and which situation obtains is already fixed and determined. If the being has already put the $*M* in the second box, and I take what is in both boxes I get $*M* + $1000, whereas if I take only what is in the second box, I get only $*M*. If the being has not put the $*M* in the second box, and I take what is in both boxes I get $1,000, whereas if I take only what is in the second box, I get no money. Therefore, whether the money is there or not, and which it is is already fixed and determined, I get $1,000 more by taking what is in both boxes rather than taking only what is in the second box. So I should take what is in both boxes.

Let me say a bit more to emphasize the pull of each of these arguments:

The First: You know that many persons like yourself, philosophy teachers and students, and so on, have gone through this experiment. All those who took only what was in the second box, including those who knew of the second argument but did not follow it, ended up with $M. And you know that all the shrewdies, all those who followed the second argument and took what was in both boxes, ended up with only $1,000. You have no reason to believe that you are any different, *vis-à-vis* predictability, than they are. Furthermore, since you know that I have all of the preceding information, you know that I would bet, giving high odds, and be rational in doing so, that if you were to take both boxes you would get only $1,000. And if you were irrevocably to take both boxes, and there were some delay in the results being announced, would not it be rational for you to then bet with some third party, giving high odds, that you will get only $1,000 from the previous transaction? Whereas if you were to take only what is in the second box, would not it be rational for you to make a side bet with some third party that you will get $M from the previous transaction? Knowing all this (though no one is actually available to bet with), do you really want to take what is in both boxes, acting against what you would rationally want to bet on?

The Second: The being has already made his prediction, placed the $M in the second box or not, and then left. This happened one week ago; this happened one year ago. Box (*B1*) is transparent. You can see the $1,000 sitting there. The $M is already either in the box (*B2*) or not (though you cannot see which). Are you going to take only what is in (*B2*)? To emphasize further, from your side, you cannot see through (*B2*), but from the other side it is transparent. I have been sitting on the other side of (*B2*), looking in and seeing what is there. Either I have already been looking at the $M for a week or I have already been looking at an empty box for a week. If the money is already there, it will stay there whatever you choose. It is not going to disappear. If it is not already there, if I am looking at an empty box, it is not going to suddenly appear if you choose only what is in the second box. Are you going to take only what is in the second box, passing up the additional $1,000 which you can plainly see? Furthermore, I have been sitting there looking at the boxes, hoping that you will perform a particular action. Internally, I am giving you advice. And, of course, you already know which advice I am silently giving to you. In either case (whether or not I see the $M in the second box), I am hoping that you will take what is in both boxes. You know that the person sitting and watching it all hopes that you will take the contents of both boxes. Are you going to take only what is in the second box, passing up the additional $1,000 which you can plainly see and ignoring my internally-given hope that you take both? Of course, my presence makes no difference. You are sitting there alone, but you know that if some friend having your interests at heart *were* observing from the other side, looking into both boxes, he *would* be hoping that you would take both. So will you take only what is in the second box, passing up the additional $1,000 which you can plainly see?

I should add that I have put this problem to a large number of people, both friends and students in class. To almost everyone it is perfectly clear and obvious what should be done. The difficulty is that these people seem to divide almost evenly on the problem, with large numbers thinking that the opposing half is just being silly.[2]

Given two such compelling opposing arguments, it will not do to rest content with one's belief that one knows what to do. Nor will it do to just repeat one of the arguments, loudly and slowly. One must also disarm the opposing argument; explain away its force while showing it due respect.

Now for an unusual suggestion. It might be a good idea for the reader to stop reading this paper at the end of this section (but do, please, return and finish it), mull over the problem for a while (several hours, days), and then return. It is not that I claim to solve the problem and do not want you to miss the joy of puzzling over an unsolved problem. It is that I want you to understand my thrashing about.

My strategy in attacking this problem is ostrich-like; that is, I shall begin by ignoring it completely (except in occasional notes) and proceed to discuss contemporary decision theory. Though the problem is not, at first, explicitly discussed, the course my discussion takes is influenced by my knowledge of the problem. Later in the paper I shall remove my head from the sand and face our problem directly, hopefully having advanced towards a solution or at least having sharpened and isolated the problem.

Writers on decision theory state two principles to govern choices among alternative actions.

> *Expected Utility Principle:* Among those actions available to a person, he should perform an action with maximal expected utility.

The expected utility of an action yielding the exclusive and exhaustive outcomes $O_1, \ldots, O_n$ with probabilities $p_1, \ldots, p_n$ respectively is:

$$p_1 \times u(O_1) + p_2 \times u(O_2) + \cdots + p_n \times u(O_n).$$

$$\text{i.e.,} \quad \sum_{i=1}^{n} p_i \times u(O_i).$$

Dominance Principle: If there is a partition of states of the world such that relative to it, action A weakly dominates action B, then A should be performed rather than B.

Action A weakly dominates action B for person P if, and only if, for each state of the world, P either prefers the consequence of A to the consequence of B or is indifferent between the two consequences, and for some state of the world, P prefers the consequence of A to the consequence of B.

There are many interesting questions and problems about the framework used or assumed by these principles and the conditions governing preference, indifference, and probability which suffice to yield the utility measure, and the exact way the principles should be formulated.[3] The problem I want to begin with is raised by the fact that for some situations, one of the principles listed above requires that one choose one action whereas the other principle requires that one choose another action. Which should one follow?

Consider the following situation, where A and B are actions, S_1 and S_2 are states of the world, and the numerical entries give the utility of the consequences, results, effects, outcomes, upshots, events, states of affairs, and so on, that obtain, happen, hold, and so on, if the action is done and the state of the world obtains.

	S_1	S_2
A:	10	4
B:	8	3

According to the dominance principle, the person should do A rather than B. (In this situation A strongly dominates B, that is, for each state of nature the person prefers the consequence of A to the consequence of B.) But suppose the person believes it very likely that if he does A, S_2 will obtain, and if he does B, S_1 will obtain. Then he believes it very likely that if he does A he will get 4, and if he does B he will get 8.

The expected utility of $A = pr(S_1/A)\,10 + pr(S_2/A)\,4$. The expected utility of $B = pr(S_1/B)\,8 + pr(S_2/B)\,3$. If, for example,

$$pr(S_1/A) = .2$$
$$pr(S_2/A) = .8$$
$$pr(S_1/B) = .9$$
$$pr(S_2/B) = .1,$$

then the expected utility of $A = 5.2$, and the expected utility of $B = 7.5$. Thus the expected utility principle requires the person to do B rather than A.[4]

The dominance principle as presented here speaks of dominance relative to a partition of the states of the world. This relativization is normally not made explicit, which perhaps accounts for the fact that writers did not mention that it may be that relative to one partition of the states of the world, one action A dominates another, whereas relative to another partition of the states of the world, it does not.

It will be helpful to have before us two facts:

First: Suppose a matrix is given, with states $S_1, \ldots, S_n$, in which action A does not dominate action B. If there is some rearrangement of the utility entries in the row for action A which gives a new row which dominates the row for action B, then there are states $T_1, \ldots, T_n$ such that in the matrix with these states, action A dominates action B.

Proof: I shall describe how one can get the appropriate states $T_1, \ldots, T_n$ in one case. It is obvious how this procedure can be used generally. Suppose that $a_1, \ldots, a_n$ and $b_1, \ldots, b_n$ are utility numbers such that, for all i, $a_i \geq b_i$, and for some i, $a_i > b_i$. We may suppose that a_i is the entry in the A row for the ith column, that is, for state S_i. We might, for example, have the following matrix:

	S_1	S_2	S_3	....	S_n
A:	a_1	a_2	a_3	....	a_n
B:	b_{12}	b_3	b_{19}	....	b_6

Let

$$T_1 = A \ \& \ S_{12} \ \text{or} \ B \ \& \ S_{15}$$
$$T_2 = A \ \& \ S_3 \ \text{or} \ B \ \& \ S_2$$
$$T_3 = A \ \& \ S_{19} \ \text{or} \ B \ \& \ S_3$$
$$\cdot$$
$$\cdot$$
$$\cdot$$
$$T_n = A \ \& \ S_6 \ \text{or} \ B \ \& \ S_n.$$

Thus we get the matrix:

	T_1	T_2	T_3	....	T_n
A:	a_{12}	a_3	a_{19}	....	a_6
B:	b_{12}	b_3	b_{19}	....	b_6

In this matrix, action A dominates action B. Since the kind of procedure followed does not depend on any specific features of the example, the point is made.

Second: Suppose there is a matrix with states $S_1, \ldots, S_n$ such that action A dominates action B. If there is some rearrangement of the utility entries in the B row so that the rearranged row is not dominated by A, then there are states $T_1, \ldots, T_n$ such that if the matrix is set up with these states, B is not dominated by A.

Proof: Suppose that $a_i \geq b_i$, for all i; $a_i > b_i$ for some i; and that some B-row value is greater than some A-row value. (Given that there is some arrangement in which A dominates B, this last supposition follows from its being possible to rearrange the B row so that it is not dominated by the A row.) Suppose, without loss of generality that $b_{12} > a_2$. Thus we have the following matrix:

	S_1	S_2	S_3	. . . .	S_n
A:	a_1	a_2	a_3	. . . .	a_n
B:	b_1	b_2	b_3	. . . .	b_n

Let

$$T_1 = S_1$$
$$T_2 = A \text{ \& } S_2 \text{ or } B \text{ \& } S_{12}$$
$$T_3 = S_3$$
$$\vdots$$
$$T_{11} = S_{11}$$
$$T_{12} = A \text{ \& } S_{12} \text{ or } B \text{ \& } S_2$$
$$T_{13} = S_{13}$$
$$\vdots$$
$$T_n = S_n.$$

Thus we get the following matrix:

	T_1	T_2	T_3	. . . .	T_{12}	. . . .	T_n
A:	a_1	a_2	a_3	. . . .	a_{12}	. . . .	a_n
B:	b_1	b_{12}	b_3	. . . .	b_2	. . . .	b_n

Since $b_{12} > a_2$, A does not dominate B.

It may seem that the states $T_1, \ldots, T_n$ defined in terms of the actions A and B, and the states $S_1, \ldots, S_n$ are contrived states which some general condition could exclude. It should be noted that — since the states $S_1, \ldots, S_n$ can be defined in terms of the actions A and B and the states $T_1, \ldots, T_n$ (I will give some examples below) — attempts to show that $T_1, \ldots, T_n$ are contrived will face many of the problems encountered in ruling out Goodman-style predicates. Furthermore, as we shall see soon, there are cases where the S states and the T states which are interdefinable in this way both seem perfectly natural and uncontrived.

The fact that whether one action dominates another or not may depend upon which particular partition of the states of the world is used would cause no difficulty if we were willing to apply the dominance principle to *any* partition of the states of the world. Since we are not, this raises the question of when the dominance principle is to be used. Let us look at some examples.

Suppose that I am about to bet on the outcome of a horserace in which only two horses, H_1 and H_2, are running. Let:

$$S_1 = \text{Horse } H_1 \text{ wins the race.}$$
$$S_2 = \text{Horse } H_2 \text{ wins the race.}$$
$$A_1 = \text{I bet on horse } H_1.$$
$$A_2 = \text{I bet on horse } H_2.$$

Suppose that I will definitely bet on one of the two horses and can only bet on one of the two horses and that the following matrix describes the situation (I might have been offered the opportunity to enter this situation by a friend. Certainly no race track would offer it to me):

	S_1	S_2
A_1 :	I win $50	I lose $5
A_2:	I lose $6	I win $49

Suppose further that the personal probability for me that H_1 wins is .2, and the personal probability for me that H_2 wins is .8. Thus the expected utility of A_1 is $.2 \times u$ (/I win $50/) + $.8 \times u$ (/I lose $5/). The expected utility of A_2 is $.2 \times u$ (/I lose $6/) + $.8 \times u$ (/I win $49/). Given my utility assignment to these outcomes, the expected utility of A_2 is greater than that of A_1. Hence the expected utility principle would have me do A_2 rather than A_1.

However, we may set the matrix up differently. Let:

$$S_3 = \text{I am lucky in my bet.}$$
$$S_4 = \text{I am unlucky in my bet.}$$

(Given that I am betting on only one horse today, we could let S_3 = The only horse I bet on today wins. Similarly for S_4, with "loses" substituted for "wins.") Thus we have the following matrix:

	S_3	S_4
A_1:	I win $50	I lose $5
A_2:	I win $49	I lose $6

But when set up in this way, A_1 dominates A_2. Therefore the dominance principle would have me do A_1 rather than A_2.[6]

In this example, the states are logically independent of which action I perform; from the fact that I perform A_1 (A_2) one cannot deduce which state obtains, and from the fact that S_1 (S_2, S_3, S_4) obtains one cannot deduce which action I perform. However, one pair of states was not probabilistically independent of my doing the actions.[7] Assuming that S_1 and S_2 are each probabilistically independent of both A_1 and A_2, $pr\,(S_3/\text{I do }A_1) = .2$; $pr\,(S_3/\text{I do }A_2) = .8$; $pr\,(S_4/\text{I do }A_1) = .8$; $pr\,(S_4/\text{I do }A_2) = .2$. Thus neither of the states S_3 or S_4 is probabilistically independent of each of the actions A_1 and A_2.[8]

In this example, it is clear that one does not wish to follow the recommendation of the dominance principle. And the explanation seems to hinge on the fact that the states are not probabilistically independent of the actions. Even though one can set up the situation so that one action dominates another, I believe that if I do A_1, the consequence will probably be the italicized consequence in its row, and I believe that if I do A_2, the consequence will probably be the italicized consequence in A_2's row. And given my assignment of utilities in this case and the probabilities I assign (the conditional probabilities of the states given the actions), it is clear why I prefer to do A_2, despite the fact that A_1 dominates A_2.

	S_3	S_4
A_1:	I win \$50	*I lose \$5*
A_2:	*I win \$49*	I lose \$6

Let us consider another example: suppose that I am playing roulette on a rigged wheel and that the owner of the casino offers me a chance to choose between actions A_1 and A_2 so that the following matrix describes the situation (where S_1 = black comes up on the next spin; S_2 = red comes up on the next spin):

	S_1	S_2
A_1:	I win \$10	I win \$100
A_2:	I win \$5	I win \$90

Finally, suppose that I know that the owner's employee, who is overseeing the wheel and who I am confident is completely loyal to the owner, has been instructed to make black come up on the next spin if I choose A_1 and to make red come up on the next spin if I choose A_2. Clearly, even though A_1 dominates A_2, given my knowledge of the situation I should choose A_2. I take it that this needs no argument. It seems that the reason that I should not be guided by dominance considerations is that the states S_1 and S_2 are not probabilistically independent of my actions A_1 and A_2. We can set up the situation so that the states are probabilistically independent of the actions. But when it is set up in this way, I am led, given my utility assignment to the outcomes, to do A_2.

Let S_3 = the fellow running the roulette wheel follows his boss's instructions; S_4 = the fellow running the roulette wheel disobeys his boss's instructions. (Note that $S_3 = A_1$ & S_1 or A_2 & S_2; $S_4 = A_1$ & S_2 or A_2 & S_1.) We then have the following matrix:

	S_3	S_4
A_1:	I win \$10	I win \$100
A_2:	I win \$90	I win \$5

Even if I am not sure that S_3 is true, so long as the personal probability of S_3 for me is sufficiently high, I will be led to do A_2, given my utility assignment to the outcomes.

These examples suggest that one should not apply the dominance principle to a situation where the states are not probabilistically independent of the actions. One wishes instead to maximize the expected utility. However, the probabilities that are to be used in determining the expected utility of an action must now be the conditional probabilities of the states given that the action is done. (This is true generally. However when the states are probabilistically independent of the actions, the conditional probability of each state given that one of the actions is done will be equal to the probability of the state, so the latter may be used.) Thus in the roulette wheel example, we may still look at the first matrix given. However, one does not wish to apply the dominance principle but to find the expected utility of the actions, which in our example are:

$$\text{E.U.}(A_1) = pr(S_1/A_1) \times u(/\text{I win \$10}/) + pr(S_2/A_1) \times u(/\text{I win \$100}/)$$
$$\text{E.U.}(A_2) = pr(S_1/A_2) \times u(/\text{I win \$5}/) + pr(S_2/A_2) \times u(/\text{I win \$90}/).[9]$$

The following position appropriately handles the examples given thus far (ignoring Newcomb's example with which the paper opens) and has intuitive appeal.[10]

(1) It is legitimate to apply dominance principles if and only if the states are probabilistically independent of the actions.

(2) If the states are not probabilistically independent of the actions, then apply the expected utility principle, using as the probability-weights the conditional probabilities of the states given the actions.

Thus in the following matrix, where the entries in the matrix are utility numbers,

	S_1	S_2	....	S_n
A:	O_1	O_2	....	O_n
B:	U_1	U_2	....	U_n

the expected utility of A is $\sum_{i=1}^{n} pr(S_i/A) O_i$, and the expected utility of B is $\sum_{i=1}^{n} pr(S_i/B) U_i$.

Is this position satisfactory? Consider the following example: P knows that S or T is his father, but he does not know which one is. S died of some terrible inherited disease, and T did not. It is known that this disease is genetically dominant, and that P's mother did not have it, and that S did not have the recessive gene. If S is his father, P will die of this disease; if T is his father, P will not die of this disease. Furthermore, there is a well-confirmed theory available, let us imagine, about the genetic transmission of the tendency to decide to do acts which form part of an intellectual life. This tendency is genetically dominant. S had this tendency (and did not have the recessive gene), T did not, and P's mother did not. P is now deciding whether (a) to go to graduate school and then teach, or (b) to become a professional baseball player. He prefers (though not enormously) the life of an academic to that of a professional athlete.

	S is P's father	T is P's father
A:	x	y
B:	z	w

$x = P$ is an academic for a while and then dies of the terrible disease; $z = P$ is a professional athlete for a while and then dies of the terrible disease; $y = P$ is an academic and leads a normal academic life; $w = P$ is a professional athlete and leads the normal life of a professional athlete, though doing a bit more reading; and P prefers x to z and y to w. However, the disease is so terrible that P greatly prefers w to x. The matrix might be as follows:

	S is P's father	T is P's father
A:	-20	100
B:	-25	95

Suppose that our well-confirmed theory tells us, and *P,* that if *P* chooses the academic life, then it is likely that he has the tendency to choose it; if he does not choose the academic life, then it is likely that he does not have the tendency. Specifically:

> $pr(P$ has the tendency$/P$ decides to do $A) = .9$
> $pr(P$ does not have the tendency$/P$ decides to do $A) = .1$
> $pr(P$ has the tendency$/P$ decides to do $B) = .1$
> $pr(P$ does not have the tendency$/P$ decides to do $B) = .9$

Since *P* has the tendency if *S* is *P*'s father, we have:

> $pr(S$ is P's father$/P$ decides to do $A) = .9$
> $pr(T$ is P's father$/P$ decides to do $A) = .1$
> $pr(S$ is P's father$/P$ decides to do $B) = .1$
> $pr(T$ is P's father$/P$ decides to do $B) = .9$

The dominance principle tells *P* to do *A* rather than *B*. But according to the position we are now considering, in situations in which the states are not probabilistically independent of the actions, the dominance principal is not to be used, but rather one is to use the expected utility principle with the conditional probabilities as the weights. Using the above conditional probabilities and the above numerical assumptions about the utility values, we get:

> The expected utility of $A = .9 \times -20 + .1 \times 100 = -8$
> The expected utility of $B = .1 \times -25 + .9 \times 95 = 83.$

Since the expected utility of *B* is greater than that of *A,* the position we are considering would have *P* do *B* rather than *A*. But this recommendation is perfectly wild. Imagine *P* saying, "I am doing *B* because if I do it it is less likely that I will die of the dread disease." One wants to reply, "It is true that you have got the conditional probabilities correct. If you do *A* it is likely that *S* is your father, and hence likely that you will die of the disease, and if you do *B* it is likely that *T* is your father and hence unlikely that you will die of the disease. But which one of them is your father is already fixed and determined and has been for a long time. The action you perform legitimately affects our estimate of the probabilities of the two states, but which state obtains does not depend on your action at all. By doing *B* you are not *making* it less likely that *S* is your father, and by doing *B* you are not making it less likely that you will die of the disease." I do not claim that this reply is without its problems.[11] Before considering another example, let us first state a principle not under attack:

> The Dominance Principle is legitimately applicable to situations in which the states are probabilistically independent of the actions.[12]

If the states are not probabilistically independent of the actions, it *seems* intuitive that the expected utility principle is appropriate and that it is not legitimate to use the dominance principle if it yields a different result from the expected utility principle. However, in situations in which the states, though not probabilistically independent of the actions, are already fixed and determined, where the actions do not affect whether or not the states obtain, then it *seems* that it is legitimate to use the dominance principle and illegitimate to follow the recommendation of the expected utility principle if it differs from that of the dominance principle.

For such situations—where the states are not probabilistically independent of the actions, though which one obtains is already fixed and determined—persons may differ over what principle to use.

Of the twelve sorts of situation in which it is not the case both that none of the states are already fixed and determined and none of the states are probabilistically independent of the actions, I shall discuss only one; namely, where each of the states is already fixed and determined and none of the states are probabilistically independent of the alternative actions.[13]

The question before us is: In this sort of situation, in which all of the states are already fixed and determined, and none of the states are probabilistically independent of the acts, and the dominance principle requires that one do one action, whereas the expected utility principle requires that one do another, should one follow the recommendation of the dominance principle or of the expected utility principle?

The question is difficult. Some may think one should follow the recommendation of the dominance principle; others may think one should follow the recommendation of the expected utility principle in such situations.

Now for the example which introduces a bit of reflexivity which I hope will soon serve us in good stead. Suppose that there are two inherited tendencies ("tendencies" because there is some small probability that it would not be followed in a specific situation):

(1) an inherited tendency to think that the expected utility principle should be used in such situations. (If P has this tendency, he is in state S_1.)

(2) an inherited tendency to think that the dominance principle should be used in such situations. (If P has this tendency, he is in state S_2.)

It is known on the basis of *post mortem* genetic examinations that:

(a) P's mother had two neutral genes. (A gene for either tendency genetically dominates a neutral gene. We need not here worry about the progeny who has a gene for each tendency.)

(b) One of the men who may be P's father had two genes for the first tendency.

(c) The other man who may be P's father had two genes for the second tendency.

So it is known that P has one of the tendencies, but it is not known which one he has. P is faced with the following choice:

	S_1	S_2
A:	10	4
B:	8	3

The choice matrix might have arisen as follows. A deadly disease is going around, and there are two effective vaccines against it. (If both are given, the person dies.) For each person, the side effects of vaccine B are worse than that of vaccine A, and each vaccine has worse side effects on persons in S_2 than either does on persons in S_1.

Now suppose that the theory about the inherited tendencies to choice tells us, and P knows this, that from a person's choice in *this* situation the probabilities of his having the two tendencies, given that he has one of the two, can be estimated, and in particular:

$$pr(S_1/A) = .1$$
$$pr(S_2/A) = .9$$
$$pr(S_1/B) = .9$$
$$pr(S_2/B) = .1.$$

What should P do? What would you do in this situation?

P may reason as follows: if I do A, then very probably S_2 obtains, and I will get 4. If I do B, then very probably S_1 holds, and I will get 8. So I will do B rather than A.

One wants to reply: whether S_1 or S_2 obtains is already fixed and determined. What you decide to do would not bring about one or the other of them. To emphasize this, let us use the past tense. For you are in S_1 if, and only if, you were in S_1 yesterday; you are in S_2 if, and only if, you were in S_2 yesterday. But to reason "If I do A then very probably I was in S_2 yesterday, and I will get 4. If I do B, then very probably, I was in S_1 yesterday, and I will get 8. So I will now do B rather than A" is absurd. What you decide to do does not affect which state you were in yesterday. For either state, over which you have no control, you are better off doing A rather than B. To do B for reasons such as the above is no less absurd than someone who has already taken vaccine B yesterday doing some other act C today because the pr (He was in S_1 yesterday/He does C today) is very high, and he wants the (delayed) side effects of the vaccine he has already taken to be less severe.

If an explanation runs from x to y, a correct explanatory theory will speak of the conditional probability $pr(y/x)$. Thus the correct explanatory theory of P's choice in this situation will speak of:

$$pr(P \text{ does } A/P \text{ is in } S_1)$$
$$pr(P \text{ does } A/P \text{ is in } S_2)$$
$$pr(P \text{ does } B/P \text{ is in } S_1)$$
$$pr(P \text{ does } B/P \text{ is in } S_2).$$

From these, the theory may enable us to determine:

$$pr(P \text{ is in } S_1/P \text{ does } A)$$
$$pr(P \text{ is in } S_2/P \text{ does } A)$$
$$pr(P \text{ is in } S_1/P \text{ does } B)$$
$$pr(P \text{ is in } S_2/P \text{ does } B)$$

but these would not be the basic explanatory probabilities. Supposing that probabilistic explanation is legitimate, we could explain why P does A by having among our antecedent conditions the statement that P is in S_2, but we cannot *explain* why P is in S_2 by having among our antecedent conditions the statement that P does A (though P's doing A may be our reason for believing he is in S_2). Given that when the explanatory line runs from x to y (x is part of the explanation of y) and not from y to x, the theory will speak of and somehow distinguish the conditional probabilities $pr(y/x)$, then the probability $pr(x/y)$ will be a *likelihood* (as, I think, this term is used in the statistical literature). Looking at the likelihoods of the states given the actions may perhaps give one the illusion of control over the states. But I suggest that when the states are already fixed and determined and the explanatory theory has the influence running from the states to the actions so that the conditional probabilities of the states on the actions are likelihoods, then if the dominance principle applies, it should be applied.

If a state is part of the explanation of deciding to do an action (if the decision is made) and this state is already fixed and determined, then the decision, which has not yet been made, cannot be part of the explanation of the state's obtaining. So we need not consider the case where pr (state/action) is in the basic explanatory theory, for an already fixed state.[14] What other possibilities are there for already fixed and determined states? One possibility would be a situation in which the states are not part of the explanation of the decision, and the decision is not part of the explanation of which state obtains, but some third thing is part of the explanation of the states obtaining, and the decision's being made. Hence neither pr (state of the matrix obtaining/P does a specific action) nor $pr(P$ does a specific action/state of the matrix obtains) would be part of the basic explanatory theory (which has conditional probabilities from antecedent to consequent going in the direction of explanation).

Let us consider a case like this, whose matrix exemplifies the structure of the Prisoner's Dilemma situation, much discussed by game theorists.[15] There are two people, (I) and (II) and the following matrix describes their situation (where the first entry in each box represents the payoff to person (I) and the second entry represents the payoff to person (II)). The situation arises just once, and the persons cannot get together to agree upon a joint plan of action.

$$
\begin{array}{c}
\qquad\qquad\qquad\text{(II)} \\[4pt]
\begin{array}{rr}
C \qquad & D \\
\end{array}
\end{array}
$$

		C	D
(I)	A:	10, 3	4, 4
	B:	8, 8	3, 10

Notice that for person (I), action A dominates action B, and for person (II), action D dominates action C. Hence if each performs his dominant action, each ends up with 4. But if each performs the non-dominant action, each ends up with 8. So, in this situation, both persons' following the dominance principle leaves each worse off than if both did not follow the dominance principle.

People may differ over what should be done in this situation. Let us, once again, suppose that there are two inherited tendencies, one to perform the dominant action in this situation and one to perform the other action. Either tendency is genetically dominant over a possible third inherited trait. Persons (I) and (II) are identical twins, who care only about their own pay-offs as represented in this matrix and know that their mother had the neutral gene, one of their two possible fathers had only the gene to perform the dominant action, and the other had only the gene not to perform the dominant action. Neither knows which man was their father nor which of the genes they have. Each knows, given the genetic theory, that it is almost certain that if he performs the dominant (dominated) action, his brother will also. We must also suppose that the theory tells us and them that given all this information upon which they base their choice, the correlation between their actions holds as almost certain, and also given *this* additional information, it holds as almost certain, and so on.

I do not wish here to discuss whether one should or should not perform the dominant action in Prisoner's Dilemma situations. I wish merely to consider the following argument for not performing the dominant action in the situation I have just described. Suppose brother I argues: "If I perform the dominant action then it is almost certain$_1$ that I have that gene, and there-fore that my brother does also, and so it is almost certain$_2$[16] that he will also perform the dominant action and so it is almost certain$_2$ that I will get 4. Whereas if I perform the dominated action, for similar reasons, it is almost certain that my brother will also, and hence it is almost certain that I will get 8. So I should perform the dominated action."

Here one surely wishes to reply that *this* argument is not a good argument for performing the dominated action. For what this brother does will not affect what the other brother does. (To emphasize this, suppose that brother II has already acted, though brother I does not yet know what he has done.) Perhaps in Prisoner's Dilemma situations one should perform the dominated action, but *this* argument does not show that one should in this situation.

The examples thus far considered lead me to believe that if the actions or decisions to do the actions do not affect, help bring about, influence, and so on *which* state obtains, then whatever the conditional probabilities (so long as they do not indicate an influence), one should perform the dominant action.

If the considerations thus far adduced are convincing, then it is clear that one should also choose the dominant action in the following situations, hav-ing the same structure (matrix) as Newcomb's and differing only in that:

(1) The being makes his prediction and sets the process going whereby the $M gets placed in the second box, or not. You then make your choice, and *after* you do, the (long) process terminates and the $M gets in the box, or not. So while you are deciding, the $M is not already there, though at this time he has already decided whether it will be or not.

(2) The being gathers his data on the basis of which he makes his predic-tion. You make your choice (for example, press one of two buttons which will open one or both boxes later by delayed action), and he then makes his prediction, on the basis of the data previously gathered, and puts the $M in, or not.

This suggests that the crucial fact is *not* whether the states are already fixed and determined but whether the actions *influence* or *affect* which state obtains.

Setting up a simple matrix,[17] we have the following possibilities (with the matrix entries being recommended decision policies for the situation).

	A dominant action is available	No dominant action is available
The actions influence which state obtains. The conditional probabilities differ.	(I) Maximize Expected Utility	(II) Maximize Expected Utility

No influence of actions on states. However conditional probabilities differ.	(III)	(IV)
No influence of actions on states. The conditional probabilities are all the same.	(V) Do dominant action (or, equivalently, Maximize Expected Utility)	(VI) Maximize Expected Utility

The standard theories make the recommendations in (V) and (VI). They do not consider (I) and (II), but (ignoring other difficulties there might be with the policy) Maximizing Expected Utility seems reasonable here. The difficulties come in the middle row. (III) is the situation exemplified by Newcomb's situation and the other examples we have listed from the person choosing whether to lead the academic life onwards. I have argued that, in these situations, one should choose the dominant action and ignore the conditional probabilities which do not indicate an influence. What then should one do in situation (IV), where which action is done does not influence which state obtains, where the conditional probabilities of the states given the actions differ, and where *no* dominant action is available. If the lesson of case (III) is that one should ignore conditional probabilities which do not indicate an influence, must not one ignore them completely in case (IV) as well?

Not exactly. What one should do, in a choice between two actions A and B, is the following.[18] Let $p_1, \ldots, p_n$ be the conditional probability distribution of action A over the n states; let $q_1, \ldots, q_n$ be the conditional probability distribution of action B over the n states. A probability distribution $r_1, \ldots, r_n$, summing to one, is between $p_1, \ldots, p_n$ and $q_1, \ldots, q_n$ if, and only if, for each i, r_i is in the closed interval (p_i, q_i) or (q_i, p_i). (Note that according to this account, $p_1, \ldots, p_n$ and $q_1, \ldots, q_n$ are each between $p_1, \ldots, p_n$ and $q_1, \ldots, q_n$.) Now for a recommendation: if relative to each probability distribution between $p_1, \ldots, p_n$ and $q_1, \ldots, q_n$, action A has a higher expected utility than action B, then do action A. The expected utility of A and B is computed with respect to the same probability distribution. It will not, of course, be the case that relative to every possible probability distribution A has a higher expected utility than B, for, by hypothesis, A does not dominate B. However, it may be that relative to each probability distribution between $p_1, \ldots, p_n$ and $q_1, \ldots, q_n$, A has a higher expected utility than B. If, on the other hand, it is not the case that relative to each probability distribution between $p_1, \ldots, p_n$ and $q_1, \ldots, q_n$, A has a higher expected utility than B (and it is not the case that relative to each, B has a higher expected utility than *A*), then we are faced with a problem of decision under constrained uncertainty (the constraints being the end probability distributions), on which kind of problem there is not, so far as I know, agreement in the literature.[19] Since consideration of the issues raised by such problems would take us far afield, we thankfully leave them.

To talk more objectively than some would like, though more intuitively than we otherwise could, since the actions do not affect or influence which state obtains, there is some one probability distribution, which we do not know, relative to which we would like to compare the action *A* and *B*. Since we do not know the distribution, we cannot proceed as in cases (V) and (VI). But since there is *one* unknown correct distribution "out there," unaffected by what we do, we must, in the procedure we use, compare each action with respect to the *same* distribution. Thus it is, at this point, an irrelevant fact that one action's expected utility computed with respect to one probability distribution is higher than another action's expected utility computed with respect to *another* probability distribution. It may seem strange that for case (IV) we bring in the probabilities in some way (even though they do not indicate an influence) whereas in case (III) we do not. This difference is only apparent, since we could bring in the probabilities in case (III) in exactly the same way. The reason why we need not do this, and need only note that *A* dominates *B*, is that if *A* dominates *B*, then relative to each probability distribution (and therefore for each one between the conditional ones established by the two actions) *A* has a higher expected utility than *B*.[20]

Now, at last, to return to Newcomb's example of the predictor. If one believes, for this case, that there is backwards causality, that your choice causes the money to be there or not, that it causes him to have made the prediction that he made, then there is no problem. One takes only what is in the second box. Or if one believes that the way the predictor works is by looking into the future, he, in some sense, sees what you are doing and hence is no more likely to be wrong about what you do than someone else who is standing there at the time and watching you and would normally see you, say, open only one box, then there is no problem. You take only what is in the second box. But suppose we establish or take as given that there is no backwards causality, that what you actually decide to do does not affect what he did in the past, and that what you actually decide to do is not part of the explanation of why he made the prediction he made. So let us agree that the predictor works as follows: he observes you sometime before you are faced with the choice, examines you with complicated apparatus, and so on , and then uses his theory to predict on the basis of this state you were in, what choice you would make later when faced with the choice. Your deciding to do as you do is not part of the explanation of why he makes the prediction he does, though your being in a certain state earlier, is part of the explanation of why he makes the prediction he does, and why you decide as you do.

I believe that one should take what is in both boxes. I fear that the considerations I have adduced thus far will not convince those proponents of taking only what is in the second box. Furthermore, I suspect that an adequate solution to this problem will go much deeper than I have yet gone or shall go in this paper. So I want to pose one question. I assume that it is clear that in the vaccine example, the person should not be convinced by the probability argument and should choose the dominant action. I assume also that it is clear that in the case of the two brothers, the brother should not be convinced by the probability argument offered. The question I should like to put to proponents of taking only what is in the second box in Newcomb's example (and hence not performing the dominant action) is: what is the difference between Newcomb's example and the other two examples which make the difference between not following the dominance principle and following it?

If no such difference is produced, one should not rush to conclude that one should perform the dominant action in Newcomb's example. For it must be granted that, at the very least, it is not *as clear* that one should perform the dominant action in Newcomb's example as in the other two examples. And one should be wary of attempting to force a decision in an unclear case by producing a similar case where the decision is clear and challenging one to find a difference between the cases which makes a difference to the decision. For suppose the undecided person, or the proponent of another decision, cannot find such a difference. Does not the forcer now have to find a difference between the cases which explains why one is clear and the other is not? And might not *this* difference then be produced by the other person as that which perhaps should yield different decisions in the two cases? Sometimes this will be implausible; for example, if the difference is that one case is relatively simple and the other has much additional detail, individually irrelevant, which prevents the other case from being taken in as a whole. But it does seem that someone arguing as I do about a case must not only: (a) describe a similar case which is clear and challenge the other to state a difference between them which should make a difference to how they are handled, but must also (b) describe a difference between the cases which explains why though one case is clear, the other is not, or one is tempted to handle the other case differently. And, assuming that all accept the difference stated in (b) as explaining what it is supposed to explain:

(I) The simplest situation is that in which all agree that the difference mentioned in (b) is not a reason for different decisions in the two cases.

(II) However, if the forcer says it is not a reason for different decisions in the two cases, and the other person says it is or may be, difficult questions arise about upon whom, if anyone, the burden of further argument falls.

What then is the difference that makes some cases clear and Newcomb's example unclear, yet does not make a difference to how the cases should be decided? Given my account of what the crucial factors are (influence, and so on), my answer to this question will have to claim that the clear cases are clear cases of no influence (or, to recall the cases which we considered at the beginning, of influence), and that in Newcomb's example there is the *illusion* of influence. The task is to explain in a sufficiently forceful way what gives rise to this illusion so that, even as we experience it, we will not be deceived by it. . . .

In closing this paper, I must muddy up the waters a bit (more?).

(1) Though Newcomb's example suggests much about when to apply the dominance principle, and when to apply the expected utility principle (and hence is relevant to formal decision theory), it is not the expected utility principle which leads some people to choose only what is in the second box. For suppose the probability of the being's predicting correctly was just .6.

> Then the expected utility of taking what is in both boxes =
> pr(he predicts correctly /I take both) $\times$ u(I receive $1,000)
> + pr(he predicts incorrectly/I take both) $\times$ u(I receive
> $1,001,000) $= .6 \times u(\$1,000) + .4 \times u(\$1,001,000)$.

The expected utility of taking only what is in the second box $= .6 \times u(\$1,000,000) + .4 \times u(\$0)$.

And given the utility I assume each of my readers assigns to obtaining these various monetary amounts, the expected utility of taking only what is in the second box is greater than the expected utility of taking what is in both boxes. Yet, I presume, if the probability of the beings predicting correctly were only .6, each of us would choose to take what is in both boxes.

So it is not (just) the expected utility argument that operates here to create the problem in Newcomb's example. It is crucial that the predictor is almost certain to be correct. I refrain from asking a proponent of taking only what is in the second box in Newcomb's example: if .6 is not a high enough probability to lead you to take only what is in the second box, and almost certainty of correct predictions leads you to take only the second, what is the minimum probability of correct prediction which leads you to take only what is in the second box? I refrain from asking this question because I am very unsure about the force of drawing-the-line arguments and also because the person who wishes to take what is in both boxes may also face a problem of drawing the line, as we shall see in a moment.

(2) If the fact that it is almost certain that the predictor will be correct is crucial to Newcomb's example, this suggests that we consider the case where it *is* certain, where you know the prediction is correct (though you do not know what the prediction is). Here one naturally argues: I know that if I

take both, I will get $1,000. I know that if I take only what is in the second, I get M. So, of course, I will take only what is in the second. And does a proponent of taking what is in both boxes in Newcomb's example, (for example, me) really wish to argue that it is the probability, however minute, of the predictor's being mistaken which makes the difference? Does he really wish to argue that if he knows the prediction will be correct, he will take only the second, but that if he knows someone using the predictor's theory will be wrong once in every twenty billion cases, he will take what is in both boxes? Could the difference between one in n, and none in n, for arbitrarily large finite n, make this difference? And how exactly does the fact that the predictor is certain to have been correct dissolve the force of the dominance argument?

To get the mind to really boggle, consider the following.

	S_1	S_2
A:	10	4
B:	8	3

Suppose that you know that either S_1 or S_2 already obtains, but you do not know which, and you know that S_1 will cause you to do B, and S_2 will cause you to do A. Now choose! ("Choose?")

To connect up again with a causalized version of Newcomb's example, suppose you know that there are two boxes, (B1) and (B2). (B1) contains $1,000. (B2) contains either a valuable diamond or nothing. You have to choose between taking what is in both boxes and taking only what is in the second. You know that there are two states: S_1 and S_2. You do not know which obtains, but you know that whichever does, it has obtained for the past week. If S_2 obtains, it causes you to take only what is in the second, and it has already caused a diamond to be produced in box (B2). If S_1 obtains, it causes you to take what is in both boxes, and does not cause a diamond to be produced in the second box. You know all this. What do you choose to do?

While we are at it, consider the following case where what you decide (and why) either (1) does affect which future state will obtain, upon which consequences depend, or (though this would not be the same problem for the view I have proposed, it might be for yours) (2) even if it does not affect which state obtains, the conditional probabilities of the states, given what you do and why, differ.

	S_1	S_2
A:	live	die
B:	die	live

(1) Apart from your decisions (if you do not know of this matrix, or know of it and cannot reach a decision), $pr\,S_1 > pr\,S_2$

(2) $pr(S_1/\text{do } A \text{ with (1) as reason}) < pr(S_2/\text{do } A \text{ with (1) as reason})$

(3) $pr(S_1/\text{do } B \text{ with (2) as reason}) > pr(S_2/\text{do } B \text{ with (2) as reason})$

.
.
.

even (n) $pr(S_1/\text{do } A \text{ with } n-1 \text{ as reason}) < pr(S_2/\text{do } A \text{ with } n-1 \text{ as reason})$

odd (n) $pr(S_1/\text{do } B \text{ with } n-1 \text{ as reason}) > pr(S_2/\text{do } B \text{ with } n-1 \text{ as reason})$

.
.
.

Also: $pr(S_1/\text{you do what you do because indifferent between } A \text{ and } B) > pr(S_2/\text{you do what you do because indifferent between } A \text{ and } B)$

$pr(S_1/\text{doing } A \text{ with all of the above as reason}) <$
$pr(S_2/\text{doing } A \text{ with all of the above as reason})$
and
$pr(S_1/\text{doing } B \text{ with all of the above as reason}) >$
$pr(S_2/\text{doing } B \text{ with all of the above as reason})$.

Finally, where "all this" refers to all of what is above this place, and reflexively, to the next two, in which it appears:

$pr(S_1/\text{doing } A \text{ with all this as reason}) <$
$pr(S_2/\text{doing } A \text{ with all this as reason})$
and
$pr(S_1/\text{doing } B \text{ with all this as reason}) >$
$pr(S_2/\text{doing } B \text{ with all this as reason})$.

What do you do?

NOTES

* It is not clear that I am entitled to present this paper. The problem of choice which concerns me was constructed by someone else, and I am not satisfied with my attempts to work through the problem. But since I believe that the problem will interest and intrigue Peter Hempel and his many friends, and since its publication may call forth a solution which will enable me to stop returning, periodically, to it, here it is. It was constructed by a physicist, Dr. William Newcomb, of the Livermore Radiation Laboratories in California. I first heard the problem, in 1963, from his friend Professor Martin David Kruskal of the Princeton University Department of Astrophysical Sciences. I have benefitted from discussions, in 1963, with William Newcomb, Martin David Kruskal, and Paul Benacerraf. Since then, on and off, I have discussed the problem with many other friends whose attempts to grapple with it

have encouraged me to publish my own. It is a beautiful problem. I wish it were mine.

1. If the being predicts that you will consciously randomize your choice, for example, flip a coin, or decide to do one of the actions if the next object you happen to see is blue, and otherwise do the other action, then he does not put the M in the second box.

2. Try it on your friends or students and see for yourself. Perhaps some psychologists will investigate whether responses to the problem are correlated with some other interesting psychological variable that they know of.

3. If the questions and problems are handled as I believe they should be, then some of the ensuing discussion would have to be formulated differently. But there is no point to introducing detail extraneous to the central problem of this paper here.

4. This divergence between the dominance principle and the expected utility principle is pointed out in Nozick (1963) and in Jeffrey (1965).

5. This is shorthand for: action A is done and state S_{12} obtains or action B is done and state S_1 obtains. The "or" is the exclusive or.

6. Note that

$$S_1 = A_1 \ \& \ S_3 \text{ or } A_2 \ \& \ S_4$$
$$S_2 = A_1 \ \& \ S_4 \text{ or } A_2 \ \& \ S_3$$
$$S_3 = A_1 \ \& \ S_1 \text{ or } A_2 \ \& \ S_2$$
$$S_4 = A_1 \ \& \ S_2 \text{ or } A_2 \ \& \ S_1$$

Similarly, the above identifies hold for Newcomb's example, with which I began, if one lets

$$S_1 = \text{The money is in the second box.}$$
$$S_2 = \text{The money is not in the second box.}$$
$$S_3 = \text{The being predicts your choice correctly.}$$
$$S_4 = \text{The being incorrectly predicts your choice.}$$
$$A_1 = \text{You take only what is in the second box.}$$
$$A_2 = \text{You take what is in both boxes.}$$

7. State S is not probabilistically independent of actions A and B if $\text{pr}(S \text{ obtains}/A \text{ is done}) \neq \text{pr}(S \text{ obtains}/B \text{ is done})$.

8. In Newcomb's predictor example, assuming that "He predicts correctly" and "He predicts incorrectly" are each probabilistically independent of my actions, then it is not the case that "He puts the money in" and "He does not put the money in" are each probabilistically independent of my actions.

   Usually it will be the case that if the members of the set of exhaustive and exclusive states are each probabilistically independent of the actions A_1 and A_2, then it will not be the case that the states equivalent to our contrived states are each probabilistically independent of both A_1 and A_2. For example, suppose $\text{pr}(S_1/A_1) = \text{pr}(S_1/A_2) = \text{pr}(S_1)$; $\text{pr}(S_2/A_2) = \text{pr}(S_2/A_1) = \text{pr}(S_2)$. Let:

$$S_3 = A_1 \ \& \ S_1 \text{ or } A_2 \ \& \ S_2$$
$$S_4 = A_1 \ \& \ S_2 \text{ or } A_2 \ \& \ S_1$$

If $\text{pr}(S_1) \neq \text{pr}(S_2)$, then S_3 and S_4 are not probabilistically independent of A_1

and A_2. For $pr(S_3/A_1) = pr(S_1/A_1) = pr(S_1)$, and $pr(S_3/A_2) = pr(S_2/A_2) = pr(S_2)$. Therefore if $pr (S_1) \neq pr(S_2)$, then $pr(S_3/A_1) \neq pr(S_3/A_2)$. If $pr(S_1) = pr (S_2) = 1/2$, then the possibility of describing the states as we have will not matter. For if, for example, A_1 can be shifted around so as to dominate A_2, then before the shifting it will have a higher expected utility than A_2. Generally, if the members of the set of exclusive and exhaustive states are probabilistically independent of both A_1 and A_2, then the members of the contrived set of states will be probabilistically independent of both A_1 and A_2 only if the probabilities of the original states which are components of the contrived states are identical. And in this case it will not matter which way one sets up the situation.

9.   Note that this procedure seems to work quite well for situations in which the states are not only not probabilistically independent of the actions but are not logically independent either. Suppose that a person is asked whether he prefers doing *A* to doing *B*, where the outcome of *A* is $/p$ if S_1 and r if $S_2/$ and the outcome of *B* is $/q$ if S_2 and r if $S_1/$. And suppose that he prefers p to q to r, and that $S_1 =$ I do *B*, and $S_2 =$ I do *A*. The person realizes that if he does *A*, S_2 will be the case and the outcome will be r, and he realizes that if he does *B*, S_1 will be the case and the outcome will be r. Since the outcome will be r in any case, he is indifferent between doing *A* and doing *B*. So let us suppose he flips a coin in order to decide which to do. But given that the coin is fair, it is now the case that the probability of $S_1 = 1/2$ and the probability of $S_2 = 1/2$. If we mechanically started to compute the expected utility of *A*, and of *B*, we would find that *A* has a higher expected utility than does *B*. For mechanically computing the expected utilities, it would turn out that the expected utility of $A = 1/2 \times u(p) + 1/2 \times u(r)$, and the expected utility of $B = 1/2 \times u (q) + 1/2 \times u(r)$. If, however, we use the conditional probabilities, then the expected utility of $A = pr (S_1/A) \times u(p) + pr(S_2/A) \times u(r) = 0 \times u(p) + 1 \times u(r) = u(r)$. And the expected utility of $B = pr (S_2/B) \times u(q) + pr (S_1/B) \times u(r) = 0 + u(q) + 1 \times u(r) = u(r)$. Thus the expected utilities of *A* and *B* are equal, as one would wish.

10. This position was suggested, with some reservations due to Newcomb's example, in Nozick (1963). It was also suggested in Jeffrey (1965).

11. I should mention what the reader has no doubt noticed; that the previous *example* is not fully satisfactory, for it seems that preferring the academic life to the athlete's life should be as strong evidence for the tendency as is choosing the academic life. And hence *P*'s choosing the athlete's life, though he prefers the academic life, on expected utility grounds does not seem to make it likely that he does not have the tendency. What the example seems to require is an inherited tendency to decide to do *A* which is such that (1) the probability of its presence cannot be estimated on the basis of the person's preferences, but only on the basis of knowing the genetic make-up of his parents or knowing his actual decisions; and (2) the theory about how the tendency operates yields the result that it is unlikely that it is present if the person decides not to do *A* in the example-situation, even though he makes this decision on the basis of the stated expected utility grounds. It is not clear how, for this example, the details are to be coherently worked out.

12. That is, the Dominance Principle is legitimately applicable to situations in which $\sim(\exists S) (\exists A) (\exists B) [pr(S \text{ obtains}/A \text{ is done}) \neq pr (S \text{ obtains}/B \text{ is done})]$.

13. The other eleven possibilities about the states are:

	Already fixed and determined		Not already fixed and determined	
	probabilistically independent of the actions	not probabilistically independent of the actions	prob. ind. of the actions	not prob. ind. of the actions
(1)	some	some	some	some
(2)	some	some	some	none
(3)	some	some	none	some
(4)	some	some	none	none
(5)	some	none	some	some
(6)	some	none	some	none
(7)	some	none	none	some
(8)	all	none	none	none
(9)	none	some	some	some
(10)	none	some	some	none
(11)	none	some	none	some

14. Unless it is possible that there be causality or influence backwards in time. I shall not here consider this possibility, though it may be that only on its basis can one defend, for some choice situations, the refusal to use the dominance principle. I try to explain later why, for some situations, even if one grants that there is no influence back in time, one may not escape the feeling that, somehow, there is.

15. Cf. Luce and Raiffa (1957), pp. 94–102.

16. Almost certainty$_1$ > almost certainty$_2$, since almost certainty$_2$ is some function of the probability that brother I has the dominant action gene given that he performs the dominant action ($=$ almost certainty$_1$) and of the probability that brother II does the dominant action given that he has the dominant action gene.

17. In choosing the headings for the rows, I have ignored more complicated possibilities, which must be investigated for a fuller theory, for example, some actions influence which state obtains and others do not.

18. I here consider only the case of two actions. Obvious and messy problems for the kind of policy about to be proposed are raised by the situation in which more than two actions are available (for example, under what conditions do pairwise comparisons lead to a linear order), whose consideration is best postponed for another occasion.

19. See Luce and Raiffa (1957), pp. 275–98 and the references therein; Ellsberg (1961) and the articles by his fellow symposiasts Raiffa and Feller.

20. If the distinctions I have drawn are correct, then some of the existing literature is in need of revision. Many of the writers might be willing just to draw the distinctions we have adumbrated. But for the specific theories offered by some personal probability theorists, it is not clear how this is to be done. For example, L. J. Savage (1954) recommends unrestricted use of dominance principles (his postulate $P2$), which would not do in case (I). And Savage seems explicitly to wish to deny himself the means of distinguishing case (I) from the others. (For further discussion, some of which must be revised in the light of this paper, of Savage's important and ingenious work, see Robert Nozick (1963) Chapter V.) And Richard Jeffrey (1965) recommends universal use of maximizing expected utility relative to the conditional probabilities of the states given

the actions (see footnote 10 above). This will not do, I have argued, in cases (III) and (IV). But Jeffrey also sees it as a special virtue of this theory that it does not utilize certain notions, and these notions look like they might well be required to draw the distinctions between the different kinds of cases.

While on the subject of how to distinguish the cases, let me (be the first to) say that I have used without explanation, and in this paper often interchangeably, the notions of influency, affecting, and so on. I have felt free to use them without paying them much attention because even such unreflective use serves to open a whole area of concern. A detailed consideration of the different possible cases with many actions, some influencing, and in different degrees, some not influencing, combined with an attempt to state detailed principles using precise "influence" notions undoubtedly would bring forth many intricate and difficult problems. These would show, I think, that my quick general statements about influence and what distinguishes the cases, are not, strictly speaking, correct. But going into these details would necessitate going into these details. So I will not.

7

Counterfactuals and Two Kinds of Expected Utility*

ALLAN GIBBARD AND WILLIAM L. HARPER

This paper develops a proposal by Robert Stalnaker.[1] We begin with a rough theory of rational decision-making. In the first place, rational decision-making involves conditional propositions: when a person weighs a major decision, it is rational for him to ask, for each act he considers, what would happen if he performed that act. It is rational, then, for him to consider propositions of the form "If I were to do *a,* then *c* would happen." Such a proposition we shall call a *counterfactual,* and we shall form count-

From Hooker, Leach, and McClennen, (eds.), *Foundations and Applications of Decision Theory,* vol. I, 125–62. All Rights Reserved. Copyright © 1978 by D. Reidel Publishing Company, Dordrecht, Holland. Reprinted with abridgement by permission of authors and publisher.

erfactuals with a connective "$\square\!\!\rightarrow$" on this pattern: "If I were to do *a,* then *c* would happen" is to be written "I do *a* $\square\!\!\rightarrow$ *c* happens."

Now ordinarily, of course, a person does not know everything that would happen if he performed a given act. He must resort to probabilities: he must ascribe a probability to each pertinent counterfactual "I do *a* $\square\!\!\rightarrow$ *c* happens." He can then use these probabilities, along with the desirabilities he ascribes to the various things that might happen if he did a given act, to reckon the expected utility of *a.* If *a* has possible outcomes $o_1, \ldots, o_n$, the expected utility of *a* is the weighted sum

$$\Sigma_i \, pr(\text{I do } a \ \square\!\!\rightarrow o_i \text{ obtains}) \ \mathcal{D}o_i,$$

where $\mathcal{D}o_i$ is the desirability of o_i. On the view we are sketching, then, the probabilities to be used in expected utility are the probabilities of certain counterfactuals.

That is not the story told in familiar Bayesian accounts of rational decision; those accounts make no overt mention of counterfactuals. We shall discuss later how Savage's account (1972) does without counterfactuals; consider first an account given by Jeffrey (1965, pp. 5-6).

A formal Bayesian decision problem is specified by two rectangular arrays (matrices) of numbers which represent probability and desirability assignments to the act-condition pairs. The columns represent a set of incompatible conditions, an unknown one of which actually obtains. Each row of the desirability matrix,

$$d_1 \ d_2 \ldots d_n$$

represents the desirabilities that the agent attributes to the *n* conditions described by the column headings, on the assumption that he is about to perform the act described by the row heading; and the corresponding row of the probability matrix,

$$p_1 \ p_2 \ldots p_n$$

represents the probabilities that the agent attributes to the same *n* conditions, still on the assumption that he is about to perform the act described by the row heading. To compute the expected desirability of the act, multiply the corresponding probabilities and desirabilities, and add:

$$p_1 d_1 + p_2 d_2 + \ldots + p_n d_n.$$

On the Bayesian model as presented by Jeffrey, then, the probabilities to be used in calculating "expected desirability" are "probabilities that the agent attributes" to certain conditions "on the assumption that he is about to perform" a given act. These, then, are conditional probabilities; they take the form $pr(S/A)$, where A is the proposition that the agent is about to perform a given act and S is the proposition that a given condition holds.

On the account Jeffrey gives, then, the probabilities to be used in decision problems are not the unconditional probabilities of certain counterfactuals, but are instead certain conditional probabilities. They take the form $pr(S/A)$, whereas on the view we sketched at the outset, they should take the form $pr(A \;\Box\!\!\rightarrow S)$. Now perhaps, for all we have said so far, the difference between these accounts is merely one of presentation. Perhaps for every appropriate A and S, we have

$$(1) \; pr\,(A \;\Box\!\!\rightarrow S) \; = \; pr\,(S/A);$$

the probability of a counterfactual $A \;\Box\!\!\rightarrow S$ always equals the corresponding conditional probability. That would be so if (1) is a logical truth. Lewis, however, has shown (1976b) that on certain very weak and plausible assumptions, (1) is not a logical truth: it does not hold in general for arbitrary propositions A and S. That leaves the possibility that (1) holds at least in all decision contexts: that it holds whenever A is an act an agent can perform and pr gives that agent's probability ascriptions at the time.

We shall state a condition that guarantees the truth of (1) in decision contexts. We shall argue, however, that there are decision contexts in which this condition is violated. The context we shall use as an example is patterned after one given by Stalnaker. We shall follow Stalnaker in arguing that in such contexts, (1) indeed fails, and it is probabilities of counterfactuals rather than conditional probabilities that should be used in calculations of expected utility. The rest of the paper takes up the ramifications for decision theory of the two ways of calculating expected utility. In particular, the two opposing answers to Newcomb's Problem (Nozick, 1969) are supported respectively by the two kinds of expected utility maximization we are discussing.

We are working in this paper within the Bayesian tradition in decision theory, in that the probabilities we are using are subjective probabilities and we suppose an agent to ascribe values to all probabilities needed in calculations of expected utilities. It is not our purpose here to defend this general tradition, but rather to work within it, and to consider two divergent ways of developing it.

COUNTERFACTUALS

What we shall be saying requires little in the way of an elaborate theory of counterfactuals. We do suppose that counterfactuals are genuine propositions. For a proposition to be a counterfactual, we do not require that its antecedent be false: on the view we are considering, a rational agent entertains counterfactuals of the form "I do $a \ \square\!\!\rightarrow\ S$" both for the act he will turn out to perform and for acts he will turn out not to perform. To say $A \ \square\!\!\rightarrow\ S$ is not to say that A's holding would bring about S's holding: $A \ \square\!\!\rightarrow\ S$ is indeed true if A's holding would bring about S's holding, but $A \ \square\!\!\rightarrow S$ is true also if S would hold regardless of whether A held.

These comments by no means constitute a full theory of counterfactuals. In what follows, we shall appeal not to a theory of counterfactuals but to the reader's intuitions about them — asking the reader to bear clearly in mind that "I do $a \ \square\!\!\rightarrow\ S$" is to be read "If I were to do a, then S would hold."

It may nevertheless be useful to sketch a theory that would support what we shall be saying; the theory we sketch here is somewhat like that of Stalnaker and Thomason (Stalnaker, 1968; Stalnaker and Thomason, 1970). Let a be an act which I might decide at time t to perform. An a-world will be a possible world which is like the actual world before t, in which I decide to do a at t and do it, and which obeys physical laws from time t on. Let W_a be the a-world which, at t, is most like the actual world at t. Thus W_a is a possible world which unfolds after t in accordance with physical law, and whose initial conditions at time t are minimally different from conditions in the actual world at t in such a way that "I do a" is true in W_a. The differences in initial conditions should be entirely within the agent's decision-making apparatus. Then "I do $a \ \square\!\!\rightarrow\ S$" is true in W_a.[2]

Two axioms that hold on this theory will be useful in later arguments. Our first axiom is just a principle of modus ponens for the counterfactual.

Axiom 1. $(A \ \& \ (A \ \square\!\!\rightarrow\ S)) \ \rightarrow\ S$.

Our second axiom is a Stalnaker-like principle.

Axiom 2. $(A \ \square\!\!\rightarrow\ \overline{S}) \ \leftrightarrow\ \overline{(A \ \square\!\!\rightarrow S)}$.

The rationale for this is that "I do $a \ \square\!\!\rightarrow\ S$" is true if S holds in W_a and "I do $a \ \square\!\!\rightarrow\ \overline{S}$ is true if, and only if, $\overline{S}$ holds in W_a. We shall also appeal to a consequence of these axioms.

Consequence 1. $A \rightarrow ((A \ \square\!\!\rightarrow S) \ \leftrightarrow\ S)$.

We do not regard Axiom 2 and Consequence 1 as self-evident. Our reason for casting the rough theory in a form which gives these principles is that circumstances where these can fail involve complications which it would be best to ignore in preliminary work.[3] Our appeals to these Axioms will be rare and explicit. For the most part in treating counterfactuals we shall simply depend on a normal understanding of the way counterfactuals apply to the situations we discuss.

TWO KINDS OF EXPECTED UTILITY

We have spoken on the one hand of expected utility calculated from the probabilities of counterfactuals and on the other hand of expected utility calculated from conditional probabilities. In what follows, we shall not distinguish between an act an agent can perform and the proposition that says that he is about to perform it; acts will be expressed by capital letters early in the alphabet. An act will ordinarily have a number of alternative outcomes, where an *outcome* of an act is a single proposition which, for all the agent knows, expresses *all* the consequences of that act which he cares about. An outcome, then, is a specification of what might eventuate which is complete in the sense that any further specification of detail is irrelevant to the agent's concerns, and it specifies something that, for all the agent knows, might really happen if he performed the act. The agent, we shall assume, ascribes a magnitude $\mathcal{D}O$ to each outcome O. He knows that if he performed the act, one and only one of its outcomes would obtain, although he does not ordinarily know which of its outcomes that would be.

Let $O_1, \ldots, O_m$ be the outcomes of act A. The *expected utility* of A *calculated from probabilities of counterfactuals* we shall call $\mathcal{U}(A)$; it is given by the formula

$$\mathcal{U}(A) = \Sigma_j \, pr(A \mathrel{\Box\!\!\rightarrow} O_i) \; \mathcal{D}O_j.$$

The *expected utility* of A *calculated from conditional probabilities* we shall call $\mathcal{V}(A)$; it is given by the formula

$$\mathcal{V}(A) = \Sigma_j \, pr(O_j/A)\mathcal{D}O_j.$$

Perhaps the best mnemonic for distinguishing $\mathcal{U}$ from $\mathcal{V}$ is this: we shall be advocating the use of counterfactuals in calculating expected utility, and we shall claim that $\mathcal{U}(A)$ is the genuine expected utility of A. $\mathcal{V}(A)$ we shall claim, measures instead the welcomeness of the news that one is about to perform A. Remember $\mathcal{V}(A)$, then, as the *value* of A *as news,* and remember $\mathcal{U}(A)$ as what the authors regard as the genuine expected utility of A.

Now clearly $\mathcal{U}(A)$ and $\gamma(A)$ will be the same if
(2) $pr(A \mathrel{\Box\!\!\rightarrow} O_j) = pr(O_j/A)$
for each outcome O_j. Unless (2) holds for every O_j such that $\mathcal{D}O_j \neq 0$, $\mathcal{U}(A)$ and $\mathcal{V}(A)$ will be the same only by coincidence. We know from Lewis's work (1976b) that (2) does not hold for all propositions A and O_j; can we expect that (2) will hold for the appropriate propositions?

One assumption, together with the logical truth of Consequence 1, will guarantee that (2) holds for an act and its outcomes. Here and throughout, we suppose that the function *pr* gives the probability ascriptions of an agent who can immediately perform the act in question, and that $pr\,\phi = 1$ for any logical truth ϕ.

Condition 1 *on act A and outcome* O_i. The counterfactual $A \,\square\!\rightarrow\, O_i$ is stochastically independent of the act *A*. That is to say,

$$pr(A \,\square\!\rightarrow\, O_i/A) = pr(A \,\square\!\rightarrow\, O_i).$$

(Read $pr(A \,\square\!\rightarrow\, O_i/A)$ as the conditional probability of $A \,\square\!\rightarrow\, O_i$ on *A*.)

Assertion 1. Suppose Consequence 1 is a logical truth. If *A* and O_i satisfy Conditon 1, and $pr(A) > 0$, then

$$pr(A \,\square\!\rightarrow\, O_i) = pr\,(O_i/A).^4$$

Proof. Since Consequence 1 is a logical truth, for any propositions *P* and *Q*,

$$pr(P \rightarrow ((P \,\square\!\rightarrow\, Q) \leftrightarrow Q)) = 1.$$

Hence if $pr\,P > 0$, then

$$pr(((P \,\square\!\rightarrow\, Q) \leftrightarrow Q)/P) = 1;$$

$$\therefore pr(P \,\square\!\rightarrow\, Q/P) = pr(Q/P).$$

From this general truth we have

$$pr(A \,\square\!\rightarrow\, O_i/A) = pr(O_i/A),$$

and from this and Condition 1, it follows that

$$pr(A \,\square\!\rightarrow\, O_i) = pr(O_i/A).$$

That proves the Assertion.

Condition 1 is that the counterfactuals relevant to decision be stochastically independent of the acts contemplated. Stochastic independence is the same as epistemic independence. For $pr(A \,\square\!\rightarrow\, O_i/A)$ is the probability it would be rational for the agent to ascribe to the counterfactual $A \,\square\!\rightarrow\, O_i$ on learning *A* and nothing else — on learning that he was about to perform that act. Thus to say that $pr(A \,\square\!\rightarrow\, O_i/A) = pr(A \,\square\!\rightarrow\, O_i)$ is to say that learning that one was about to perform the act would not change the probability one ascribes to the proposition that if one were to perform the act, outcome O_i

would obtain. We shall use the terms "stochastic independence" and "epistemic independence" interchangeably.

The two kinds of expected utility $\mathcal{U}$ and $\mathcal{V}$ can also be characterized in a way suggested by Jeffrey's account of the Bayesian model. Let acts $A_1, \ldots,$ A_m be open to the agent. Let states $S_1, \ldots, S_n$ partition the possibilities in the following sense. For any propositions $S_1, \ldots, S_n$, the truth-function *aut* $(S_1, \ldots, S_n)$ will be their exclusive disjunction: *aut* $(S_1, \ldots, S_n)$ holds in and only in circumstances where exactly one of $S_1, \ldots, S_n$ is true. Let the agent know *aut* $(S_1, \ldots, S_n)$. For each act A_i and state S_j, let him know that if he did A_i and S_j obtained, the outcome would be O_{ij}. Let him ascribe each outcome O_{ij} a desirability $\mathcal{D}O_{ij}$. This will be a *matrix formulation* of a decision problem; its defining features are that the agent knows that $S_1, \ldots, S_n$ partition the possibilities, and in each of these states $S_1, \ldots, S_n$, each act open to the agent has a unique outcome. A set $\{S_1, \ldots, S_n\}$ of states which satisfy these conditions will be called *the states of a matrix formulation* of the decision problem in question.

Both $\mathcal{U}$ and $\mathcal{V}$ can be characterized in terms of a matrix formulation:

$$\mathcal{U}(A_i) = \Sigma_j \, pr(A_i \,\square\!\!\rightarrow S_j) \;\; \mathcal{D}O_{ij};$$
$$\mathcal{V}(A_i) = \Sigma_j \, pr(S_j/A_i) \;\; \mathcal{D}O_{ij}.$$

If $\mathcal{D}O_{ij}$ can be regarded as the desirability the agent attributes to S_j "on the assumption that" he will do A_i, then $\mathcal{V}(A_i)$ is the desirability of A_i as characterized in the account we quoted from Jeffrey.

On the basis of these matrix characterizations of $\mathcal{U}$ and $\mathcal{V}$, we can state another sufficient condition for the $\mathcal{U}$-utility and $\mathcal{V}$-utility of an act to be the same.

Condition 2 *on act A_i, states $S_1, \ldots, S_n$, and the function pr.* For each A_i and S_j,

$$pr(A_i \,\square\!\!\rightarrow S_j/A_i) = pr(A_i \,\square\!\!\rightarrow S_j).$$

Assertion 2. Suppose Consequence 1 is a logical truth. If a decision problem satisfies Condition 2 for act A_i, then $\mathcal{U}(A_i) = \mathcal{V}(A_i)$. The proof is like that of Assertion 1.

ACT-DEPENDENT STATES IN THE SAVAGE FRAMEWORK

Savage's representation of decision problems (1954) is roughly the matrix formulation just discussed. Ignorance is represented as ignorance about which of a number of states of the world obtains. These states are mutually exclusive, and as specific as the problem requires (p. 15). The agent ascribes desirability to "consequences," or what we are calling *outcomes*. For each act open to the agent, he knows what outcome obtains for each state of the world; if he does not, the problem must be reformulated so that he does. Savage indeed defines an act as a function from states to outcomes (p. 14).

It is a consequence of the axioms Savage gives that a rational agent is disposed to choose as if he ascribed a numerical desirability to each outcome and a numerical probability to each state and then acted to maximize expected utility, where the expected utility of an act A is

(3) $\Sigma_s \, pr(S) \, \mathcal{D}O(A,S).$

(Here $O(A,S)$ is the outcome of act A in state S.) Another consequence of Savage's axioms is the principle of dominance: if for every state S, the outcome of act A in S is more desirable than the outcome of B in S, then A is preferable to B.

Consider this misuse of the Savage apparatus; it is of a kind discussed by Jeffrey (1965,pp.8–10).

> *Case* 1. David wants Bathsheba, but since she is the wife of Uriah, he fears that summoning her to him would provoke a revolt. He reasons to himself as follows: "There are two possibilities: R, that there will be a revolt, and $\bar{R}$, that there won't be. The outcomes and their desirabilities are given in Matrix 1, where B is that I take Bathsheba and A is that I abstain from her. Whether or not there is a revolt, I prefer having Bathsheba to not having her, and so taking Bathsheba dominates over abstaining from her.

	R	$\bar{R}$
A	$R\bar{B}(0)$	$\bar{R}\bar{B}(9)$
B	$RB(1)$	$\bar{R}B(10)$

Matrix 1

This argument is of course fallacious: dominance requires that the states in question be independent of the acts contemplated, whereas taking Bathsheba may provoke revolt. To apply the Savage framework to a decision problem, one must find states of the world which are in some sense act-independent. . . .

ACT-DEPENDENT COUNTERFACTUALS

Should we expect Condition 2 to hold? In the case of David, it seems that we should. Suppose David somehow learned that he was about to send for

Bathsheba; that would give him no reason to change the probability he ascribes to the proposition "If I were to send for Bathsheba, there would be a revolt." Similarly, if David learned that he was about to abstain from Bathsheba, that would give him no reason to change the probability he ascribes to the proposition "If I were to abstain from Bathsheba, there would be a revolt." In the case of David, it seems, the pertinent counterfactuals are epistemically act-independent, and hence for each act he can perform, the $\mathcal{U}$-utility and the $\mathcal{V}$-utility are the same.

When, however, a common factor is believed to affect both behavior and outcome, Condition 2 may fail, and $\mathcal{U}$-utility may diverge from $\mathcal{V}$-utility. The following case is patterned after an example used by Stalnaker to make the same point.[5]

> *Case* 2. Solomon faces a situation like David's, but he, unlike David, has studied works on psychology and political science which teach him the following: kings have two basic personality types, charismatic and uncharismatic. A king's degree of charisma depends on his genetic make-up and early childhood experiences and cannot be changed in adulthood. Now charismatic kings tend to act justly and uncharismatic kings unjustly. Successful revolts against charismatic kings are rare, whereas successful revolts against uncharismatic kings are frequent. Unjust acts themselves, though, do not cause successful revolts; the reason that uncharismatic kings are prone to successful revolts is that they have a sneaky, ignoble bearing. Solomon does not know whether or not he is charismatic; he does know that it is unjust to send for another man's wife.

Now in this case, Condition 2 fails for states R and $\bar{R}$. The counterfactual $B \square \!\!\rightarrow R$ is not epistemically independent of B: we have

$$pr(B \square \!\!\rightarrow R/B) > pr(B \square \!\!\rightarrow R).$$

For the conditional probability of anything on B is the probability Solomon would rationally ascribe to it if he learned that B. Since he knows that B's holding would in no way tend to bring about R's holding, he always ascribes the same probability to $B \square \!\!\rightarrow R$ as to R. Hence both $pr(B \square \!\!\rightarrow R) = pr(R)$ and $pr(B \square \!\!\rightarrow R/B) = pr(R/B)$. Now if Solomon learned that B, he would have reason to think that he was uncharismatic and thus revolt-prone. Hence $pr(R/B) > pr(R)$, and therefore

(6) $pr(B \square \!\!\rightarrow R/B) = pr(R/B) > pr(R) = pr(B \square \!\!\rightarrow R).$

Here, then, the counterfactual is not epistemically act-independent.

(6) states also that $pr(B \square \!\!\rightarrow R) < pr(R/B)$, so that in this case, the prob-

ability of the counterfactual does not equal the corresponding conditional probability. By similar argument we could show that $pr(A \,\Box\!\!\rightarrow R) > pr(R/A)$. Indeed in this case a $\mathcal{U}$-maximizer will choose to send for his neighbor's wife whereas a $\mathcal{V}$-maximizer will choose to abstain from her — although we shall need to stipulate the case in more detail to prove the latter.

Consider first $\mathcal{U}$-maximization. We have that

$$\mathcal{U}(B) = pr(B \,\Box\!\!\rightarrow \bar{R}) \,\mathcal{D}\bar{R}B + pr(B \,\Box\!\!\rightarrow R) \,\mathcal{D}RB;$$
$$\mathcal{U}(A) = pr(A \,\Box\!\!\rightarrow \bar{R}) \,\mathcal{D}\bar{R}B + pr(A \,\Box\!\!\rightarrow R) \,\mathcal{D}R\bar{B}.$$

We have argued that $pr(B \,\Box\!\!\rightarrow R) = pr(R)$. Similarly, $pr(A \,\Box\!\!\rightarrow R) = pr(R)$, and so $pr(A \,\Box\!\!\rightarrow R) = pr(B \,\Box\!\!\rightarrow R)$. Likewise, $pr(A \,\Box\!\!\rightarrow \bar{R}) = pr(B \,\Box\!\!\rightarrow \bar{R})$. We know that $\mathcal{D}\bar{R}B > \mathcal{D}\bar{R}\bar{B}$ and $\mathcal{D}RB > \mathcal{D}R\bar{B}$. Therefore $\mathcal{U}(B) > \mathcal{U}(A)$. This is in effect an argument from dominance, as we shall discuss later.

Now consider $\mathcal{V}$-maximization. Learning that A would give Solomon reason to think he was charismatic and thus not revolt-prone, whereas learning that B would give him reason to think that he was uncharismatic and revolt-prone. Thus $pr(R/B) > pr(R/A)$. Suppose the difference between these probabilities is greater than 1/9, so that where $pr(R/A) = \alpha$ and $pr(R/B) = \alpha + \epsilon$, we have $\epsilon > 1/9$. From Matrix 1, we have

$$\mathcal{V}(A) = pr(\bar{R}/A) \,\mathcal{D}\,\bar{R}\bar{B} + pr(R/A) \,\mathcal{D}R\bar{B} = 9(1-\alpha) + 0.$$
$$\mathcal{V}(B) = pr(\bar{R}/B) \,\mathcal{D}\bar{R}B + pr(R/B) \,\mathcal{D}RB = 10(1-\alpha-\epsilon) + 1(\alpha + \epsilon).$$

Therefore $\mathcal{V}(A) - \mathcal{V}(B) = 9\epsilon - 1$, and since $\epsilon > 1/9$, this is positive. We have shown that if $\epsilon > 1/9$, then although $\mathcal{U}(B) > \mathcal{U}(A)$, we have $\mathcal{V}(A) > \mathcal{V}(B)$. Thus $\mathcal{U}$-maximization and $\mathcal{V}$-maximization in this case yield conflicting prescriptions.

Which of these prescriptions is the rational one? It seems clear that in this case it is rational to perform the $\mathcal{U}$-maximizing act: unjustly to send for the wife of his neighbor. Solomon cares only about getting the woman and avoiding revolt. He knows that sending for the woman would not cause a revolt. To be sure, sending for her would be an indication that Solomon lacked charisma, and hence an indication that he will face a revolt. To abstain from the woman for this reason, though, would be knowingly to bring about an indication of a desired outcome without in any way bringing about the desired outcome itself. That seems clearly irrational.

For those who find Solomon too distant in time and place or who mistrust charisma, we offer the case of Robert Jones, rising young executive of International Energy Conglomerate Incorporated. Jones and several other young executives have been competing for a very lucrative promotion. The company brass found the candidates so evenly matched that they employed a psychologist to break the tie by testing for personality qualities that lead to long-run successful performance in the corporate world. The test was administered to the candidates on Thursday. The promotion decision is made on the basis of the test and will be announced on Monday. It is now Friday. Jones learns, through a reliable company grapevine, that all the candidates have scored equally well on all factors except ruthlessness and that the promotion will go to whichever of them has scored highest on this factor, but he cannot find out which of them this is.

On Friday afternoon Jones is faced with a new problem. He must decide whether or not to fire poor old John Smith, who failed to meet his sales quota this month because of the death of his wife. Jones believes that Smith will come up to snuff after he gets over his loss provided that he is treated leniently and that he can convince the brass that leniency to Smith will benefit the company. Moreover, he believes that this would favorably impress the brass with his astuteness. Unfortunately, Jones has no way to get in touch with them until after they announce the promotion on Monday.

Jones knows that the ruthlessness factor of the personality test he has taken accurately predicts his behavior in just the sort of decision he now faces. Firing Smith is good evidence that he has passed the test and will get the promotion, while leniency is good evidence that he has failed the test and will not get the promotion. We suppose that the utilities and probabilities correspond to those facing Solomon. $\mathcal{V}$-maximizing recommends firing Smith, while $\mathcal{U}$-maximizing recommends leniency. Firing Smith would produce evidence that Jones will get his desired promotion. It seems clear, however, that to fire Smith for this reason despite the fact that to do so would in no way help to bring about the promotion and would itself be harmful is irrational.

THE SIGNIFICANCE OF $\mathcal{U}$ AND $\mathcal{V}$

From the Solomon example, it should be apparent that the $\mathcal{V}$-utility of an act is a measure of the welcomeness of the news that one is about to perform that act. Such news may tend to be welcome because the act is likely to have desirable consequences, or tend to be unwelcome because the act is likely to have disagreeable consequences. Those, however, are not the only reasons an act may be welcome or unwelcome: an act may be welcome because its being performed is an indication that the world is in a desired state. Solomon, for instance, would welcome the news that he was about to abstain from his neighbor's wife, but he would welcome it not because he thought just acts any more likely to have desirable consequences than unjust acts, but because he takes just acts to be a sign of charisma, and he thinks that charisma may bring about a desired outcome.

$\mathcal{U}$-utility, in contrast, is a measure of the expected efficacy of an act in bringing about states of affairs the agent desires; it measures the expected value of the consequences of an act. That can be seen in the case of Solomon. The $\mathcal{U}$-utility of sending for his neighbor's wife is greater than that of abstaining, and that is because he knows that sending for her will bring about a consequence he desires — having the woman — and he knows that it will not bring about any consequences he wishes to avoid: in particular, he knows that it will not bring about a revolt.

What is it for an act to bring about a consequence? Here are two possible answers, both formulated in terms of counterfactuals.

In the first place, roughly following Sobel (1970, p.400), we may say that act A brings about state S if $A \ \square\!\!\rightarrow S$ holds, and for some alternative A^* to A, $A^* \square\!\!\rightarrow S$ does not hold.[6] (An *alternative* to A is another act open to the agent on the same occasion.) Now on this analysis, the $\mathcal{U}$-utility of an act as we have defined it is the sum of the expected value of its consequences plus a term which is the same for all acts open to the agent on the occasion in question; this latter term is the expected value of unavoidable outcomes. A state S is *unavoidable* if, and only if, for every act A^* open to the agent, $A^* \square\!\!\rightarrow S$ holds. Thus $A \square\!\!\rightarrow S$ holds if, and only if, S is a consequence of A or S is unavoidable. Hence in particular, for any outcome O,

$$pr(A \square\!\!\rightarrow O) = pr(O \text{ is a consequence of } A)$$
$$+ \ pr(O \text{ is unavoidable}),$$

and so we have

$$\mathcal{U}(A) = \Sigma_O \ pr(A \square\!\!\rightarrow O) \ \mathcal{D}O$$
$$= \Sigma_O \ pr(O \text{ is a consequence of } A) \ \mathcal{D}O$$
$$+ \ \Sigma_O \ pr(O \text{ is unavoidable}) \ \mathcal{D}O.$$

The first term is the expected value of the consequences of A, and the second term is the same for all acts open to the agent. Therefore on this analysis of the term "consequence," $\mathcal{U}$-utility is maximal for the act or acts whose consequences have maximal expected value.

Here is a second possible way of analyzing what it is to be a consequence. When an agent chooses between two acts A and B, what he really needs to know is not what the consequences of A are and what the consequences of B are, but rather what the consequences are of A as opposed to B and vice versa. Thus for purposes of decision-making, we can do without an analysis of the clause "S is a consequence of A," and analyze instead the clause "S is a consequence of A as opposed to B." This we can analyze as

$$(A \;\Box\!\!\rightarrow S) \; \& \; \sim (B \;\Box\!\!\rightarrow S).$$

Now on this analysis, $\mathcal{U}(A) > \mathcal{U}(B)$ if, and only if, the expected value of the consequences of A as opposed to B exceeds the expected value of the consequences of B as opposed to A. For any state S, $A \;\Box\!\!\rightarrow S$ holds if, and only if, either S is a consequence of A as opposed to B or $(A \;\Box\!\!\rightarrow S)$ & $(B \;\Box\!\!\rightarrow S)$ holds.

Thus
$$
\begin{aligned}
\mathcal{U}(A) &= \Sigma_o \; pr(A \;\Box\!\!\rightarrow O) \; \mathcal{D}O \\
&= \Sigma_o \; pr(O \text{ is a consequence of } A \text{ as opposed to } B) \; \mathcal{D}O \\
&\quad + \Sigma_o \; pr((A \;\Box\!\!\rightarrow O) \; \& \; (B \;\Box\!\!\rightarrow O)) \; \mathcal{D}O \\
\mathcal{U}(B) &= \Sigma_o \; pr(O \text{ is a consequence of } B \text{ as opposed to } A) \; \mathcal{D}O \\
&\quad + \Sigma_o \; pr((A \;\Box\!\!\rightarrow O) \; \& \; (B \;\Box\!\!\rightarrow O)) \; \mathcal{D}O
\end{aligned}
$$

The second term is the same in both cases, and so $\mathcal{U}(A) > \mathcal{U}(B)$ if, and only if,

$$\Sigma_o pr(O \text{ is a consequence of } A \text{ as opposed to } B) \; \mathcal{D}O >$$
$$\Sigma_o pr(O \text{ is a consequence of } B \text{ as opposed to } A) \; \mathcal{D}O.$$

The left side is the expected value of the consequences of A as opposed to $B;$ the right side is the expected value of the consequences of B as opposed to A. Thus for any pair of alternatives, to prefer the one with the higher $\mathcal{U}$ -utility is to prefer the one the consequences of which as opposed to the other have the greater expected value.

We can now ask whether $\mathcal{U}$ or $\mathcal{V}$ is more properly called the "utility" of an act. The answer seems clearly to be $\mathcal{U}$. The "utility" of an act should be its expected genuine efficacy in bringing about states of affairs the agent wants, not the degree to which news of the act ought to cheer the agent. Since $\mathcal{U}$-utility is a matter of what the act can be expected to bring about whereas $\mathcal{V}$-utility is a matter of the welcomeness of news, $\mathcal{U}$-utility seems best to capture the notion of utility.

Jeffrey (1965, pp. 73–74) writes, "If the agent is deliberating about performing act A or act $B,$ and if AB is impossible, there is no effective difference between asking whether he prefers A to B as a news item or as an act, for he makes the news." It should now be clear why it may sometimes be rational for an agent to choose an act B instead of an act $A,$ even though he would welcome the news of A more than that of B. The news of an act may furnish evidence of a state of the world which the act itself is known not to produce. In that case, though the agent indeed makes the news of his act, he does not make all the news his act bespeaks.

TWO SURE-THING PRINCIPLES

Case 3. Upon his accession to the throne, Reoboam wonders whether to announce that he will reign severely or to announce that he will reign leniently. He will be bound by what he announces. He slightly prefers a short severe reign to a short lenient reign, and he slightly prefers a long severe reign to a long lenient reign. He strongly prefers a long reign of any kind to a short reign of any kind. Where L is that he is lenient and D, that he is deposed early, his utilities are as in the Matrix 3.

$$\begin{array}{c|cc} & D & \bar{D} \\ \hline L & 0 & 80 \\ \bar{L} & 10 & 100 \end{array}$$

Matrix 3

The wise men of the kingdom give him these findings of behavioral science: there is no correlation between a king's severity and the length of his reign. Severity, nevertheless, often causes early deposition. The reason for the lack of correlation between severity and early deposition is that on the one hand, charismatic kings tend to be severe, and on the other hand, lack of charisma tends to elicit revolts. A king's degree of charisma cannot be changed in adulthood. There is at present no indication of whether Reoboam is charismatic or not.

These findings were based on a sample of one hundred kings, 48 of whom had their reigns cut short by revolt. On post mortem examination of the pineal gland, 50 were found to have been charismatic and 50 uncharismatic. 80 per cent of the charismatic kings had been severe and 80 per cent of the uncharismatic kings had been lenient. Of the charismatic kings, 40 per cent of those who were severe were deposed whereas only 20 per cent of those who were lenient were deposed. Of the uncharismatic kings, 80 per cent of those who were severe were deposed whereas only 55 per cent of those who were lenient were deposed. The totals were as in Table 1. This is Reoboam's total evidence on the subject.[7]

TABLE 1

	Charismatic	Uncharismatic	Total
Severe	16 deposed (40%) 24 long-reigned	8 deposed (80%) 2 long-reigned	24 deposed (48%) 26 long-reigned
Lenient	2 deposed (20%) 8 long-reigned	22 deposed (55%) 18 long-reigned	24 deposed (48%) 26 long-reigned

Reoboam's older advisors argue from a sure-thing principle. There are two possibilities, they say: that Reoboam is charismatic and that he is uncharismatic; what he does now will not affect his degree of charisma. On the assumption that he is charismatic, it is rational to prefer lenience. For since 40 per cent of severe charismatic kings are deposed, the expected utility of severity in that case would be

$$0.4 \, \mathscr{D}SD + 0.6 \, \mathscr{D}S\bar{D} = 0.4 \times 10 + 0.6 \times 80 = 52,$$

whereas since only 20 per cent of lenient charismatic kings are deposed, the expected utility of lenience in that case would be

$$0.2 \, \mathscr{D}LD + 0.8 \, \mathscr{D}L\bar{D} = 0.2 \times 0 + 0.8 \times 10 = 64.$$

On the assumption that he is uncharismatic, it is again rational to prefer lenience. For since 80 per cent of severe uncharismatic kings are deposed, the expected utility of severity in this case would be

$$0.8 \, \mathscr{D}SD + 0.2 \, \mathscr{D}S\bar{D} = 0.8 \times 10 + 0.2 \times 100 = 28,$$

whereas since only 55 per cent of lenient uncharismatic kings are deposed, the expected utility of lenience in this case would be

$$0.55 \, \mathscr{D}LD + 0.45 \, \mathscr{D}L\bar{D} = 0.55 \times 0 + 0.45 \times 80 = 36.$$

Thus in either case, lenience is to be preferred, and so by a sure-thing principle, it is rational to prefer lenience in the actual case.

Reoboams's youthful friends argue that, on the contrary, sure-thing considerations prescribe severity. Severity is indeed the dominant strategy. There are two possibilities: D, that Reoboam will be deposed, and $\bar{D}$, that he will not be. These two states are stochastically independent of the acts contemplated: both $pr(D/S)$ and $pr(D/L)$ are 0.48. Therefore, his youthful friends urge, one can without fallacy use the states D and $\bar{D}$ in an argument from dominance. On the assumption that he will be deposed, he prefers to be severe, and likewise, on the assumption that he will not be deposed, he prefers to be severe. Thus by dominance, it is rational for him to prefer severity.

Here, then, are two sure-thing arguments which lead to contrary prescriptions. One argument appeals to the finding that charisma is causally independent of the acts contemplated; the other appeals to the finding that being deposed is stochastically independent of the acts. The old advisors and youthful companions are in effect appealing to different versions of a sure-thing principle, one of which requires causal independence and the other of which requires stochastic independence. The two versions lead to incompatible conclusions.

The sure-thing principle is this: if a rational agent knows *aut* $(S_1, \ldots, S_n)$ and prefers A to B in each case, then he prefers A to B. If the propositions $S_1, \ldots, S_n$ are required to be states in a matrix formulation of the decision problem, so that each pair of state and act determine a unique outcome, the sure-thing principle becomes the principle of dominance to be discussed below; the principle of dominance is thus a special case of the sure-thing principle. Now the principle of dominance, we have said, requires a proviso that the states in question be act-independent. The sure-thing principle should presumably include the same proviso. The sure-thing principle, then, should be this: if a rational agent knows that precisely one of the propositions $S_1, \ldots, S_n$ are independent of the acts A and B, then he prefers A to B.

The problem in the case of Reoboam is that his two groups of advisors appeal to different kinds of independence to reach opposing conclusions. The older advisors appeal to causal independence; they cite the finding that a king's degree of charisma is unaffected by his adult actions. His youthful companions appeal to stochastic independence; they cite the finding that there is no correlation between severity in kings and revolt. The two appeals yield opposite conclusions.

It seems, then, that the sure thing principle comes in two different versions, one of which requires that the propositions in question be causally independent of the acts, and the other of which requires the propositions to be stochastically independent of the acts. . . .

TWO KINDS OF DOMINANCE

We have said that the principle of dominance is the sure-thing principle restricted to a special case and that the sure-thing principle has two versions, one of which holds for $\mathcal{U}$-maximization and the other for $\mathcal{V}$-maximization. There should, then, be two versions of the principle of dominance, one for each kind of utility maximization. The principles can be formulated as follows.

Definition. Let $S_1, \ldots, S_n$ be the states of a standard decision matrix, and let A and B be acts. Then A *strongly dominates B with respect to $S_1, \ldots, S_n$* if for each S_i, the outcome of A in S_i is more desirable than the outcome of B in S_i.

Principle of Dominance with Causal Independence. Suppose act A strongly dominates act B with respect to states $S_1, \ldots, S_n$. If for each state S_i, the agent knows that $(A \;\square\!\!\rightarrow S_i) \leftrightarrow S_i$ and $(B \;\square\!\!\rightarrow S_i) \leftrightarrow S_i$, then it is rational for him to prefer A to B.

Principle of Dominance with Stochastic Independence. Suppose act A strongly dominates act B with respect to states $S_1, \ldots, S_n$. If for each state S_i, $pr(S_i/A) = pr(S_i) = pr(S_i/B)$, then it is rational for him to prefer A to B.

The principle of Dominance with Causal Independence holds if rationality requires maximization of $\mathcal{U}$, and the Principle of Dominance with Stochastic Independence holds if rationality requires maximization of $\mathcal{V}$[8]. . . .

ACT-INDEPENDENCE IN THE SAVAGE FORMULATION

We said above that to apply the Savage framework to a decision problem, one must find states of the world that are in some sense act-independent. In the last section, we distinguished two kinds of independence, causal and epistemic. Which kind is needed in the Savage formulation of decision problems?

The answer is that the Savage formulation has both a $\mathcal{U}$-maximizing interpretation and a $\mathcal{V}$-maximizing interpretation. On the $\mathcal{U}$-maximizing interpretation, the states must be causally independent of the acts, whereas on the $\mathcal{V}$-maximizing interpretation, the states must be epistemically independent of the acts. That is to say, if the states are causally act-independent, then utility as calculated by the Savage method is $\mathcal{U}$-utility, whereas if the states are epistemically act-independent, then utility as calculated by the Savage method is $\mathcal{V}$-utility. If the states are both causally and epistemically act-independent, then the $\mathcal{U}$-utility of each act equals its $\mathcal{V}$-utility. Thus the Savage formulation itself is not committed to either kind of utility: the kind of utility it yields depends on the way it is applied to decision problems.

The expected utility of an act A in the Savage theory is

$$(3) \quad \Sigma_s pr(S) \, \mathcal{D}O(A, S).$$

If the states S are all known to be causally independent of A, so that for each state S, the agent knows that $(A \;\square\!\!\rightarrow S) \leftrightarrow S$, then for each S, we have $pr(S) = pr(A \;\square\!\!\rightarrow S)$. (3) thus becomes

$$\Sigma_s pr(A \;\square\!\!\rightarrow S) \, \mathcal{D}O(A,S),$$

and this, we said earlier, is $\mathcal{U}(A)$. If, on the other hand, the states S are stochastically independent of A, so that for each S, $pr(S) = pr(S/A)$, then (3) becomes

$$\Sigma_s pr(S/A) \, \mathcal{D}O(A,S),$$

which is $\mathcal{V}(A)$.

The Newcomb paradox discussed by Nozick (1969) has the same structure as the case of Solomon. Nozick treats it as a conflict between the principle of expected utility maximization and the principle of dominance. On the views we have propounded in this paper, the problem is rather a conflict between two kinds of expected utility maximization. The problem is this. There are two boxes, transparent and opaque; the transparent box contains a thousand dollars. The agent can perform A_1, taking just the contents of the opaque box, or A_2, taking the contents of both boxes. A Predictor has already placed a million dollars in the opaque box if he predicted A_1 and nothing if he predicted A_2. The agent knows all this, and he knows the Predictor to be highly reliable in that both pr (he has predicted A_1/A_1) and pr (he has predicted A_2/A_2) are close to one.

To show how the expected utility calculations work, we must add detail to the specification of the situation. Suppose, somewhat unrealistically, that getting no money has a utility of zero, getting one thousand dollars a utility of 10, that getting one million has a utility of 100, and that getting one million and one thousand has a utility of 101. Let M be "there are a million dollars in the opaque box," and suppose $pr(M/A_1) = 0.9$ and $pr(M/A_2) = 0.1$. The calculation of $\mathcal{V}(A_1)$ and $\mathcal{V}(A_2)$ is familiar.

$$\mathcal{U}(A_1) = pr(M/A_1) \, \mathcal{D}\$1,000,000 + pr(\bar{M}/A_1) \, \mathcal{D}\$0$$
$$= 0.9 (100) + 0.1 (0) = 90.$$
$$\mathcal{U}(A_2) = pr(M/A_2) \, \mathcal{D}\$1,001,000 + pr(\bar{M}/A_2) \, \mathcal{D}\$1,000$$
$$= 0.1 (101) + 0.9 (10) = 19.1$$

Maximization of $\mathcal{V}$, as is well known, prescribes taking only the contents of the opaque box.[9]

$\mathcal{U}(A_1)$ and $\mathcal{U}(A_2)$ depend on the probability of M, which in turn depends on the probabilities of A_1 and A_2. For any probability of M, though, we have $\mathcal{U}(A_2) > \mathcal{U}(A_1)$. For let the probability of M be μ; then since M is causally act-independent, $pr(A_1 \,\square\!\!\rightarrow M) = \mu$ and $pr(A_2 \,\square\!\!\rightarrow M) = \mu$. Therefore

$$\mathcal{U}(A_1) = pr(A_1 \,\square\!\!\rightarrow M) \;\mathcal{D}\$1,000,000 + pr(A_1 \,\square\!\!\rightarrow \bar{M}) \;\mathcal{D}\$0$$
$$= 100\mu + 0(1-\mu) = 100\mu.$$
$$\mathcal{U}(A_2) = pr(A_2 \,\square\!\!\rightarrow M) \;\mathcal{D}\$1,001,000 + pr(A_2 \,\square\!\!\rightarrow \bar{M}) \;\mathcal{D}\$1,000$$
$$= 101\mu + 10(1-\mu) = 91\mu + 10.$$

Thus $\mathcal{U}(A_2) - \mathcal{U}(A_1) = 10 - 9\mu$, and since $\mu \leq 1$, this is always positive. Therefore whatever probability M may have, $\mathcal{U}(A_2) > \mathcal{U}(A_1)$, and $\mathcal{U}$-maximization prescribes taking both boxes.

To some people, this prescription seems irrational.[10] One possible argument against it takes roughly the form "If you're so smart, why ain't you rich?" $\mathcal{V}$-maximizers tend to leave the experiment millionaires whereas $\mathcal{U}$-maximizers do not. Both very much want to be millionaires, and the $\mathcal{V}$-maximizers usually succeed; hence it must be the $\mathcal{V}$-maximizers who are making the rational choice. We take the moral of the paradox to be something else: if someone is very good at predicting behavior and rewards predicted irrationality richly, then irrationality will be richly rewarded.

To see this, consider a variation on Newcomb's story: the subject of the experiment is to take the contents of the opaque box first and learn what it is; he then may choose either to take the thousand dollars in the second box or not to take it. The Predictor has an excellent record and a thoroughly accepted theory to back it up. Most people find nothing in the first box and then take the contents of the second box. Of the million subjects tested, one per cent have found a million dollars in the first box, and strangely enough only one per cent of these—one hundred in ten thousand—have gone on to take the thousand dollars they could each see in the second box. When those who leave the thousand dollars are later asked why they did so, they say things like "If I were the sort of person who would take the thousand dollars in that situation, I wouldn't be a millionaire."

On both grounds of $\mathcal{U}$-maximization and of $\mathcal{V}$-maximization, these new millionaires have acted irrationally in failing to take the extra thousand dollars. They know for certain that they have the million dollars; therefore the $\mathcal{V}$-utility of taking the thousand as well is 101, whereas the $\mathcal{V}$-utility of not taking it is 100. Even on the view of $\mathcal{V}$-maximizers, then, this experiment will almost always make irrational people and only irrational people millionaires. Everyone knows so at the outset.

Return now to the unmodified Newcomb situation, where the subject must take or pass up the thousand dollars before he sees whether the opaque box is full or empty. What happens if the subject knows not merely that the Predictor is highly reliable, but that he is infallible? The argument that the $\mathcal{U}$-utility of taking both boxes exceeds that of taking only one box goes through unchanged. To some people, however, it seems especially apparent in this case that it is rational to take only the opaque box and irrational to take both. For in this case the subject is certain that he will be a millionaire if and only if he takes only the opaque box. If in the case where the predictor is known to be infallible it is irrational to take both boxes, then, $\mathcal{U}$-maximization is not always the rational policy.

We maintain that $\mathcal{U}$-maximization is rational even in the case where the Predictor is known to be infallible. True, where R is "I become a millionaire," the agent knows in this case that R holds if A_1 holds: he knows the truth-functional proposition $R \leftrightarrow A_1$. From this proposition, however, it does not follow that he *would* be a millionaire if he did A_1, or that he *would* be a non-millionaire if he did A_2.

If the subject knows for sure that he will take just the opaque box, then he knows for sure that the million dollars is in the opaque box, and so he knows for sure that he will be a millionaire. But since he knows for sure that the million dollars is already in the opaque box, he knows for sure that even if he were to take both boxes, he would be a millionaire. If, on the other hand, the subject knows for sure that he will take both boxes, then he knows for sure that the opaque box is empty, and so he knows for sure that he will be a non-millionaire. But since in this case he knows for sure that the opaque box is empty, he knows for sure that even if he were to take just the opaque box, he would be a non-millionaire.

If the subject does not know what he will do, then what he knows is this: either he will take just the opaque box and be a millionaire, or he will take both boxes and be a non-millionaire. From this, however, it follows neither that (i) if he took just the opaque box, he would be a millionaire, nor that (ii) if he took both boxes he would be a non-millionaire. For (i), the subject knows, is true if, and only if, the opaque box is filled with a million dollars, and (ii), the subject knows, is true if, and only if, the opaque box is empty. Thus, if (i) followed from what the agent knows, he could conclude for certain that the opaque box contains a million dollars, and if (ii) followed from what the agent knows, he could conclude that the opaque box is empty. Since the subject, we have supposed, does not know what he will do, he can conclude neither that the opaque box contains a million dollars nor that it is empty. Therefore neither (i) nor (ii) follows from what the subject knows.

Rational choice in Newcomb's situation, we maintain, depends on a comparison of what would happen if one took both boxes with what would happen if one took only the opaque box. What the agent knows for sure is this: if he took both boxes, he would get a thousand dollars more than he would if he took only the opaque box. That, on our view, makes it rational for someone who wants as much as he can get to take both boxes and irrational to take only one box.

Why, then, does it seem obvious to many people that if the Predictor is known to be infallible, it is rational to take only the opaque box and irrational to take both boxes? We have three possible explanations. The first is that a person may have a tendency to want to bring about an indication of a desired state of the world, even if it is known that the act that brings about the indication in no way brings about the desired state itself. Taking just the opaque box would be a sure indication that it contained a million dollars, even though taking just the opaque box in no way brings it about that the box contains a million dollars.

The second possible explanation lies in the force of the argument "If you're so smart, why ain't you rich?" That argument, though, if it holds good, should apply equally well to the modified Newcomb situation, with a predictor who is known to be highly accurate but fallible. There the conclusion of the argument seems absurd: according to the argument, having already received the million dollars, one should pass up the additional thousand dollars one is free to take, on the grounds that those who are disposed to pass it up tend to become millionaires. Since the argument leads to an absurd conclusion in one case, there must be something wrong with it.

The third possible explanation is the fallacious inference we have just discussed, from

> Either I shall take one box and be a millionaire, or I shall take both boxes and be a non-millionaire

to the conclusion

> If I were to take one box, I would be a millionaire, and if I were to take both boxes, I would be a non-millionaire.

If, to someone who is free of fallacies, it is still intuitively apparent that the subject should take only the opaque box, we have no further arguments to give him. If in addition he thinks the subject should take only the opaque box even in the case where the predictor is known to be somewhat fallible, if he also thinks that in the modified Newcomb situation the subject, on receiving the extra million dollars, should take the extra thousand, if he also thinks that it is rational for Reoboam to be severe, and if he also thinks it is rational for Solomon to abstain from his neighbor's wife, then he may genuinely have the intuitions of a $\mathscr{V}$-maximizer: $\mathscr{V}$-maximization then provides a systematic account of his intuitions. If he thinks some of these things but not all of them, then we leave it to him to provide a systematic account of his views. Our own views are systematically accounted for by $\mathscr{U}$-maximization.

STABILITY OF DECISION

When a person decides what to do, he has in effect learned what he will do, and so he has new information. He will adjust his probability ascriptions accordingly. These adjustments may affect the $\mathscr{U}$-utility of the various acts open to him.

Indeed, once the person decides to perform an act A, the $\mathscr{U}$-utility of A

will be equal to its $\mathscr{V}$-utility.[11] Or at least this holds if Consequence 1 that $A \rightarrow ((A \;\square\; C) \leftrightarrow C)$, is a logical truth. For we saw at the beginning of this chapter in the proof of Assertion 1 that if Consequence 1 is a logical truth, then for any pair of propositions P and Q, $pr(P \;\square\!\!\rightarrow Q/P) = pr(Q/P)$. Now let $\mathscr{U}_A(A)$ be the $\mathscr{U}$-utility of act A as reckoned by the agent after he has decided for sure to do A, let pr give the agent's probability ascriptions before he has decided what to do. Let pr_A give the agent's probability ascriptions after he has decided for sure to do A. Then for any proposition P, $pr_A(P) = pr(P/A)$. Thus

$$
\begin{aligned}
\mathscr{U}_A(A) &= \Sigma_O\, pr_A(A \;\square\!\!\rightarrow O)\,\mathscr{D}O \\
&= \Sigma_O\, pr(A \;\square\!\!\rightarrow O/A)\,\mathscr{D}O \\
&= \Sigma_O\, pr(O/A)\,\mathscr{D}O \\
&= \mathscr{V}(A).
\end{aligned}
$$

The $\mathscr{V}$-utility of an act, then, is what its $\mathscr{U}$-utility would be if the agent knew he were going to perform it.

It does not follow that once a person knows what he will do, $\mathscr{V}$-maximization and $\mathscr{U}$-maximization give the same prescriptions. For although for any act A, $\mathscr{U}_A(A) = \mathscr{V}(A)$, it is not in general true that for alternatives B to A, $\mathscr{U}_A(B) = \mathscr{V}(B)$. Thus in cases where $\mathscr{U}(A) < \mathscr{U}(B)$ but $\mathscr{V}(A) > \mathscr{V}(B)$, it is consistent with what we have said to suppose that $\mathscr{U}_A(A) < \mathscr{U}_A(B)$. In such a case, $\mathscr{V}$-maximization prescribes A regardless of what the agent believes he will do, but even if he believes he will do A, $\mathscr{U}$-maximization prescribes B. The situation is this:

$$
\mathscr{U}_A(B) > \mathscr{U}_A(A) = \mathscr{V}(A) > \mathscr{V}(B).
$$

Even though, once an agent knows what he will do, the distinction between the $\mathscr{U}$-utility of that act and its $\mathscr{V}$-utility disappears, the distinction between $\mathscr{U}$-maximization and $\mathscr{V}$-maximization remains.

That deciding what to do can affect the $\mathscr{U}$-utilities of the acts open to an agent raises a problem of stability of decision for $\mathscr{U}$-maximizers. Consider the story of the man who met death in Damascus.[12] Death looked surprised, but then recovered his ghastly composure and said "I am coming for you tomorrow." The terrified man that night bought a camel and rode to Aleppo. The next day, death knocked on the door of the room where he was hiding and said "I have come for you."

"But I thought you would be looking for me in Damascus," said the man.

"Not at all," said death, "that is why I was surprised to see you yesterday. I knew that today I was to find you in Aleppo."

Now suppose the man knows the following. Death works from an appointment book which states time and place; a person dies if, and only if, the book correctly states in what city he will be at the stated time. The book is made up weeks in advance on the basis of highly reliable predictions. An appointment on the next day has been inscribed for him. Suppose, on this basis, the man would take his being in Damascus the next day as strong evidence that his appointment with death is in Damascus, and would take his being in Aleppo the next day as strong evidence that his appointment is in Aleppo.

Two acts are open to him: A, go to Aleppo, and D, stay in Damascus. There are two possibilities: S_A, death will seek him in Aleppo, and S_D, death will seek him in Damascus. He knows that death will find him if, and only if, death looks for him in the right city, so that, where L is that he lives, he knows $(D \Box\!\!\rightarrow L) \leftrightarrow S_A$ and $(A \Box\!\!\rightarrow L) \leftrightarrow S_D$. He ascribes conditional probabilities $pr(S_A/A) \approx 1$ and $pr(S_D/D) \approx 1$; suppose these are both 0.99 and that $pr(S_D/A) = 0.01$ and $pr(S_A/D) = 0.01$. Suppose $\mathscr{D}(\bar{L}) = -100$ and $\mathscr{D}(L) = 0$. Then where α is $pr(A)$, his probability of going to Aleppo, and $1 - \alpha$ is his probability of going to Damascus,

$$pr(A \Box\!\!\rightarrow L) = pr(S_D) = \alpha pr(S_D/A) + (1-\alpha) pr(S_D/D)$$
$$= 0.01\alpha + 0.99(1-\alpha) = 0.99 - 0.98\alpha$$
$$pr(A \Box\!\!\rightarrow \bar{L}) = pr(S_A) = 1 - pr(S_D) = 0.01 + 0.98\alpha.$$

Thus

$$\mathscr{U}(A) = pr(A \Box\!\!\rightarrow L)\ \mathscr{D}(L) + pr(A \Box\!\!\rightarrow \bar{L})\ \mathscr{D}(\bar{L})$$
$$= (0.01 + 0.98\alpha)(-100) = -1 - 98\alpha.$$

By a like calculation, $\mathscr{U}(D) = -99 + 98\alpha$. Thus if $\alpha = 1$, then $\mathscr{U}(D) = -1$ and $\mathscr{U}(A) = -99$, and thus $\mathscr{U}(D) > \mathscr{U}(A)$. If $\alpha = 0$, then $\mathscr{U}(D) = -99$ and $\mathscr{U}(A) = -1$, so that $\mathscr{U}(A) > \mathscr{U}(D)$. Indeed we have $\mathscr{U}(D) > \mathscr{U}(A)$ whenever $pr(A) > 1/2$, and $\mathscr{U}(A) > \mathscr{U}(D)$ whenever $pr(D) > 1/2$.

What are we to make of this? If the man ascribes himself equal probabilities of going to Aleppo and staying in Damascus, he has equal grounds for thinking that death intends to seek him in Damascus and that death intends to seek him in Aleppo. If, however, he decides to go to Aleppo, he then has strong grounds for expecting that Aleppo is where death already expects him to be, and hence it is rational for him to prefer staying in Damascus. Similarly, deciding to stay in Damascus would give him strong grounds for thinking that he ought to go to Aleppo: once he knows he will stay in Damascus, he can be almost sure that death already expects him in Damascus, and hence that if he had gone to Aleppo, death would have sought him in vain.

$\mathscr{V}$-maximization does not lead to such instability. What happens to $\mathscr{V}$-utility when an agent knows for sure what he will do is somewhat unclear.

Standard probability theory offers no interpretation of $pr_A(O/B)$ where $pr(B/A) = 0$, and so, on the standard theory, once an agent knows for sure what he will do, the $\mathscr{V}$-utility of the alternatives ceases to be well-defined. What we can say about $\mathscr{V}$-utility is this: as long as an act's being performed has non-zero probability, its $\mathscr{V}$-utility is independent of its probability and the probabilities of alternatives to it. For the $\mathscr{V}$-utility of an act A depends on conditional probabilities of the form $pr(O/A)$. This is just the probability the agent would ascribe to O on learning A for sure, and that is independent of how likely he now regards A. Whereas, then, the $\mathscr{U}$-utility of an act may vary with its probability of being performed, its $\mathscr{V}$-utility does not. $\mathscr{U}$-maximization, then, may give rise to a kind of instability which $\mathscr{V}$-maximization precludes: in certain cases, an act will be $\mathscr{U}$-maximal if, and only if, the probability of its performance is low.

Is this a reason for preferring $\mathscr{V}$-maximization? We think not. In the case of death in Damascus, rational decision does seem to be unstable. Any reason the doomed man has for thinking he will go to Aleppo is a reason for thinking he would live longer if he stayed in Damascus, and any reason he has for thinking he will stay in Damascus is reason for thinking he would live longer if he went to Aleppo. Thinking he will do one is reason for doing the other. That there can be cases of unstable $\mathscr{U}$-maximization seems strange, but the strangeness lies in the cases, not in $\mathscr{U}$-maximization: instability of rational decision seems to be a genuine feature of such cases.

APPLICATIONS TO GAME THEORY

Game theory provides many cases where $\mathscr{U}$-maximizing and $\mathscr{V}$-maximizing diverge; perhaps the most striking of these is the Prisoner's Dilemma, for which a desirability matrix is shown.

	A_0	A_1
B_0	1 1	0 10
B_1	10 0	9 9

Here A_0 and B_0 are respectively A's and B's options of confessing, while A_1 and B_1 are the options of not confessing. The desirabilities reflect these facts: (1) if both confess, they both get long prison terms; (2) if one confesses and the other does not, then the confessor gets off while the other gets an even longer prison term; (3) if neither confesses, both get off with very light sentences.

Suppose each prisoner knows that the other thinks in much the same way he does. Then his own choice given him evidence for what the other will do. Thus, the conditional probability of a long prison term on his confessing is greater than the conditional probability of a long prison term on his not confessing. If the difference between these two conditional probabilities is sufficiently great, then $\mathscr{V}$-maximizing will prescribe not confessing.

The $\mathscr{V}$-utilities of the acts open to B will be as follows.

$$\mathscr{V}(B_0) = pr(A_0/B_0) \times 1 + pr(A_1/B_0) \times 10$$
$$\mathscr{V}(B_1) = pr(A_0/B_1) \times 0 + pr(A_1/B_1) \times 9.$$

If $pr(A_1/B_1) - pr(A_1/B_o)$ is sufficiently great (in this case 1/9 or more), then $\mathscr{V}$-maximizing recommends that B take option B_1 and not confess. If the probabilities for A are similar, then $\mathscr{V}$-maximizing also recommends not confessing for A. The outcome if both $\mathscr{V}$-maximize is $A_1 B_1$, the optimal one of mutual co-operation.[13]

For a $\mathscr{U}$-maximizer, dominance applies because his companion's choice is causally independent of his own. Therefore, $\mathscr{U}$-maximizing yields the classical outcome of the Prisoner's Dilemma. This suggests that $\mathscr{U}$-maximizing and not $\mathscr{V}$-maximizing corresponds to the kind of utility maximizing commonly assumed in game theory.

NOTES

* An earlier draft of this paper was circulated in January 1976. A much shorter version was presented to the 5th International Congress of Logic, Methodology, and Philosophy of Science, London, Ontario, August 1975. There, and at the earlier University of Western Ontario research colloquium on Foundations and Applications of Decision Theory we benefited from discussions with many people; in particular we should mention Richard Jeffrey, Isaac Levi, Barry O'Neill and Howard Sobel.

1. Stalnaker made his proposal in 1972 in a letter to David Lewis, since published in Harper, Stalnaker, and Pearce (1981), and at a symposium of the Canadian Philosophical Association. He was responding to the result of David Lewis that was later published as Lewis (1976).

2. Although the rough treatment of counterfactuals we propose is similar in many respects to the theories developed by Stalnaker and Lewis, it differs from them in some important respects. Stalnaker and Lewis each base their accounts on comparisons of overall similarity of worlds. On our account, what matters is comparative similarity of worlds at the instant of decision. Whether a given

a-world is selected as W_a depends not at all on how similar the future in that world is to the actual future; whatever similarities the future in W_a may have to the actual future will be a semantical consequence of laws of nature, conditions in W_a at the instant of decision, and actual conditions at that instant. (Roughly, then, they will be consequences of laws of nature and the similarity of W_a to the actual world at the instant of decision.) We consider only worlds in which the past is exactly like the actual past, for since the agent cannot now alter the past, those are the only worlds relevant to his decision. Lewis (1973b, p. 566 and in conversation) suggests that a proper treatment of overall similarity will yield as a deep consequence of general facts about the world the conditions we are imposing by fiat.

3.   In characterizing our conditional we have imposed the Stalnaker-like constraint that there is a unique world W_a which would eventuate from performing a at t. Our rationale for Axiom 2 depends on this assumption and on the assumption that if a is actually performed then W_a is the actual world itself. Consequence 1 is weaker than Axiom 2, and only depends on the second part of this assumption. In circumstances where these assumptions break down, it would seem to us that using conditionals to compute expected utility is inappropriate. A more general approach is needed to handle such cases.

4.   This is stated by Lewis (1976b, note 10).

5.   Meeting of the Canadian Philosophical Association, 1972. Nozick gives a similar example (1969, p. 125).

6.   Sobel actually uses "$A * \Box\!\!\rightarrow \overline{S}$ does hold" where we use "$A * \Box\!\!\rightarrow S$ does not hold." With Axiom 2, these are equivalent.

7.   We realize that a Bayesian king presented with these data would not ordinarily take on degrees of belief that exactly match the frequencies given in the table; nevertheless, with appropriate prior beliefs and evidence, he would come to have those degrees of belief. Assume that he does.

8.   Nozick (1969) in effect endorses the Principle of Dominance with Stochastic Independence (p. 119 in this volume), but not $\mathcal{V}$-maximization: in cases of the kind we have been considering, he considers the recommendations of $\mathcal{V}$-maximization "perfectly wild" (p. 118). Nozick also states and endorses the principle of dominance with causal independence (p. 124).

9.   For $\mathcal{V}$ maximizing treatments of Newcomb's Problem, see Bar Hillel and Margalit (1972) and Levi (1975).

10.   Levi (1975) reconstructs Nozick's argument for taking both boxes in a way which uses $pr(M)$ rather than $pr(M/A_1)$ and $pr(M/A_2)$ as the appropriate probabilities for computing expected utility in Newcomb's Problem. This agrees with $\mathcal{U}$-maximizing in that the same probabilities are used for computing expected utility for A_1 as for A_2 and results in the same recommendation to take both boxes. Levi is one of the people to whom this recommendation seems irrational.

11.   We owe this point to Barry O'Neill.

12.   A version of this story quoted from Somerset Maugham's play *Sheppey* (New York, Doubleday 1934) appears on the facing page of John O'Hara's novel *Appointment in Samarra*. (New York, Random House 1934). The story is undoubtedly much older.

13.   Nozick (1969), Brams (1975b), Grofman (1975) and Rapoport (1975), have all suggested a link between Newcomb's Problem and the Prisoner's Dilemma. Brams, Grofman and Rapoport all endorse cooperative solutions, Rapoport (1975, p. 619) appears to endorse $\mathcal{V}$-maximizing.

8

Counterfactuals and Newcomb's Problem*

TERENCE HORGAN

Newcomb's Problem concerns a being with enormous predictive powers. You have overwhelming confidence in these powers; he has already correctly predicted your own choices in numerous situations and the choices of many others in the situation you now face. There are two boxes before you: box 1 contains $1,000 and box 2 contains either $1 million or nothing. You have two choices: to take the contents of both boxes or to take the contents of box 2 only. You know that the contents of box 2 depend on the being's prediction, in the following way. If he predicted that you will choose both boxes, then he put nothing in box 2; and if he predicted that you will choose only box 2, then he put $1 million in box 2. What do you do?

There is a sensible argument for choosing only box 2: if you do so, then the being will have predicted this choice and you will get $1 million; whereas if you choose both boxes then the being will have predicted *this* choice and you will end up with only $1,000. On the other hand, there is also a sensible argument for taking both boxes: either the $1 million is present in box 2 or else nothing is there, and either way you do better by $1,000 if you choose both boxes.

I maintain that one-box reasoning is correct here, and that two-box reasoning is mistaken; thus the rational choice is box 2 only. I shall defend this view, and I shall investigate the implications of my argument for the foundations of decision theory. Counterfactual conditionals will play a central role throughout. (Following recent practice, I shall regard a conditional as a counterfactual provided it has the same kind of truth conditions as contrary-to-fact subjunctive conditionals—whether or not its antecedent is false, and whether or not it is grammatically subjunctive.)

From *The Journal of Philosophy* 78, no. 6 (June 1981): 331–56. Reprinted by permission of the author and publisher.

THE TWO COMPETING ARGUMENTS

I begin by formulating, in intuitive nonquantitative terms, the one-box argument and the two-box argument. At present I shall not explicitly invoke decision-theoretic concepts like expected utility and dominance; these notions will be discussed in later sections. The one-box argument runs as follows:

(*1_o) If I were to choose both boxes, then the being would have predicted this.

(2_o) If I were to choose both boxes and the being had predicted this, then I would get $1,000.

(3_o) So if I were to choose both boxes, then I would get $1,000.

(*4_o) If I were to choose box 2, then the being would have predicted this.

(5_o) If I were to choose box 2 and the being had predicted this, then I would get $1 million.

(6_o) So if I were to choose box 2, then I would get $1 million.

(7_o) If (3) and (6) are true, then I ought to choose box 2.

(8_o) Hence, I ought to choose box 2.

Premises 1_o and 4_o are starred because they will prove crucial in the subsequent analysis. Lines 1–6 are all counterfactuals; although their *grammatical* form (subjunctive, rather than indicative) is not important, it is crucial to interpret them as having the *logical* form of counterfactual conditionals rather than mere material conditionals. Suppose I believe that I will in fact choose box 2 and that I will in fact get one million. Then I believe the following material conditionals:

($3'$) I choose both boxes → I get $1,000.

($6'$) I choose box 2 → I get $1 million.

Yet I also might believe, despite $3'$ and $6'$, that if I *were* to choose both boxes then I *would* get $1,001,000. If so, then surely it is not true that I ought to choose box 2. Thus, lines 3_o and 6_o must be interpreted as counterfactuals in order for the normative premise, 7_o, to be plausible.[1]

The two-box argument may be formulated as follows, with the crucial nonnormative premises again starred:

(1_t) Either box 2 contains $1 million or it contains nothing.

(*2_t) If it contains $1 million, then I would get $1,001,000 if I chose both boxes.

(3_t) If it contains $1 million, then I would get $1 million if I chose box 2.

(4_t) If it contains nothing, then I would get $1,000 if I chose both boxes.

(*5_t) If it contains nothing, then I would get $0 if I chose box 2.

(6_t) So *either* I would get $1,001,000 if I chose both boxes and I would get $1 million if I chose box 2, *or* I would get $1,000 if I chose both boxes and I would get $0 if I chose box 2.

(7,) If (6) is true, then I ought to choose both boxes.

(8,) Hence, I ought to choose both boxes.

Line (6,) may be called the *disjunctive basis* for the inference to the normative conclusion (8,). The four conditionals within (6,) must be interpreted as counterfactuals; otherwise, for reasons analogous to those involved in the one-box argument, the normative premise (7,) loses its plausibility. Accordingly, the connectives in the consequent-clauses of (2,) through (5,), respectively, each must be interpreted counterfactually. The *main* connectives in (2,–5,), however, can be construed either materially or counterfactually; the inference from (1,–5,) to (6,) is valid either way. I shall interpret these main connectives materially, since this weaker construal suffices.[2]

In order to assess the one-box argument and the two-box argument as here formulated, we require a semantic analysis of counterfactuals. I shall adopt the influential possible-worlds analysis of Stalnaker (1968) and Lewis (1973a). According to Lewis, a counterfactual $P \square \rightarrow Q$ is true (at a possible world w) if, and only if, either (1) there are no possible worlds at which P is true (the vacuous case), or (2) some P-world at which Q is true is *more similar,* over all, to w than is any P-world at which Q is not true. Stalnaker assumes, as Lewis does not, that, for any world w and any proposition P, if there are any possible P-worlds, then there is a unique P-world closest to w. This assumption is not really required for my purposes here, but I shall adopt it as an expository convenience. So we can take a counterfactual $P \square \rightarrow Q$ to be (nonvacuously) true if, and only if, Q is true at the closest P-world. (I also shall assume, in all that follows, that none of the counterfactuals I discuss are vacuous.)

The notion of comparative overall similarity among possible worlds is inherently vague, and this vagueness will prove crucial in assessing the one-box argument and the two-box argument. Lewis now maintains that there is a "standard resolution" of vagueness which is appropriate in most contexts, but that certain unusual contexts favor a nonstandard resolution (1979b). In discussing whether events in the past are dependent upon events in the present, he writes:

We know that present conditions have their past causes. We can persuade ourselves, and sometimes do, that if the present were different then these past causes would have to be different, else they would have caused the present to be as it actually is. Given such an argument — let us call it a *back-tracking argument* — we willingly grant that if the present were different, the past would be different too. . . . But the persuasion does not last. We very easily slip back into our usual sort of counterfactual reasoning, and implicitly assume . . that facts about earlier times are counterfactually independent of facts about later times. . . . What is going on, I suggest, can best be explained as follows. (1) Counterfactuals are infected with vagueness, as everyone agrees. Different ways of (partly) resolving the vagueness are appropriate in different contexts . . . (2) We ordinarily resolve the vagueness of counterfactuals in such a way that counterfactual dependence is asymmetric (except perhaps in cases of time travel or the like). Under this standard resolution, back-tracking arguments are mistaken. . . . (3) Some special contexts favor a different resolution of vagueness, one under which the past depends counterfactually on the present and some back-tracking arguments are correct. . . . (4) A counterfactual saying that the past would be different if the present were somehow different may come out true under the special resolution of its vagueness, but false under the standard resolution (1979b, 456–57).

These remarks bear directly on our present concern, because the one-box argument in Newcomb's Problem is a backtracking argument. Under the *standard* resolution of vagueness, as Lewis calls it, the nonnormative premises of the one-box argument cannot all be true. On the other hand, we shall see that there is a contextually appropriate nonstandard resolution of vagueness under which they *are* all true and under which the nonnormative premises of the two-box argument cannot all be true. Thus, the crux of Newcomb's Problem concerns the question of how best to resolve the vagueness of similarity, for purposes of practical decision making.

TWO RESOLUTIONS OF VAGUENESS

Lewis develops his account of the standard resolution of vagueness on the basis of a putative counterexample to his proposed semantics for counterfactuals, due to Kit Fine (1975). Fine writes:

The counterfactual "If Nixon had pressed the button there would have been a nuclear holocaust" is true or can be imagined to be so. Now suppose that there never will be a nuclear holocaust. Then that counterfactual is, on Lewis's analysis, very likely false. For given any world in which antecedent and consequent are both true it will be easy to imagine a closer world in which the antecedent is true and the consequent is false. For we need only imagine a change that prevents the holocaust but that does not require such a great divergence from reality (1975, p. 452).

Lewis replies that our offhand judgments about similarities and differences among possible worlds are not to the point here; we need to consider specific counterfactuals that we consider clearly true (or clearly false), and to determine, on the basis of these, the parameters of similarity and difference which are *actually employed* when counterfactuals are interpreted in the standard way. He takes Fine's counterfactual as such a test case, and he uses it to uncover what he takes to be the key parameters and their relative importance. He concludes that the standard resolution obeys the following system of weights or priorities:

(1) It is of the first importance to avoid big, complicated, varied, widespread violations of law.
(2) It is of the second importance to maximize the spatiotemporal region throughout which perfect match of particular fact prevails.
(3) It is of the third importance to avoid even small, simple, localized violations of law.
(4) It is of little or no importance to secure approximate similarity of particular fact, even in matters that concern us greatly (1979b, 472).

So, under the standard resolution of vagueness, if the antecedent of a counterfactual $A \;\Box\!\!\rightarrow\; C$ is a statement describing a particular event or act, then the A-world w most similar to actuality will have these features: (i) there is perfect match of particular fact between w and our actual world until a moment very shortly before the A-event in w; (ii) a small, simple, localized violation of actual-world law occurs in w very shortly before the A-event — just enough of a miracle to bring about the A-event itself; and (iii) no other violations of actual-world law occur, either major or minor.[3] Thus, under the standard resolution of vagueness, it is *true* that if Nixon had pressed the button there would have been a nuclear holocaust.

Henceforth I shall assume that there is indeed a standard resolution of the vagueness of similarity among worlds and that Lewis's account of it is essentially correct. Returning to Newcomb's Problem, it is clear that premises (1_o) and (4_o) of the one-box argument cannot both be true under the standard resolution. For the being has made his prediction about my choice and has either put the $1 million in box 2 or not, well before I choose. Thus, his *actual-world* prediction and the *actual-world* state of box 2 remain intact in the closest world in which I take both boxes and also in the closest world in which I take box 2 only. This being so, either (1_o) or (4_o) must be false.

On the other hand, the nonnormative premises of the two-box argument are all true under the standard resolution. Premise (2_t), for instance, is true if, and only if, either there is not $1 million in box 2 or I get $1,001,000 in the closest world w to actuality in which I take both boxes. Suppose in fact there is $1 million in box 2. Then since perfect match of particular fact prevails between our actual world and w until very shortly before my choice in w (in particular, since the being predicts in w that I will choose only box 2, and therefore puts $1 million into box 2), I do indeed get $1,001,000 in w. Of course, in w the being is *mistaken* in his prediction, but under the standard resolution of vagueness this does not matter.

But although the two-box argument fares better than its rival under the standard resolution, the intuitive plausibility of the one-box argument rests upon a nonstandard resolution of vagueness, one which seems quite appropriate in this context. It differs from the standard resolution to the extent that it gives top priority to maintaining the being's *predictive correctness* in the nearest possible world where I take both boxes, and also in the nearest world where I take box 2.[4] Under this *backtracking resolution,* as I shall call it, premises (1_o) and (4_o) are both true: the closest world in which I take both boxes is one in which the being correctly predicted this and put nothing in box 2, and the closest world in which I take only box 2 is one in which he correctly predicted *this* and put $1 million in box 2. Of course one of these worlds — whichever one will turn out to be nonactual — is one in which the being's prediction and act differ from what they were in the actual world. But, under the backtracking resolution, the being's predictive correctness is a more important parameter of similarity than is maximization of the spatiotemporal region through which perfect match of particular fact prevails.[5]

Under the backtracking resolution, furthermore, line (6_t) of the two-box argument — the disjunctive basis for the normative conclusion — is false. The left counterfactual clause within the left disjunct is false: in the closest world in which I take both boxes, the being correctly predicts this and I get only $1,000 rather than $1,001,000. And the right counterfactual clause within the right disjunct of (6_t) is also false: in the closest world in which I take box 2, the being correctly predicts this and I get $1 million rather than $0.

The falsity of (6_o) results from the fact that premises (2_t) and (5_t) cannot both be true under the backtracking resolution. Suppose there is $1 million in box 2. Then, since the being predicts my choice correctly in our actual world and since preservation of this predictive correctness now has greater weight of similarity than does preservation of his actual prediction, I get only $1,000 in the closest world where I take both boxes — not $1,001,000.

Thus (2_t) is false if there is $1 million in box 2. And, for analogous reasons, (5_t) is false if there is nothing in box 2.[6]

So we have arrived at a deadlock. In Newcomb's Problem there are two alternative resolutions of the vagueness of similarity, and each has some claim to contextual appropriateness. Under the standard resolution, the nonnormative premises of the two-box argument are all true, but those of the one-box argument are not. Under the backtracking resolution, the non-normative premises of the one-box argument are all true, but those of the two-box argument are not. Furthermore, the normative premise in each argument should be understood in relation to the vagueness resolution that makes that argument's nonnormative premises true. Thus, 7_o of the one-box argument says that if (3_o) and (6_o) are true under the backtracking resolution, then I should choose box 2. And (7_t) of the two-box argument says that, if (6_t) is true under the standard resolution, then I should choose both boxes. Of course, (7_o) and (7_t) cannot both be correct.

In order to break the deadlock, we must determine which of the two competing resolutions is *pragmatically* appropriate in Newcomb's Problem — that is, is the one to be used in making a practical inference. If the backtracking resolution if pragmatically appropriate, then (7_o) is true and (7_t) is false. But if the standard resolution is pragmatically appropriate, then (7_t) is true and (7_o) is false.

THE SOLUTION TO NEWCOMB'S PROBLEM

Breaking the deadlock is no simple matter, however. We can expect the dispute to continue at the meta level: the one-boxers will defend the backtracking resolution as pragmatically appropriate, and the two-boxers will defend the standard resolution. The two sides each can be expected to give plausible arguments for their respective stances, and these arguments are likely to be similar in spirit to the original object-level arguments set forth above. This dialectical situation is unavoidable, as far as I can tell; neither side will be able to refute the other decisively. Nevertheless, I think we can still make progress through semantic ascent. I shall set forth what I take to be the most plausible meta-level argument available to each side, and I shall show that the two-boxer's argument suffers from a kind of circularity that the one-boxer's lacks. On this basis, I shall contend that the backtracking resolution has a stronger claim to pragmatic appropriateness than does the standard resolution.

In comparing the two resolutions, we shall focus our attention on four key possible worlds. Let A_1 and A_2, respectively, be the act of choosing both boxes and the act of choosing only box 2; and let S_1 and S_2, respectively, be the state of $1 million being present in box 2 and the state of $0 being there. The four worlds that will concern us are these: w_1, the closest (A_1 & S_1)-world to actuality, under the standard resolution; w_2, the closest (A_2 & S_1)-world; w_3, the closest (A_1 & S_2)-world; and w_4, the closest (A_2 & S_2)-world.

The one-boxer's meta-level argument for the pragmatic relevance of the backtracking resolution can now be formulated as follows. When I consider whether to perform A_1 or A_2, I should not be particularly interested in what happens in certain worlds that I am quite sure are not actual (or will not *become* actual, if you like) — provided that my confidence in their nonactuality is independent of any beliefs I have as to the likelihood of my doing A_1 or the likelihood of my doing A_2. And, given my overwhelming confidence that the being has correctly predicted what I will do, I am virtually certain that our actual world will turn out to be either w_2 or w_3, rather than either w_1 or w_4. The worlds w_1 and w_4 therefore ought to be regarded as essentially irrelevant, for purposes of practical decision-making. Thus, the backtracking resolution is pragmatically appropriate, because, under this resolution, w_2 is the closest A_2-world and w_3 is the closest A_1-world.

The two-boxer's meta-level argument for the pragmatic relevance of the standard resolution, on the other hand, is this. For practical purposes, I should regard a possible world as the "closest" A_i-world if, and only if, I would *actualize* it (that is, render it actual) by doing A_i. But in Newcomb's Problem my act cannot causally influence the state of box 2. Hence, if S_1 obtains, I would actualize w_1 by taking both boxes, and I would actualize w_2 by taking only box 2; and, if S_2 obtains, I would actualize w_3 by taking both boxes, and I would actualize w_4 by taking only box 2. Thus the standard resolution is the pragmatically appropriate one, because, under this resolution, the closest A_1-world and the closest A_2-world are the worlds I would actualize by performing A_1 or A_2, respectively.

I said that the two-boxer's meta-level argument suffers from a form of circularity. The circularity rests upon two facts. First, consider his key nonnormative contention:

(M,)   *Either* I would actualize w_1 if I chose both boxes and I would actualize w_2 if I chose box 2, *or* I would actualize w_3 if I chose both boxes and I would actualize w_4 if I chose box 2.

This assertion, though undeniably true (under the standard resolution), is *equivalent* to (6,), the crucial nonnormative contention of the original two-box argument. (The first component counterfactual in M,, like the corresponding one in (6,), is true if, and only if, w_1 is the closest A_1-world, and similarly for the other corresponding components of (6,) and (M,).) Second, in light of the undeniable fact that (6,) is true under the standard resolution, the assertion that the standard resolution is pragmatically appropriate in Newcomb's Problem is essentially equivalent to the assertion that the agent ought to choose both boxes; the two assertions stand or fall together.

Circularity enters when the two-boxer claims that *if* (M,) is true, then the standard resolution ought to be adopted as pragmatically appropriate in Newcomb's Problem. Given the two facts just noted, this claim turns out to be essentially equivalent to the claim that *if* (6,) is true then the agent ought to take both boxes. That is, it is essentially equivalent to the normative premise (7,) of the original two-box argument. Thus, the two-boxer really has no independent meta-level grounds for adopting the standard resolution as pragmatically appropriate, over and above the intuitive plausibility of (7,) itself.

We one-boxers can do better, however. Not only does our original normative premise (7,) also possess substantial intuitive plausibility, but our meta-level defense of the pragmatic relevance of the backtracking resolution is no mere mirroring of the original one-box argument. Our reasoning, as presented four paragraphs ago, rests upon the following principle, which employs no meta-level counterfactuals:

(M,) I am virtually certain, independently of any beliefs I have as to the likelihood of my doing A_1 or the likelihood of my doing A_2, that either w_2 or w_3 will become actual.

This principle constitutes an independent justification for adopting the backtracking resolution for pragmatic purposes. The two-boxers have no comparable justification of their own position, however: they can only fall back, at the meta level, upon precisely the kinds of standard-resolution counterfactuals whose pragmatic relevance is in question. (Note that it is no independent justification to point out that my act cannot causally influence the state of box 2. For, as the above formulation of the two-boxer's object-level and meta-level arguments makes clear, the significance of causal independence is that it makes (6,) and (M,) *true* under the standard resolution. The question, however, is whether the standard resolution is pragmatically appropriate.)

I conclude that the backtracking resolution is superior to the standard resolution for purposes of decision-making in Newcomb's Problem. The upshot, as regards the original object-level arguments set forth in the first section, is this. Under the backtracking resolution of vagueness, the non-normative premises of the one-box argument are all true, and the normative premise (7,) is true as well. Under the standard resolution, the nonnormative premises of the two-box argument are all true, but the normative premise (7,) is false. Therefore, the one-box argument is sound and the two-box argument is unsound. So the rational choice is to take box 2 and collect a million bucks.

Against this conclusion, it will perhaps be replied that I have committed the blunder of assuming that one's present choice in Newcomb's problem can causally influence the being's previous prediction, backward through time. But I have made no such assumption. I do recommend acting *as if* one's present choice could causally influence the being's prior prediction, but my argument does not presuppose backward causation.

ON CONFLICTING INTUITIONS CONCERNING RATIONALITY

Psychologically, Newcomb's Problem is maddeningly paradoxical. Two deep-seated intuitions come head to head, and both refuse to budge: (1) the intuition that it is crazy to choose both boxes in the belief that you will get only $1,000, rather than choosing only box 2 in the belief that you will get $1 million; and (2) the intuition that it is crazy to choose only box 2, since choosing both cannot affect the contents of box 2. You may find, as I do, that intuition 2 persists despite the argument of the preceding section. I don't think either intuition can be made to go away; thus, insofar as its *psychological* force is concerned, Newcomb's Problem remains a brainteaser.

Nonetheless, two-boxers and one-boxers each stand to gain by presenting considerations designed to show that the opposite camp's fundamental intuition is rationally suspect despite its psychological appeal. In this section I seek to defuse one such consideration sometimes used by two-boxers against intuition 1; I then present two considerations aimed at undermining intuition 2.

Two-boxers sometimes suggest that many people are drawn intuitively to the one-box choice by a subtle form of wishful thinking. Gibbard and Harper (1978, pp. 152–53 in this volume) describe the alleged psychological syndrome this way: "a person may have a tendency to want to bring about an indication of a desired state of the world, even if it is known that the act that brings about the indication in no way brings about the desired state itself." Choosing just box 2 would be a strong *indication* that it contained $1 million, even though this choice in no way causally influences the contents of the box. But the very description of this psychological syndrome seems to lay bare the fact that it is not rationally defensible: *giving myself evidence* that the desired state of the world obtains is simply not a good reason for acting in a certain way if I know that the act will not have any tendency to *cause* that state to obtain.

This psychological diagnosis misrepresents intuition 1, I think. The one-boxer does not find the choice of box 2 appealing because of a standard-resolution counterfactual asserting that if he were to choose box 2 then he would *obtain evidence* that he was about to receive $1 million. (If standard-resolution counterfactual considerations were uppermost in his mind, he would indeed do well to heed the two-box argument, keeping in mind that his choice cannot causally influence the contents of box 2.) Rather, he is moved by counterfactual considerations of the backtracking kind: to wit, that choosing one box would very likely be followed by getting $1 million.

His intuition is based not upon the causal *efficacy* of his act (that is, providing evidence that he will obtain $1 million), but rather upon his confidence that the being has already correctly predicted what he will do. It is the two-boxers, not the one-boxers, who maintain that decision-making in Newcomb's Problem should be based upon causal efficacy—a contention which presupposes the pragmatic appropriateness of the standard resolution of vagueness.

I turn now to two considerations aimed at casting suspicion upon intuition 2. First, consider the "limit case" of Newcomb's Problem—where I know that the being is infallible, and, therefore, I am *completely certain* that our actual world will turn out to be either w_2 or w_3.[7] In this situation, it seems patently irrational to act on the basis of the possibility that w_1 or w_4 might become actual, since I am positive that neither will. Rather, it is preferable to regard only w_2 and w_3 as pragmatically relevant worlds and thus to choose box 2 in the certainty that I thereby actualize w_2. But if this approach is rational in the limit case, why should there be an abrupt switch when we move to the situation where I attach not certainty but overwhelmingly high *probability* to the being's predictive correctness? It is difficult to see what theoretical basis there could be for this switch—a fact which renders intuition 2 theoretically suspect.

Admittedly, intuition 2 tends to persist even in the limit case. Here, however, the intuition seems clearly outweighed by the certainty that either w_2 or w_3 will become actual. So, if the two-boxer opts for the choice of both boxes even in the limit case, he purchases theoretical consistency at the price of intuitive irrationality—a high price to pay.[8]

My second observation is closely related to the first. It is true that the state of box 2 is not causally dependent upon my act in Newcomb's Problem. But another kind of dependence relation obtains which is at least as important as causal independence and which seems to take clear precedence in the limit case. If I am completely certain that the being has predicted correctly, then the state of box 2 depends *logically* upon my current beliefs together with my act. That is, from the relevant propositions about the setup of the problem (including the proposition that the being has correctly predicted my choice) together with the proposition that I choose both boxes, it follows that I get $1,000. And from those relevant propositions together with the proposition that I choose only box 2, it follows that I get $1 million. (This logical dependence, of course, is the reason why the two-box choice seems patently irrational in the limit case.)

Furthermore, the same inferences go through in probabilistic form. If I attach probability r to the proposition that the being has correctly predicted my choice, then my background beliefs together with the proposition that I will choose both boxes entail that there is probability r that I will get $1,000; and likewise for choosing box 2 and getting $1 million. Thus, a significant degree of logical dependence exists even when I am less than totally certain about the being's predictive correctness. And since logical dependence coexists with causal independence in Newcomb's Problem, there is strong reason — especially in the limit case — to regard intuition 2 as suspect.

So the reasons for rejecting intuition 2 can be summarized this way. The choice of both boxes is patently irrational in the limit case, despite intuition 2; here logical dependence clearly takes pragmatic precedence over causal independence. And there is no evident theoretical basis for saying that rationality abruptly switches to the two-box choice when we move downward from the limit case to cases involving high probability; thus, intuition 1 ought rationally to prevail over intuition 2 in the nonlimit cases as well.

COUNTERFACTUALS AND EXPECTED UTILITY

In this and the next section I shall consider the implications of the above discussion for the foundations of decision theory. A standard version of the Bayesian model of rational action, of the sort given by Jeffrey (1965), runs as follows. Let acts $A_1, \ldots, A_m$ be open to the agent. Let states $S_1, \ldots, S_n$ be mutually exclusive and jointly exhaustive possible states of the world, and let the agent know this. For each act A_i and each state S_j, let him know that if he performed A_i and S_j obtained, the outcome would be O_{ij} and let him assign to each outcome O_{ij} a desirability D_{oij}. These conditions define a *matrix formulation* of a decision problem.

In any decision problem of this kind, it is claimed, rationality consists in performing an act with maximal *expected utility*. Jeffrey defines expected utility this way:

$$V(A_i) = \Sigma_j \, pr \, (S_j/A_i) \, DO_{ij}$$

More recently, however, Gibbard and Harper (1978, reprinted in this volume) have argued that the concept thus defined is best characterized as the *value of the act as news* — that is, the welcomeness to the agent (not the usefulness to him) of learning that he is about to perform A_i. ("*V*" is their symbol, not Jeffrey's). They maintain that the genuine expected utility of A_i, $U(A_i)$, is to be calculated from probabilities of counterfactuals rather than from conditional probabilities:

$$U(A_i) = \Sigma_j \, pr(A_i \,\square\!\!\rightarrow S_j) \, DO_{ij}{}^9$$

David Lewis (1976b) has shown that, under certain weak and natural assumptions, the proposition

$$pr(P \square \rightarrow Q) = pr(Q/P)$$

is not a logical truth. And, if we follow Gibbard and Harper in imposing (by fiat) a vagueness resolution on the relevant counterfactuals which is essentially Lewis's standard resolution, there are decision problems where U and V diverge from each other. The Prisoner's Dilemma is one such problem: V-maximization recommends the cooperative strategy, whereas U-maximization recommends the noncooperative dominance strategy. Newcomb's Problem is another: V-maximization recommends taking only box 2, whereas U-maximization recommends taking both boxes.

To see how this divergence works in Newcomb's Problem, consider the following payoff matrix. (As before, A_1 and A_2 are the acts of choosing both boxes and choosing only box 2, respectively; S_1 and S_2 are the presence of $1 million in box 2 and the presence of $0 there, respectively.)

	S_1	S_2
A_1	1,001,000	1,000
A_2	1,000,000	0

Assume that the desirabilities of the payoffs are reflected in their monetary values. Since the agent is extremely confident that the being's prediction will turn out correct, for him $pr(S_1/A_2)$ and $pr(S_2/A_1)$ are near 1, whereas $pr(S_1/A_1)$ and $pr(S_2/A_2)$ are near 0. Hence V-maximization recommends A_2, since $V(A_2)$ is near 1 million whereas $V(A_1)$ is near 1,000. On the other hand, the actual-world past is held constant under the standard resolution of vagueness. Hence, under this resolution, the following identities obtain:

$$pr(A_1 \square \rightarrow S_1) = pr(A_2 \square \rightarrow S_1) = pr(S_1)$$
$$pr(A_1 \square \rightarrow S_2) = pr(A_2 \square \rightarrow S_2) = pr(S_2)$$

So, letting x be $pr(S_1)$ and y be $pr(S_2)$, we have:

$$U(A_1) = 1,001,000x + 1,000y$$
$$U(A_2) = 1,000,000x + 0y$$

Thus, $U(A_1)$ exceeds $U(A_2)$ for any permissible values of x and y.

Although I think Gibbard and Harper are wrong in advocating the choice of two boxes in Newcomb's Problem, I do not deny that act-to-state counterfactuals can be used to calculate expected utility. Indeed, the one-box argument in section 1 is essentially an expected-utility argument. (Strictly speaking, it is the "limit case" argument; if the agent is not totally certain that the being has predicted correctly, he really should begin lines (1_o), (3_o),

(4_o), and (6_o) with a phrase like "It is extremely probable that . . . .")

What I do deny, however, is Gibbard and Harper's assumption that the counterfactuals in expected-utility calculations should always be interpreted under the standard resolution of vagueness. I claim, rather, that in certain exceptional decision problems, a nonstandard resolution is pragmatically appropriate. In Newcomb's Problem, of course, it is the backtracking resolution. Under this resolution, U and V do not diverge, because the agent's subjective probability for each act-to-state counterfactual is determined in the same way as the corresponding subjective conditional probability—that is, by his subjective probability for the proposition that the being's prediction will turn out correct. That is, under the backtracking resolution,

$$pr(A_1 \,\square\!\rightarrow S_1) = pr(S_1/A_1) = pr(A_2 \,\square\!\rightarrow S_2) = pr(S_2/A_2) \approx 0$$
$$pr(A_1 \,\square\!\rightarrow S_2) = pr(S_2/A_1) = pr(A_2 \,\square\!\rightarrow S_1) = pr(S_1/A_2) \approx 1$$

I maintain that this convergence of U and V is in fact the distinguishing characteristic of the pragmatically appropriate resolution of vagueness for *any* decision problem. Let the *conditionalized* resolution R, relative to a given decision problem, be the resolution with these two features: (i) under R, $pr(A_i \,\square\!\rightarrow S_j) = (S_j/A_i)$, for each A_i and S_j; and (ii) R otherwise differs minimally from the standard resolution. Let $U_s(A_i)$ be $U(A_i)$ with the act-to-state counterfactuals interpreted under the standard resolution; and let $U_c(A_i)$ be $U(A_i)$ with those counterfactuals interpreted under the conditionalized resolution. I claim that the genuine expected utility of A_i is given not by U_s but by U_c—and hence by V, since U_c and V never diverge. (Note that different vagueness resolutions count as the conditionalized resolution in different decision problems. Usually, but not always, the conditionalized resolution will just be the standard resolution itself.)

This approach can be defended by harnessing, and then generalizing upon, the considerations I employed earlier in arguing that the backtracking resolution is pragmatically appropriate in Newcomb's Problem. The agent facing Newcomb's Problem is virtually certain, independently of any beliefs he might have regarding the probability of his doing A_1 or the probability of his doing A_2, that the being's prediction will turn out correct. Accordingly, his calculation of the expected utility of act A_i should not be based upon the probability of S_1 and the probability of S_2 in an A_i-world where the being's correctness is seriously in doubt; rather, it should be based upon the respective probabilities of S_1 and S_2 in an A_i-world where the overwhelmingly high actual-world probability of the being's predictive correctness remains intact. Thus he should not construe the expected utility of A_i as $U_s(A_i)$, because the probability is only about .5 that the being predicts correctly in the world that is "closest" under the standard resolution. Rather, he should construe the expected utility of A_i as $U_c(A_i)$, because the A_i-world that is "closest" under the conditionalized resolution is one where the overwhelmingly high actual-world probability of the being's predictive correctness remains intact.

These considerations are readily generalized. In any decision problem, conditionalizing on A_i is the right way to relativize the probabilities of the respective states for purposes of calculating the expected utility of the act A_i. Conditionalization, after all, reflects the interconnections the agent believes obtain *in our actual world* between $pr(A_i)$ and $pr(S_j)$ for each S_j. Accordingly, the agent should take $V(A_i)$ as the genuine expected utility of A_i — or equivalently, $U_c(A_i)$.

One might wonder what point there is in introducing counterfactuals into decision theory, if U_c and V never diverge. Why not simply stick to the principle of V-maximization? One answer is that people do *in fact* reason counterfactually in real-life decision problems, and this sort of reasoning seems to be part of what gets formally represented in normative decision theory. Accordingly, it is appropriate to build into decision theory an account of how counterfactuals are properly employed in expected-utility calculations. Furthermore, counterfactuals are not really theoretically superfluous under my account. For, as I shall argue presently, they provide significant theoretical insight into the nature of dominance considerations in decision problems.[10]

COUNTERFACTUALS AND DOMINANCE

An act A is said to *strongly dominate* an act B with respect to states $S_1, \ldots, S_n$ if, and only if, for each S_i, the outcome of A in S_i is more desirable than the outcome of B in S_i. A is said to *weakly dominate* B with respect to $S_1, \ldots, S_n$ if, and only if, for each S_i, the outcome of A in S_i, is at least as desirable as the outcome of B in S_i, and, for some S_i, the outcome of A in S_i is more desirable than the outcome of B in S_i. The *dominance principle* is this:

DOM   If there is a partition of states of the world such that relative to it, act A weakly dominates act B, then A should be performed rather than B.

In Newcomb's Problem, the act of taking both boxes dominates the act of taking only box 2, relative to the states S_1 and S_2 in the above matrix. Thus DOM recommends taking both boxes, whereas the traditional expected-utility principle (the V-maximization principle, in Gibbard and Harper's terminology) recommends taking only box 2. Robert Nozick, in his seminal paper on this topic (1969, reprinted in this volume), saw Newcomb's Problem as posing a conflict between these two principles of choice. He argued persuasively that in certain decision problems the dominance principle ought not to be followed, and he then considered two restricted versions. One version asserts that DOM holds when the states are probabilistically independent of the acts A and B—that is, when $pr(S_j/A) = pr(S_j/B) = pr(S_j)$, for each S_j. This principle does not sanction taking both boxes in Newcomb's Problem. Another version, though, asserts that DOM holds when the states are *causally* independent of the acts A and B, as they are in Newcomb's Problem. Nozick opted, somewhat reluctantly, for this latter version—and thus for taking both boxes. This committed him to the view that DOM prevails over V-maximization whenever the two principles conflict and the states are causally independent of the acts, whereas V-maximization remains correct in other decision problems.[11]

Gibbard and Harper, on the other hand accommodate Nozick's restricted version of the dominance principle into a theoretically uniform framework. They construe causal independence of a state S_j from an act A_i as *counterfactual* independence, under the standard resolution of vagueness—that is, as the condition that $((A_i \,\square\!\!\rightarrow S_j) \leftrightarrow S_j)$ is true under the standard resolution. Let us call this *s-independence;* and let us refer to probabilistic independence as *p-independence*. Then the two restricted versions of DOM considered by Nozick are these:

DOM$_s$ Principle DOM holds if the states are

s-independent of the acts A and B.

DOM$_p$ Principle DOM holds if the states are

p-independent of the acts A and B.
Gibbard and Harper show that the principle of U_s-maximization entails DOM$_s$ and that the principle of V-maximization entails DOM$_p$. They opt for DOM$_s$ along with U_s-maximization, which eliminates any conflict between dominance reasoning and expected-utility reasoning.

I myself have defended V-maximization rather than U_s-maximization; thus I am commited to DOM$_p$ rather than DOM$_s$. I am also committed to the following principle (letting *c-independence* be counterfactual independence under the conditionalized resolution of vagueness):

DOM$_c$ Principle DOM holds if the states are

c-independent of the acts A and B.
This too follows from the V-maximization principle, by virtue of (i) the equivalence of V and U_c, and (ii) the fact that DOM$_c$ follows from the principle of U_c-maximization. (The proof of (ii) is exactly like Gibbard and Harper's derivation of DOM$_s$ from the U_s-maximization principle.) Neither DOM$_p$ nor DOM$_c$ sanctions taking both boxes in Newcomb's Problem because the states S_1 and S_2 in the above matrix are neither p-independent nor c-independent of the acts.

Although DOM$_p$ and DOM$_c$ both follow from the V-maximization principle, they are not equivalent. C-independence entails p-independence, but not conversely; thus DOM$_c$ is stronger than DOM$_p$.[12] This asymmetry is important, because it bears directly upon a form of argument in decision-making which

I shall call a *direct dominance argument* — a form exemplified, for instance, by the two-box argument in Newcomb's Problem as formulated above.

In a direct dominance argument, the agent relies not merely on the fact that one act dominates another, but also on a statement of the following form. (This is the form of premise (6,) of the two-box argument in Newcomb's Problem; call it the *disjunctive basis* for the normative conclusion.)

$$((A_1 \mathbin{\Box\!\!\rightarrow} O_1) \, \& \ldots \& \, (A_m \mathbin{\Box\!\!\rightarrow} O_{m1}))$$
$$\mathrm{v} \ldots \mathrm{v} \, ((A_1 \mathbin{\Box\!\!\rightarrow} O_{1n}) \, \& \ldots \& \, (A_m \mathbin{\Box\!\!\rightarrow} O_{mn}))$$

In 2×2 decision problems (that is, problems involving two acts and two states), the disjunctive basis has this form:

$$((A_1 \mathbin{\Box\!\!\rightarrow} O_{11}) \, \& \, (A_2 \mathbin{\Box\!\!\rightarrow} O_{21})) \, \mathrm{v} \, ((A_1 \mathbin{\Box\!\!\rightarrow} O_{12}) \, \& \, (A_2 \mathbin{\Box\!\!\rightarrow} O_{22}))$$

When the agent facing a 2×2 problem reasons that he would do better with the dominant act no matter whether S_1 holds or S_2 holds, he obviously has in mind that the left disjunct of the disjunctive basis is true if S_1 holds and that the right disjunct is true if S_2 holds. Thus, a direct dominance argument corresponds to what we intuitively think of as "reasoning from dominance"; such an argument assumes the truth of the appropriate disjunctive basis.

One might think that the disjunctive basis just follows logically from the conditions that define a decision problem. In a 2×2 problem, the relevant conditions are $S_1 \, \mathrm{v} \, S_2$ plus the following four counterfactuals:

I. $(A_1 \, \& \, S_1) \mathbin{\Box\!\!\rightarrow} O_{11}$
II. $(A_2 \, \& \, S_1) \mathbin{\Box\!\!\rightarrow} O_{21}$
III. $(A_1 \, \& \, S_2) \mathbin{\Box\!\!\rightarrow} O_{12}$
IV. $(A_2 \, \& \, S_2) \mathbin{\Box\!\!\rightarrow} O_{22}$

But in fact the disjunctive basis does not follow from these conditions alone.[13] Rather, the following supplementary premises, whose truth is not guaranteed by the matrix structure of a 2×2 decision problem, must be invoked:

I'. $S_1 \rightarrow (A_1 \mathbin{\Box\!\!\rightarrow} S_1)$
II'. $S_1 \rightarrow (A_2 \mathbin{\Box\!\!\rightarrow} S_1)$
III'. $S_2 \rightarrow (A_1 \mathbin{\Box\!\!\rightarrow} S_2)$
IV'. $S_2 \rightarrow (A_2 \mathbin{\Box\!\!\rightarrow} S_2)$

And from I'-IV' together, along with the fact that the states S_1 and S_2 meet the Partition Condition (see n. 10), the four corresponding biconditionals follow; that is, $((A_i \;\Box\!\!\rightarrow S_j) \leftrightarrow S_j)$ follows, for each A_i and S_j. And the same is true for all decision problems, not just 2×2 problems. That is, a direct dominance argument in any decision problem presupposes that the states are counterfactually independent of the acts.

What *kind* of counterfactual independence is presupposed: s-independence or c-independence? The latter, if my earlier discussion was correct; I claimed that in any decision problem, the conditionalized resolution of vagueness is pragmatically appropriate. Thus, the trouble with the two-box direct dominance argument in the first section can be put this way: although the states are s-independent of the acts, they are not c-independent of them.

Newcomb's Problem is controversial, of course. But we can expect direct dominance reasoning to be obviously and uncontroversially incorrect in cases where (i) the conditionalized resolution of vagueness coincides with the standard resolution, and (ii) the states are not counterfactualy independent of the acts (that is, not s-independent and not c-independent, since the two kinds of independence coincide). An example of this kind is provided by Nozick (1969, in this volume, pp. 114–15. Suppose I am about to bet on a horserace in which only two horses, H_1 and H_2, are running. Let A_1 and A_2, respectively, be the act of betting on horse H_1 and the act of betting on horse H_2; let S_1 and S_2, respectively, be the state consisting in H_1 winning the race, and the state consisting in H_2 winning it. Suppose I will definitely bet on one and only one horse and that the payoff matrix is this:

	S_1	S_2
A_1	I win $50	I lose $5
A_2	I lose $6	I lose $49

Suppose further that, for me, $pr\,(S_1) = .2$, and $pr\,(S_2) = .8$. Thus, assuming that the monetary value of the outcomes reflects their utilities, the expected utility of A_2 exceeds the expected utility of A_1. (Note that U_s coincides with V and U_c here, since the standard resolution of vagueness is the conditionalized resolution.)

But we can set up the matrix differently. Let S_3 and S_4, respectively, be the states described by "I am lucky in my bet" and "I am unlucky in my bet." Then we have the following matrix:

	S_3	S_4
A_1	I win $50	I lose $5
A_2	I lose $49	I lose $6

A_1 dominates A_2, relative to states S_3 and S_4. Yet it would be crazy to do A_1 rather than A_2 on this basis because S_3 and S_4 are just not the kinds of states that support direct dominance reasoning. The trouble is that they are not counterfactually independent of the acts (that is, they are neither s-independent nor c-independent, since the two coincide here). Thus, the relevant disjunctive basis,

Either I would win \$50 if I bet on horse H_1 and I would win \$49 if I bet on horse H_2, *or* I would lose \$5 if I bet on horse H_1 and I would lose \$6 if I bet on horse H_2.

cannot be assumed true. Indeed, it is false — which explains why an argument from dominance is so obviously crazy in this case.

I said earlier that DOM_c is stronger than DOM_p and that this asymmetry is relevant to direct dominance arguments. The relevance lies in the fact that such arguments presuppose that the states are c-independent of the acts, and not merely p-independent. This means that there can be cases where direct dominance reasoning is mistaken, even though the states are p-independent of the acts. To be sure, in such cases the dominant act will be the *correct* act to choose, since DOM_p follows from the two equivalent expected-utility principles I have endorsed here — that is, V-maximization and U_c-maximization. However, the correctness of the act will not be supportable by direct dominance considerations.

We can obtain such a case by modifying Nozick's horserace example: let the probability for the agent that horse H_1 wins be .5, and let the probability that horse H_2 wins be .5. Then the states S_3 and S_4 are p-independent of the acts. However, they still fail to be counterfactually independent of the acts, and thus the above disjunctive-basis statement is still false. Hence, the choice of A_1 over A_2 is no more supportable by a *direct dominance* argument here than it was in the original example. Of course, the agent ought to do A_1 in this modified example; but he should do so because the expected utility of A_1 now exceeds the expected utility of A_2 — *not* because of a direct dominance argument.

A PUTATIVE COUNTEREXAMPLE TO V-MAXIMIZATION

In defending their approach to expected utility, Gibbard and Harper claim that there are decision problems where V-maximization is clearly irrational and where U_s-maximization yields the correct recommendation. Cartwright (1979) and Skyrms (1980b) have given similar examples, and they each propose ways of redefining expected utility which, like Gibbard and Harper's way, imply that the two-box choice in Newcomb's Problem has maximal expected utility.

I am unpersuaded by the putative counterexamples to traditional V-maximization offered by these revisionist two-boxers. There is more to say about their various cases than I have room to say here, so I shall only comment on one fairly representative example described by Gibbard:

> It is discovered that the reason for the correlation between smoking and lung cancer is not that smoking tends to cause lung cancer. Rather, the cause of lung cancer is a certain genetic factor, and a person gets lung cancer if and only if he has that factor. The reason for the correlation of lung cancer with smoking is that the same genetic factor predisposes people to smoke.
>
> A smoker who knows these facts is trying to decide whether to give up smoking.... He likes to smoke, but wants much more to avoid cancer than to continue to smoke.[14]

We may specify the agent's desirabilities as follows:

	S_1 genetic factor present	S_2 genetic factor lacking
A_1 continue smoking	smoking and cancer (10)	smoking without cancer (100)
A_2 give up smoking	abstinence and cancer (8)	abstinence without cancer (80)

Gibbard claims that the states in this matrix are far from being stochastically independent of the acts: "Learning that he was about to continue to smoke would be evidence to the agent that the genetic factor was present, whereas learning that he was about to stop would be evidence to him that the genetic factor was not present. Thus his subjective conditional probability for S_1 given that he continues smoking is greater than his subjective conditional probability for S_1 given that he stops smoking"(1979, p. 5). Assuming that this difference in probabilities is great enough, V-maximization will dictate giving up smoking—which is surely irrational, given the agent's preferences and given his belief that this act would have absolutely no causal efficacy in relation to his subsequently getting (or not getting) lung cancer.

I am not convinced that V-maximization would really dictate stopping smoking. For the agent's desirability assignments in the given decision matrix (and his past history of smoking) provide him with a crucial piece of information: that he is inclined to smoke and therefore is likely to get lung cancer. If he did not have this information about himself, then for him $pr(S_1/A_1)$ would indeed exceed $pr(S_1/A_2)$. But, since he does have it, the information that he will quit smoking (or will continue to smoke) should not make any difference to his subjective probabilities regarding the lung cancer. That is, he should adjust $pr(S_1)$ upward and $pr(S_2)$ downward on the basis of the information provided by his desirabilities (and his smoking history); thereafter, he should set $pr(S_1/A_1)$ equal to $pr(S_1/A_2)$, and $pr(S_2/A_1)$ equal to $pr(S_2/A_2)$. And then V-maximization will recommend A_1, not A_2.

In short, the flaw in the example is the assumption that the agent needs to *act* before he has the relevant information to determine the likelihood of getting lung cancer. He does not, because his own desirabilities (and past behavior) give him the bad news already. This same problem arises in most of the putative counter-examples to V-maximization offered by the revisionist two-boxers.

Perhaps, though, the example can be modified to avoid this objective. Let the agent believe that the genetic factor in question induces in smokers a tendency to choose to continue smoking when confronted with the present decision problem; and let him believe (implausible though this may be) that smokers who lack the genetic factor have a tendency to choose to stop smoking when confronted with this problem. Under *these* assumptions $pr(S_1/A_1)$ will be significantly higher than $pr(S_1/A_2)$, and $pr(S_2/A_1)$ will be significantly lower than $pr(S_2/A_2)$, even after the agent takes into account the information provided by his desirabilities (and his smoking history). And if the differences are great enough, then V-maximization will recommend stopping smoking.

I concede that this modified story avoids my objection, but I deny that stopping smoking would now be irrational. Supose that 95 per cent of the smokers who are confronted with this decision problem and decide to continue smoking subsequently die of lung cancer and that 95 per cent of those who are confronted with it and decide to stop end up dying of other causes. If the agent knows these statistics and if he believes that they reflect the causal influence of the genetic factor (or its absence) upon the choosers, then I think he acts rationally if he decides to stop smoking.

Of course, this decision does not rest on the belief that stopping smoking will *cause* him not to have the genetic factor. But rationality in this case need not rest upon a belief in the causal efficacy of one's act any more than the rationality of the one-box decision in Newcomb's Problem rests upon such a belief. Rather, it rests upon *counterfactual* beliefs — with the vagueness of similarity being resolved in the pragmatically appropriate way. The agent says to himself, "It's quite probable that if I were to keep smoking then I would have the genetic factor; and it's quite probable that if I were to stop smoking then I would not have the genetic factor." He concludes, quite reasonably, that he ought to stop.

THE PRISONER'S DILEMMA

These last remarks are applicable, *mutatis mutandis,* to the classical Prisoner's Dilemma. Two prisoners, A and B, each have an option of confessing (A_1 and B_1, respectively) or not confessing (A_2 and B_2, respectively). If they both confess, they each get long prison terms. If one confesses and the other does not, the confessor is released and the other gets an even longer prison term. And if neither confesses, they both get light sentences. Let the desirability matrix be as follows:

	B_1	B_2
A_1	1,1	10,0
A_2	0,10	9,9

What should you do in this situation, if you are A or B? This dilemma is structurally parallel to Newcomb's Problem[15] and to the (modified) lung cancer problem. U_s-maximization recommends confessing, because (i) the other prisoner's acts are causally independent of your own, and (ii) confessing dominates not confessing, relative to the "states" consisting in his available acts. But suppose you believe that the other prisoner thinks in much the same way as you do. (Perhaps this belief is based upon knowledge of psychological similarities; or perhaps it merely reflects the fact that you consider both yourself and the other prisoner to be rational.) Then you can reasonably assert the following, with the vagueness of similarity being resolved in the pragmatically appropriate way: "It is probable that if I were to confess then the other prisoner would confess too; and it is probable that if I were to refrain from confessing then he would refrain too." On this basis, it is reasonable to opt for the cooperative strategy of not confessing – the strategy recommended by V-maximization. (Not confessing is V-maximal for prisoner B as long as $pr\,(A_2/B_2) - pr\,(A_2/B_1)$ is sufficiently great – in this case 1/9 or more. Parallel remarks hold regarding prisoner A.) You know that your act will not causally influence the other prisoner's act, of course. But rationality does not require a belief in causal efficacy here, just as it requires no such belief in Newcomb's Problem.

NOTES

*I am grateful to Allan Gibbard, Alvin Goldman, and Arthur Kuflik for helpful comments on an earlier version of this paper, and to a number of people – especially Gibbard, Robert Barrett, Michael Gorr, Paul Lyon, and Ned McClennen – for enlightening discussion.

1. At any rate (3_o) and (6_o) cannot be interpreted as mere material conditionals. If ordinary indicative conditionals are distinct in logical form from both material conditionals and counterfactuals, then it might be appropriate to construe the conditionals in the one-box argument as semantically indicative. I shall not explore this possibility here. (I have in mind specifically Ernest Adams's treatment of indicative conditionals in Adams (1976).)

2. Under the possible-worlds semantics for counterfactuals I shall adopt, a counterfactual $P \;\Box\!\!\rightarrow Q$ logically implies $P \rightarrow Q$, but not conversely.

3. Condition iii obtains under the standard resolution, says Lewis, because only a "big, complicated" miracle could completely wipe out all the rapidly outward-spreading effects of the minor A-initiating miracle mentioned in ii. (This is not an analytic truth, in his view, but a rather a *de facto* asymmetry which prevails in possible worlds with fundamental laws like those of our world.) This claim about the size of the second miracle might be questioned; but, if it is incorrect, then Lewis's account of the standard resolution will have to be revised to accommodate iii and not vice versa. Conditions i–iii seem to reflect our actual usage of counterfactuals like Fine's and actual usage in Lewis's touchstone in determining the standard resolution. Indeed, if we restrict ourselves to counterfactuals whose antecedent clauses describe some particular act (and these are the kind I am primarily concerned about in this paper), we may think of conditions i–iii themselves as determining the standard resolution of vagueness.

4. Strictly speaking, top priority goes to maintaining the *relation* that obtains in our world between the being's prediction and my eventual act — be this correctness or incorrectness. But it is simpler, for expository purposes, not to speak strictly.

5. The notion "perfect match of particular fact" is not unproblematic. If we keep intact the facts concerning the being's specific prediction and act, we must sacrifice the fact that he predicted correctly. Still, this latter fact seems to be not unequivocally about the past, but rather about the *relation* between the being's specific past prediction and my future choice.

6. In the extremely unlikely event that the being will turn out to be mistaken in his prediction of my actual-world choice, 2_t and 5_t would both be true, whereas either 3_t or 4_t would be false. 6_t would still be false, however.

7. By "infallibility" I mean that the being's predictions are always correct *in our actual world*. He would be infallible in a much stronger sense if his predictions were always correct in *all* possible worlds. If I knew him to be infallible in this strong sense, then I would know that the putative worlds w_1 and w_4 did not even exist; thus the premises (2_t) and (5_t) of the two-box argument would collapse even under the standard resolution of vagueness (that is, their component counterfactuals would be false). Mere actual-world infallibility, on the other hand, is compatible with the existence of w_1 and w_4; hence it is compatible with the standard-resolution truth of the two-boxer's nonnormative premises.

8. Gibbard and Harper (1978) defend the two-box choice even in the limit case. Nozick, who initiated the philosophical debate about Newcomb's Problem with Nozick (1969), reprinted in this volume, opted for one-box choice in the limit case and the two-box choice in all nonlimit cases. He confessed uneasiness with this position, however, pointing out (1) that it is not clear why the difference between complete certainty and very high probability should be theoretically important, and (2) that it is not clear how complete certainty about the being's correctness dissolves the force of the two-box argument.

9. Gibbard and Harper do not distinguish between an act $A,$ and the proposition

that the agent performs A_i, or between a state S_j, and the proposition that S_i obtains; thus they can write the corresponding act-to-state counterfactual as "$A_i \,\square\!\!\rightarrow S_j$." I shall follow this practice here.

10. Counterfactuals also are important in characterizing decision matrices themselves. Recall how the notion of "outcome" was introduced: the agent believes that if A_i and S_j *were* the case, the O_{ij} *would* result. Gibbard claims (1979), I think correctly, that decision matrices must also satisfy the following Partition Condition: The agent believes not only that one and only one state from S_1, ..., S_n obtains, but also that one and only one of them *would* obtain no matter which available act he performed.

11. Actually, Nozick's position was more complicated than this. As I remarked in n. 8, he held that the agent in Newcomb's problem should choose box 2 if he is *completely certain* that the being has predicted correctly.

12. DOM$_p$ is equivalent not to DOM$_c$ but to the following weaker principle: DOM holds if $pr(A \,\square\!\!\rightarrow S_j) = pr(B \,\square\!\!\rightarrow S_j) = pr(S_j)$, under the conditionalized resolution of vagueness, for each S_j.

13. To see this, let W be our actual world, and let w_1, w_2, and w_3 be non-actual worlds such that w_1 is closer to W than is w_2, and w_2 is closer to W than is w_3. Let A_2, S_1, AND O_{21} hold at W; let w_1 be the closest A_1-world to W, and let S_2 and O_{12} hold at w_1; let w_2 be the closest $(A_1 \& S_1)$-world to W, and let O_{11} hold at w_2; let w_3 be the closest $(A_2 \& S_2)$-world to W, and let O_{22} hold at w_3. Let one only of O_{11}, O_{12}, O_{21}, and O_{22} hold at each of the four worlds. Under these conditions, $(S_1 \text{ v } S_2)$ and (I)-(IV) are all true. Yet the disjunctive basis is false, because $(A_1 \,\square\!\!\rightarrow O_{11})$ and $(A_2 \,\square\!\!\rightarrow O_{22})$ are both false, although $(A_2 \,\square\!\!\rightarrow O_{21})$ and $(A_1 \,\square\!\!\rightarrow O_{12})$ are both true.

The invalidity of the inference from $(S_1 \text{ v } S_2)$ and (I)-(IV) to the disjunctive basis is closely related to the invalidity of the inference from $((P \& Q) \,\square\!\!\rightarrow R)$ to $(Q \rightarrow (P \,\square\!\!\rightarrow R))$. If we could perform this form of exportation on (I)-(IV), the disjunctive basis would follow immediately by truth-functional logic.

14. Gibbard (1979). This example is from R. A. Fisher. See the references in Levi's essay, chapter 13. A similar example is discussed in Nozick (1969). Such cases sometimes are presented (as in Nozick) as putative counterexamples to DOM$_p$; but DOM$_p$ follows from the principle of V-maximization, as noted earlier.

15. Lewis argues (1979a, reprinted in this volume) that Newcomb's problem and the Prisoner's Dilemma differ only in "inessential trappings" (p. 251 in this volume). A similar view is strongly suggested in Gibbard and Harper (1978). Lewis, like Gibbard and Harper, thinks it is rational to take both boxes in Newcomb's Problem, no matter how reliable the predictor might be, and that it is rational to confess in the Prisoner's Dilemma, no matter how confident you are that the other prisoner will act the same way you do.

9

Causality, Decision, and Newcomb's Paradox

ELLERY EELLS

Recently a number of *prima facie* counterexamples to the Principle of Maximizing Conditional Expected Utility (*PMCEU*), all inspired by Newcomb's paradox,[1] have been constructed. These involve decision problems that seem to establish a conflict between the Principle of Dominance (*PDOM*) and *PMCEU* in which it seems that only the former gives the correct prescriptions. Central to the alleged counterexamples is the observation that *PMCEU* seems not to be appropriately sensitive to causal beliefs of a certain kind that a decision-maker might have.

In the first section of this paper, I will state *PMCEU* in the framework of Jeffrey's decision model and give a simple version of *PDOM*. In the second section, I will present two *prima facie* counterexamples to *PMCEU* of the kind I have in mind, and clarify some aspects of their common causal structure. The third section contains a brief presentation of two recent solutions to the problem: namely, Skyrms's *K*-expectation approach and Gibbard and Harper's *U*-maximization approach. In that section, I will argue that a successful *CEU* approach to the problem would have advantages over the other two approaches. In the fourth section, after giving a more than usually detailed analysis of the causal structure of the relevant decision problems, I will argue that *PMCEU*, if fully and properly exploited, actually gives the correct prescriptions — indeed, the same as those given by *PDOM* and by the rules proposed by Gibbard and Harper and by Skyrms. Finally, I turn to the Newcomb Problem itself, concerned there not with what the prescription of *PMCEU* is, but with what the correct act is in the first place. There I argue that, contrary to an interesting and intricate analysis recently advanced by Horgan, the rational act is in fact the dominant, two-box, act.

From Ellery Eells, *Rational Decision and Causality* Copyright © by Cambridge University Press, 1982, Chs. 3–6, abridged and revised by Ellery Eells, reprinted by permission of author and publisher; and from Ellery Eells, "Newcomb's Many Solutions," *Theory and Decision* 16 (1984): 59–105, Sec. 4, reprinted by permission of the author and D. Reidel Publishing Company.

1. In Jeffrey's decision model (1965; second edition, 1983), acts, states and outcomes are considered to be entities of the same kind: propositions.[2] *Acts,* or *act-propositions,* are propositions to the effect that the agent performs certain acts. *States,* or *state-propositions,* are propositions that say that certain states of affairs obtain. Let $(S_1, \ldots, S_n)$ be the finite set of mutually exclusive and collectively exhaustive states considered by the decision-maker. *Outcomes,* or *outcome-propositions,* say that certain outcomes, or consequences, obtain (or will obtain). Let $(O_1, \ldots, O_m)$ be the finite set of mutually exclusive and collectively exhaustive outcomes the agent considers in his decision situation. Outcomes can be distinguished from states by thinking of them as more directly related to the happiness of the agent than states. Thus "It will rain today" is a state, and "I will be caught in the rain today" is an outcome. The distinction is not sharp, and it will be convenient at times to blur the distinction and consider outcomes to be states of a kind. Propositions in the Boolean closure of the set of acts, states, and outcomes will be called *decision-relevant propositions.*

The agent has a subjective probability (subjective degree of belief) assignment (symbolized by *"pr"*), and a desirability, or utility, assignment (symbolized by *"D"*) whose domains include the set of decision-relevant propositions. The functions *pr* and *D* are assumed to satisfy the standard probability axioms and the *Desirability Axiom:* for any two propositions X and Y, if $pr(X \ \& \ Y) = 0$, then

$$pr(X \lor Y)D(X \lor Y) = pr(X)D(X) + pr(Y)D(Y).$$

Some consequences of Jeffrey's axioms are:

(1) $D(A) = \sum_{i=1}^{n} pr(S_i/A)D(S_i \ \& \ A),$

(2) $D(A) = \sum_{j=1}^{m} pr(O_j/A)D(O_j \ \& \ A),$

(3) $D(A) = \sum_{i=1}^{n} pr(S_i/A) \sum_{j=1}^{m} pr(O_j/S_i \ \& \ A)D(O_j \ \& \ S_i \ \& \ A),$

(4) $D(A) = \sum_{i=1}^{n} \sum_{j=1}^{m} pr(S_i \ \& \ O_j/A)D(S_i \ \& \ O_j \ \& \ A),$

where A is any proposition — typically an act — and $pr(X/Y)$ is the probability of X conditional on Y, or $pr(X \ \& \ Y)/pr(Y)$. Terms in (1)–(4) involving probabilities conditional on a proposition whose probability is 0 are not counted as part of the summation.

For the purposes of this paper, I define an agent's conditional expected utility of an act A as follows: if the states and outcomes considered by an agent are as above, then his *conditional expected utility* of the act A, in symbols, *CEU(A)*, is given by the expression on the right in (3) (or, equivalently, the expression on the right in (4)). Thus, the agent's conditional expected utility of an act is calculated from his desirabilities for maximally specific decision-relevant propositions and his subjective probability assignment.[3] Jeffrey's axioms guarantee that the expressions on the right in (1)–(4) are all equal to $CEU(A)$ and to $D(A)$, the agent's desirability for the act A. The *Principle of Maximizing Conditional Expected Utility* states that a rational agent chooses an act that has the greatest conditional expected utility. Thus, *PMCEU* tells you how to figure out what the rational act is from your desirabilities over a set of maximally specific propositions and your subjective probability assignment. The principle can be thought of as a descriptive principle or as a normative principle or both.

Before stating the simple version of *PDOM* which I shall use, I must give the following definition. For any two acts A and B, A *dominates* B *in the agent's preferences* if, and only if, for any two maximally specific decision-relevant propositions of the forms A & S_i & O_j and B & S_i & O_j, $D(A$ & S_i $\&O_j) > D(B$ & S_i & $O_j)$. Then *PDOM* states: If (i) A dominates every other act in your preferences and (ii) you believe that which act you perform does not causally affect which proposition of the form S_i & O_j is true, then do A. For a simple two-act (A and B), two-state (S and $-S$) decision problem, *PDOM* can be simply stated as follows: If (i) $D(A$ & $S) > D(B$ & $S)$ and $D(A$ & $-S) > D(B$ & $-S)$ and (ii) you believe that which of A and B you do will not affect which of S and $-S$ obtains (or will obtain), then do A. *PDOM* can be thought of as a descriptive principle or as a normative principle or both.

PDOM is intuitively attractive. I believe that it accurately prescribes and describes rational behavior. But it is not very broadly applicable. It is far from common that one finds oneself confronting a decision problem in which one act dominates all the others and all the relevant causal irrelevancies obtain. But it was long thought that for situations in which *PDOM is* applicable, *PMCEU* would agree with the prescriptions of *PDOM*. This was based on the assumption that if a proposition X is believed to be *causally* independent of an act A (in the sense that whether or not A is performed does not causally affect whether or not X obtains or will obtain), then X will be (subjectively) *probabilistically* independent of A. It is easy to see that if this assumption were true, then *PMCEU* would always agree with *PDOM*. Suppose that act A dominates all the other acts B in the agent's preferences and that each S_i & O_j is believed by him to be causally independent of each act. Then *PDOM* prescribes act A, and given the above assumption relating causal independence of acts to probabilistic independence, we have:

$$CEU(A) = \sum_{i=1}^{n} \sum_{j=1}^{m} pr(S_i \text{ \& } O_j/A) D(S_i \text{ \& } O_j \text{ \& } A)$$
$$= \sum_{i=1}^{n} \sum_{j=1}^{m} pr(S_i \text{ \& } O_j) D(S_i \text{ \& } O_j \text{ \& } A),$$

and

$$CEU(B) = \sum_{i=1}^{n} \sum_{j=1}^{m} pr(S_i \ \& \ O_j) \, D(S_i \ \& \ O_j \ \& \ B).$$

Clearly, since A dominates B, $CEU(A) > CEU(B)$ and *PMCEU* agrees with *PDOM*.

The *prima facie* counterexamples described in the next section involve decision problems in which the assumption relating causal independence of acts to probabilistic independence of acts seems to fail—in such a way that while *PDOM* gives the right answers, *PMCEU* seems not to.

2. Skyrms asks us to suppose the following about the connection between hardening of the arteries and cholesterol intake:

> Hardening of the arteries is not caused by cholesterol intake like the clogging of a water pipe; rather it is caused by a lesion in the artery wall. In an advanced state these lesions will catch cholesterol from the blood, a fact which has deceived previous researchers about the causal picture. Moreover, imagine that once someone develops the lesion, he tends to increase his cholesterol intake. We do not know what mechanism accounts for this effect of a lesion. We do, however, know that the increased cholesterol intake is beneficial; it somehow slows the development of the lesion. Cholesterol intake among those who do not have the lesion appears to have no effect on vascular health. (1980b, p. 129).

Skyrms then asks what a rational person who believed all this would do if offered eggs benedict for breakfast.

It appears that if he wanted to maximize his *CEU,* he would abstain from the eggs. Supposing he believes that almost all cases of high cholesterol intake are caused by the lesion and that the lesion is very efficacious in producing high cholesterol intake, it seems plausible that his subjective probabilities would be such that the probability of having the lesion is higher conditional on high cholesterol intake than conditional on low to medium cholesterol intake. And since the probability of hardening of the arteries conditional on having the lesion is very high and the desirablility of hardening of the arteries is very low, it seems that *PMCEU* recommends not eating the eggs benedict.

But it is clear that it would be irrational not to eat the eggs, assuming that the man likes eggs benedict. (Let us assume, in fact, that eating the eggs dominates not eating the eggs in the man's preferences: in each of the four possible states of affairs corresponding to having or not having the lesion *and* developing or not developing hardening of the arteries, eating the eggs is at least slightly better than not eating them.) For even though the probability of the lesion's being present (and thus of hardening of the arteries) may be higher conditional on high cholesterol intake than on low to medium cholesterol intake, eating the eggs does not *cause* the lesion or hardening of the arteries: the probabilistic relations do not mirror the causal relations in the natural way. *PDOM* prescribes eating the eggs; refraining from the eggs in order to maximize *CEU* is "a futile attempt to manipulate the cause by suppressing its symptoms" (Skyrms, 1980b, p. 129). (One might want to modify the example by assuming that the man must decide between a *life-long policy* of eggs benedict for breakfast and *life-long policy* of fruit and juice for breakfast.)

Gibbard and Harper (1978, reprinted in this volume) present the following counterexample. King Solomon wants another man's wife. But he is not sure whether he should summon her, because that would be an unjust act and kings who act unjustly usually face revolts. Where "J" symbolizes that Solomon abstains from the woman and '*R*" symbolizes that there will be a revolt, suppose Solomon's desirabilities are as follows: $D(R \& J) = 0$, $D(R \& -J) = 1$, $D(-R \& J) = 9$ and $D(-R \& -J) = 10$. Also suppose that

> Solomon ... has studied works on psychology and political science which teach him the following: Kings have two basic personality types, charismatic and uncharismatic. A king's degree of charisma depends on his genetic makeup and early childhood experiences, and cannot be changed in adulthood. Now charismatic kings tend to act justly and uncharismatic kings unjustly. Successful revolts against charismatic kings are rare, whereas successful revolts against uncharismatic kings are frequent. Unjust acts themselves, though, do not cause successful revolts; the reason that uncharismatic kings are prone to successful revolts is that they have a sneaky, ignoble bearing. Solomon does not know whether or not he is charismatic; he does know that it is unjust to send for another man's wife (1978, p. 141 in this volume).

Since the charismatic, non-revolt-prone kings tend to act justly and the uncharismatic, revolt-prone kings tend to act unjustly and since *J* is a just act and $-J$ is an unjust act, Solomon's probabilities are such that $pr(R/J) < pr(R/-J)$. Suppose that $pr(R/J) = a$ and $pr(R/-J) = a + \epsilon$ and $\epsilon > 1/9$. Then

$$CEU(J) = pr(R/J)D(R \& J) + pr(-R/J)D(-R \& J)$$
$$= 0 + 9(1 - a) = 9 - 9a,$$

$$CEU(-J) = pr(R/-J)D(R \& -J) + pr(-R/-J)D(-R \& -J)$$
$$= 1(a + \epsilon) + 10(1 - a - \epsilon) = 10 - 9a - 9\epsilon.$$

$CEU(J) - CEU(-J) = 9\epsilon - 1$, which is positive, since $\epsilon > 1/9$. So $CEU(J) > CEU(-J)$.

But again it is clear that J is the wrong prescription. Solomon knows that unjust acts like sending for the woman do not cause successful revolts. So, since all Solomon wants in this decision situation is to have the woman and not to have a revolt and since sending for the woman would in no way tend to produce a revolt, he should, as *PDOM* prescribes, send for her. Again, *PMCEU* seems to recommend a course of action that is a futile attempt to manipulate the cause (of revolts) by suppressing its symptoms (unjust acts). As Gibbard and Harper put it,

> Sending for her would be an indication that Solomon lacked charisma, and hence an indication that he will face a revolt. To abstain from the woman for this reason, though, would be knowingly to bring about an indication of a desired outcome without in anyway bringing about the desired outcome itself. That seems clearly irrational. (1978, p. 142 in this volume).

Note that Skyrms's cholesterol case and Gibbard and Harper's charisma case are, in a sense, "isomorphic." For the cholesterol case, let *"L," "T,"* and *"I"* symbolize propositions to the effect that the lesion is present, that hardening of the arteries develops, and that high cholesterol foods are eaten, respectively. For the charisma case, let *"C"* symbolize that Solomon has charisma. We already know what *"R"* and *"J"* symbolize. *L, T,* and *I* play the same role in the cholesterol case as *C, −R,* and *J* play in the charisma case, respectively. *L* and *C* are factors that are not within the agent's control and that cause, independently of what the agent does, *T* and *−R,* respectively. *L* and *C* also cause the acts *I* and *J,* respectively. (I shall freely use expressions like *"L* causes *T"* and *"L* causes *I,"* meaning, of course, that the lesion causes atherosclerosis and the lesion causes high cholesterol intake, respectively.) I shall call states that play the same role as *L* and *C* in situations of the kind in question *common causes.* I shall call propositions that play the same role as *I* and *J*−acts that are symptomatic of the presence of the common cause−in situations of the kind in question *symptomatic acts.* And propositions like *T* and *−R*−outcomes that are symptomatic of the presence of the common cause−will be called *symptomatic outcomes.* When I wish to speak of an arbitrary decision problem of the kind in question−the general case−I will use the expressions *"CC," "SA,"* and *"SO"* to symbolize propositions to the effect that the common cause is present, the symptomatic act is performed, and the symptomatic outcome obtains, respectively. I shall call such decision problems *Newcomb problems.* And finally, let *"DM"* be a name for the ideally rational decision-maker to whom I shall often refer.

Thus, the causal structure of Newcomb problems can be diagrammatically represented as follows:

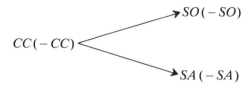

$$CC(-CC) \begin{array}{c} \nearrow SO(-SO) \\ \\ \searrow SA(-SA) \end{array}$$

The diagram is to be interpreted as meaning that *CC* causes *SO* and *SA* and (possibly) $-CC$ causes $-SO$ and $-SA$. I do not know if *CC*'s causing *SO* and *SA* implies that $-CC$ causes $-SO$ and $-SA$; for instance, it is unclear that the absence of the lesion in the cholesterol case actually *causes* one *not* to have hardening of the arteries. Thus, perhaps, in some Newcomb problems not all of the causal relations indicated in the above diagram will hold; in others, they will all clearly hold. But this does not seem to me to mark an important difference between kinds of Newcomb problems.

Since the distinction between states and outcomes is blurry, the decision situations discussed above can be characterized in a variety of ways: two-state (*CC* and $-CC$) two-outcome (*SO* and $-SO$) two-act (*SA* and $-SA$); four-state (*CC* & *SO*, *CC* & $-SO$, $-CC$ & *SO*, $-CC$ & $-SO$) two-act (*SA* and $-SA$), four-outcome two-act (as above, considering the states to be outcomes); two-state (*CC* and $-CC$) two-act (*SA* and $-SA$), or two-outcome (*SO* and $-SO$) two-act (*SA* and $-SA$). In the last two cases, the utility or disutility of the outcomes or states not explicitly considered is to be thought of as attaching appropriately — given the agent's causal and probabilistic beliefs — to the states or outcomes explicitly considered. All of the above characterizations of Newcomb situations will be used in the ensuing discussion.

Perhaps it will be illuminating to present a recipe for concocting two-state two-act Newcomb situations. This will help to clarify their structure and show that they are probably not uncommon. I shall say (loosely) that a state *S swamps an act A in an agent's preferences* if $D(-S\&A) - D(S\&A)$ and $D(-S\& -A) - D(S\& -A)$ both have the same sign and are large compared to $D(-S\&A) - D(-S\& -A)$ and $D(S\&A) - D(S\& -A)$, which are also of the same sign. Then, to construct a Newcomb situation, just find a state *S* and an act *A* such that

    (5) *A* dominates $-A$ in the agent's preferences,
    (6) *S* swamps *A* in the agent's preferences,
    (7) *S* is very bad compared to $-S$,
    (8) *A*, like $-A$, causes neither *S* nor $-S$,

and

    (9) $pr(S/A) > pr(S/-A)$.

(5), (6) and (7) together are equivalent to (6) plus the assumption that the differences used in defining "swamps" are all positive. The rationale for (9) is that the agent believes that state S is a cause of the act A. This belief makes it *prima facie* plausible that his subjective probabilities are such that $pr(A/S) > pr(A/-S)$. And by symmetry of positive probabilistic relevance, (9) follows.[4] By (5), (8), and *PDOM*, A is the rational act. But $CEU(-A) > CEU(A)$ if, and only if,

$$pr(S/-A)D(S \& -A) + pr(-S/-A)D(-S \& -A)$$
$$> pr(S/A)D(S \& A) + pr(-S/A)D(-S \& A),$$

if, and only if,

$$pr(S/-A)D(S \& -A) + (1 - pr(S/-A))D(-S \& -A)$$
$$> pr(S/A)D(S \& A) + (1 - pr(S/A))D(-S \& A),$$

if, and only if,

$$pr(S/-A)(D(S \& -A) - D(-S \& -A)) + D(-S \& -A)$$
$$> pr(S/A)(D(S \& A) - D(-S \& A)) + D(-S \& A),$$

if, and only if,

$$pr(S/A)(D(-S \& A) - D(S \& A)) - D(-S \& A)$$
$$> pr(S/-A)(D(-S \& -A) - D(S \& -A)) - D(-S \& -A).$$

It is easy to see that this last relationship holds if S sufficiently swamps A, S is bad enough compared to $-S$, and the difference between $pr(S/A)$ and $pr(S/-A)$ is great enough. In that case, S is the common cause and A is the symptomatic act in a two-state, two-act Newcomb situation.

Although *PDOM* gives the right answers in Newcomb problems, we cannot simply give up *PMCEU* in favor of *PDOM* because, as pointed out earlier, *PDOM*, unlike *PMCEU*, is not broadly applicable. This raises the following problem of the form of a dilemma. *Either* try to devise a new decision rule that has all of the advantages of *PMCEU*, such as its broad applicability, *or* try to show that the *prima facie* counterexamples to *PMCEU* are in fact not genuine. In the next section, I describe two approaches of the first kind, and in the section after that, I will take the second approach.

3. Skyrms and Gibbard-Harper offer different solutions to the problem. Both accounts agree that Newcomb situations are genuine counterexamples to *PMCEU*. And both solutions recommend the maximization of a different kind of expectation. I shall first present the solutions and then briefly consider their merits.

Skyrms suggests that in a decision situation some factors are "outside the influence of our action." For example, in the cholesterol case, whether the agent has the atherosclerosis lesion is a factor that is outside the influence of his available acts. Skyrms suggests (1980b, p. 133) the following:

Let K_i s be maximally specific specifications of the factors outside our influence at the time of decision which are casually relevant to the outcome of our action, and let C_j s be specifications of factors which may be influenced by our actions. Then I suggest that we should maximize the K-expectation:

$$U_K(A) = \sum_i pr(K_i) \sum_j pr(C_j \text{ given } K_i \& A) \text{ Utility} (C_j \& K_i \& A)$$
$$= \sum_{i,j} pr(K_i) pr(C_j \text{ given } K_i \& A) \text{ Utility} (C_j \& K_i \& A)$$

For the cholesterol case, where L and T are the factors outside the influence of the agent's actions, we have

$$U_K(I) = pr(L \& T)D(L \& T \& I) + pr(L \& -T)D(L \& -T \& I)$$
$$\quad + pr(-L \& T)D(-L \& T \& I) + pr(-L \& -T)D(-L \& -T \& I),$$
and
$$U_K(-I) = pr(L \& T)D(L \& T \& -I) + pr(L \& -T)D(L \& -T \& -I)$$
$$\quad + pr(-L \& T)D(-L \& T \& -I) + pr(-L \& -T)D(-L \&$$
$$\quad -T \& -I).$$

Clearly, having the eggs benedict maximizes K-expectation, since I dominates $-I$. And in the charisma case, where C and R are outside the influence of the available acts and $-J$ dominates J in Solomon's preferences, it is easy to check that maximizing K-expectation agrees with our intuitions — and with *PDOM* — that Solomon should send for the woman.

Of course, K-expectation has to get more complicated than characterized above, for in some decision situations an agent may not know which factors are outside his influence. To handle this, Skyrms says that we should construct hypotheses about what is outside our influence whose truth values are also outside our influence. The suggestion is to get a set of mutually exclusive and collectively exhaustive hypotheses H_n such that according to H_n, K_{ni}'s are maximally specific and collectively exhaustive factors that are outside the agent's influence and C_{nj}'s are mutually exclusive and collectively exhaustive factors that are within the agent's influence. Then the K expectation of act A is:

$$\sum_{nij} pr(H_n \& K_{ni}) pr(C_{nj}/H_n \& K_{ni} \& A) D(C_{nj} \& H_n \& K_{ni} \& A).$$

I shall call Skyrms's rule, the rule that says that one should choose an act that has the greatest K-expectation, the *Principle of Maximizing K-Expectation* (hereafter, *PMKE*).

The solution proposed by Gibbard and Harper (1978) is based on using probabilities of counterfactual (or subjunctive) conditionals in the evaluation of expected utility instead of conditional probabilities. Where $A \mathbin{\square\!\!\rightarrow} C$ symbolizes the counterfactual conditional "If A were, then C would be" and $O_1, \ldots, O_m$ is a set of mutually exclusive and collectively exhaustive outcomes containing the possible outcomes of the act A, the U-expectation of A, $U(A)$, is given by:

$$U(A) = \sum_j pr(A \mathbin{\square\!\!\rightarrow} O_j) D(O_j).$$

I shall call the Gibbard-Harper rule, the rule that says that one should choose an act that has the greatest U-expectation, the *Principle of Maximizing U-Expectation* (hereafter, *PMUE*).

In the charisma case, the U-expectations are as follows:

$$U(J) = pr(J \mathbin{\square\!\!\rightarrow} R) D(J \,\&\, R) + pr(J \mathbin{\square\!\!\rightarrow} -R) D(J \,\&\, -R),$$
$$U(-J) = pr(-J \mathbin{\square\!\!\rightarrow} R) D(-J \,\&\, R) + pr(-J \mathbin{\square\!\!\rightarrow} -R) D(-J \,\&\, -R).$$

(The outcomes can be thought of as really of the form $(A \,\&\, O_j)$, and we can assume that $pr(A \mathbin{\square\!\!\rightarrow} (A \,\&\, O_j)) = pr(A \mathbin{\square\!\!\rightarrow} O_j)$.) Since unjust acts do not in any way tend to bring about revolts, $-J$'s holding would not tend to bring about R. Thus $pr(-J \mathbin{\square\!\!\rightarrow} R) = pr(R)$.[5] Similarly, $pr(J \mathbin{\square\!\!\rightarrow} R) = pr(R)$ and $pr(-J \mathbin{\square\!\!\rightarrow} -R) = pr(J \mathbin{\square\!\!\rightarrow} -R) = pr(-R)$. So,

$$U(J) = pr(R) D(J \,\&\, R) + pr(-R) D(J \,\&\, -R),$$
$$U(-J) = pr(R) D(-J \,\&\, R) + pr(-R) D(-J \,\&\, -R).$$

Since $D(-J \,\&\, R) > D(J \,\&\, R)$ and $D(-J \,\&\, -R) > D(J \,\&\, -R)$, $U(-J) > U(J)$, agreeing with the recommendations of *PMKE, PDOM* and our intuitions.

Note that if we blur the distinction between outcomes and states, the K-expectation and the U-expectation of an act can be seen to be equal, at least for the simple examples of Newcomb situations presented above. That is, if we set

$$U(A) = \sum_{i,j} pr(A \mathbin{\square\!\!\rightarrow} (S_i \,\&\, O_j)) D(A \,\&\, S_i \,\&\, O_j),$$

then the K- and U-expectations of acts considered in the two main examples of section 2 are equal. For instance, in the cholesterol case,

$$
\begin{aligned}
U(I) &= pr(I \mathbin{\square\!\!\rightarrow} (L \,\&\, T)) D(L \,\&\, T \,\&\, I) \\
&\quad + pr(I \mathbin{\square\!\!\rightarrow} (L \,\&\, -T)) D(L \,\&\, -T \,\&\, I) \\
&\quad + pr(I \mathbin{\square\!\!\rightarrow} (-L \,\&\, T)) D(-L \,\&\, T \,\&\, I) \\
&\quad + pr(I \mathbin{\square\!\!\rightarrow} (-L \,\&\, -T)) D(-L \,\&\, -T \,\&\, I) \\
&= pr(L \,\&\, T) D(L \,\&\, T \,\&\, I) + pr(L \,\&\, -T) D(L \,\&\, -T \,\&\, I) \\
&\quad + pr(-L \,\&\, T) D(-L \,\&\, T \,\&\, I) + pr(-L \,\&\, -T) D(-L \,\&\, -T \,\&\, I),
\end{aligned}
$$

and similarly for $U(-I)$.

It is clear that both *PMUE* and *PMKE* give the right recommendations in the Newcomb problems discussed. Their success in this is owing to the fact that these rules are sensitive to some causal aspects of such decision problems in a way in which it appears that *PMCEU* is not.

The Gibbard-Harper rule assimilates such causal information through the use of probabilities of counterfactual conditionals rather than conditional probabilities in the evaluation of expected utility. As Jeffrey (1981a) and Skyrms (1980b, p. 132, n.) point out, the counterfactuals used in evaluating *U*-expectation must be given a "nonbacktracking" interpretation. That is, an appropriate interpretation must disallow the following kind of reasoning: it is highly probable that if Solomon were to send for the woman, he would be the kind of person who would, that is, uncharismatic and thus revolt-prone; it is less probable that he would be the kind of person who would send for her, that is, uncharismatic and thus revolt-prone, if he were to abstain from her; therefore, $pr(-J \boxright R) > pr(J \boxright R)$. The interpretation must be such that if an act A has no causal efficacy in producing either the state S or the state $-S$, then $pr(A \boxright S)$ must equal $pr(-A \boxright S)$. It is their nonbacktracking interpretation that makes *U*-expectation sensitive to the relevant causal information that the agent has in Newcomb problems.

While it is easy to express what is required of an interpretation of counterfactuals for it to be appropriate for Gibbard and Harper's purpose, it is quite a different problem to construct a plausible theory of counterfactuals that has the desired nonbacktracking effect. Gibbard and Harper state that they do not appeal to any theory of counterfactuals, but rather to their readers' intuitions. However, it is not clear that this is satisfactory for, in the first place, our intuitions are weak here (at least mine are), and, in the second place, our intuitions must be constrained to be consistent with the desired nonbacktracking effect, which may be highly unintuitive in some cases. I think this point can be borne out by looking at the sketch of a Stalnaker-like theory of counterfactuals that Gibbard and Harper give to guide our intuitions. However, I shall not do that here.[6] I just want to point out that it is not clear that an adequate theory of counterfactuals that is appropriate for Gibbard and Harper's approach can be constructed and that without such a theory it is not clear that, for some decision problems, our intuitions would not need to be *strained* for their analysis to work. And even if such a theory could be constructed, we must still allow for the possibility of others. As Skyrms points out, "the latitude for interpretation that subjunctives allow makes this a kind of minimal theory, to the effect that there is a way of resolving the ambiguity of the subjunctive that gives the right answer" (1980b, p. 132).

As to *K*-expectation, I have argued elsewhere[7] that *PMKE* will always give the right recommendation if the K_i's and C_j's satisfy the appropriateness conditions (or, where *K*-expectation involves the hypotheses H_n, if each

H_n implies that the K_{ni}'s and C_{nj}'s satisfy the appropriateness conditions):

(10)   while the available acts may be within the influence of the K_i's, the K_i's are not within the influence of the acts (all according to the agent's beliefs);

(11)   while the C_j's may be within the influence of the available acts, the acts are not within the influence of the C_j's once some K_i is fixed (all according to the agent's beliefs);

and

(12)   the acts are not within the influence of any cause of any C_j once some K_i is fixed (according to the agent's beliefs).

But the problem is this: given that the agent knows the causal structure of the decision problem in which he finds himself, or that he has a number of hypotheses as to what that causal structure is, how is he to *find* partitions that satisfy the appropriateness conditions? It is not clear that this will not sometimes be an enormously difficult task, requiring a special kind of creativity or imagination or skill that not all rational decision-makers can be expected to have. For example, the agent cannot always just take what he initially, naively considered to be all the decision-relevant propositions and construct appropriate partitions from them using the Boolean operations. It should be noted in addition that we have, as yet, no theoretical guarantee that appropriate partitions will always even exist. Indeed, consider this example of David Lewis's:

> Consider an agent with eccentric beliefs. He thinks the influence of his actions ramifies but also fades, so that everything in the far future is within his influence but only a little bit. Perhaps he thinks that his actions raise and lower the chances of future occurrences, but only very slightly. Also, he thinks that time is circular, so that the far future includes the present and the immediate past and indeed all of history.[8]

Suppose, for instance, that the man in the cholesterol case is thoroughly convinced that his act has some very slight influence over whether he currently has the lesion. What would be an appropriate choice of partitions for this situation?

These considerations indicate several advantages that a successful *CEU* approach would have over the approaches of Skyrms and of Gibbard and Harper. First, a *CEU* approach would have the advantage over Skyrms's approach that the *CEU* of an act does not vary according to how the space of probabilities is partitioned. On Skyrms's approach, one must find appropriate partitions, since the K-expectation of an act varies according to which partitions are taken as the K_i's and C_j's. If Jeffrey's axioms are correct, then $CEU(A)$ is equal to $D(A)$, the agent's true desirability of the act

A, so that it does not matter what partition of states and outcomes the agent calculates $CEU(A)$ relative to.

Second, both Skyrms's and Gibbard and Harper's approach introduce into decision theory certain concepts, absent in a *CEU* approach, that are controversial and not very well understood. On a *CEU* approach, we have only the logical connectives, addition and multiplication, the decision-relevant propositions, and the ideas of subjective probability (*pr*) and desirability (*D*). On the Gibbard-Harper approach, we have all this plus the connective $\square\!\!\rightarrow$, connecting acts and outcomes. And if Skyrms's hypotheses H_n are taken to assert of partitions of K_i's and C_j's that they satisfy the appropriateness conditions laid down above, then, on his approach, we have all the primitives of a *CEU* approach plus the connective "is within the causal influence of." In view of the controversial nature of our understanding of counterfactual conditionals and of causality, these observations would seem to indicate important advantages which a *CEU* approach to Newcomb problems would have over the approaches considered in this section.

Third, we have nothing like a theoretical guarantee that *PMKE* or *PMUE* is broadly applicable. For *PMCEU,* however, there exist numerous proven relations between calculations of expected utility and very intuitive, empirically testable theories of qualitative preference. My purpose here is not to discuss these theorems in detail—see Bolker (1967), Jeffrey (1977), and Domotor (1978)—but just to point out that the axioms of the relevant theories of preference are very compelling, which gives some evidence that *PMCEU* is broadly applicable, and if not broadly applicable, then at least empirically testable. The connection between *PMCEU* and the various attractive axiomatizations of qualitative preference provides further incentive to consider carefully whether the counterexamples are genuine.[9]

Indeed, there are several intuitive reasons for doubting that the counterexamples are genuine. First, it is a fundamental tenet of Bayesianism—accepted by the authors of the *prima facie* counterexamples to *PMCEU*—that conditionalization models learning, that is, that the way in which rational people revise their degrees of belief on learning some proposition to be true is by adopting the probability assignment that is gotten from their prior assignment by conditionalization on the proposition learned. But the truth of this tenet together with the assumption that is essential to the counterexamples—namely, that $pr(CC/SA) > pr(CC/-SA)$, so that $pr(SO/SA) > pr(SO/-SA)$, has some rather peculiar consequences. Consider the charisma case. If conditionalization models learning and if—as is essential to the counterexamples—the probability of Solomon's having charisma, and thus of having a revolt-free reign is greater conditional on his abstaining from the woman than on sending for her, then, if Solomon abstains, we would expect Solomon's degrees of belief in the propositions that he has charisma and that he will have a revolt-free reign to increase. But, since Solomon knows that what he will do will have no effect on whether or not he has charisma and whether or not he will have a revolt-free reign, it seems that his probabilities would not change in this way, if he is rational. If this is unconvincing, consider another Newcomb problem offered by Gibbard and Harper (precisely analogous with respect to the agent's desirabilities and the causal facts to the other Newcomb situations discussed):

> the case of Robert Jones, rising young executive of International Energy Conglomerate Incorporated. Jones and several other young executives have been competing for a very lucrative promotion. The company brass found the candidates so evenly matched that they employed a psychologist to break the tie by testing for personality qualities that lead to long run successful performance in the corporate world. The test was administered to the candidates on Thursday. The promotion decision is made on the basis of the test and will be announced on Monday. It is now Friday. Jones learns, through a reliable company grapevine, that all the candidates have scored equally well on all factors except ruthlessness and that the promotion will go to whichever of them has scored highest on this factor, but he cannot find out which of them this is.
>
> On Friday afternoon Jones is faced with a new problem. He must decide whether or not to fire poor old John Smith, who failed to meet his sales quota this month because of the death of his wife. Jones believes that Smith will come up to snuff after he gets over his loss provided that he is treated leniently and that he can convince the company brass that leniency to Smith will benefit the company.... Unfortunately, Jones has no way to get in touch with them until after they announce the promotion on Monday.
>
> Jones knows that the ruthlessness factor of the personality test he has taken accurately predicts his behavior in just the sort of situation ·he now faces. (1978, pp. 142–43 in this volume)

In this example, *PMCEU* allegedly prescribes firing Smith, but *PMUE* prescribes leniency. Here, the probability of Jones's being ruthless and thus of having scored high at ruthlessness and thus of getting the promotion is supposed to be higher conditional on firing Smith than on being lenient. But again, if conditionalization models learning, then it would seem that Jones could make himself more and more confident about his promotion prospects by firing Smith and, presumably, by engaging in other ruthless activities (such as kicking his cat and firing his maid) between Friday and Monday. But again, since Jones knows that such activities do not affect his chances for promotion, it seems irrational for his degrees of belief to change in this way.

Second, there are some not obviously unreasonable ways in which an agent could figure his probabilities such that the condition essential to the counterexamples — that is, $pr(SO/SA) > pr(SO/-SA)$ — must fail. Take the charisma case again for example. One way in which Solomon might go about evaluating $pr(R/J)$ and $pr(R/-J)$ is by equating them with something like hypothetical relative frequencies. Solomon imagines two long sequences of decision situations that he finds himself in — that he actually might find himself in in the future — that are identical to the one he now finds himself in in all respects that he considers relevant to rational decision-making. In the situations of sequence 1, of length u, Solomon does not send for the woman. In the situations of sequence 2, of length v, Solomon sends for her. Let u' (v') be the number of situations in sequence 1 (2) in which Solomon imagines that a revolt ensues. Solomon sets $pr(R/J)$ equal to u'/u and $pr(R/-J)$ equal to v'/v. Because of the causal information that Solomon has (uncharisma, not unjust acts, causes revolts and Solomon has either charisma eternally or uncharisma eternally), it seems clear that $pr(R/J)$ should equal $pr(R/-J)$. As another possibility, Solomon bases his probabilities on imagined proportions taken from a hypothetical group of kings who are exactly like him in all ways up to the time of decision.

Finally, it seems that on any plausible account of how a common cause can cause a rationally acting person to perform an act, the common cause could only cause the act indirectly: by causing the person to have *reasons* for performing the act. But this suggests that it is not the performing of the act that should be taken as evidence for the presence of the common cause, but rather the nature of the reasons the agent has for performing it, where, given the presence of those reasons, the act itself is evidentially irrelevant. It seems to me that any approach to the *prima facie* counterexamples that does not deal directly with the nature of the causal relation between the common cause and the symptomatic act in Newcomb problems cannot really go to the heart of the matter. In the next section, I will follow up this idea and its implications for a possible *CEU* resolution of the matter.

4. It is essential to the counterexamples that the agent's subjective probabilities be such that[10]

(13) $pr(CC/SA) > pr(CC/-SA)$.

Then, either CC can be thought of as carrying the bad news, or, from (13), it can be argued that $pr(SO/SA)$ must be greater than $pr(SO/-SA)$. (13) is equivalent to

(14) $pr(SA/CC) > pr(SA/-CC)$.

Is it plausible that our rational agent's beliefs be such that they are accurately characterized by (13) and (14)? Now the agent does not know whether or not he has the common cause. Let us assume that the agent knows that he does not know whether or not he has the common cause and that he believes that he is rational. And let us abbreviate the expression "rational people who do not know whether or not they have the common cause" by "agent-like people." Then it is relevant to ask: Is it plausible that (13) and (14) characterize the agent's beliefs about the behavior of agent-like people?[11]

One thing that might make us think that this *is* plausible is that the agent, of course, thinks that the common cause causes the symptomatic act. It is natural to think that an event is more probable given that a cause of it obtains than given that the cause does not obtain. Thus, the fact that our rational agent believes that the common cause causes agent-like people to perform the symptomatic act would seem to make it plausible that he would (rationally) believe that agent-like people behave in such a way that the probability of their performing the symptomatic act is higher given that they have the common cause than given that they do not.

On the other hand, it is natural to think that a rational person's act (the rational act, let us assume) is determined by the body of information the person has at hand (by his subjective beliefs and desires) and not, beyond this, by what in fact is the case. An act is rational relative to a possessed body of information; the quality of the information and the actual facts are both irrelevant.[12] Let us assume that our agent believes this. The fact that he believes *this* would seem — at least initially — to make it implausible that (13) and (14) characterize his (rational) beliefs about the behavior of agent-like people. The difference between having and not having the common cause is a difference between one thing's being the case and another thing's being the case: it is not itself a difference between one body of information and another. So how could the agent rationally believe that agent-like people with the common cause are more likely to perform the symptomatic act than agent-like people without the common cause when they are all alike with respect to knowledge about whether the common cause, in each his own case, obtains?

It is, of course, very easy to reconcile the natural view, sketched above, about rational behavior and the rationality of acts with the belief that agent-like people behave in such a way that the symptomatic act is more probable given that the common cause obtains than given that the common cause does not obtain. And the obvious and natural way to make this reconciliation is to point out that while the difference between the common cause's obtaining and its not obtaining is not *itself* a difference between two bodies of information, still such a difference can *account* for a difference in bodies of information. I propose that the only way in which a common cause can cause an agent-like person to perform the symptomatic act is by appropriately affecting his body of possessed information. I shall assume that the way in which a common cause causes a rational person to perform a symptomatic act is by causing him to have such beliefs and desires that a rational evaluation of the available acts in light of these beliefs and desires leads to the conclusion that the symptomatic act is the best act. And I shall assume that our agent believes this hypothesis about how the common cause causes the symptomatic act.

According to this hypothesis, the causal structure of Newcomb problems is more complex than indicated earlier. The causal structure can be represented in more detail by the following diagram:

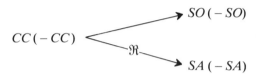

Here, interpret $\Re$ as the set of propositions describing the possible sets of beliefs and desires a person might have in the relevant decision situation (more on such propositions later). Then the lower chain is to be interpreted as meaning that $CC(-CC)$ causes $SA(-SA)$ indirectly, by affecting which element of $\Re$ is true: $CC(-CC)$ causes some element of $\Re$, which, in turn, causes $SA(-SA)$.

The plausibility of this hypothesis — and thus of our agent's subscribing to it — would seem, if anything, to reinforce the plausibility of his beliefs being accurately characterized by (13) and (14). However, (13) and (14) are ambiguous (which I have been deliberately ignoring up until now). There are two possible readings of (13) and (14). Under one reading, (13) and (14) characterize beliefs, the agent's possession of which is very plausible. And, indeed, the plausibility of the agent's possessing these beliefs might reasonably be thought to be reinforced by the plausibility of his subscribing to our hypothesis about how the common cause causes the symptomatic act. But, as we shall see, it is inappropriate to draw conclusions about which act maximizes *CEU* from (13) and (14) taken as characterizations of these beliefs. On the other hand, it would be appropriate to draw conclusions about which act maximizes *CEU* from (13) and (14) if the agent had the beliefs characterized by (13) and (14) under the alternative reading. But we shall see that the assumption that he has *these* beliefs is very implausible given my assumption about how he believes the common cause causes the symptomatic act.

The two readings of (13) and (14) that I have in mind are as follows. Let us concentrate first on (13). According to one reading, (13) characterizes a belief that is roughly equivalent to, or closely approximated by, the belief that

$$\#(w : CC(w) \ \& \ SA(w)) \ / \ \#(w : SA(w) >$$
$$\#(w : CC(w) \ \& \ -SA(w)) \ / \ \#(w : -SA(w)),$$

where "#" indicates cardinality, "w" ranges over all agent-like people — or perhaps just those in some set of agent-like people that the agent thinks is representative of the incidence of the common cause and the symptomatic act — and $CC(w)$ and $SA(w)$ are propositions that say that w has the common cause and w does the symptomatic act, respectively. I shall say that under this reading of (13), (13) characterizes a *type-A* belief. Thus, the type-*A* belief that (13) characterizes is the belief that the common cause occurs with greater frequency among people who do the symptomatic act than among those who do not. Similarly, the type-*A* belief that (14) characterizes is the belief that the symptomatic act is more common among those who have the common cause than among those who do not have it. Henceforth, a characterization of a type-*A* belief will be intended if the relevant symbols in a probabilistic statement are followed by "(a)":

(13′) $pr(CC(a)/SA(a)) > pr(CC(a)/ - SA(a))$,

(14′) $pr(SA(a)/CC(a)) > pr(SA(a)/ - CC(a))$.

It will be convenient to associate propositions with symbols like "$CC(a)$" and "$SA(a)$" so that there will be no difficulty of interpretation when such a symbol occurs in a probability statement along with symbols that stand for propositions. "$CC(a)$" and "$SA(a)$" can be thought of as symbolizing the propositions "If I were to randomly select a rational person a right now, a would have the common cause" and "If I were to randomly select a rational person a right now, a would be a doer of the symptomatic act," respectively. Of course, "a" is to be thought of as denoting the same rational person in each of the above propositions, as "right now" is to be thought of as referring to the same time in each of the above propositions. A more elegant method might be to interpret "$CC(a)$" and "$SA(a)$" simply as "a has the common cause" and "a does the symptomatic act," respectively, and think of all probabilities as conditional on the proposition "a is a randomly selected rational person."[13]

According to the other reading of (13), (13) characterizes a belief that is also characterizable as

(13″) $pr(CC(DM)/SA(DM)) > pr(CC(DM)/ - SA(DM))$,

where $CC(DM)$ and $SA(DM)$ are the propositions to the effect that *DM*, our decision-maker, has the common cause and does the symptomatic act, respectively. I shall say that under this reading of (13), (13) characterizes a *type-B* belief. A characterization of a type-*B* belief of our agent will be intended if the relevant symbols in a probability statement are followed by "(DM)," as in (13″) and

(14″) $pr(SA(DM)/CC(DM)) > pr(SA(DM)/ - CC(DM))$.

The distinction between type-*A* and type-*B* beliefs will become clearer as the discussion unfolds.

I will argue that the assumption that the agent believes my hypothesis about how the common cause causes the symptomatic act makes it plausible that he has the type-*A* beliefs that (13′) and (14′) characterize, but makes it implausible that he has the type-*B* beliefs characterized by (13″) and (14″) and, in fact, makes it very plausible that he has the following (equivalent) type-*B* beliefs:

(15) $pr(CC(DM)/SA(DM)) = pr(CC(DM)/-SA(DM))$,

(16) $pr(SA(DM)/CC(DM)) = pr(SA(DM)/-CC(DM))$.

As argued below, it is clear that agents' type-*B* beliefs, and not their type-*A* beliefs, should figure in calculations of expected utility. Also, it is obvious that (15) and (16) (each) imply that, for simple two-state ($CC(DM)$ and $-CC(DM)$), two-act ($SA(DM)$ and $-SA(DM)$) Newcomb problems such as those discussed in the last section, *CEU* will agree with *K*-expectation and *U*-expectation and thus also *PDOM,* for (15) implies that the probabilities of the two states conditional on the act are equal to their unconditional probabilities, which are equal to the values used in the formulas for *K*- and *U*-expectation.[14]

It is easy to see why the assumption that the agent believes my hypothesis about how a common cause can cause a symptomatic act makes it plausible that he has the type-*A* beliefs characterized by (13′) and (14′). The agent believes that *CC* causes beliefs and desires that rationally lead to act *SA*. So, such beliefs and desires, our agent should reason, are more likely to be possessed by an arbitrary rational agent, *a,* on the assumption that $CC(a)$ than they are on the assumption that $-CC(a)$. And if a person *a* is more likely to have beliefs and desires that lead rationally to $SA(a)$ given that $CC(a)$ is the case than given that $-CC(a)$ is the case, then it should be more likely that a person *a* will *do* $SA(a)$ given that $CC(a)$ is the case than it is given that $-CC(a)$ is the case. And that is just what (14′), which is equivalent to (13′), states.[15]

So, it is plausible that our agent, *DM,* has the type-*A* beliefs characterized by (13′) and (14′). This, however, clearly does not justify using (13) and (14) to draw conclusions about which act, $SA(DM)$ or $-SA(DM)$, maximizes *DM*'s *CEU,* for a type-*A* belief is about the behavior of a group of people, not of our agent. But what is relevant to our agent in his deliberation is the probability of *his* having the common cause conditional on *his* performing (or not performing) the symptomatic act, and not the frequency with which the common cause is present among people who perform (or do not) the symptomatic act. And these two values may be different, for, as we shall see, the agent may know things about himself — in particular about why he would perform the symptomatic act if he would — that have implications for the first value but not the second.

The argument that our rational agent should have the type-*B* beliefs characterized by (15) and (16), rather than the type-*B* beliefs characterized by (13″) and (14″), will involve a number of assumptions that are idealizations, but not unreasonable ones, I believe. Indeed, I shall argue that the assumptions I shall make are little, if any, more idealistic than those commonly made in current Bayesian decision theories. Also, several of them can be considerably weakened, as will be noted in what follows.

The first assumption is, basically, that the agent knows what his beliefs and desires are. Let ϕ be the set of propositions that *DM* explicitly considers in his decision problem. In the cholesterol case, for example, this set may include some or all of the following: I, L, "L is outside the influence of I," $I \square\!\!\rightarrow L$. Now *DM* has degrees of belief over the members of ϕ. Let $R\phi(DM)$ be the (true) proposition that says what these subjective probabilities and desirabilities are at the time of decision. I assume that, near the time of decision,

(17) $pr(R\phi(DM)) = 1$.

At least if decision theory is to be prescriptive, this assumption should be unobjectionable. For, if an agent is to be able to *apply any* of the competing decision theories, he must, at some time before the decision takes place, know what the relevant probabilities and desirabilities are — without them, he cannot calculate the relevant kind of expectation.[16]

Let "$B_{SA}(DM)$" ("$B_{-SA}(DM)$") stand for the proposition that *DM* will (rationally) determine the $SA(DM)$ ($-SA(DM)$) is the correct act. I assume that *DM* will determine that one of the two acts is the correct one and that he fully believes this, so that $B_{-SA}(DM)$ should be thought of as equivalent to $-B_{SA}(DM)$. My second assumption is:

(18) $pr(B_{SA}(DM) \leftrightarrow SA(DM)) = 1$.

That is, the agent is certain that: he will perform $SA(DM)$ ($-SA(DM)$) if, and only if, he determines that $SA(DM)$ ($-SA(DM)$) is the correct act. This assumption seems reasonable as an idealization.[17] One may object, however, that (18) assumes that *DM* believes he has no "weakness of will"[18] and that it is very unrealistic of us to assume that our rational agent is so unrealistic about himself. But it seems that if the agent believed that he has or might have weakness of will, then whatever utility he may attach to giving in to it should enter into his deliberation about which is best for him in light of that. If so, then it seems that (18) can accurately characterize his beliefs even if he acknowledges weakness of will.

Given (18), if the common cause is to cause an act, then it must affect at least some aspects of people's deliberation as to which act is best. But my last assumption is:

(19) $pr(B_{sA}(DM)/R\phi(DM)$ & $CC(DM))$
$= pr(B_{sA}(DM)/R\phi(DM)$ & $-CC(DM))$.

Why is this a reasonable assumption? According to Bayesian decision theories, the act that a rational person determines is best turns on just three things: his subjective probabilities, his desirabilities over the maximally specific propositions he explicitly considers in his deliberation, and a decision rule. So if CC is to affect our rational agent's determination of which act is best, it must affect at least some of these three things that the determination turns on. Let us assume that our agent, knowing some decision theory, believes this. Now, which of these three things can our agent believe the common cause can affect in him, *consistently with his belief that he is rational?* Clearly, the common cause could affect (or have affected) the agent's *desirabilities* without affecting his rational capacity, for these are more a matter of taste than of rationality — on the Bayesian view of rationality. And it would not be unreasonable to suppose that the common cause could, to some extent, affect the agent's *probabilities* without affecting his rational capacity. According to the subjective interpretation of probability, two rational people with the same information can disagree in their probability assessments, and perhaps the presence or absence of factors like our common cause could account for this in some cases.

But can the presence or absence of the common cause make a difference in the agent's *choice of decision rule* without affecting his rational capacity? Unlike one's subjective probabilities and desirabilities, it seems that the correctness of a decision rule is not a subjective matter. Indeed, this is presupposed in all decision theories that endorse decision rules that take as input an agent's probabilities and desirabilities and give as output the correct act: the rational act for a given agent is a *function* of his subjective probabilities and desirabilities. So at least the following is clear (or clearly presupposed by all Bayesian decision theories): given that an agent is rational and that he has some particular pair of probability and desirability assignments, whether a common cause is present or absent is irrelevant to which act is (rationally) determined by him to be the correct one. Of course, this is consistent with the common cause having an effect on which of a number of decision rules, each of which yields the same prescription, is used. But, while it is not essential to my argument, the assumption that an agent is rational should be enough to ensure that the presence or absence of a common cause will not affect which decision rule is used.[19]

Thus, the agent believes that the way the common cause causes the symptomatic act is by causing people to conclude that it is the rational act and that the way in which it does this is by affecting their probabilities or desirabilities (or both) in such a way that their decision rules (which the common cause plays no role in their choosing) yield the prescription of the symptomatic act. Note that since, in decision theory, subjective probabilities model beliefs and desirabilities model desires and decision rules model rational evaluation of alternatives in light of beliefs and desires, this is just a more formal decision-theoretic formulation of the hypothesis that I have already assumed that the agent believes: the common cause causes the symptomatic act by causing such beliefs and desires that a rational evaluation of the available acts in light of them leads to the conclusion that the symptomatic act is the correct act.

It follows from (18) and (19) that,

(20) $pr(SA\,(DM)/R\phi(DM)\ \&\ CC(DM))$
$= pr(SA\,(DM)/R\phi(DM)\ \&\ -CC(DM)).$

This reflects the idea that since probabilities, desirabilities, and decision rule determine the act and since the common cause does not affect the decision rule, the probability of the symptomatic act should be the same given the common cause as it is given its absence once particular probabilities and desirabilities are specified, as in $R\phi\,(DM)$. From (20) together with (17) it follows that,

(16) $pr(SA\,(DM)/CC(DM)) = pr(SA\,(DM)/-CC(DM))$
and
(15) $pr(CC(DM)/SA(DM)) = pr(CC(DM)/-SA\,(DM)).$

Thus, what is essential to the development of Newcomb problem counterexamples to *PMCEU*—that the agent should have the type-*B* beliefs that (13″) and (14″) characterize—is false. I would like to emphasize the generality of this argument: it applies to all Newcomb problems of the simple kind where the symptomatic act has no causal influence on the common cause, and establishes (15) and (16) for such problems and thus that *PMCEU* gives the right answers in such problems.[20]

As to "diagnosing" the *prima facie* conflict between *PMCEU* on the one hand and *PDOM* and the various causal decision theories on the other, I have the following suggestions. First, the appearance that Newcomb problems constitute counterexamples to *PMCEU* may have arisen from a *failure to distinguish* between type-*A* beliefs (such as those given by (13′) and (14′)) and type-*B beliefs* (such as those given by (13″) and (14″)). Second, it may have arisen from an *unwarranted inference* from the reasonableness of our agent's holding the type-*A* beliefs characterized by (13′) and (14′) to the reasonableness of his holding the type-*B* beliefs characterized by (13″) and (14″). And third, it may have arisen from an unwarranted inference from our holding certain type-*A* like beliefs *about DM,* thinking of him as an "arbitrary agent," to the reasonableness of his holding corresponding type-*B* beliefs about himself. That is, the fact that, for example, (15) and (16) might be false, and (13″) and (14″) true, if *"pr"* is interpreted as *our* subjective probability assignment does not imply that the same should hold when *"pr"* is interpreted, appropriately for analyzing *DM*'s deliberation, as *DM*'s subjective probability assignment.[21] *PMCEU* requires the use of all the relevant available information, and it appears that in some cases some of the information is not very easily accessible to persons other than the decision-maker.

5. In the decision problems considered so far, it is fairly uncontroversial that the appropriate act is the dominant (in the sense of *PDOM*) act; what is controversial is whether those decision problems constitute counterexamples to *PMCEU*. In Newcomb's Problem, however, it *is* somewhat controversial what the appropriate act is (hence the common reference to "Newcomb's *Paradox*"), as well as what the prescription of *PMCEU* is. I have elsewhere argued that, in Newcomb's Problem, the rational act is the dominant (two-box) act, and that *PMCEU,* properly applied, prescribes this act.[22] Here, I shall consider an argument recently advanced by Horgan (1981, reprinted in this volume) to the effect that the appropriate act is the *nondominant* (one-box) act.[23] I shall argue that Horgan fails to establish this and, this time in the framework of Horgan's analysis, that the rational act is the dominant act in Newcomb's Problem as well. (All page references from here on are to the printing of Horgan's article in this volume; I shall assume it is at the reader's hand, and that the reader is familiar with the Newcomb problem.)

Horgan's strategy is to consider a one-box argument and a two-box argument (pp. 160–61 in this volume) and to argue that when the counterfactuals involved in the arguments are appropriately construed, the one-box argument turns out to be valid and the two-box argument invalid.[24] The two competing construals of the counterfactuals involved are the "standard" and "backtracking" resolutions of the vagueness of the relevant counterfactuals (explained on pp. 161–63). Under the standard resolution of vagueness, the two-box argument Horgan considers is valid and the one-box argument is not; and under the backtracking resolution, the one-box argument he considers is valid and the two-box argument is not. Horgan argues that the backtracking resolution is the "pragmatically appropriate" resolution, that is, "the one to be used in making a practical inference." And his strategy is to "set forth what I take to be the most plausible meta-level argument available to each side, and ... show that the two-boxer's argument suffers from a kind of circularity that the one-boxer's lacks" (p. 165).

Following Horgan's notation, let A_1 and A_2 be the two-box and one-box act, respectively; let S_1 and S_2 be, respectively, the states of the $1 million's being present and absent in the second (opaque) box; and let w_1, w_2, w_3, and w_4 be, respectively, the closest $(A_1$ & $S_1)$-world, the closest $(A_2$ & $S_1)$-world, the closest $(A_1$ & $S_2)$-world, and the closest $(A_2$ & $S_2)$-world.

The meta-level two-box argument Horgan considers concludes that the standard resolution is the pragmatically appropriate resolution, from the premise:

(M_t): *Either* I would actualize w_1 if I chose both boxes and I would actualize w_2 if I chose box 2, *or* I would actualize w_3 if I chose both boxes and I would actualize w_4 if I chose box 2. (p. 166)

Given this premise, the argument goes, the standard resolution is correct because, under this resolution, the closest A_1- and A_2-worlds are the ones the agent would actualize, that is, render actual, by performing A_1 and A_2, respectively. But, Horgan claims, (M_t) "is *equivalent* to (6_t) (see p. 166), the crucial nonnormative contention of the original (object-level) two-box argument," so that the meta-level two-box argument provides no independent meta-level grounds for the appropriateness of the standard resolution.

The meta-level one-box argument Horgan considers concludes that the backtracking resolution is pragmatically appropriate, from the premise:

(M_o): I am virtually certain, independently of any belief I have as to the likelihood of my doing A_1 or the likelihood of my doing A_2, that either w_2 or w_3 will become actual. (p. 167)

The rationale for the premise is that the agent is supposed to be enormously confident in the Predictor's ability to predict the agent's action, and that in w_1 and in w_4, the Predictor errs. The argument, as I understand it, proceeds from (M_o) as follows: "The worlds w_1 and w_4 therefore ought to be regarded as essentially irrelevant, for purposes of practical decision making. Thus, the backtracking resolution is pragmatically appropriate, because, under this resolution, w_2 is the closest A_2-world and w_3 is the closest A_1-world" (p. 166).

Later I will argue that the two-box meta-level argument Horgan considers can be improved and made noncircular. But let us first examine this one-box meta-level argument.

First, it seems to me that M_o does not at all favor the backtracking resolution over the standard resolution. Indeed, it does not even imply that one should be *virtually certain* that w_2 is the closest A_2-world and that w_3 is the closest A_1-world. For the purposes of discussing Newcomb's Problem, the standard resolution can be characterized by the proposition that: *either* (a) w_1 is the closest A_1-world and w_2 is the closest A_2-world *or* (b) w_3 is the closest A_1-world and w_4 is the closest A_2-world, where (a) is the the case if, and only if, S_1 obtains and (b) is the case if, and only if, S_2 obtains. Suppose our agent, adopting the standard resolution as pragmatically appropriate, is certain or virtually certain of this proposition. Now if the agent's subjective probabilities are such that $pr(S_1/A_2)$ and $pr(S_2/A_1)$ are both very close to

1, as those who maintain that *PMCEU* prescribes the one-box act some-times maintain, then clearly the agent's probabilities will be such that $pr(w_1$ is the closest A_1-world & w_2 is the closest A_2-world/A_2) and $pr(w_3$ is the closest A_1-world & w_4 is the closest A_2-world/A_1) are both very close to one. This in turn implies that $pr(w_2$ will become actual/A_2) and $pr(w_3$ will become actual/A_1) are also very close to one. Thus, since the disjunc-tion of the two conditioning propositions in these two probabilities has probability one, the unconditional probability of the disjunction of the two conditioned propositions is very close to one, that is, the agent is virtually certain that one of w_2 and w_3 will become actual. And this reasoning is com-pletely independent of what the subjective probabilities of A_1 and of A_2 are — that is, of any beliefs the agent has about the likelihood of A_1 or of A_2.

Thus, (M_o) is true for this agent, who adopts the standard resolution. One who believes that the standard resolution is pragmatically appropriate need not be moved to reconsider by its being pointed out that (M_o) is true of him. One can be virtually certain (independently of one's beliefs about the likeli-hood of performing A_1 or of performing A_2) that one of w_2 and w_3 will turn out to be actual and at the same time reasonably adopt the standard resolu-tion of the relevant counterfactuals. Indeed, such a person need not even be virtually certain that w_2 is the closest A_2-world and that w_3 is the closest A_1-world — as long as the first is held to be virtually certain *given* A_2 (but not necessarily given A_1) and the second is held to be virtually certain *given* A_1 (but not necessarily given A_2). Thus, if one's subjective probabilities for A_1 and A_2 are intermediate (one is quite uncertain about what will be decid-ed), then one can assign an intermediate probability to the proposition that w_2 and w_3 are the closest A_2- and A_1-worlds, respectively, and still be quite certain that one of w_2 and w_3 will become actual.

I think this meta-level one-box argument goes wrong by incorporating the wrong independence clause in (M_o). One can be virtually certain that one of w_2 and w_3 will become actual independently of beliefs about the likelihoods of A_1 and A_2 even if one believes that (roughly) *were* one to do the act that one *will in fact not* do, one of w_1 and w_4 *would* become actual. Thus, we saw above that (M_o) was consistent with the agent's beliefs being such that, for example, $pr(w_1$ is the closest A_1-world & w_2 is the closest A_2-world / A_2) is very close to one, where this can hold for any value of the subjective probability of A_2. So, supposing that one does A_2, it will be w_2 that one is virtually certain will become actual, though in this case w_1 is virtually cer-tainly the closest A_1-world. For the meta-level one-box argument to have a chance at establishing its conclusion, the premise must assert that the agent is virtually certain that one of w_2 and w_3 will become actual independently of *which act will be performed* (rather than independently of one's *beliefs* about which act will be performed). Thus, let us rewrite (M_o) to reflect this change — and another. It seems that, strictly speaking, the premise should be about the relation between the acts and the worlds and not about the agent's beliefs regarding such relations. It will not follow that a certain world *is* the closest A_1- or A_2-world from the fact that the agent *believes* such and such about the acts and worlds. So let the premise state what the agent believes, rather than that he believes it, so that his virtual certainty about the premise is supposed to be transferred to belief in the pragmatic appropriateness of the backtracking resolution *via* the meta-level one-box argument:

(M'_o): Independently of which of A_1 and A_2 is performed (that is, no matter which is performed), either w_2 or w_3 will become actual.

But now that the premise of the meta-level one-box argument has been formulated in such a way as to tell the standard and backtracking resolutions apart, it turns out that the meta-level one-box argument suffers from the same sort of circularity that Horgan claims the meta-level two-box argument suffers from. Premise (M'_o) has two parts, as follows:

(i) one of w_2 and w_3 will become actual,

and

(ii) the fact that one of w_2 and w_3 will become actual is independent of which of A_1 and A_2 is performed.

A natural characterization of the relevant kind of independence would seem to be the following:

X is *independent* of *Y* if, and only if, the following are equivalent (that is, all true or all false): *X*, *Y* $\Box\!\!\rightarrow$ *X*, and $\sim$ *Y* $\Box\!\!\rightarrow$ *X*.

It is easy to see that for any propositions *X* and *Y*, *X*, together with *X*'s independence from *Y* (in the above sense of independence), is equivalent to: *Y* $\Box\!\!\rightarrow$ *X* and $\sim$ *Y* $\Box\!\!\rightarrow$ *X*. Thus, (M'_o) (that is, the conjunction of (i) and (ii)) is equivalent to:

I do A_1 $\Box\!\!\rightarrow$ one of w_2 and w_3 will become actual *and* I do A_2 $\Box\!\!\rightarrow$ one of w_2 and w_3 will become actual.

And it is easy to see that this is equivalent to:

I do A_1 $\Box\!\!\rightarrow$ w_3 will become actual *and* I do A_2 $\Box\!\!\rightarrow$ w_2 will become actual.

So, just as the premise of Horgan's version of the meta-level two-box argument was equivalent to (6_t) of his version of the object-level two-box argument, (M'_o) is equivalent to the conjunction of (3_o) and (6_o) of the object-level one-box argument (see p. 160). And just as (M_t) is true only under the standard resolution of $\Box\!\!\rightarrow$, so also (M'_o) is true only under the backtracking resolution. And no independent meta-level grounds have been given for the pragmatic appropriateness of the backtracking resolution. But it seems that the move from (M_o) to (M'_o) is just what is needed for the premise to tell the standard and backtracking resolutions apart. Perhaps one could avoid this circularity of the meta-level one-box argument if an appropriate sense of the relevant kind of independence can be characterized independently of counterfactuals, but I cannot see how this can be done.

I mentioned earlier that I would argue that the two-boxer's meta-level argument can be improved in such a way that it will not suffer from the circularity Horgan sees in the version he considers. First note that Horgan agrees with the two-boxer that which act I perform does not causally affect the contents of the second (opaque) box. His complaint is just that this fact does not *justify* the standard resolution as pragmatically appropriate: it only makes the relevant two-boxer's counterfactuals (in (M_i) and in (6_i)) *true under the standard resolution* (p. 166). Also, it seems that he does not wish to dispute the two-boxer's claim that "I should regard a possible world as the 'closest' A_i-world if and only if I would *actualize* it (that is, render it actual) by doing A_i." (p. 166). Rather, his complaint is that the truth of the two-boxer's counterfactual claims regarding *which* worlds would be actualized, were A_1 or A_2 performed, depends upon the standard resolution of those counterfactuals.

But it seems to me that Horgan has missed the casual spirit that a two-boxer *should* intend by the word "actualize" or the words "render it actual." Consider the (meta-linguistic) counterfactual schemes "If I were to do A, then w would become actual" and "If I were to do A, then I would actualize w (or render w actual, or *thereby cause w* to become actual)." It is possible for a counterfactual of the first form to be true and the corresponding one of the second form false, even if we apply the same resolution of vagueness in each case. What I have in mind is this: for a counterfactual of the second form to be true, the corresponding counterfactual of the first form must be true *and* all the differences between w and the actual world (if any) must be causally traceable to the occurrence of A in w.[25] Then, if we adopt a backtracking resolution of vagueness, yet give high priority to the avoidance of backwards causation, then it is clear, intuitively,[26] that a counterfactual of the first form can be true while the corresponding one of the second form is false. Just let A be A_1 and w be w_3, for example. Then if the one million dollars is *in fact* in the opaque box, w_3 nevertheless *does* become actual on the performance of A_1 (on the backtracking resolution) even though A_1 does not *cause* the difference between the actual world and w_3 consisting in the different contents of the opaque box (since we are giving very high priority to avoiding backwards causation).

Let us give a partial (and I think uncontroversial) resolution to the vagueness of counterfactuals — which I shall call "the *c*-resolution" — that (i) incorporates the intuition that I should regard a possible world as the closest A_i-world only if I would actualize it (in the causal sense) by doing A_i and (ii) is neutral between the standard and the backtracking resolution of vagueness (that is, there will be remaining vagueness that may be resolved either way). Let us give the following factor the highest priority in judging the relative closeness of various A_i-worlds to the actual world: all the differences between a close A_i-world and the actual world (if any) must be causal results of the occurrence of A_i in the A_i-world. Giving this factor top priority is not as stringent as may at first appear, for some worlds may have quite different causal laws from those of the actual world. And giving this factor highest priority is neutral between the standard and the backtracking resolution of vagueness, for it does not *itself* rule out the possibility that some relatively close worlds will exhibit *backwards* causation.

Now consider this version of premise (6_t) of the object-level two-box argument (or call it a version of (M_t) if you like), where the subscript "*c*" in "$\Box\!\!\rightarrow_c$" indicates that any resolution of the (remaining) vagueness of the counterfactuals must be consistent with the *c*-resolution:

(M_t^*): $((A_1 \Box\!\!\rightarrow_c S_1)\&(A_2 \Box\!\!\rightarrow_c S_1) \text{ v } (A_1 \Box\!\!\rightarrow_c S_2)\&(A_2 \Box\!\!\rightarrow_c S_2))$.

Clearly (M_t^*) is true under the standard resolution of the remaining vagueness. Indeed, it is true on any resolution of the remaining vagueness that gives high enough priority to the acts' not influencing the contents of the opaque box. So, (M_t^*) will be true on any resolution of the remaining vagueness that gives high enough priority to the avoidance of backwards causation. Thus, (6_t) will be true on any resolution of the vagueness of the counterfactuals involved on which (i) high priority is given to the idea that differences (if any) between close A_i-worlds and the actual world are causal results of A_i and (ii) high priority is given to the avoidance of backwards causation.

As to backwards causation, Horgan states: "I do recommend acting as if one's present choice could influence the being's prior prediction, but my argument does not presuppose backward causation" (pp. 167–68). But the only way (M_t^*) could be false under a backtracking resolution (or any other resolution) is if some close worlds have backwards causation, that is, if we give low enough priority to avoiding backwards causation. Also, given high priority for the avoidance of backwards causation, I cannot see how the first part of Horgan's statement can be reconciled with the seemingly un-disputed claim that I should regard a possible world as the closest A_i-world only if performing A_i would actualize it (in the causal sense of "actualize").

At the meta-level, the two-boxer should take seriously the premise:

(M_t^{**}): For $i = 1,2$, the only differences between the actual world and the closest A_i-world (if there are any differences) are with respect to features of the A_i-world which A_i is, at least in part, causally responsible for; and performing A_i cannot causally affect the past.

It is (M_t^{**}), and not (M_t), which should be utilized as the crucial premise of the meta-level two-box argument. And clearly, (M_t^{**}) implies that if the one million dollars is in the second (opaque) box, then w_1 is the closest A_1-world and w_2 is the closest A_2-world; and it implies that if the \$1 million is not there, then w_3 is the closest A_1-world and w_4 is the closest A_2-world. And since the standard resolution agrees with these implications of the highly pragmatically relevant premise (M_t**), and the backtracking resolution does not, the standard resolution is the pragmatically appropriate resolution, the meta-level two-box argument concludes. Note that this meta-level two-box argument is *noncircular,* as the crucial premise (M_t**) contains no counterfactuals and makes use of no concepts that cannot be characterized without appeal to counterfactuals standardly resolved.[27] Also, (M_t**) constitutes *independent* meta-level grounds for the appropriateness of the standard resolution, since it specifies *causal* conditions which an appropriate resolution must accommodate, ideas which played no explicit role in the object-level arguments Horgan considers.

NOTES

1. For a detailed discussion of Newcomb's paradox, see Robert Nozick's classic paper (1969), reprinted in this volume. I will not here address the issue of whether Newcomb's Problem itself is a genuine counterexample to *PMCEU* (although Newcomb's Paradox is discussed in the last section of this paper from a different perspective). In this connection, I shall consider only some of the less fantastic examples inspired by Newcomb's Paradox. Chapter 8 of my (1982) shows how analysis similar to that given in this paper can be applied to Newcomb's Problem.
2. The discussion of Jeffrey's system in this section is roughly patterned after the description of Jeffrey's system in Adams and Rosenkrantz (1980).
3. Relative to a set W of propositions that is closed under the usual logical (sentential) connectives, I shall call a proposition S *maximally specific* if S is a member of W and there is no proposition S' in W such that S' truth-functionally implies, but is not truth-functionally implied by, S. Relative to a set W of propositions, a proposition is maximally specific if it is maximally specific relative to the closure of W under the usual connectives. A maximally specific proposition relative to a set is always equivalent to a conjunction of members and negations of members of the set. The set of propositions maximally specific relative to a set of propositions (modulo equivalence) is always a set of mutually exclusive and collectively exhaustive propositions. If ($W_1, \ldots, W_n$) are sets of mutually exclusive and collectively exhaustive propositions, then a proposition is maximally specific relative to the union of the W_i's if, and only if, it is equivalent to a conjunction $S_1 \& \ldots \& S_n$, where each $S_i \in W_i$.
4. Henry Kyburg has argued that probabilistic independence is not in general symmetric for the relevant kind of subjective probabilities (the kind which corresponds to what I below say characterizes "type-B," as opposed to "type-A," beliefs), from which it follows that positive and negative probabilistic relevance are not symmetric either for the relevant kind of subjective probabilities. See his (1974), pp. 287–90, and his (1980) p. 153. But see my (1984a) for an argument that Kyburg's *prima facie* counterexamples to symmetry are not genuine. Throughout this paper I will assume that probabilistic independence and positive and negative probabilistic relevance are all symmetric for our agent's subjective probabilities.
5. This depends on a "nonbacktracking" interpretation of counterfactuals. This feature of the Gibbard-Harper solution will be discussed below.
6. For this, see my (1982), pp. 98–105.

7. See Eells (1982), p. 117 f., for the argument and for details on why finding "appropriate" partitions may sometimes be a very tricky problem in itself.
8. Lewis (1981), p. 19. In this article, Lewis advances his own version of what has come to be known as "causal decision theory" and compares it with the versions of Gibbard and Harper and Skyrms. For further discussion of these three theories, see my (1982), Chapter 5.
9. I do not mean to say that causal decision theorists will never find "representation theorems" for their theories. But when they are found, it seems that more than just qualitative preference will have to be represented: the theorems will need an idea in addition to preference that can capture the force of judgments expressed in terms of the counterfactual conditional, or the relation "is outside the influence of," which must be made before calculations of expected utility can be made.
10. The discussion in this section will be on a general level. That is, I shall refer to "the common cause" rather than to, for example, the lesion or charisma, to "the symptomatic act" rather than to high cholesterol intake or Solomon's sending for the woman, and so forth. The reader who prefers more specificity may think lesion when he reads "common cause," high cholesterol intake when he reads "symptomatic act," L when he reads *"CC,"* and so forth.
11. Below I shall discuss in detail two kinds of belief that (13) and (14) can be taken to characterize.
12. Of course, this is true only within certain limits. We can reasonably insist that the agent's beliefs be consistent and that his degrees of belief be coherent (obey the probability axioms).
13. This was suggested by Charles Chihara.
14. Note that the equality between K-expectation, U-expectation, and *CEU* will hold even if *CEU* is evaluated relative to a different selection of decision-relevant propositions. As pointed out earlier, *CEU* does not vary according to how the space of probabilities is partitioned.
15. A more formal (and tedious) version of this argument is given in Eells (1981) and Eells (1982), Chapter 6.
16. In Chapter 7 of Eells (1982), the argument is repeated for the case in which the agent is uncertain about what his true beliefs and desires are.
17. In "Common Causes and Decision Theory" (forthcoming), Elliott Sober and I relax this assumption and argue that given certain reasonable conditions, even if the agent entertains the possibility of his "slipping"—either between his intentions and the act or between his beliefs and desires and the rational intention based on them—*PMCEU* will still yield the correct prescriptions.
18. Ernest Adams suggested this to me as a possible characterization of 18.
19. It is worth noting that the argument does not assume that *DM* actually will apply *PMCEU,* or even that *DM* knows what decision rule he will use. The argument is intended to show that *PMCEU* would, *if applied,* give the right answer.
20. In Chapter 7 of Eells (1982), I both weaken the assumptions and argue that *PMCEU* also gives the right answers in more complex Newcomb-like Problems. Several objections are considered and dealt with in Chapter 6 and in my (1984b) and in Elliott Sober's and my "Common Causes and Decision Theory" (forthcoming).
21. This "inner-outer" part of the third diagnosis is based on comments of Ernest Adams and Charles Chihara.
22. See Chapter 8 of my (1982).

23. Most, but not all, of my criticisms of Horgan's argument here are based on Section 4 of my (1984a).
24. It is curious that Horgan does not consider *other* two-box arguments, which for some may be more intuitively compelling—for example, an argument of Nozick's (1969, in this volume, p. 125 ff.) and one discussed by Schlesinger (1974, p. 211). In the first kind of argument, parallels are drawn between Newcomb's Problem and others in which the correct act is clearly the analogue of the two-box act in Newcomb's Problem, that is, the dominant act. See also my (1982), pp. 210-14 for a version of this kind of argument. In the second kind of argument, Newcomb's Problem is modified so that the back of the opaque box is transparent, where a friend who wishes you well sits behind the box and can see whether or not the $1 million is in that box, although you still cannot; but he is not allowed to communicate with you. Clearly, no matter what is in the opaque box, the well-wisher knows that it is in your best interest to take both boxes, and you should know that he knows that. And it seems that whether or not there actually is a well-wisher and whether or not the back of the opaque box actually is transparent should not control which act is correct.
25. That is, with the exception of any "miracle" in *w* that is required for the occurrence of *A* in *w*. See Lewis (1979b) on such miracles. To be sensitive to the possibility that a small miracle is required in *w*, I should insist just that all differences between *w* and the actual world (if any) must be causally traceable to the occurrence of *A* in *w* or to the small miracle (if any) that occurs shortly before the occurrence of *A* in *w*.
26. The reason for the qualification is that we would need semantics for metalinguistic counterfactuals for a precise investigation of the truth values of the meta-linguistic counterfactuals in question. Note also that this point is relevant to Horgan's assertion that M_t and 6_t are equivalent, for the former is meta-linguistic and the latter is object-linguistic. But below, I reformulate the idea so as to make it apply to object-linguistic counterfactuals.
27. David Lewis (1973b) has advocated an analysis of causation in terms of non-backtracking counterfactuals, but of course this is not the only kind of analysis of causation. Also, Cindy Stern (1981) has argued in effect that Lewis's analysis is circular because it must presuppose causal relations in its delineation of which possible worlds are close, or similar, to the actual world.

10

Where the Tickle Defense Goes Wrong

FRANK JACKSON AND ROBERT PARGETTER

For our purposes it is enough to specify Conditional Decision Theory as the conjunction of a definition and a rule.
Definition of Expected Utility:

$$U(A) = \sum_i pr(O_i/A) \, V(O_iA)$$

where A is a proposed action, O_i the possible outcomes of A, and pr and V are the agent's subjective probability and value functions, respectively. *Rule of Action:* The right act out of a set of options available to an agent is that act having greatest expected utility.

A number of authors[1] have urged that there are clear cases where Conditional Decision Theory, *CDT,* gives the wrong answers. Unlike Newcomb's Paradox, these cases are both realistic and ones about which there is near unanimity of opinion. Accordingly, they have been regarded as constituting a very powerful reason for looking for a new decision theory (perhaps Subjunctive Decision Theory, *SDT,* got by leaving the rule as is, and replacing the definition by: $U(A) = \sum_i pr(A \,\Box\!\!\to O_i)V(O_iA)$).[2]

The waters have, however, been considerably muddied by what has come to be known as the Tickle Defense of *CDT.*[3] Its effect is that the cases cease to be *clear* counter-examples; and, further, even if they succeed, it comes to seem that *CDT* only fails in distinctly recherché situations. This paper aims to clear the waters.

We argue that considerations of the proper scope of decision theories show that, despite the Tickle Defense, there are clear cases where *CDT* fails. (We say nothing in support of *SDT* succeeding where *CDT* fails, though we in fact believe that it does.)

From *Australasian Journal of Philosophy* 61 (1983): 295–99, with postscript added. Reprinted by permission.

THE CASES AND THE TICKLE DEFENSE

Smokers have fantasized that smoking is good for you, and that the statistics suggesting the contrary are due to the fact that the kind of genes that predispose people to smoke are also the kind that predispose towards early death: it is not the smoking that causes the early deaths, but the genes which cause both the smoking and the early deaths; and, moreover, smoking does in fact counteract slightly the bad effects of these genes. Let's suppose this is true and known to be true.

Straight off our smokers' fantasy appears to be a decisive objection to *CDT*. (i) The case is realizable in that we know the kind of evidence that would establish it — the cigarette companies have been looking for same for years. (ii) It is clear that in this case it would be right to smoke. (iii) It seems that *CDT* yields the incorrect answer that it is wrong to smoke because, despite smoking's beneficial effects, the probability of early death given you smoke is higher than that of early death given you do not smoke. And (iv) it is clear that this is not an isolated case; a whole host of similar ones can be constructed along similar lines. (Imagine that jogging is not good for you — the opposite in fact — but the only people who can stomach it are naturally pretty tough, which is why joggers live longer; and so on and so forth.)

The Tickle Defense accepts that in such a case it would be right to smoke, but challenges the claim that *CDT* gives the opposite answer. The essence of the defense is that decision theory deals with voluntary actions, not involuntary movements; and it is plausible that actions necessarily have mental causes. Hence the genes in the fantasy case must act through the mind if the case is to trouble *CDT*. Suppose the genetic predisposition to smoke (and to early death) does so by inducing a particular craving to smoke, the "tickle." (Other suppositions could have been made; the kind of psychological state induced is not important; what matters is that there must be some psychological state or other.) The advocate of the Tickle Defense points out that cravings are things we know about, and, in particular, things agents know about before acting. Hence, in applying *CDT* to the case in question, total evidence requires that we conditionalize the probabilities on the existence or otherwise of the craving. But once this is done, *CDT* no longer recommends not smoking; the relevant inequalities among the probabilities are reversed. Although pr (early death given I smoke) $>$ pr (early death given I do not smoke), we have both pr (early death given I crave and smoke) $<$ pr (early death given I crave and do not smoke) and pr (early death given I smoke and do not crave) $<$ pr (early death given I do not smoke and do not crave). The craving, and equally its absence, "screens off" (and more) the connection between smoking and early death.

It is tempting to reply to the Tickle Defense[4] "What if the agent lacks the requisite self-knowledge about the role of the relevant psychological state- —the craving in our case?" There seem to us to be three problems with this reply to the Tickle Defense. First, some have held the mind to be transparent. If they are right, the requisite self-knowledge cannot be lacking. They are probably wrong, but it is strange that one should have to take a stance against the transparency of the mind in order to refute *CDT*. Secondly, all extant decision theories — *SDT* as much as *CDT* — involve a very considerable degree of idealization. No one actually has degrees of belief and wants that have the properties of the probability and value functions, respectively, which feature in them. The amount of self-knowledge required by the Tickle Defense is a minor idealization by comparison. Finally, this reply to the Tickle Defense invites the response that what the smokers' fantasy shows is not that *CDT* should be abandoned, but that it should be modified slightly. Leave the rule of action as is, and instead of defining expected utility in terms of the agent's probability function, define it in terms of what the agent's probability function would be if he were self-knowing (the two will often be the same, anyway). Our conclusion, therefore, is that, at the very least, the Tickle Defense has muddied the waters; it has made it seem that cases where *CDT* goes wrong are recherché ones involving ignorance of self.

There is, however, another reply available against the Tickle Defense. As we now proceed to show, unless we curtail the scope of *CDT* to an unacceptable extent, the Defense cannot save *CDT* from giving manifestly wrong answers in realizable cases.

THE SCOPE OF DECISION THEORIES

Decision theories are about what it is right to do, but what does "right" mean? Advocates of *CDT* — and of *SDT,* if it comes to that — are typically fairly silent on this question. They make clear that it is not moral rightness they are talking about, and leave the rest pretty much to our pre-analytical intuitions. This is fair enough. Usually nothing vital for their purposes hangs on the question. The Tickle Defense is an exception. To see where it goes wrong, we need to look briefly at the relevant notion of rightness.

In Ethics it is common to distinguish subjective from objective rightness.[5] The same kind of distinction can be drawn in non-ethical cases. I go into the bank. Just two tellers' windows are open. The queue at one window is significantly shorter than at the other, and I join it. It turns out in a way which I did not and could not foresee, that the people in front of me in the short queue have complicated bits of banking to do, while those in the long queue do not. As a result, it takes me much longer to get to a teller's window than it would have had I joined the initially-longer queue. Did I do the right or the wrong thing in joining the short queue? Obviously the correct response is not to insist on one answer or the other, but to distinguish: I did the subjectively right, but objectively wrong thing in joining the short queue.[6] (A defensible view about Chamberlain is that he did the subjectively right, though objectively wrong thing at Munich; the indefensible view is that he did the objectively right thing.)

Now decision theories — *CDT, SDT,* and company — are to do with subjective rightness. Otherwise it would be nonsense for them to be formulated, as they are, in terms of subjective probability. Decision theories deal with what it is right for me to do by my own lights, thus it is my (the agent's) subjective probability function that is used in calculating expected utilities. But as well as what is right by my own lights, there is what is right by another's lights. As well as asking what it is right (subjectively so, but we will take the qualification as understood from now on) for *X* to do by *X*'s lights, we can ask what it is right for *X* to do by *Y*'s lights. We naturally tend to have a special interest in our own decisions, and so it is often what it is right for an agent to do by his own lights that particularly concerns us. But the other question is askable, and asked. We often concern ourselves with what it is right for someone else to do by our lights — too often, in the case of busybodies!

What we have in mind is not assessing the options available to another in terms of his value and probability functions, but in terms of his value and *our* probability functions. "Given what Fred wants, I think he should buy an imported car instead of a local one. He disagrees, though; he thinks it more likely than I that spare parts for imported cars will become scarce." I have Fred's interests at heart, I want for him what he wants for himself; the disagreement is over which course of action by him is most likely to achieve his ends.

A good decision theory gives answers to both sorts of question. It would be an unacceptable restriction of scope to have a theory which only gave answers for what it is right to do by the agent's own lights. We want also answers to what Harry should hold about what it is right for Fred to do.

The smoker's fantasy case *does* show that *CDT* gives the wrong answers to the latter kind of question, and the Tickle Defense does not even get started as a reply. Suppose *I* want the answer to whether my aunt in Scotland should smoke. In the smoker's fantasy case, my answer is clearly that she should. Smoking is good for her; though of course I would be sad to hear that she is smoking, as this would mean that she probably has bad genes. But *CDT* gives as my answer the wrong one that she should not smoke, for my probability of her dying early given she smokes is greater than that given she does not. In sum, in the smoker's fantasy case, what it is right for my aunt to do by my lights is smoke, and *CDT* fails by virtue of giving the opposite answer.

And, moreover, there is no mileage to be gained on behalf of *CDT* out of the Tickle Defense. I know nothing of my aunt's cravings or "tickles," no matter how transparent her mind is to herself.

Of course I might if she rang me up just before putting the cigarette to her lips and told all. But to observe that *CDT* might give the right answer in a considerable variant on our case merely highlights that it gives the wrong answer in our case as it actually is.

POSTSCRIPT

Ellery Eells[7] has recently sought to generalize the Tickle Defense of *CDT*. The essence of the Tickle Defense is that an agent's subjective probabilities just before acting (or anyway after the arrival of the "tickle") are such as to make *CDT* recommend smoking in the smoker's fantasy case. Eells seeks to show quite generally that, in all cases like the smoker's fantasy, a rational agent's subjective probabilities *and* desirabilities *must* make *CDT* recommend the intuitively right action.

He starts from the following premise

> the way in which a common cause [for example, one's genes] causes a rational person to perform a symptomatic act [for example, smoking] is by causing him to have such beliefs and desires that a rational evaluation of the available acts . . . leads to the conclusion that the symptomatic act is the best act.[8]

We do not need to consider his interesting and intricate argument from this premise. We can see immediately that his generalization of the Tickle Defense cannot meet our objection. For it is all about the *agent's* probabilities and desirabilities. And this is no incidental feature that might easily be removed. The common cause—the genetic predisposition or whatever—is *in the agent* and does not affect an outside observer's deliberations concerning what, by his lights, the agent should do. My aunt's genes do not affect my rational deliberation about what she ought to do, whatever effect it may have on her deliberations via her beliefs and desires.

NOTES

1. See, e.g., Skyrms (1980b), p. 128 f; Lewis (1981) and the reference therein.
2. On this and related rivals to *CDT,* see Gibbard and Harper (1978), Lewis (1981), and Skyrms (1980b).
3. Skyrms (1980 b, p. 130) cites Frank Jackson, Richard Jeffrey, David Lewis, and Isaac Levi as having put this defense to him at one time or another. At

least two of these think that the defense ultimately fails: Lewis for reasons given in (1981), pp. 10–11; Jackson for the reasons to be given here.
4. Lewis (1981), pp. 10–11; see also Skyrms (1980b), pp. 130–31.
5. See Brandt (1959), p. 364–65. (Different authors mark the distinction with different terms.)
6. Those who believe in objective chances (other than 0 and 1) can distinguish two sorts of objective rightness, because opinion about the chance of something happening and about it in fact happening are both opinions about objective matters.
7. Eells (1982), especially Chapter 6, and Chapter 9 of this volume.
8. Eells (1982), p. 152.

11

Reply to Jackson and Pargetter*

ELLERY EELLS

Jackson and Pargetter (1983, 1985) claim that tickle, and "metatickle," defenses of evidential decision theory do not work in decision problems of their second kind: what should *I* think this *other* person should do, given the other's desires. I am only concerned here with "metatickle" defenses, where I understand metatickles to be pieces of information about our deliberation that, according to such defenses, are supposed to screen off the evidential relevance of the acts to factors which the acts do not cause or prevent (such as causes of the acts).[1] The reason they give is that the information available to the other about his deliberation (which includes knowledge of his desires *and his* beliefs) is not available to *me,* deliberating on the other's behalf. My reply to their argument is in two parts. First, I will argue, by way of an example, that contrary to a conjecture of Jackson and Pargetter's, causal decision theory is (equally) vulnerable to the same sort of objection — albeit in different sorts of decision problems.[2] And second, I will describe a procedure that is available to me when deliberating on behalf of the other which should pay metatickles their due and result in both the causal and the evidential decision theory's delivering the appropriate prescriptions in the relevant decision problems.

Here is a decision problem in which causal decision theory, without accommodation of metatickles, will, for many people, prescribe the wrong action. It is built up from two others. The first is the original Newcomb's Problem, where A_1 is the one-box act, A_2 is the two-box act, and in which it is, at least initially, highly subjectively probable to the agent that the predictor has predicted A_i, conditional on the agent's choosing A_i, for both $i = 1$ and $i = 2$. Call this decision problem I. In decision problem II, the predictor waits until *after* your action before filling or not filling the opaque box with the $1,000,000: If you do A_1, he puts the $1,000,000 in, and if you do A_2, he does not. This predictor is, according to the agent's beliefs, infallible. In decision problem III, there are three available acts, A_1 and A_2 as above, and A_o: take neither box. The invariable outcome of A_o is getting $999. Call the predictors of decision problems I and II "Predictor I" and "Predictor II," respectively. In decision problem III, there is a third predictor, Predictor III. This predictor predicts whether or not you will choose A_o, and he is also believed to be highly accurate — in a way which makes the prediction of an act subjectively very probably conditional on that act's being chosen. If this predictor predicts A_o, then he lets Predictor II control the contents of the opaque box; and if he predicts that you will *not* do A_o, he lets Predictor I control the opaque box. The agent believes that Predictor I always makes a prediction either of A_1 or of A_2, no matter what Predictor III does: Predictor I predicts, very accurately, what people who in fact do one of A_1 and A_2 do; but he is no good at all at predicting whether or not you will in fact do one of A_1 and A_2 (rather than doing A_o). Think of Predictor I's prediction as based on what he thinks you *would* do if you *were* to do one of A_1 and A_2. (Or perhaps Predictor I believes you are in decision problem I, rather than in decision problem III.)

Letting F_0 be the prior state of Predictor III's having predicted A_0 in problem III, and letting G_1 and G_2 be the prior states of Predictor I's having predicted A_1 and A_2, respectively, and assuming monetary utilities, the causal expectations of the three acts are as follows:

$$U_K(A_0) = 999;$$
$$U_K(A_1) = pr(F_0)\,1,000,000 + pr(\sim F_0 \ \& \ G_1)\,1,000,000;$$
$$U_K(A_2) = pr(F_0)\,1,000 + pr(\sim F_0 \ \& \ G_1)\,1,001,000$$
$$\qquad\qquad + pr(\sim F_0 \ \& \ G_2)\,1,000$$

Letting $r = pr(F_0)$ and $p = pr(G_1)$ and assuming — plausibly, for reasons given at the end of the previous paragraph — that F_0 and G_1 are subjectively probabilistically independent of each other, we have:

$$U_K(A_0) = 999;$$
$$U_K(A_1) = 1{,}000{,}000r + 1{,}000{,}000(1-r)p$$
$$= 1{,}000{,}000r + 1{,}000{,}000p - 1{,}000{,}000rp;$$
$$U_K(A_2) = 1{,}000r + 1{,}001{,}000(1-r)p + 1{,}000(1-r)(1-p)$$
$$= 1{,}000{,}000p - 1{,}000{,}000rp + 1{,}000;$$

so that

$$U_K(A_1) > U_K(A_2) \text{ if, and only if, } r > 1/1000.$$

(Note also that, no matter what the values of r and p are, $U_K(A_2)$ is at least 1,000, so that it is always greater than $U_K(A_0)$.)

Thus, it is quite plausible that causal decision theory will (at least initially) prescribe A_1 in decision problem III. Suppose the agent chooses A_1 on this basis. Should he then be happy with his choice (prior to action, or at least to outcome)? Given the way in which we have assumed that the agent believes Predictor III to be accurate, the agent's choice of A_1 should cause his subjective probability of F_0, that is, the value of r, to decrease. And if it gets below $1/1000$, then the causal expectation of A_2 will then be greater than that of A_1. The agent's *choice* of A_1 *itself* makes him regret it.

On the other hand, a choice of A_2 will not result in post-choice regret. If A_2 is causally superior, then the agent's subjective probability of F_0 is less than $1/1000$. And if the agent *chooses* A_2 on this basis, then the effect of this on the probability of F_0 could only be to decrease it even further, in which case A_2 becomes causally even better relative to A_1 than it was before the choice.

By similar reasoning, a choice of A_0 should lead to regret that one did not do A_1, since A_0 is evidence that one will be, essentially, in decision problem II (except that one has that third alternative of taking no boxes), in which A_1 is best. But, as we have seen, a choice of A_1 would make A_2 look better. Act A_2 is the only act whose choice does not cause one to wish to have chosen some other act: it is the only act whose choice is not self-defeating.[3] On this basis—A_2's being the only act one's choice of which one would then like to live by—it seems that A_2 is the unique appropriate action.

How can causal decision theory avoid the prescription of A_1? By the accommodation of metatickles of some kind. Note that it is because of the *evidential* relations between the acts and the prior states that one would regret a choice of A_1 (or of A_0) and that a choice of A_2 should enhance the agent's assessment of its choiceworthiness. It seems that the only hope is for the agent's knowledge of his desires and beliefs (including beliefs about how his deliberation is going, possibly after some preliminary calculations of causal expectation) to result, eventually, in the acts' becoming evidentially irrelevant to the prior states—or at least for this knowledge (these metatickles) eventually to land the decision maker on an act whose choice will not defeat its own choiceworthiness.[4]

But suppose now that *my uncle* is in decision problem III, that I know this, and that I know that he wants to walk away with as much money as possible. *I* am wondering what would be the best action for *him* given what *he* wants. If my subjective probability that he is in state F_0 is greater than $1/1000$, then causal decision theory will tell me that he should do A_1. But this is the wrong act, as argued above. Indeed, both my uncle and I should be unhappy (for him) if he chooses it. As suggested above, my uncle's metatickles should eventually cause him to come around to the correct act, A_2, in his causal reasoning. But, if Jackson and Pargetter's point is valid, these metatickles will not help me, deliberating on his behalf. For again, these metatickles are not accessible to me. Thus, Jackson and Pargetter's objection is as applicable to the causal theory as it is to the evidential theory.

This might seem to indicate that decision theory is narrower in scope than Jackson and Pargetter conceive it to be. However, there is a procedure that I can adopt, when deliberating in my uncle's behalf, that would seem to give metatickles their due. My decision problem about what my uncle should do (or my aunt, in Jackson and Pargetter's example) can be turned into a hypothetical decision problem about what *I* should do, *were* I in his (or her) position as far as the decision problem and desirabilities are concerned and still in my own position as far as subjective probabilities go. That is, I can "pretend" that I am a person in my *uncle's* (or *aunt's*) decision problem who has *his* (or *her*) desirabilities and *my* probabilities. I then deliberate. And this (actual) deliberation should take into account the fact that I have (hypothetically) such and such beliefs and desires, and so forth. This actual deliberation in terms of the hypothetical set of beliefs and desires should generate, for me, metatickles that should work to the same effect as the metatickles available to a decision maker deliberating in his own behalf in terms of his own beliefs and desires, namely to the effect of breaking the evidential connection between the acts and the prior states. If the metatickle defense works in the case of my aunt's or uncle's deliberation on her or his own behalf, then it should, if I adopt this procedure, work for the case of *my* deliberation on *her* or *his* behalf.

Of course, there may be decision problems for which, by using this procedure, I will eventually land on an act that would be irrational for the other to perform in light of the other's beliefs and desires. But this will be because we start out with *different beliefs* (which, incidentally, can result in different metatickles). And the question, recall, was: What is the rational act in light of the other's desires and *my* beliefs? And this procedure should give the right answer for someone with such beliefs and desires.

NOTES

*I thank the University of Wisconsin-Madison Graduate School for financial support and Elliott Sober for useful discussion.

1. I will not present such a defense here. For several versions of the defense, see Eells (1981, 1982, 1984b, 1985a,c) and Jeffrey (1981b, 1983).
2. Jackson and Pargetter say, "We say nothing in support of (causal decision theory) succeeding where (evidential decision theory) fails, though we in fact believe that it does" (1983, p. 295; 1985, in this volume, p. 214). For several versions of causal decision theory, see the references cited in my previous essay of this volume.
3. That is, the act is "ratifiable," as Jeffrey would say (1981b; 1983, pp. 15–20). For difficulties with this theory of ratifiability, see the second reference cited and Eells (1985c), the latter of which defends the theory against one sort of difficulty and revises it in light of the two others.
4. Space does not allow me elaborate on exactly how this may come about. See Eells (1985c) for suggestions on how metatickles may be accommodated in causal decision theory in examples of this kind.

12

Newcomb's Problem: A Stalemate

TERENCE HORGAN

My reasoning in Horgan (1981) has recently come under attack in separate papers by Isaac Levi (1982) and Ellery Eells (1984a). In this paper I shall examine their objections. I also shall explore some connections between Newcomb's Problem and the notion "having an outcome within one's power."

In accordance with the notation in my original paper, let A_1 and A_2 be the acts of choosing both boxes and choosing only the second box, respectively;

and let S_1 and S_2 be the presence of $1 million in box 2 and the presence of $0 there, respectively. As before, let w_1 be the closest (A_1 & S_1)-world to actuality, w_2 the closest (A_2 & S_1)-world, w_3 the closest (A_1 & S_2)-world, and w_4 the closest (A_2 & S_2)-world — where similarity to actuality is understood in accordance with the standard resolution of the vagueness of counterfactuals.

Levi first accuses me of fallaciously inferring, from the fact that pr (A_1/S_2) and pr (A_2/S_1) are both high in Newcomb's Problem, that the converse probabilities pr (S_2/A_1) and pr (S_1/A_2) are both high as well. He holds that Newcomb's Problem simply fails to provide any information about probabilities of the form pr (S_j/A_i), the probabilities needed to calculate the V-utility of the acts A_1 and A_2.

I admit that in the usual formulation of the problem, and in my own formulation at the beginning of my paper, what is explicitly stipulated is that most of the being's two-box predictions and most of his one-box predictions have been correct and that the agent knows this. Levi rightly points out, as he did in Levi (1975), that these conditions really only bear directly on pr (A_1/S_2) and pr (A_2/S_1). And he also rightly observes that these latter probabilities both can have high values even if the converse probabilities are not both high — for instance, in a situation where the agent knows not only that the being was correct in 90 per cent of his two-box predictions and in 90 per cent of his one-box predictions, but also that he predicted the one-box choice in 99.9 per cent of the past cases. (In this situation, the vast majority of those who chose both boxes received $1,001,000. Thus premise 1_o of the one-box argument is false even under the backtracking resolution of vagueness; furthermore, the V-maximization principle and the dominance principle both recommend taking both boxes.)

But I plead not guilty to the fallacy charge. I construe Newcomb's Problem as implicitly involving some further conditions which unfortunately I failed to state: that is, (1) that almost all of those who have chosen both boxes in the past have received $1,000, (2) that almost all of those who have chosen only the second box have received $1 million, and (3) that the agent knows these facts. That is, I take it to be *built into* Newcomb's Problem that for the agent, pr (S_2/A_1) and pr (S_1/A_2) are both high. And I think it is reasonable and natural to construe the problem this way because only then do there arise the commonsense and theoretical conflicts that make the problem paradoxical — that is, the conflict between the one-box argument and the two-box argument and between the V-maximization principle and the dominance principle. In any case, the problem so construed is the one to which my paper was addressed. I should have said so explicitly. (I suppose there is no prior fact of the matter as to whether the implicit conditions just mentioned are part of Newcomb's Problem or not. Very well, I hereby *stipulate* that the conditions are included, as I use the term "Newcomb's Problem." I choose to individuate the problem this way because otherwise it becomes a conglomeration of many problems only some of which I find interesting.)

Levi's second objection is directed against the following principle, which lies at the heart of my defense of one-boxism:

> (M_o) I am virtually certain, independently of any beliefs I have as to the likelihood of my doing A_1 or the likelihood of my doing A_2, that either w_2 or w_3 will become actual.

When I set forth this principle, unfortunately, I neglected to explain either the meaning of, or the rationale for, the phrase between commas. My intended meaning is made explicit by the second clause of the following reformulation:

> (M_o') It is highly probable that either w_2 or w_3 will become actual; and this proposition follows from some set of propositions in my belief-corpus which contains no proposition concerning the probability that I will perform A_1 or the probability that I will perform A_2.

The reason for the qualification is that it would not be appropriate to restrict one's decision-making purview to the worlds w_2 and w_3 if one's near-certainty that one of these worlds would become actual were based upon a prior near-certainty about which act one was about to perform; for the other act might be preferable.

Levi, however, interprets M_o as asserting that the propositions A_1 and A_2 are each *probabilistically independent* of the proposition that either w_2 or w_3 will become actual. And he claims that in order for $pr(S_2/A_1)$ and $pr(S_1/A_2)$ both to be high, given that $pr(A_1/S_2)$ and $pr(A_2/S_1)$ are both high, $pr(A_1)$ and $pr(A_2)$ cannot be too near 0 or too near 1. He concludes that (M_o) as he interprets it must be rejected.

The principle thus rejected, however, is not the one I meant to assert. His objection does not affect (M_o'), and hence does not affect (M_o) as I intended it.[1]

After attacking my attempt to turn aside two-box reasoning, Levi goes on to present arguments of his own that purport to impugn the cogency of the two-boxers' principle of U-maximization. I think these arguments are effectively refuted, however, in a recent reply by Lewis (1983).

I turn now to the objections raised by Eells. First, he too focuses on principle (M_o). He begins by saying that (M_o) should not be *about* my beliefs, but instead should just *state* the relevant belief. In accordance with this suggestion, my reformulated principle says "It is highly probable that either w_2 or w_3 will become actual," rather than saying "I am virtually certain that either w_2 or w_3 will become actual." It seems to me that either formulation will serve, particularly since I conceive of probability, at least insofar as it figures in decision theory, as degree of belief.

In any case, Eells's substantive claim concerning (M_o) is that, by virtue of the clause between commas, (M_o) suffers from precisely the kind of meta-level circularity which I claim it avoids. For, he interprets (M_o) this way:

> $(M_o")$ It is highly probable that either w_2 or w_3 will become actual; and this latter proposition is independent of which of A_1 and A_2 is performed (where X is *independent* of Y if, and only if, the following are all (materially) equivalent: X, Y $\square\!\!\rightarrow$ X, and $-Y$ $\square\!\!\rightarrow$ X).

But the notion of independence I intended in (M_o) is not counterfactual independence (under the backtracking resolution), any more than it is probabilistic independence. Rather, it is independence in the sense of "not belonging to the premises." What I intended to assert in (M_o) was that the agent in Newcomb's Problem has a set of premises which not only implies that it is highly probable that either w_2 or w_3 will become actual, but which also includes no propositions about the probability of his doing A_1 or the probability of his doing A_2. This notion of independence involves no counterfactuals, and is captured by (M_o') rather than $(M_o")$.

Incidentally, it should be noted that the agent's premises do not themselves include any backtracking counterfactuals either; thus circularity does not enter that way. The premises are (1) our earlier characterization of the worlds w_1, w_2, w_3, and w_4 (a characterization which appeals to the *standard* resolution of vagueness, not the backtracking resolution); and (2) the conditions that define Newcomb's Problem.

Eells's second point concerns my formulation of the two-boxer's meta-level argument for the pragmatic aproppriateness of the standard resolution of vagueness and my claim that this argument suffers from a form of circularity from which the one-boxer's meta-level argument is immune. I suggested that the two-boxer's key meta-level premise is this:

> (M_t) Either I would actualize w_1 if I chose both boxes and I would actualize w_2 if I chose box 2, or I would actualize w_3 if I chose both boxes and I would actualize w_4 if I chose box 2.

The problem I raised is that this premise, as I understand it, is just equivalent to the meta-level premise (6_t): hence the claim "If (M_t) is true then the standard resolution of vagueness is the pragmatically appropriate one" is essentially equivalent to premise (7_t) of the two-box argument. What was wanted, though, was a defense of the pragmatic relevance of the standard resolution of vagueness and thus by implication a defense of (7_t) which does not resort all over again to counterfactuals resolved in the standard way.

Eells attempts to avoid this circularity problem by proposing a vagueness resolution that is allegedly different from both the standard resolution and the backtracking resolution. Under his *causal resolution* (*c-resolution*), every difference between the closest A_i-world and the actual world must be either (a) the occurrence of A_i itself, or (b) a minimal "minor miracle" sufficient to smoothly graft A_i onto the actual world's past, or (c) some causal result of the occurrence of A_i in the given world. (Eells actually only mentions (c), but I think this is an oversight.) He suggests that the c-resolution is neutral between the standard resolution and the backtracking resolution. And the appropriate premise for defending two-boxism, he claims, is the following — where the counterfactual connective is to be understood in a way that (i) is consistent with the c-resolution and (ii) has its remaining vagueness resolved any way we like:

$$((A_1 \;\Box\!\!\rightarrow S_1) \;\&\; (A_2 \;\Box\!\!\rightarrow S_1)) \;v\; ((A_1 \;\Box\!\!\rightarrow S_2 \;\&\; (A_2 \;\Box\!\!\rightarrow S_2)).$$

Now, this principle is not a meta-level claim, but instead is just premise (6_i) of the object-level two-box argument — with the counterfactuals understood according to the c-resolution. So I take it that Eells is offering us a new object-level argument, rather than a new justification for the pragmatic appropriateness of the standard resolution of vagueness; it is the object-level two-box argument all over again, with the counterfactuals understood in accordance with the c-resolution. (I *think* this is the argument he is offering us. I find the structure of his discussion somewhat confusing.)

But I just do not see how this new argument is supposed to help the two-boxer's case. Our original object-level one-box argument stands in the same relation to the new object-level two-box argument as it stood to the original object-level two-box argument — that is, stalemate. Although Eells claims that the c-resolution is *neutral* between the standard resolution and the backtracking resolution, the fact is that it allows backtracking only if the nearest c-resolution worlds should happen to contain backwards causation; and none of them do (at least none that are relevant to the counterfactuals in the one-box argument and the two-box argument). Thus, the c-resolution conflicts with the backtracking resolution every bit as much as the standard resolution does. Indeed, one wonders how exactly the c-resolution and the standard resolution are supposed to differ, relative to the counterfactuals that interest us; I cannot see that they differ significantly at all. So we are back to square one, wondering whether the pragmatically relevant resolution of vagueness is the backtracking resolution or the c-resolution. As far as I can tell, this question is not really any different from the parallel question concerning the backtracking resolution and the standard resolution. And I claimed in my paper that the one-boxers can provide a non-circular meta-level defense of the appropriateness of the backtracking resolution, whereas the two-boxers must beg the question by resorting to meta-level counterfactuals resolved in their favored way.

So I don't think that Eells's appeal to the so-called c-resolution evades the problem of object-level stalemate or my charge of meta-level circularity. However, at the end of his discussion he make a different point, which I think is more telling. He suggests that the following sort of principle, rather than (M_t), should be the basis for the two-boxer's meta-level argument. (I am altering his formulation a bit, in a way which I think improves it.)

> (M_t') (1) For $i = 1, 2$, the closest A_i-world, under the standard resolution of vagueness, is either the actual world or else a world which differs from the actual world only with respect to (a) the occurrence of A_i itself, (b) the occurrence, if need be, of a minor last-second miracle just sufficient to smoothly graft A_i onto the actual world's past, and (c) features for which A_i is, at least in part, causally responsible; (2) the remaining two worlds from the set (w_1, w_2, w_3, and w_4) contain a past that is different from the actual world's past; and (3) my present actions cannot causally influence the past.

I think it must be conceded that (M_t') provides very strong intuitive grounds for saying that the standard resolution, rather than the backtracking one, is pragmatically appropriate. Under the backtracking resolution, after all, one of the two closest worlds from the set (w_1, w_2, w_3, w_4) is a world with a past that is *different* from our actual world's past; and one of the worlds *not* counted as closest is a world in which the only differences from our actual world are either the act A_i itself (grafted onto the actual past with minimal disruption) or else features for which A_i is at least partially causally responsible.

Is (M_t') guilty of the brand of circularity which I attributed to (M_t)? Not in any obvious way, since (M_t') does not employ meta-level standard-resolution counterfactuals the way (M_t) does. Of course, if one follows Lewis (1973b) in construing causation in terms of counterfactual dependence, then standard-resolution counterfactuals will ultimately re-emerge in (M_t') once the causal locutions are "analyzed out." But here I think the two-boxers can fairly make two points. First, one need not adopt Lewis's treatment of causation; and if one does not, then the circularity does not apply against (M_t'). But second, even if one does adopt Lewis's counterfactual account of causation (or something like it), the circularity charge simply loses its bite. (M_t') provides an intuitively very strong reason (for many, a compelling reason) for the pragmatic appropriateness of the standard resolution. Thus, consider the claim

> If (M_t') is true then I ought to adopt the standard resolution for decision-making purposes.

The two-boxer who understands causation in terms of standard-resolution counterfactual dependence can, I think, simply *concede* that this claim might ultimately turn out to be "circular" in the sense I describe in my paper; that is, that it might turn out to be "essentially equivalent" to premise

(7_t) of the object-level one-box argument. I think he can live with this fact, simply by saying that he *accepts* both (7_t) and the above meta-level normative principle — and leaving it at that.

Indeed, although I think that (M_t') is preferable to (M_t) as an expression of the two-boxer's fundamental reasons for regarding the standard resolution of vagueness as the pragmatically appropriate one, I think it is also open to him simply (i) to cite (M_t) in support of the standard resolution, then (ii) to concede that his meta-level normative premise is essentially equivalent to (7_t) and then (iii) to say that despite these facts, he regards (7_t) and its meta-level counterpart as *true*. There is no inconsistency in this, but rather a refusal to play the game of seeking a meta-level defense of the standard resolution which does not itself appeal to counterfactuals. The two-boxer does not have to play this game, after all, and does not have to concede that success at the game is what really determines the pragmatically appropriate resolution of vagueness.[2]

My considered opinion, therefore, is that one cannot really hope to overcome the object-level stalemate I described. It does not really help to ascend to the meta-level and consider arguments about which vagueness resolution ought to be regarded as pragmatically appropriate. Stalemate simply re-emerges at this level: one-boxers will defend the backtracking resolution by appealing to the probability considerations expressed in (M_o'), whereas two-boxers will defend the standard resolution by appealing either to the counterfactual considerations in (M_t) or to the causal considerations in (M_t') (which might or might not reduce in turn to standard-resolution counterfactual considerations).[3]

Viewing the issue as a stalemate is both liberating and frustrating. It is liberating to the extent that one now feels justified in not worrying about the opposition and in just going ahead and constructing a decision theory that consistently yields the answers which one has already decided are the right ones. But it is frustrating both because it involves the concession that there is no way to establish definitively what the *truly* rational act is in Newcomb's Problem and also because it suggests the disturbing possibility that there is really no such thing as the rational act *simpliciter,* but only the V-rational act and the U-rational act.

I remain a one-boxer, though. I will take my million and then regret that I passed up the chance to get an extra thousand. I would much rather do that than take my thousand and then regret that I had no chance for more.

I shall conclude with some brief reflections concerning the notion of having a certain outcome within one's power. Consider the following two-box argument:

> *Either* (1) I have the power to choose both boxes and receive $1,001,000, and also the power to choose the second box and receive $1 million, whereas (2) I lack either the power to choose both boxes and

receive $1,000 or the power to choose the second box and receive $0; *or* (3) I have the power to choose both boxes and receive $1,000, and also the power to choose the second box and receive $0, whereas (4) I lack either the power to choose both boxes and receive $1,001,000 or the power to choose the second box and receive $1 million. Hence the outcome I have the power to achieve by choosing both boxes is preferable to the outcome I have the power to achieve by choosing the second box—whatever those outcomes are. And if this is so then I ought to choose both boxes. Hence I ought to choose both boxes.

How might the one-boxer deal with this argument, and are there any lessons to be learned concerning the concept of an agent's power?

Ordinarily, we associate power with the potential causal efficacy of an agent's potential acts. Accordingly, we ordinarily think that an agent never has within his power an outcome involving a past which differs from the actual world's past. Now, the one-boxer might accede to this way of conceiving power and so might grant the non-normative premise of the above argument. If so, he will then be obliged to deny the normative premise. He will be committed to saying that, for decision-making purposes, w_2 and w_3 are the appropriate worlds to consider—even though one of these worlds (that is, whichever one will turn out not to be actual) contains an outcome that is not even within the agent's power (since the being's past prediction in that world is different than his actual past prediction and thus the contents of box 2 in that world are different than their actual contents).

But another approach the one-boxer might take would be to counter with his own argument concerning power. Suppose we are dealing with the "limit case" of Newcomb's Problem, where the agent is completely certain that the being has correctly predicted what he will do. Then the agent might reason as follows:

Either I will choose both boxes and then obtain $1,000, *or* I will choose only the second box and then obtain $1 million; and this proposition follows from propositions which I know are true and which say nothing about which act I shall perform (or about the probability of either act). Hence I lack the power to falsify the being's prediction. But I have the power to take both boxes, and also the power to take only the second box. Hence I have the power to choose both boxes and then obtain $1,000, and also the power to choose the second box and then obtain $1 million; while I lack either the power to choose both boxes and then obtain $1,001, 000 or the power to choose the second box and then obtain $0. So the outcome I have the power to achieve by choosing only the second box is preferable to the outcome I have the power to achieve by choosing both boxes. And if this is so then I ought to choose only the second box. Hence I ought to choose only the second box.

Now, one might insist that the ordinary notion of power inevitably involves causal efficacy and precludes power over the past and hence that it is simply fallacious for the agent to infer from the conditions of the limit-case of Newcomb's Problem that he cannot falsify the being's prediction. The agent certainly *can* falsify the being's prediction since the state of box 2 is already fixed and yet he can perform either act. It is just that he will not falsify the prediction, even though he *can*.

Indeed, the one-boxer himself might take this line and might repudiate the present one-box argument as fallacious while still standing by the original one-box argument involving backtracking counterfactuals.

But I think it must be admitted that there is something very natural about saying that the agent simply cannot falsify the being's prediction. After all, he knows that he is bound to fail, no matter how hard he tries. Furthermore, pre-assured failure will not be a matter of simple bad luck; luck does not enter into it at all, since the probability that the being will be wrong is dead zero.

The naturalness of using "can" this way, I suggest, reflects the fact that our ordinary notion of power is actually more flexible than it initially appears to be. One way of employing this notion—in numerous contexts the only appropriate way—is to build in causal efficacy and to deny such a thing as power over the past. But another possible usage, one which has a strong air of appropriateness in the present context at least, is to employ the term in such way that the conditions of the limit-case of Newcomb's Problem do indeed imply that the agent cannot falsify the being's prediction and do indeed imply that he has the power to obtain for himself either the $1,000 outcome or the $1 million outcome.

One can imagine various treatments of the semantics of "can" that would accomodate this suggestion. For instance, in Horgan (1979) I proposed that "Person S can ϕ" is true if, and only if, "$S\phi$'s" is true in some *circumstantially similar* possible world—where the relevant notion of circumstantial similarity is largely context-dependent. This sort of approach allows us to acknowledge that in most contexts, the actual-world past is to be held constant in all the circumstantially similar worlds; but it also allows for the possibility of contexts in which the appropriate resolution of the vagueness of circumstantial similarity is a backtracking resolution.

For the one-boxer, Newcomb's Problem provides the latter kind of context. This is because the notion of power is conceptually intertwined with practical decision-making: we weigh potential outcomes in our deliberations insofar as we think that they are within (or that there is an adequate probability that they are within) our power. Thus, from the one-boxer's point of view it is entirely appropriate for the agent in Newcomb's Problem to deploy the above one-box argument involving power. The relevant notion of power is an unusual one to be sure: under this notion, a pair of outcomes are both within one's power even though one of them involves a non-actual prior prediction by the being and a non-actual state of box 2. But this is the appropriate notion of power in this situation, says the one-boxer, because the agent knows that he is bound to act as the being predicted he would. For practical purposes, therefore (and practical purposes are what count here), the agent *cannot* falsify the being's prediction; so he should act accordingly.

Meanwhile, of course, the two-boxer has his own argument employing the notion of power — the argument cited earlier. And the conflict between this argument and the one-boxer's power argument is structurally parallel to the conflict between the two object-level counterfactual arguments I described in my original paper. The salient facts are these: (1) Two competing notions of power are at work, a standard one and a backtracking one. (2) The non-normative premises in each argument are true and the inferences in each argument are valid, when the notion of power is understood in the way appropriate to the given argument. (3) Thus the crux of the dispute concerns the normative premises of the two arguments: the two-boxer claims that the agent ought to perform the act which yields the better of the outcomes that are within his *standard* power; while the one-boxer says he ought to choose the act with the better of the outcomes that are within his *backtracking* power.

Again I see no way to avoid stalemate. But let me conclude by trying to make the one-boxer's notion of power more vivid. Imagine being in a Newcomb situation with the following features. (1) You are a hungry prisoner, condemned to die tomorrow. (2) You are completely certain that the being has correctly predicted what you will do. (The limit case.) (3) Box 1 contains a delicious meal, which you may eat immediately if you choose both boxes. (4) If the being predicted that you will choose only box 2, then he put a note into box 2 which will cause the authorities to cancel your execution and set you free. (5) If the being predicted that you will choose both boxes, then he put nothing into box 2. (6) You know all these facts.

If you choose both boxes, you will do so in the full knowledge that you will be executed tomorrow. Likewise, if you choose only the second box, you will do so in the full knowledge that you will be set free. Now surely, in such a situation you would have a strong tendency to view yourself as having the power to choose your own fate — notwithstanding the fact that your choice will not causally influence the contents of box 2.

Two-boxers seem to predominate among those who are currently working on the foundations of decision theory. But I think it is not unreasonable to speculate that most of them, if faced with the situation just described, would swallow hard and choose one box. No doubt they would grumble afterwards about having irrationally passed up a chance for a good meal when their happy fate was sealed in advance. But would you really choose two boxes in the certain knowledge that you will subsequently die, just to prove you mean business?[4]

NOTES

1. The objection is mistaken anyway, as the following example demonstrates. Let $pr(A_1 \& S_1) = 0.1$, $pr(A_1 \& S_2) = .9$, $pr(A_2 \& S_1) = .08$, and $pr(A_2 \& S_2) = .01$. Then each of the conditional probabilities in question will be high: $pr(A_1/S_2) = pr(S_2/A_1) = 90/91$, and $pr(A_2/S_1) = pr(S_1/A_2) = 8/9$. And yet, contrary to Levi, $pr(A_1)$ and $pr(A_2)$ are near 1 and 0, respectively; $pr(A_1) = .91$, and $pr(A_2) = .09$. (This example, due to Howard Sobel, was brought to my attention by Richmond Campbell.) What does appear true is this: if we set either the two probabilities $pr(S_2/A_1)$ and $pr(S_1/A_2)$, or else the two probabilities $pr(A_1/S_2)$ and the $pr(A_2/S_1)$, equal to the *same* high value, then if the two members of the other pair both remain high then $pr(A_1)$ and $pr(A_2)$ cannot be too near 1 or too near 0.

   Incidentally, the behavior of these four conditional probabilities becomes very important in the dynamics of the agent's deliberation concerning Newcomb's Problem. As I conceive of the problem, the agent is supposed to consider it highly probable that the predictor has foreseen the agent's *entire* deliberative process, and not merely certain tentative decisions which the agent might over-rule in the course of his deliberations. Thus, even as the agent becomes confident about what he will do, the probabilities $pr(S_2/A_1)$ and $pr(S_1/A_2)$ — the ones that are crucial in calculating the V-maximal act — should remain identical, and should retain their initial high value. This means that $pr(A_1/S_2)$ will drop as the agent becomes confident that he will perform A_2, or else $pr(A_2/S_1)$ will drop as he becomes confident that he will perform A_1. But these latter changes won't affect the V-rationality of the one-box choice. For further relevant discussion of this issue, see Gillespie (forthcoming).

2. In this connection, let me comment briefly on an argument that was not originally part of Eells' paper, but is included in the version of the paper that appears in this volume. He remarks that (M_o) does not imply that one should be virtually certain that w_2 is the closest A_2-world and that w_3 is the closest A_3-world. I agree. But I never meant to claim that (M_o) *implies* this. After all, the question of which worlds are "closest" depends upon which vagueness-resolution one adopts, and my prior claim was that in contexts like Newcomb's problem, this is partly a matter of *choice*. Thus, my argument that we ought, for decisionmaking purposes, to choose the backtracking resolution, was a (meta-level) *normative* argument. Its form was really this:

   > If (M_o) is true, then one ought to adopt the backtracking resolution for purposes of deciding how to act in Newcomb's problem. (M_o) is true. Hence, one ought to adopt the backtracking resolution.

   Now, I also defended the meta-level normative premise of this argument, as against the two-boxer's corresponding meta-level normative premise involving (M_t), with the following *meta-meta*-level normative argument:

   > For purposes of choosing a vagueness-resolution to adopt in practical decisionmaking, one ought to act on the basis of a meta-level normative premise that makes no appeal to counterfactuals; for the question of how to resolve the vagueness of counterfactuals is precisely what is at issue. The premise 'If (M_o) is true, then one ought to adopt the backtracking resolution' makes no appeal to counterfactuals whereas the two-boxer's meta-level normative premise *does* appeal to counterfactuals. Hence, one ought to adopt the one-boxer's meta-level normative premise, rather than the two-boxer's meta-level normative premise.

But my present point is that the two-boxer need not accept the (meta-meta-level) normative principle that one ought to adopt a meta-level normative principle that avoids reference to counterfactuals. Instead, the two-boxer can simply rest content with his object-level normative principle and his meta-level normative principle, even if they both contain (standard-resolution) counterfactuals.
3. By the time my paper was published I had already come to regard the debate between the one-boxers and the two-boxers as a hopeless stalemate. David Lewis (1981) also expresses this view, and my own reluctant acceptance of it came about partly as a result of discussing the matter with him.
4. I thank Norman Gillespie for helpful discussion, and Richmond Campbell for the example mentioned in note 1.

13

Common Causes, Smoking, and Lung Cancer*

ISAAC LEVI

One of the attractive features of Bayesian doctrine is its generality. Other approaches to decision-making and statistical inference often appear eclectic or partial. To those who love system, Bayesianism has seemed just right.

Yet critics of Bayesian doctrine have complained since the nineteenth century that the probability numbers used by Bayesians to represent probabilities and utilities are excessively arbitrary. Not the least among such critics has been the great British statistician R. A. Fisher. Those of us who are sympathetic to worries like those expressed by Fisher have also sympathized with efforts to replace Bayesian theology with accounts of statistical inference and decision-making that will compete with the systematic virtues of Bayesianism without insisting that we pull numbers out of a hat.

Recently, however, Bayesianism has been challenged from another quarter. Advocates of causal decision theory complain that Bayesians sometimes neglect relevant causal fine structure of decision problems. Sometimes supporters of this view mention Fisher's speculations concerning the causal relations between smoking and lung cancer when developing illustrative applications of their approach.

We should not, however, take Fisher to be guilty of causal decision theory by association. Fisher himself wrote precious little on decision-making. But the stands he took on probability judgment and statistical inference pose problems for Bayesian decision theory, and there have been proposals around for a long time for responding to these problems. These proposals are suggestive of alternatives to Bayesian decision theory which address serious difficulties with Bayesian doctrine—difficulties which Fisher understood quite well.

By way of contrast, the critique of Bayesianism undertaken by causal decision theory has mislocated the soft underbelly of Bayesian dogma. Worse yet, it has diverted the attention of those bemused by the artifacts of modal and causal realism from the important troubles with Bayesianism.

In this discussion, I hope to show how gratuitously diversionary causal decision theory is through a quick review of the predicament of someone deliberating as to whether to quit smoking cigarettes because of experimental correlations between smoking and lung cancer. One of the conclusions I mean to draw from all of this is that even in those contexts where causal decision theory allegedly challenges Bayesian decision theory, the most sensible accounts of what one ought to do reject the assumptions of both Bayesianism and causal decision theory.

In 1957, R. A. Fisher published the first in a series of notes and essays in which he protested against the exaggerated conclusions being drawn concerning the causal links between smoking and lung cancer from the retrospective studies of Doll, Hill, and Hammond.[1] These studies revealed a correlation between smoking and lung cancer in the samples observed. Fisher was concerned to warn against taking an observed correlation to be an indicator of causation. He thought that embarking on a campaign to urge people to stop smoking based on evidence which, at best, suggested that further study of the conjectured link between lung cancer and smoking is in order was an abuse of statistical data and could lead to the discrediting of the use of statistical methods of the sort that he and his colleagues had worked so hard to develop in the 1920s and 1930s.

Fisher pointed out that one possible explanation of the observed correlations would be obtained through positing a common cause—conceivably genetic. Fisher did not claim that the available data offered adequate evidence for the truth of this conjecture. Just as he thought that the data provided some reason for exploring the conjecture that smoking caused cancer, he thought it also provided some reason for exploring the conjecture of a common cause. He seemed inclined to believe that some twin studies done in Germany and England which suggested a genetic component contributing to smoking habits favored some version of the genetic common cause hypothesis—but still only as a conjecture meriting further study.

Fisher thought that if it could be shown that there is no causal dependence between smoking and lung cancer and, in particular, if there were a common genetic cause, it would be inappropriate to undertake a campaign to urge people to stop smoking. Indeed, he insisted that as long as we can only claim a serious possibility that smoking causes lung cancer, we should not raise an alarm. Sensible people whose smoking habits are not important to them may be prepared to give up the habit "as a kind of insurance" against a danger they cannot assess. But others deeply caught up in the toils of the habit may suffer a considerable psychic cost (so Fisher argued) in order to break the habit. We should not put them through the anguish which a stern warning would engender without having solid evidence that smoking does, indeed, cause lung cancer—evidence which he claimed had not, as yet, been supplied.[2]

Thus, the kind of recommendation about what people should do that interested Fisher concerned public policy. Fisher thought that should evidence come in indicating that smoking did cause lung cancer so that reducing the incidence of smoking would reduce the incidence of lung cancer, a policy designed to induce such a reduction in smoking might be in order. But if the evidence supported a common cause hypothesis, no such campaign would be warranted. If we sought to reduce the incidence of lung cancer then, we would have to manipulate the gene pool. Fisher was a eugenicist; but at the time he wrote (and perhaps now) genetic engineering was not sufficiently well developed to make this a viable option.

Public policy recommendations aimed at reducing the incidence of lung cancer are one thing. Recommendations as to whether a cigarette smoker, given his or her aims and predilections, should continue to smoke or not is quite another. Fisher did say that someone with very little interest in smoking might reasonably drop the habit as long as there is the bare possibility that smoking causes lung cancer. He did not, however, make any recommendation as to whether someone who has the smoking habit should take steps to break it if that agent knew that smoking and lung cancer were induced by a common cause.

Of course, one might well conjecture that Fisher would have agreed that an agent who enjoyed smoking would have no good reason to stop. So would most of us. But this does not suggest that Fisher can be enlisted on the side of causal decision theorists.

Fisher was no admirer of Bayesianism—a point of view which he rightly condemned for its tendency to oscillate between dogmatism and wilful arbitrariness.[3] But the features he thought objectionable in Bayesianism are retained in causal decision theory. Causal decision theorists, like Bayesians, introduce subjective probability judgments when there is no warrant for so doing.

But let us make no further conjectures as to what Fisher might have said just yet. Instead let us explore the ramifications for decision-making of the conjecture that Fisher himself argued ought to be worth investigating – to wit, that genetic endowment is a contributing factor both to smoking and to lung cancer.

Causal decision theorists appear sometimes to be motivated to explore cases like smoking and lung cancer because they seek realistic cases of decision problems where the recommendations of causal decision theory differ from those of Bayesian decision theory. I have always thought this motivation misguided, not because predicaments exemplified by the smoking-lung cancer case are unrealistic under the assumption of common genetic cause or contributing causal factor, but because realistic versions of such cases fail to constitute the conflict with Bayesianism that is sought.

If this is so, causal decision theory has few ramifications for practical applications in real life different from Bayesianism. The fact that versions of Newcomb's Problem or David Lewis's Prisoner's Dilemma for space cadets (as Richard Jeffrey so delicately puts it) do illustrate conflicts between Bayesianism and causal decision theory has not seemed terribly important to some devotees of Bayesian dogma as long as prospects for realistic applications remain remote.

But as long as examples of such conflict can be coherently and consistently described, as I think they can, the causal decision theorist can still insist that his theory may have use in some contexts in real life which we have not as yet anticipated. My previous remarks on causal decision theory have been designed to argue that causal decision theory gives bad advice even to space cadets. I have offered reasons elsewhere.[4] Although I shall rehearse them briefly at the end of this paper, they are not my chief concern here.

In this discussion, I shall consider the smoking-lung cancer case under the assumption that there is a genetic factor contributing both to the incidence of cancer and to smoking. Discussion of this example will explain why I think realistic confrontations between causal decision theory and Bayesian decision theory are going to be difficult to come by. If this is right, complaints about the realism of treatments of Newcomb's Problem will be shown to be misplaced. In the course of these remarks, I hope to make it clear that my chief purpose is not to criticize causal decision theory. In itself, causal decision theory is not that important. My chief target is Bayesian decision theory which, in my view, promotes a dogmatism about probability judgment and utility judgment which ought to be a focus of philosophical attention. Causal decision theory diverts attention from these matters by directing the interests of philosophers to alleged troubles with Bayesianism in the labyrinths of causal metaphysics. I hope to remind students of causal decision theory that the serious troubles with Bayesianism are to be found elsewhere.[5]

Suppose that Jones takes for granted that there are two genotypes *G* and *not-G* such that the statistical probability of becoming a lifelong smoker (*S*) on living a life is high (say, .9) if *G* holds and is low (say, .1) if *not-G* holds. Jones also knows that the statistical probability of contracting lung cancer (*C*) on living a life is .9 if *G* holds and is .1 if *not-G* holds. Finally, Jones knows that the chance of *C* on living a life of smoking (*S*) given *G* (given *not-G*) is equal to the chance of *C* on living life given *G* (given *not-G*). Regardless of the genotype, smoking and lung cancer are stochastically independent variables.

For the sake of the argument, assume that Jones is age thirty and has been smoking cigarettes for a dozen years. He is contemplating an effort to break the habit. His preferences are such that he favors smoking all his life and contracting cancer to stopping smoking and contracting cancer (that is, he prefers *S&C* to *not-S&C*). Also he prefers *not-C&S* to *not-C&not-S*. Relative to *C* and *not-C* as states of nature, smoking for a lifetime dominates not smoking for a lifetime.

Breaking the cigarette habit is notoriously difficult and success is by no means guaranteed. Of course, breaking the habit is not the sort of thing one does overnight. It involves undertaking some regimen such as participating in Smokenders. Let the regimen be *R*. For the sake of simplicity, I shall suppose that the chance of stopping smoking (*not-S*) on following the regimen (*R*) is equal to 1. Following the regimen assures success. I assume that this is so regardless of whether he has genotype *G* or *not-G*.

I am not supposing that doing *R* is equivalent to *not-S*. Not smoking a lifetime can come about because one has never smoked at all or, alternatively, even if one has, like Jones, smoked until age thirty, one might not stop owing to following some regimen but because of a loss of appetite for smoking.

Finally I am assuming that given *G* (*not-G*) doing *R* is stochastically independent of contracting cancer. That is to say that the chance of *C* on living a life with genotype *G (not-G)* and doing *R* is the same as the chance of *C* on living a life with genotype *G(not-G)* which equals .9 (.1).

Because *R* is not equivalent to not-*S*, it does not follow from the fact that smoking a lifetime is stochastically dependent on genotype that smoking up to age thirty and then doing *R* is stochastically dependent on genotype. There are two cases to consider.

Case 1: By far the more realistic of the two cases is the one where Jones takes for granted that whether he goes to Smokenders or not is stochastically independent of his genotype.

If the requirements of direct inference consonant with Bayesian doctrine are faithfully observed in determining subjective or credal probabilities from knowledge of chances or statistical probabilities, the credal probability *pr(G/R&not-S)* = *pr(G)*. Also *pr(C/G&R)* = *pr(C/G)* and *pr(C/not-G&R)* = *pr(C/not-G)*. Hence, *pr(C/R&not-S)* = *pr(C/R)* = *pr(C)*. Contracting cancer is probabilistically independent of going to Smokenders.

In such a case, the Bayesian recommendation is that Jones should not bother undertaking a regimen to break his habit. Causal decision theorists agree.

Thus Case 1 is not an example where causal decision theory and Bayesian decision theory cross swords—even though it is an example of a common cause predicament—quite likely of the sort that Fisher envisaged.

Case 2: Imagine that Jones believes that whether he goes to Smokenders or not does depend stochastically on genotype. To simplify, suppose that the chance of *not-R* on a life with genotype *G* (*not-G*) equals the chance of *S* on a life with gene *G* (*not-G*) equals .9 (.1). I doubt it is likely that Jones would adopt such probability judgments—surely not without strong resistance. Even so, we have simply lost some of the realism which we might attribute to Case 1. The question now is whether in Case 2 we can find a conflict between Bayesian and causal decision theory.

In a footnote to his original paper on Newcomb's Problem, Nozick observed that even in Case 2, we need not have a conflict between Bayesian and causal decision theory.[6] Eells has recently written a book which essentially elaborates Nozick's point.[7]

When contemplating a decision whether to break the habit, agent Jones may have a symptom (a "tickle") which is evidence for his being of type *G* or of type *not-G*. Jones should use this evidence together with Bayes's theorem to compute a posterior probability for *G* and for *not-G* and, hence, values for *pr(C/R&E)* and *pr(C/notR&E)* (where *E* is the evidence of the tickle). It will then turn out that these two probabilities are equal to the value of *pr(C/E)*. Once more Bayesian doctrine recommends taking the dominating options and refusing to break the habit. We have failed to find a conflict between causal decision theory and Bayesian decision theory.

Of course, we need to consider whether we can suppose that Jones does endorse some sort of tickle hypothesis or that he should do so. It is sometimes suggested that if nothing else will serve as a tickle, the fact that Jones has the preferences for smoking he does can function as the evidence *E*. Indeed, it may be argued that if Jones can consistently view himself as having a choice in the matter, he should have available to him some sort of tickle data *E*.

I do not see why this should be so. We may regard Jones as having a choice in the matter as long as he goes or does not go to Smokenders owing to the outcome of his deliberation. We need not suppose that any particular feature of the deliberation is itself symptomatic of the genotype—only the outcome—which is the conclusion to go to Smokenders or not as the case may be. There may be no feature of the deliberation which Jones can recognize until the conclusion which is a serviceable tickle capable of "screening off" any dependence between his choice and his contracting cancer.

Let us be clear about this. All I mean to claim is that there is no incoherence or inconsistency in this. I do think that Case 2 predicaments are highly unrealistic, tickle or no tickle. I do not think, however, that cases where there is no tickle are, for that reason, less realistic (whatever this can mean to us in such bizarre situations) than cases where there are tickles.

Thus, if we are going to find conflict between Bayesian decision theory and causal decision theory in common cause examples like the smoking-lung cancer case, we should have to think of Case 2 and under the non-tickle hypothesis.

However, there are other problems of a type which do have a practical bearing on realistic predicaments which suggest further obstacles in the way of constructing good examples of conflict between causal and Bayesian decision theory.

In our example with the probability numbers specified (the analysis would be different if we used different numbers but the main points would be the same), Bayesian decision theory requires that we compute a value for $pr(C/R) = pr(C/R \& not\text{-}S)$ and $pr(C/not\text{-}R)$. But given the specifications of the problem, we need to invoke some "prior" or unconditional probability $pr(G)$ for the probability that the agent Jones has genotype G. If in our example the value of $pr(G)$ is somewhere near .5, a conflict between the recommendations of Bayesian decision theory and causal decision theory will occur. Otherwise it will not. I have explained essentially the same point in the context of Newcomb's Problem elsewhere.[8] Is it realistic to assign some particular prior credal probability to G?

I think I know and can document Fisher's answer to this question. Fisher, followed by Neyman and Pearson and other pioneers in modern statistical theory, argued (as did Venn and Peirce in the nineteenth century) that unless one can show that Jones's genotype is itself the outcome of a stochastic process and, moreover, Jones knows that the chance of his being a G on a process of that type is r (where r is a standard designator for a real number), Jones cannot justifiably assign $pr(G)$ the value r.[9]

Those in the Laplacian tradition (whose modern day advocates are Carnap, Jeffreys, and Jaynes) are guilty of disguising the arbitrariness of their verdicts in the cloak of intuition and inductive logic. Personalists differ from these authors only insofar as they disown this particular form of self-deception, come out of the closet, and admit the arbitrariness of their numerically definite probability judgments.

I have discussed views like Fisher's extensively elsewhere[10] and shall not repeat myself here. Speaking very roughly, I deny that one must always have knowledge of numerically definite probability to ground judgments of credal probability. In the absence of such knowledge, it will be sensible to endorse highly indeterminate states of credal probability judgment. Even if this view is not as extreme as Fisher's would have been, it is extreme enough to suggest the conclusion that, for the most part, the only times one could be justified in assigning a prior probability to G is when Jones knows (i) that he was selected at random from some given population and (ii) he knew the distribution of G and *not-G* in that population. I want to emphasize that this remark must be heavily qualified and that more accurate statements of what I think about this are to be found elsewhere. However, in the present context, I think this formulation reasonably serviceable.

The important point to emphasize is that whether one considers the realistic Case 1 version of the smoking-lung cancer problem or the more bizarre Case 2 version, it will be extremely unlikely that Jones will have the knowledge that he is a random sample from a given population and that he has precise information about the percentages of G's and *not-G*'s in that population. Furthermore, it would be even still more remarkable if the percentages of the two genotypes were equal or nearly equal.

What should the agent Jones do in Case 2 if he does not have the knowledge of chances of G and *not-G* as is quite realistic to suppose? In such cases, I suggest, Jones should adopt a credal state which allows as permissible a wide range of probability values going nearly from 0 to nearly 1. Jones cannot use Bayesian calculations to determine whether he should break the habit or not. Some permissible distributions argue in favor of doing so. Others do not. In the absence of a verdict, Jones may appeal to criteria for decision-making under uncertainty. A review of the criteria considered in Luce and Raiffa[11] indicate that they all agree that one should choose the dominating option. I myself favor maximin. No matter, just as this line of reasoning favors the two box solution in the classical Newcomb's Problem (as I noted a decade ago[12]), it favors refusal to break the habit in Case 2.

Notice that we are now considering not two but three varieties of decision theory: Bayesian decision theory, causal decision theory, and a third hybrid of Bayesian decision theory and principles for decision-making under uncertainty. In situations where credal probability judgment goes indeterminate, neither Bayesian decision theory nor causal decision theory can, as a general rule, make recommendations as to which among feasible options to choose. Hybrid theory offers Bayesian answers in those special cases where credal probability judgment is determinate. When credal probability goes indeterminate, hybrid theory invokes criteria for decision making under uncertainty (I have favored maximin or leximin criteria) to decide between options which have not been ruled out by Bayesian criteria.[13] In the extreme case where credal probability judgment is maximally indeterminate, hybrid decision theory coincides with decision theory for decision making under uncertainty.

The hybrid theory was not designed to handle Newcomb-like problems. It is a far more serious enterprise than that. Decision-making under uncertainty has been a matter of concern to those who think probability judgment ought to be grounded in knowledge of chance for a very long time. The hybrid theory is designed to give Bayesian answers in those contexts where Bayesian theory can be applied while deviating from Bayesianism when considerations of expected utility cannot render a verdict simply because probability and utility assessments are not definite enough.

The fact that the hybrid theory gives the same answer as the causal decision theory in Case 2 when Jones has no definite credal probability that he is of genotype *G* brings out the fact that the attraction many people find in the recommendations of causal decision theory has little to do with questions of causal dependency and has much to do with reluctance to follow anything other than a conservative course when they cannot calculate expectations.

Still it might be said that causal decision theory does differ from Bayesian decision theory in this case. Bayesian decision theory cannot give an answer because of the indeterminacy of the credal probability that Jones has genotype *G*. Causal decision theory recommends the dominating option no matter what that probability is—just as maximin does.

But the difference is negligible. Causal decision theory does, after all, aim to give answers in contexts where one option fails to dominate the other. In those contexts, indeterminacy in credal probability judgment renders causal decision theory as impotent as Bayesian decision theory as a means for narrowing down the set of admissible options. Hybrid decision theory can still give more definite verdicts even in such cases.

Of course, just as we have a hybrid Bayesian decision theory, we can envisage a hybrid causal decision theory so that we can say that hybrid causal decision theory and hybrid Bayesian decision theory both give answers even in the case where one option fails to dominate the other. Once we grant this, it seems sensible to focus on the comparison between hybrid Bayesian decision theory and hybrid causal decision theory.

What emerges from our discussion thus far when we have shifted to the hybrid versions of Bayesian and causal decision theory is that the version of Case 2 considered thus far does not reveal any difference between the two. Both the hybrid Bayesian and causal decision theories recommend that Jones not break his habit.

Let us now shift to variants of Case 2 where Jones knows that he has been selected at random from a population with known percentages of *G*'s and *non-G*'s or where, perhaps, he knows the genotypes of his parents, the appropriate linkage parameters, and so forth, so that he knows the chance of his being a *G*. This version of Case 2 is more farfetched than the previous one. Yet it is the type of case where Jones could legitimately ground his credal probability judgment that he is a *G* in knowledge of chance and come up with numerically precise credal probabilities.

Of course, we might also consider the case where Jones does not claim knowledge of the chance of his being a *G* but assigns a numerically definite credal probability to his being a *G* without grounding it on knowledge of chances. This version of Case 2 is less farfetched than the previous one; but Jones's probability judgments in this case are more vulnerable to the charge of being arbitrary. To the extent that he takes this point seriously, he will modify the credal probabilities he takes seriously so that they become indeterminate as in the first version of the Case 2 we considered.

Still and all someone can coherently endorse a view where his credal probability judgments are not grounded in knowledge of chances. So I shall consider this version of Case 2 along with the version where numerically definite credal probabilities are assigned on the basis of chances. Both versions of the situation are problematic—albeit for somewhat different reasons. That is all that need be of concern to us.

When the credal probabilities for the hypothesis that the genotype is *G* go determinate, both hybrid theories collapse to their corresponding pure forms. Hybrid causal decision theory reduces to causal decision theory and hybrid Bayesian decision theory reduces to Bayesian decision theory.

As I pointed out a long time ago, in the context of Newcomb's Problem, the Bayesian decision theory recommends two boxes for some versions of the problem and one box for others. Causal decision theory recommends two boxes for all cases (as long as the payoffs remain fixed). The same is true in the Case 2 version of the smoking-lung cancer predicament. Given the payoff structure we have stipulated for that problem and the chances of *C* and of *S* given *G* and *not-G* we have supposed, if the probability of *G* and of *not-G* are roughly equal, causal decision theory recommends that Jones keep on smoking whereas Bayesian decision theory recommends that Jones try to break the habit. Otherwise, the two theories agree that Jones keep on smoking.

We have reached the Promised Land. The version of the smoking-lung cancer predicament where causal decision theory and Bayesian decision theory clash has been discovered. Unfortunately Zion is not as attractive as it was advertised to be. Either Jones knows that there is a roughly equal chance of his being of genotype *G* as there is of his being of genotype *not-G* and can ground his subjective probability that he is a *G* on such knowledge of chance or he must assign *pr*(*G*) the value 0.5 without such knowledge. The former scenario is just not credible. The second scenario implies that Jones's probability judgments are unabashedly arbitrary or are grounded on something like the discredited principle of insufficient reason.

One thing more can be said about these cases. They are sufficiently rarefied and bizarre to render appeals to "intuitions" about what ought to be done in such predicaments questionable as "data" on the basis of which one can render a verdict concerning the merits of Bayesian and causal decision theory. So we have not found clashes between causal decision theory and Bayesian decision theory which can be used as the basis for making a critical assessment of their relative merits.

I have alluded elsewhere to a kind of predicament which is a special version of Newcomb's Problem in which causal decision theory gives a different verdict from Bayesian theory and where it seems clear (to me at any rate) that causal decision theory leads to absurdity. That predicament arises when the demon is perfectly infallible and known to be so.[14]

There is a corresponding version of the smoking-lung cancer problem. Suppose that genotype *G* yields lifetime smokers 100 per cent of the time and likewise yields sufferers of cancer 100 per cent of the time. Genotype *not-G* never yields lifetime smokers and never yields sufferers of cancer. Jones can know this about himself and also regard himself as free to choose whether to break the habit or not without contradiction or incoherence.

I grant that this scenario is strange; but, given the weird presuppositions we have already swallowed, I cannot see why we should refuse to consider this predicament in exploring the merits of Bayesian decision theory and causal decision theory.

There is one advantage to exploring it. The problem is a problem of decision-making under certainty, and the verdict is one which ought to be clear. Jones ought to try to break the habit. But causal decision theory recommends that he refrain from doing so. Here we have a case where one would expect intuitions to be clear and to run against causal decision theory.

Still there are many who resist the objection or the intuition invoked. So there is yet another objection which, in my judgment, cuts still deeper. Causal decision theory is excessively sensitive to the way states and consequences of options are described in making evaluations of feasible options. Bayesian decision theory does not have this sensitivity.[15] This means that Bayesian decision theory can be applied without presupposing in advance some controversial view in causal metaphysics. Causal decision theory relies on conditional analyses of causality in ways which must seem questionable to all but rabid partisans of such views.

Strictly speaking, hybrid Bayesianism is also sensitive to the way states and consequences are described. The reason is that the maximin criteria can apply only when security levels or "worst possible consequences" are identified for each feasible option; and this determination depends on the way possible consequences are identified.

However, it should be remembered that hybrid Bayesianism begins by first assessing expected utility and invokes maximin only when considerations of expected utility fail to render a verdict. In assessing expected utility, the sensitivity to the way states and consequences are described does not obtain. Moreover, when invoking the maximin criterion, the determination of security levels can be seen as a function of the agent's values and interests. Hence the sensitivity here does not depend on any causal metaphysics but on questions of value.[16]

Causal decision theory of the hybrid variety can also claim that the application of maximin invokes determinations of security levels depending on the agent's values and not on his causal metaphysics.

But the first criterion invoked by causal decision theory involves an assessment of expected value which, unlike the Bayesian approach, is sensitive to the way states and consequences are described in a manner reflecting controversial views concerning causality.

Even though these considerations ought to show that causal decision theory is a curious intellectual aberration of the past decade, my aim in this essay has not been to defend this view. I have hoped to show that there is no support in the concerns of Fisher for causal decision theory. I have also tried to suggest how difficult it is to obtain a realistic predicament where causal decision theory clashes with Bayesian decision theory.

However, the most important point I wish to make is that the serious deficiencies in Bayesian dogma are not to be found by pursuing the directions favored by causal decision theorists. Bayesian decision theory presupposes views of probability judgment and utility judgment which entail that rational agents have states of belief and desire which are representable by probability measures and utility measures unique up to positive affine transformations. Fisher understood very well how untenable such views are and sought in the domain of statistics to develop approaches to inference which do not fall into the trap of Bayesian dogma. Philosophers interested in problems of rational choice would be well advised to turn away from the frivolities of causal decision theory and the dogmatism of strict Bayesianism. The wisdom encased in the dogmatic husk of Bayesianism ought to be combined with the insights of the great anti-Bayesian critics, like Venn, Peirce, Fisher, Neyman, Pearson, and Wald, to provide us with a more general perspective on issues of rational choice.

NOTES

*Thanks are due to Teddy Seidenfeld for critical comments on the first draft.

1. Fisher's writings on smoking and lung cancer were collected in a booklet Fisher (1959b). The papers are all reprinted in Fisher (1974) v.5 as items 269, 270, 272, 274, 275, 276, and 276a. My references are to the papers as they appear in (1974).
2. Fisher (1974), item 274, pp. 408-9.

3. Fisher (1959a), pp. 14–20 and Fisher (1974), item 273, pp.398–406.
4. Levi (1975), (1982), and (1983).
5. See especially my Levi (1980). For some mysterious reason, my views in that book are sometimes called "Bayesian." Although in special cases, my theory urges Bayesian recommendations, in other cases, my theory makes anti-Bayesian recommendations. My proposals may be hybrid; but they are not Bayesian in any sense faithful to the basic principles of the Bayesian tradition.
6. Nozick (1969), in this volume: p.131, (note 11).
7. Eells (1982).
8. Levi (1975) as reprinted in Hooker (1978), pp.372–73, 375. In Case 2, the argument runs as follows. In Case 2, we are given in effect, that $pr(C/R\&not\text{-}S) = pr(C/not\text{-}S)$ and $pr(C/not\text{-}R) = pr(C/S)$. More generally, all the specifications of probabilities supplied for S obtain when $not\text{-}R$ is substituted.

By the calculus of probabilities, we know the following:

(a) $pr(C/R) = pr(C/R\&G)pr(G/R) + pr(C/R\&not\text{-}G)pr(not\text{-}G/R)$.

We also know

(b) $pr(C/R\&G) = pr(C/G) = 0.9$
  and $pr(C/R\&not\text{-}G) = pr(C/not\text{-}G) = 0.1$

(c) $pr(R/G) = pr(not\text{-}S/G) = 0.1$ and
  $pr(R/not\text{-}G) = pr(not\text{-}S/not\text{-}G) = 0.9$

Hence, we have

(d) $pr(G/R) = (pr(R/G)pr(G))/pr(R) = 0.1pr(G)/pr(R)$.
  $pr(not\text{-}G/R) = (pr(R/not\text{-}G)pr(not\text{-}G))/pr(R) = 0.9\,pr(not\text{-}G)/pr(R)$.

(e) $pr(R) = pr(R/G)pr(G) + pr(R/not\text{-}G)pr(not\text{-}G)$
   $= 0.1pr(G) + 0.9pr(not\text{-}G)$.

Making substitutions from (b)-(e) into (a), we obtain the following:

(f) $pr(C/R) = .09/(.1pr(G) + .9pr(not\text{-}G))$.

By similar calculation, we have

(g) $pr(not\text{-}C/not\text{-}R) = .09/(.9pr(G) + .1pr(not\text{-}G))$.

From (f) and (g) it is easy to see that if $pr(G) = pr(not\text{-}G) = 0.5$, $pr(C/R) = pr(not\text{-}C/not\text{-}R) = 0.18$. On the other hand, if $pr(G)$ is near 1, $pr(C/R)$ is near 0.9 as is $pr(C/not\text{-}R)$ so that we approach a situation where the decision whether to follow the regimen R or not is probabilistically independent of whether one gets cancer or not. In this latter case even a Bayesian would favor the dominating option of smoking. Only when $pr(G)$ is sufficiently near equality with $pr(not\text{-}G)$ will we obtain a clash. How near is sufficiently near will, of course, depend on the character of the payoff matrix and the details of the stochastic model. But even if these details are varied, the main point remains the same. Bayesians will favor the dominating option for some values of $pr(G)$ and not for others.

9. See the references in note 3.
10. See the various references to objectivist necessitarianism in Levi (1980).
11. Luce and Raiffa (1958), p.298.
12. Levi (1975) as reprinted in Hooker (1978), p.381–82.
13. See Levi (1980), Chapter 7, for considerations favoring maximin and leximin criteria. My approach in Levi (1980) invokes three "tests" for admissibility: test for E-admissibility grounded on considerations of expected utility (4.8), tests for P-admissibility (ch. 6) and tests for S-admissibility and lex-admissibility (pp.148–49 and 154–55). In most contexts of practical decision-making, P-admissibility is vacuous so that the sequence of tests reduces to E-admissibility followed by S-admissibility (or lex-admissibility). This is the form in which I am presenting the theory in this discussion. I first outlined the theory of Levi (1980) in Levi (1974) which is reprinted in Hooker (1978).
14. See Levi (1975) printed in Hooker (1978), p.380.
15. Levi (1982), pp.338–42 and Levi (1983), pp. 541–42.
16. See the addenda to Levi (1974) printed in Hooker (1978), p. 259.

IV

IS THE PRISONER'S DILEMMA
A NEWCOMB PROBLEM?

14

Prisoners' Dilemma Is a Newcomb Problem

DAVID LEWIS

Several authors have observed that Prisoners' Dilemma and Newcomb's Problem are related — for instance, in that both involve controversial appeals to dominance.[1] But to call them "related" is an understatement. Considered as puzzles about rationality, or disagreements between two conceptions thereof, they are one and the same problem. Prisoners' Dilemma *is* a Newcomb Problem — or rather, two Newcomb Problems side by side, one per prisoner. Only the inessential trappings are different. Let us make them the same.

You and I, the "prisoners," are separated. Each is offered the choice: to rat or not to rat. (The action of 'ratting" is so called because I consider it to be *rat*ional — but that is controversial.) Ratting is done as follows: one reaches out and takes a transparent box, which is seen to contain a thousand dollars. A prisoner who rats gets to keep the thousand. (Maybe ratting is construed as an act of confessing and accusing one's partner, much as taking the Queen's shilling was once construed as an act of enlisting — but that is irrelevant to the decision problem.) If either prisoner declines to rat, he is not at all rewarded; but his partner is presented with a million dollars, nicely packed in an opaque box. (Maybe each faces a long sentence and a short sentence to be served consecutively; escape from the long sentence costs a million, and escape from the short sentence costs a thousand. But it is irrele-

From David Lewis, "Prisoners' Dilemma Is a Newcomb Problem," *Philosophy and Public Affairs* 8, no. 3 (Spring 1979): 235–40. Copyright © 1979 by Princeton University Press. Reprinted by permission of Princeton University Press.

vant how the prisoners propose to spend their money.) So the payoff matrix looks like this.

	I rat	I don't rat
You rat	I get \$1,000 You get \$1,000	I get \$0 You get \$1,001,000
You don't rat	I get \$1,001,000 You get \$0	I get \$1,000,000 You get \$1,000,000

There we have it: a perfectly typical case of Prisoners' Dilemma. My decision problem, in a nutshell, is as follows; yours is exactly similar.

(1) I am offered a thousand – take it or leave it.

(2) Perhaps also I will be given a million; but whether I will or not is causally independent of what I do now. Nothing I can do now will have any effect on whether or not I get my million.

(3) I will get my million if and only if you do not take your thousand.

Newcomb's Problem is the same as regards points (1) and (2). The only difference – if such it be – is that point (3) is replaced by

(3′) I will get my million if and only if it is predicted that I do not take my thousand.

"Predicted" need not mean "predicted in advance." Not so in English: we credit new theories with success in "predicting" phenomena already observed. And not so in Newcomb's Problem. While it dramatizes the problem to think of the million *already there,* or else already *not* there, in the opaque box in front of me as I deliberate, it is agreed all around that what really matters is (2), and hence that the "prediction" should be causally independent of my decision. Making the prediction ahead of time is one good way to secure this causal independence. But it is not the only way.[2] Provided that I can have no effect on it, the prediction could just as well be made simultaneously with my decision or even afterwards, and the character of Newcomb's Problem would be unchanged.[3] Likewise in the case of Prisoners' Dilemma nothing need be assumed – and in my telling of the story, nothing was assumed – about whether the prisoners are put to the test simultaneously or one after the other.

Also it is inessential to Newcomb's Problem that any prediction – in advance, or otherwise – should actually take place. It is enough that some potentially predictive process should go on and that whether I get my million is somehow made to depend on the outcome of that process. It could all be automated: if the predictive computer sends a pulse of current to the money-putting machine I get my million, otherwise not. Or there might be people who put the million in the box or not depending on the outcome of the process, but who do not at all think of the outcome as a prediction of my choice or as warrant for a prediction. It makes no difference to my decision problem whether someone — the one who gives the million or perhaps some bystander — does or does not form beliefs about what I will do by inference from the outcome of the predictive process.

Eliminating inessentials, then, Newcomb's Problem is characterized by (1), (2), and

(3″) I will get my million if and only if a certain potentially predictive process (which may go on before, during, or after my choice) yields the outcome which could warrant a prediction that I do not take my thousand.

The potentially predictive process *par excellence* is *simulation*. To predict whether I will take my thousand, make a replica of me, put my replica in a replica of my predicament, and see whether my replica takes *his* thousand. And whether or not anybody actually makes a prediction about me by observing my replica, still my replica's decision is a potentially predictive process with respect to mine. Disregarding predictive processes other than simulation, if such there be, we have this special case of (3″):

(3‴) I will get my million if and only if my replica does not take his thousand.

There are replicas and replicas. Some are the same sort of thing that I am, others are less so. A flesh-and-blood duplicate made by copying me atom for atom would be one good sort of replica. A working scale model of me, smaller perhaps by a ratio of 1:148, also might serve. So might a pattern of bits in a computer, or beads on an abacus, or marks on paper, or neuron firings in a brain, even though these things are unlike me and replicate me only by way of some complicated isomorphism.

Also, some replicas are more reliable than others. There may be grounds for greater or lesser degrees of confidence that my replica and I will decide alike in the matter of the thousand. A replica that matches me perfectly in the respects relevant to my decision (whether duplicate or isomorph) will have more predictive power than a less perfect replica; but even a poor replica may have some significant degree of predictive power.

As Newcomb's Problem is usually told, the predictive process involved is extremely reliable. But that is inessential. The disagreement between conceptions of rationality that gives the problem its interest arises even when the reliability of the process, as estimated by the agent, is quite poor — indeed, even when the agent judges that the predictive process will do little better than chance. More precisely, define *average estimated reliability* as the average of (A) the agent's conditional degree of belief that the predictive process will predict correctly, given that he takes his thousand, and (B) his conditional degree of belief that the process will predict correctly, given that he does not take his thousand. (When the predictive process is a simulation, for instance, we have the average of two conditional degrees of belief that the agent and his replica will decide alike.) Let r be the ratio of the value of the thousand to the value of the million: .001 if value is proportional to money, perhaps somewhat more under diminishing marginal value. We have a disagreement between two conceptions of rationality if and only if the expected value[4] of taking the thousand is less than that of declining it, which is so if and only if the average estimated reliability exceeds $\frac{(1 + r)}{2}$. (That is .5005 if value is proportional to money.) This is not a very high standard of reliability. So there can be a fully problematic case of Newcomb's Problem in which the predictive process consists of simulation by some very imperfect and very unreliable replica.

The most readily available sort of replica of me is simply another person, placed in a replica of my predicament. For instance: you, my fellow prisoner. Most likely you are not a very exact replica of me, and your choice is not a very reliable predictive process for mine.[5] Still, you might well be reliable enough (in my estimation) for a Newcomb Problem.[6] So we have this special case of (3'''):

(3) I will get my million if and only if you do not take your thousand. Inessential trappings aside, Prisoners' Dilemma is a version of Newcomb's Problem, *quod erat demonstrandum*.

Some who discuss Newcomb's Problem think it is rational to decline the thousand if the predictive process is reliable enough. Their reason is that they believe, justifiably, that those who decline their thousands will probably get their millions. Some who discuss Prisoners' Dilemma think it is rational not to rat if the two partners are enough alike.[7] Their reason is that they believe, justifiably, that those who do not rat will probably not be ratted on by their like-thinking partners. These two opinions are one opinion in two guises.

But some—I, for one—who discuss Newcomb's Problem think it is rational to take the thousand no matter how reliable the predictive process may be. Our reason is that one thereby gets a thousand more than he would if he declined, since he would get his million or not regardless of whether he took his thousand. And some—I, for one— who discuss Prisoners' Dilemma think it is rational to rat no matter how much alike the two partners may be, and no matter how certain they may be that they will decide alike. Our reason is that one is better off if he rats than he would be if he did not, since he would be ratted on or not regardless of whether he ratted. These two opinions also are one.

Some have fended off the lessons of Newcomb's Problem by saying, "Let us not have, or let us not rely on, any intuitions about what is rational in goofball cases so unlike the decision problems of real life." But Prisoners' Dilemmas are deplorably common in real life. They are the most down-to-earth versions of Newcomb's Problem now available.

1. Nozick (1969), pp. 122–23 in this volume; Brams (1975b); Davis (1977), p. 58 in this volume; Sobel (1978), pp. 167–68.
2. And perhaps not an infallible way. See Lewis (1976a).
3. That is noted by Nozick (1969), p. 123 in this volume, and I have not seen it disputed.
4. As calculated according to the non-casual sort of decision theory presented for instance in Jeffrey (1965).
5. On the other hand, you might be an extremely perfect and reliable replica, as in the Prisoners' Dilemma between twins described by Nozick (1969), pp. 122–23 in this volume.
6. If you do not meet even the low standard of estimated reliability just considered, either because you are unlike me or because you and I alike are apt to choose at random or because the payoffs are such as to set *r* rather high, then we have a situation with no clash between conceptions of rationality; on *any* conception, it is rational to rat. But even this non-problem might legitimately be called a version of Newcomb's Problem, since it satisfies conditions (1), (2), and (3″).
7. For instance, Davis (1977), reprinted in this volume. He considers the case in which the partners are alike because they are both rational; but there is also the case where they are alike because they are given to the same sorts of irrationality.

15

Is the Symmetry Argument Valid?

LAWRENCE H. DAVIS

The basic argument for cooperating presented in "Prisoners, Paradox, and Rationality" (pp. 45–59 in this volume) contains the following steps:

(1) An alternative X is rationally prescribed for an agent y if y knows that there are just two possible outcomes m and n, such that if y takes X then the outcome is m, if y does not take X then the outcome is n, and m is better (in y's judgment) than n.

(2) Each prisoner knows that each knows that each will take the ra-

tionally prescribed alternative (recall the independent argument that there *is* just one rationally prescribed alternative).
(3) Each knows that an alternative is rationally prescribed for one of them just in case it is also rationally prescribed for the other of them.
(4) Each knows that he will maintain silence just in case the other does, and that he will confess just in case the other does.
(5) Each knows that if silence is rationally prescribed and he maintains silence, then the outcome will be (*c, c*); and that if confessing is rationally prescribed and he confesses, then the outcome will be (*b, b*).
(6) Each knows that (*c, c*) and (*b, b*) are the only possible outcomes.
(7) Each knows that he judges (*c, c*) to be better than (*b, b*).
(8) Therefore, maintaining silence is rationally prescribed for each.

I now think that this argument is indeed valid, for three reasons: I have not come across a persuasive objection to it, it or an equivalent argument has been endorsed by some who have searched more than I, and in at least two cases the endorsements seem virtually against the wills of their authors. The notion of "possible outcome" that bothered me so much now strikes me as dispensable. The word "possible" can simply be dropped from principle (1) along with the whole of step (6). Alternatively, "possible outcome" can be thought of as adequately defined by the material conditionals following the "such that" in (1).[1] This is how the phrase should be understood in the following remarks, in which I consider the positions of some of the other contributors to this volume.

1. One should not lose sight of the fact that the basic argument for co-operating has the unrealistic (2) for a premise. All is certain, given that premise. Dominance reasoning does not apply, since there are only two possible outcomes, and there is no need to calculate expected utilities. The rationally prescribed alternative is to cooperate. Russell Hardin—whose remarks on the absence of paradox from Prisoner's Dilemma, by the way, match my own in the second section of my paper—sketches a similar argument from symmetry and apparently endorses its conclusion. But his is one of the endorsements that seem unenthusiastically given, to put it mildly. For he hastens to add that the required situation is an impossibility:

[The agent] would be acting as though [he knew] what [he] could not know—that [his] adversary would also act as though bound by the deduction from symmetry. A sophisticated player knows one can know no such thing about one's unknown adversary, not least because one would probably not put absolute trust in anyone, but surely not in an unknown and presumably self-interested adversary (1982a, pp. 151–52).

In his haste to distract attention from his concession, Hardin has failed perhaps to notice that he has given no reason for thinking the situation impossible, no reason for thinking you could not know of a *known* adversary that he is perfectly rational and knows the same about you. But suppose Hardin is right, and neither you nor anyone could know this. All that follows is that the basic argument for cooperating has a false premise. So it is not sound, but it is still valid, and that is all that had been claimed.

2. James H. Fetzer is cited by Eells as offering the following analysis of Newcomb's Problem:[2]

> [I]f the agent takes seriously the premise that the predictor will make the correct prediction in every case, then the agent should not list among the possible outcomes of his action his getting $1,001,000 or his getting $0. [And so] dominance reasoning is not applicable.[3]

This reasoning is quite parallel to the basic argument for cooperating in the Prisoner's Dilemma, and so I count Fetzer as giving a second endorsement to my position. Notice the premise, corresponding to my (2), that the agent believes the predictor makes no error.[4]

Eells himself writes "I agree that if the agent assigned probability 0 to some relevant outcome-proposition, then the principle of dominance may not apply" (p. 208). I count this as a third endorsement of the basic argument for cooperating. But it is the second of the reluctant ones because Eells commits himself only to "dominance *may* not apply," and because he does not even say this much before first insisting that an agent who behaved this way "would, in virtue thereof, be irrational." Note that this claim is as irrelevant as Hardin's. Even if the agent is irrational, he does believe the predictor is infallible; and Fetzer's argument shows that, given this belief, the action rationally prescribed for this agent is to take just the opaque box.

A word should be said about Eells's defense of his irrelevant claim, despite its irrelevance. He cites Lewis (1981) to the effect that assigning probability 0 to a proposition "is tantamount to a firm resolve never to change your mind, and that is objectionable." But this is strange. I have not firmly resolved never to change my mind about the proposition "Zeus will strike me dead unless I beg him to spare me within the next 30 seconds." I (think I) can even imagine evidence that would persuade me of its truth. Yet I simply do not consider it in deliberating what to do. Nor is this a matter of assigning it a *low* probability. I assign it a *zero* probability. I *have* entertained the proposition (and so, now, have you), but I *do not consider it at all* in planning my actions (and nor will you, if you are rational). Surely there are propositions such as this one about Zeus, hence logically possible outcomes, that it is not irrational to exclude from consideration – that is, they may be assigned zero probability. And surely we can ask what it is rational for an agent to do who thinks that "The predictor sometimes errs" is such a proposition.

Eells's only other objection to Fetzer's argument is to insist that it does not apply if the agent's confidence in the predictor's infallibility falls just shy of certainty. Granting this for now, and assuming that "taking the contents of both boxes is correct for this agent, then it is hard to see why it would not also be correct for an agent whose degree of belief in the proposition that the predictor will predict correctly is higher by a mere 0.000001" (p. 208). True. It is hard to see. But this is just the Problem of the Heap—faced in particular by anyone who believes subjective probabilities can be treated as continuously varying quantities. (What of the man whose degree of confidence that the Lady (rather than the Tiger) is behind the right-hand door is 50.0000001, versus the one whose degree of confidence is only 49.9999999? How can a difference of a mere 0.0000002 make it rational for the first, but not the second, to choose the right-hand door?)

3. Fetzer's argument has the agent reason

(9) If I take just the opaque box, I will receive a million dollars.

and

(10) If I take both boxes, I will receive just a thousand dollars.

These certainly follow from the description of the Newcomb situation and the agent's premise that the predictor never errs. And given the principle (1) stated in the fourth section of my paper, it follows that taking just the opaque box is rationally prescribed for this agent:

(1) An alternative X is rationally prescribed for an agent y if y knows that there are just two possible outcomes m and n, such that if y takes X then the outcome is m, if y does not take X then the outcome is n, and m is better (in y's judgment) than n.

(Well, the "knows" in (1) can be replaced with "believes.") Gibbard and Harper (1978), however, insist that the relevant principle is that of maximizing expected utility; and, as they favor interpreting this principle, its application requires attention to the counterfactuals

(9') If I were to take just the opaque box, I would receive a million dollars.

and

(10') If I were to take both boxes, I would receive merely a thousand.

But as they analyze counterfactuals, (9') or (10') is false. Suppose the million is there, in the opaque box. Given the predictor's infallibility, I *will* take just that box and so receive the million. But, they believe, if I *were* to take both boxes, the million would not disappear. I would still get it, along with the additional thousand in the transparent box. Similarly, if the million is not there, my taking just the opaque box will not make it appear. So the rational course is to take both boxes, just as dominance and the principle of maximizing expected utility as they understand it dictate.

Now whatever be said about counterfactuals, I still say they need not be considered here at all. My principle (1) and the material conditionals (3) and (4) settle the issue (cf. the end of the fifth section "Prisoners, Paradox, and Rationality").[5]

But I also want to protest their assessment of (9′) and (10′). Belief in the predictor's infallibility—a "given" of the situation—requires the agent to suppose that even if the opaque box *is* empty, if he *were* to take just it, then it *would not have been* empty. Compare: "There is Sirius in the night sky. I *will* not see any change in its appearance. But if I *were* to see it suddenly increase in brightness, then it *would have exploded* some eight years ago." If this is right, then even according to their (ultimately undefended) understanding of rationality in terms of considering counterfactuals like these, it is rational for the agent to take just the opaque box.

4. Eells (1982) criticizes Gibbard and Harper along these lines (pp. 98-105) but later (p. 209) fails to notice that he thereby refutes an objection he attributes to Schlesinger (1974). Stripped of narrative details, that objection boils down to the claim that whatever is in the opaque box, it *is* in the agent's best interest to take both boxes. But this is so only if the content of the opaque box is the same whatever the agent does; and this is false. Bear in mind: it is not being claimed that there is any causal relation between the agent's act and the content of the opaque box. In particular, the million would not disappear if the agent took both boxes. Rather, it would never have been there to begin with. Similarly in Prisoner's Dilemma, where my (2) holds. The agent does not *make* the other behave as he does; rather, it is a "given" of his decision problem that they *will* behave alike. If he were to confess (*per impossibile,* given (2) and my argument), it would be the case that the other also confesses.

5. I believe this disposes of all the direct objections to the basic argument for cooperating in Prisoner's Dilemma and the parallel argument for taking just the opaque box in Newcomb's Problem. Again I stress that these arguments only apply where the agent is certain enough about the relation between his action and the situation he faces to make my principle (1) applicable.

But there is an indirect objection that is worth considering. There are similar cases where, it is maintained, the rational alternative is "obviously" the one corresponding to confessing or taking both boxes. The challenge to my position is to explain the relevant difference between the cases.

Suppose, for example, that consuming a great deal of cholesterol does not itself cause hardening of the arteries, but that both are caused by a certain physical condition C. More specifically, suppose a rational agent believes that C invariably leads to hardening of the arteries and is highly correlated with high cholesterol consumption—henceforth "H." What eating habits will he cultivate, if he likes high cholesterol foods but would prefer to avoid hardening of the arteries? Well, either *C* obtains or it does not. The agent knows that *H* does not itself cause *C;* the causal connection is in the other direction. And so, conclude Brian Skyrms (1980b) and Eells (1982, pp. 89–90), it would be irrational for him to forego the foods he likes.

An obvious difference between this case and the cases where (1) applies is the absence of *certainty* about the relation between the act and the possible outcomes. High cholesterol intake can have causes other than *C;* the two are not *invariably* correlated (as, for simplicity, we have assumed *C* and hardening of the arteries to be). The agent cannot then reason

(9*) If *H,* I will suffer hardening of the arteries.

or

(10*) If − *H,* I will avoid hardening of the arteries.

If the case is changed so the agent is certain enough of (9*) and (10*) to warrant ignoring their negations, then (1) applies, and it would indeed be rational for this agent to avoid cholesterol, assuming nothing else is at stake.

But there is a second difference between the cholesterol case and cases where (1) applies, which makes it very difficult to convert the former to the latter.[6] As emphasized by Eells (1982, pp. 149, 152), the connection between *C* and *H* is most plausibly mediated by psychological factors. If the agent is entirely and inflexibly rational (including immunity from "weakness of the will"), these factors will be exclusively *reasons* he takes himself to have – for example, relevant beliefs and desires. But the agent may plausibly be assumed to know these and hence to have adequate evidence for or against the presence of *C* before he decides what action he will take. In fact, he can *use this extra information to help decide* which action to take. And the impact of the information will be to block one of the material conditionals needed to make (1) applicable.[7]

Suppose, for example, his liking for high-cholesterol foods is fairly intense, even if not stronger than his aversion to hardening of the arteries. He may reason that this yen of his is already a strong indication that *C* is present in him, since it is a psychological factor which gives him a powerful reason for *H.* And so he may come to believe (9*), but not (10*). Already possessing evidence strong enough to convince him that *C* is present, he will not think that deciding now on − *H* will change things.

Alternatively, suppose he is indifferent to high-cholesterol foods, but someone offers him an enormous amount of money if he commits himself irrevocably to *H.* He knows he now has a strong reason for deciding on *H,* quite possibly strong enough to outweigh whatever reasons he has not to do so. But notice that his having *this* reason is not plausibly regarded as evidence for the presence of *C* in him. It is implausible to suppose that *C* caused him to be made the offer (or to believe that he had been made the offer). This time he may believe (10*), but he has no reason for believing (9*).

To get a case where (1) applies, we must introduce fairly wild beliefs. Suppose the agent believes that *C* and only *C* causes otherwise rational agents to consume high-cholesterol foods *against their better judgments*. If the agent thinks his eating these foods is rationally acceptable, then his doing so is no proof that *C* is present. But suppose someone has offered him a large amount of money to *stop* eating them; and suppose his considered judgment is that he should accept this offer. The next day he feels a strong temptation to eat some eggs surreptitiously, though he still judges doing so to be unwise. *Now* he may reason that if he successfully combats this temptation, it is a sure sign that *C* is not present in him; while if he gives in, it is a sure sign that it is present. That is, he may reason

(9*′) If I eat these eggs, I will suffer hardening of the arteries.
and
(10*′) If I forego these eggs, I will avoid hardening of the arteries.

He now has even more reason not to eat the eggs, and (1) clearly applies to his situation. Unfortunately, if (and only if) *C* is present, he will be unable to resist the temptation, irrational though it be.

For a case in which (1) applies but "weakness of the will" is not relevant, suppose the agent believes quite simply (and however irrationally)

(11) It is rational (in the light of my beliefs, desires, etc.) for me to decide on *H,* if, and only if, *C* is present in me.

Now if someone offers the agent a million dollars to adopt a high-cholesterol diet, and the agent prefers getting the million to avoiding hardening of the arteries, he will also think that for sure he will get hardening of the arteries. For (11) is such that the agent believes he would not have received the offer if *C* were not present in him. Strange to think *C* could be so powerful; but rationality of belief in (11) is not our present concern. What will the agent decide, rationally, if he has been offered no million, likes high-cholesterol foods, but prefers avoiding hardening of the arteries? The situation is now exactly parallel to the Prisoner's Dilemma with (2) assumed, and Newcomb's Problem with the agent believing in the predictor's infallibility. The agent believes he will act rationally, and together with (11) this implies both (9*) and (10*). There are only two possible outcomes, dominance reasoning is irrelevant, and since we are not to question his beliefs, we must acquiesce in the rationality of his foregoing the foods he likes.

NOTES

1. But see note 5, below.
2. I am taking familiarity with Newcomb's Problem for granted. For a description, see the Introduction to this volume and the essay by Robert Nozick.
3. Eells (1982), pp. 207–8; from correspondence of March 1, 1980, and discussion.
4. Notice also that the agent need not believe that he *or* the Predictor is rational. Only that the predictor *makes no error.* Similarly in Prisoner's Dilemma: state-

ments (2) and (3) can simply be dropped from the basic argument for cooperating along with the clauses with "rationally prescribed" in statement (5). I came to appreciate this point with the help of Lewis (1979), reprinted in this volume, and correspondence with him. But altered this way, the Prisoner's Dilemma is no longer as illuminating about rationality. Or perhaps it illuminates a different aspect of rationality.

5. Principle (1) is not intended as a general analysis of "rationally prescribed"; it gives just one sufficient condition applying to a narrow range of cases, and it may well be that counterfactuals are required elsewhere. But even so, is it really correct as it stands? Suppose an agent *already believes* that he will not take a certain alternative X. He can then infer the material conditional "If I take X, the outcome will be o," where o is an outcome he judges better than anything else possible. It apparently follows, by (1), that X is rationally prescribed for him. Notice however that if the agent is astute enough to infer the conditional mentioned from his belief that he will not take X, he should be astute enough to infer, with equal validity, the conditional 'If I take X, then the outcome will be o','" where o' is an outcome he judges worse than anything else possible. If this is the situation, it seems that (1) does not apply. For it is not true that the agent believes or knows "that there are *just two* possible outcomes." So the case is no counterexample to (1). But what of an agent who can see one inference of this sort, but no more, from "I will not take X"? Perhaps there is no problem. Perhaps there are no such agents; or if there are, perhaps X really is rationally prescribed for them. (Or not-X, depending on just which conditional is the lucky one inferred.) But if this is unacceptable, we may need to stipulate in (1) that the agent not know or believe either of the relevant conditionals *just because* he already knows or believes he will take a certain one of the relevant alternatives or *just because* he already knows or believes he will not take it. Such a stipulation may seem *ad hoc*. But I am not offering any explanation or justification for (1) even without this stipulation. I claim only that it is true — at least with this stipulation.

My thanks to Don Hubin for calling this putative counterexample to my attention and corresponding with me about it. For Hubin's views, see Hubin and Ross (forthcoming).

6. Essentially this difference is present also in all other Newcomb problems known to me in which the first difference, concerning the agent's certainty, is absent. It is especially blatant in the variation presented by Gibbard and Harper (1978), p. 151 in this volume; and it is imported into the genuine Newcomb problem by Eells (1982), pp. 211-16.

7. Contrast this analysis with Eells (1982), pp. 152-69, and in this volume, pp. 197-205. Eells thinks the relevance of the agent's knowledge of his reasons for acting is that it renders his knowledge of the correlation of H with C irrelevant to his *estimate of the probability of H:* The agent he thinks,

> will base his probability of [H being the rational response to the reasons he has] on the current state of his evaluation of the alternatives in the light of [these reasons]. The *cause* of [these reasons] is irrelevant to what the rational response to [these reasons] is, and [the agent] can be assumed to know this.

Let "R" stand for his having the reasons he has and knowing that he has them. Then Eells's conclusion is that for this agent,

$$pr(H/R\&C) = pr(H/R\&-C) = pr(H/R)$$

(1982, pp.160–62, and in this volume, pp.203–4, substituting my notation) is a reasonable assumption. But this cannot be right. If the agent has not completed his evaluation of the alternatives, he may be still unsure whether the rational response to the reasons he has is H or $-H$. But if he is informed of C's presence, he may be quite confident that when he does finish evaluating, he will decide on H. And if he *has* completed his evaluation, reasoning like Eells's gives us

$$pr(H/R) \; = \; pr(H/-R) \; = \; pr(H),$$

where R is *any* condition obtaining just prior to his action. But this is problematic. For suppose he has just decided on H, and let *"R"* be "I do not believe H to be unreasonable." It is unclear how *"$pr(H/-R)$"* is even to be *defined*, much less equated with *"$pr(H/R)$,"* given the agent's knowledge that he is rational. (Cf. 1982, pp. 185–86. Eells's reasoning on p. 216 is vitiated by the same sort of problem.)

16

Not Every Prisoner's Dilemma
Is a Newcomb Problem*

JORDAN HOWARD SOBEL

Newcomb's Problem and the Prisoner's Dilemma are alike in several ways. In each problem there is a dominant action whose choice-relevant value excels in all possible circumstances. And in each problem, possible circumstances are certainly causally independent of possible actions. Furthermore, in connection with each problem there is a sense (though not the same sense) in which agents who rejected the dominant action could expect to do better than agents who employed it. And finally, it can seem that maximizers *would* reject the dominant action not only in Newcomb's Problem, which problem was designed for this result, but also in the Prisoner's Dilemma, or at least in one in which "each prisoner knows that the other thinks in much the same way he does."[1] It can seem that these problems are not merely very similar, but that at least such Prisoner's Dilemmas *are* Newcomb problems "or rather two Newcomb problems side by side, inessential trappings aside."[2] But this is not quite right, for though some such Prisoner's Dilemmas are Newcomb problems, *some* are *not*.[3] Whether or not one *is* will depend in large part on *why* each prisoner is convinced that the other thinks in much the same way he does—on *why* he is convinced that as far as ways of thinking are concerned the other and he are near perfect replicas of one another. Whether or not such a Prisoner's Dilemma is a Newcomb problem will depend on what opinions lie behind and around this conviction.

It is mainly—though not only—Prisoner's Dilemmas in which each prisoner is nearly sure that the other will act as he does that have been thought to be Newcomb problems—they have been thought to be "near-certainty Newcomb problems." I first set conditions for such Newcomb problems and Prisoner's Dilemmas, and then discuss how these are related.

NEAR-CERTAINTY NEWCOMB PROBLEMS

Let a Newcomb's Problem be defined by conditions: (1) An *expected utility matrix*[4] of a Newcomb's Problem has the structure,

circumstances

		c_1	c_2
actions	a_1	x	w
	a_2	z	y

wherein $x = \mathcal{U}(a_1 \& c_1)$, $w = \mathcal{U}(a_1 \& c_2)$, and so on, and $w > y > x > z$. And a *news value matrix* has the same structure, so that in it $x = \mathcal{N}(a_1 \& c_1)$, $w = \mathcal{N}(a_1 \& c_2)$, and so on. In Newcomb's Problem itself, if values are linear with monetary payoffs, expected utility and news value matrices can be,

	There is nothing in Box 2	There is $M in Box 2
Take both boxes	1	1001
Take only Box 2	0	1000

(2) Circumstances c_1 and c_2 in a Newcomb's Problem are certainly *causally* independent of actions a_1 and a_2. (3n) In a Newcomb's Problem circumstances are *not* to be *epistemically* independent of actions. In a *near-certainty* Newcomb Problem circumstances will be nearly *maximally* dependent on actions epistemically:

$$pr(c_1/a_1) \cong 1 \cong pr(c_2/a_2),$$
and since $\quad pr(c_1 \ \& \ c_2) = 0$ and $pr(c_1 \ v \ c_2) = 1,$
$$pr(c_2/a_1) \cong 0 \cong pr(c_1/a_2).$$

In a near-certainty Newcomb's Problem, a_1 and a_2 will be near-certain potential signs respectively of c_1 and c_2. And finally, mainly because of the epistemic dependence of circumstances, (4), in a Newcomb's Problem, the *news value* of a_2 exceeds that of a_1:

$$pr(c_1/a_2) \ \mathcal{N}_{\!\!\!0} \ (a_2 \ \& \ c_1) \ + \ pr(c_2/a_2) \ \mathcal{N}_{\!\!\!0} \ (a_2 \ \& \ c_2) \ >$$
$$pr(c_1/a_1) \ \mathcal{N}_{\!\!\!0} \ (a_1 \ \& \ c_1) \ + \ pr(c_2/a_1) \ \mathcal{N}_{\!\!\!0} \ (a_1 \ \& \ c_2)$$

In Newcomb's Problem itself,

$$(pr(\text{nothing/only Box 2}) \cdot 0 \ + \ pr(\$M/\text{only Box 2}) \cdot 1000) \ \cong \ 1000,$$

while

$$(pr(\text{nothing/both}) \cdot 1 \ + \ pr(\$M/\text{both}) \cdot 1001) \ \cong \ 1.$$

In a Newcomb's Problem a_2 would maximize *news value,* or what Jeffrey has termed *desirability.* In contrast, by conditions (1) and (2) — the dominance of a_1 and the certain causal independence of circumstances from actions — a_1 would maximize *expected utility.* According to a simple causal theory of expected utility, using "$\Box\!\!\rightarrow$" as the causal conditional connective,

$$\mathcal{U}(a_1) = pr(a_1 \ \Box\!\!\rightarrow c_1) \ \mathcal{U}(a_1 \ \& \ c_1) \ + \ pr(a_1 \ \Box\!\!\rightarrow c_2) \ \mathcal{U}(a_1 \ \& \ c_2),$$
and
$$\mathcal{U}(a_2) = pr(a_2 \ \Box\!\!\rightarrow c_1) \ \mathcal{U}(a_2 \ \& \ c_1) \ + \ pr(a_2 \ \Box\!\!\rightarrow c_2) \ \mathcal{U}(a_2 \ \& \ c_2);$$

condition (2) entails that

$$pr(a_1 \ \Box\!\!\rightarrow c_1) = pr(c_1) = pr(a_2 \ \Box\!\!\rightarrow c_1),$$
and
$$pr(a_1 \ \Box\!\!\rightarrow c_2) = pr(c_2) = (a_2 \ \Box\!\!\rightarrow c_2),[5]$$
and by (1),

$$\mathcal{U}(a_1 \ \& \ c_1) > \ \mathcal{U}(a_2 \ \& \ c_1) \text{ and } \ \mathcal{U}(a_1 \ \& \ c_2) > \ \mathcal{U}(a_2 \ \& \ c_2);$$

from which it follows that

$$\mathcal{U}(a_1) > \ \mathcal{U}(a_2).$$

In Newcomb's Problem itself, taking both boxes would maximize expected utility, though taking only Box 2 would maximize news value. And so a temptation to wishful willing is apt to obscure the authority, in this problem, of the fact that the agent can be sure (and presumably is sure) that he would do better taking both boxes than he would do taking just the second. Exactly $1000 better.

NEAR-CERTAINTY PRISONER'S DILEMMAS

Let a near-certainty Prisoner's Dilemma be defined by three conditions: (1) An expected utility matrix of a Prisoner's Dilemma has the structure displayed above. Similarly as regards a news value matrix of a Prisoner's Dilemma. For the Prisoner's Dilemma itself, Jeffrey's version,[6] if values are linear with negative inverses of prison-terms, expected utility and news value matrices can be,

	The other prisoner will confess	The other prisoner will not confess
Confess	-5	0
Do not confess	-10	-1

(2) Circumstances c_1 and c_2 in a Prisoner's Dilemma are certainly causally independent of actions a_1 and a_2. And, (3p), in a near-certainty Prisoner's Dilemma, it is nearly certain that "the other will do as I do," or, more abstractly, that

$$pr((a_1 \& c_1) \lor (a_2 \& c_2)) \cong 1;$$

and, since $pr(c_1 \& c_2) = 0$

$$pr((a_2 \& c_1) \lor (a_1 \& c_2)) \cong 0.$$

Condition (3p) is specific to *near-certainty* Prisoner's Dilemmas. Neither it nor anything like it is essential to the Prisoner's Dilemma. That problem was designed to dramatize the possibility of dominance/optimality confrontations, and condition (3p) is not needed for that purpose. *No* "other-regarding" epistemic condition is needed for that purpose. It *is* a feature of standard versions of the Prisoner's Dilemma that the prisoners are in separate cells, but this is so that it should be clear that they cannot enter into agreements that would make a difference, and not so that it should be clear that neither will know what the other is up to, or know that the other knows what he is up to.

NEAR-CERTAINTY NEWCOMB'S PROBLEMS AND PRISONER'S DILEMMAS

Near-certainty Newcomb's Problems and Prisoner's Dilemmas while alike in their first two conditions differ in their third conditions. Also, there is no fourth condition for Prisoner's Dilemmas. Even so, every near-certainty

Newcomb's Problem is a near-certainty Prisoner's Dilemma. Since (a_1, a_2) and (c_1, c_2) determine a news value matrix for a decision problem, $pr(a_1 \vee a_2) = 1$, $pr(a_1 \& a_2) = 0$, $pr(c_1 \vee c_2) = 1$, and $pr(c_1 \& c_2) = 0$. So from (3n),

$$pr(c_1/a_1) \cong 1 \cong pr(c_2/a_2),$$

and

$$pr(c_2/a_1) \cong 0 \cong pr(c_1/a_2),$$

it follows that (3p),

$$pr((a_1 \& c_1) \vee (a_2 \& c_2)) \cong 1.$$

Every near-certainty Newcomb's Problem is a near-certainty Prisoner's Dilemma. But not every such Prisoner's Dilemma is a Newcomb Problem. The important point here is that (3p) does *not* in context entail (3n). Even if I am nearly certain that the other prisoner will do what I do, my conditional probabilities for actions like mine on his part need not *both* be high. Whether or not they are both high will depend on *why* I am nearly certain that we will act alike.

A KIND OF PRISONER'S DILEMMA THAT IS NOT A NEWCOMB PROBLEM.

Let me be nearly certain that I will confess,

$$pr(a_1) \cong 1,$$

and *on quite independent grounds* nearly certain that you will confess,

$$pr(c_1) \cong 1.$$

Perhaps, for example, I have decided to confess, and have heard through channels I consider reliable that you have come to the same decision. I could then be nearly certain you too were going to confess even if I had no idea what sort of person you were or why you were going to confess. And if I arrived at my own decision without *regard* to what you were going to do, my certainty concerning what you would do could possibly have *nothing* to do with my certainty concerning what I was going to do.

In the case under construction I am to be nearly certain that I will confess and, on quite independent grounds of *some* sort (not necessarily the sort described above), nearly certain that you will confess. Suppose further that *as* a consequence of these near-certainties, though I am not quite so confident of the conjunction, I am still nearly certain of it — I am to be nearly certain that we will both confess:

$$pr(a_1 \& c_1) \cong 1.$$

In the case I am to come by *this* near-certainty entirely by way of the first two. It follows from this last near certainty that I am nearly certain that we will act alike (I am nearly certain of more than that):

$$pr((a_1 \,\&\, c_1) \lor (a_2 \,\&\, c_2)) \cong 1.$$

Continuing with stipulations for the case, though I am to think it very unlikely that I will not confess, I am to consider it much *more* unlikely that *both* of us will not confess than that I *alone* will not: let ">!" mean "is much greater than," so that for positive numbers j and k, $j >! k$ if, and only if, $j/(j + k) \cong 1$; it is to be part of the case that,

$$pr(a_2 \,\&\, c_1) >! pr(a_2 \,\&\, c_2).$$

Why? Because I have *independent* grounds for my opinions about what you and I will do and so consider it much more likely that I am mistaken just about *myself* than that I am mistaken about *both* of us. It follows, given that $pr(c_1 \lor c_2) = 1$ and that $pr(c_1 \,\&\, c_2) = 0$, that my probability for your not confessing conditional on my not confessing is very *low:*

$$pr(c_2/a_2) = pr(a_2 \,\&\, c_2)/(pr(a_2 \,\&\, c_1) + pr(a_2 \,\&\, c_2)),$$

so

$$pr(c_2/a_2) \cong 0$$

contrary to (3n).

Are such cases possible, logically possible? Are the constraints imposed on probabilities jointly consistent? Yes. One class of cases of the kind described is determined by the following plainly consistent probabilities:

$pr(a_1 \,\&\, a_2) = 0$
$pr(c_1 \,\&\, c_2) = 0$
$pr(a_1 \,\&\, c_1) = .9$
$pr(a_1 \,\&\, c_2) = (\sqrt{.9} - .9)$
$pr(a_2 \,\&\, c_1) = (\sqrt{.9} - .9)$
$pr(a_2 \,\&\, c_2) = 1 - (.9 + 2(\sqrt{.9} - .9))$

Given these probabilities, circumstances are probabilistically independent of actions:

$$\begin{aligned}
pr(c_1) &= .9 + (\sqrt{.9} - .9) = \sqrt{.9} \\
pr(c_1/a_1) &= .9/(.9 + (\sqrt{.9} - .9)) = \sqrt{.9} \\
pr(c_1/a_2) &= (\sqrt{.9} - .9)/((\sqrt{.9} - .9) + (1 - (.9 + 2(\sqrt{.9} - .9)))) \\
&= (\sqrt{.9} - .9)/(1 - \sqrt{.9}) \\
&= \sqrt{.9}
\end{aligned}$$

$$pr(c_2) \quad = (\sqrt{.9} - .9) + (1 - (.9 + 2(\sqrt{.9} - .9)))$$
$$= 1 - \sqrt{.9}$$
$$pr(c_2/a_1) = (\sqrt{.9} - .9)/[.9 + (\sqrt{.9} - .9)]$$
$$= 1 - \sqrt{.9}$$
$$pr(c_2/a_2) = (1 - (.9 + 2(\sqrt{.9} - .9)))/((\sqrt{.9} - .9)$$
$$+ (1 - (.9 + 2(\sqrt{.9} - .9))))$$
$$= (1 + .9 - 2\sqrt{.9})/(1 - \sqrt{.9})$$
$$= 1 - \sqrt{.9}$$

And given these probabilities, the other conditions of our case hold, if we assume that $x \cong 1$ if, and only if, $.9 \le x \le 1$, and that $y \cong 0$ if, and only if, $0 \le y \le .1$:

$$pr(a_1) = P(c_1) = \sqrt{.9} \cong 1$$
$$pr(a_1 \,\&\, c_1) = .9 \cong 1$$
$$pr((a_1 \,\&\, c_1) \,\text{v}\, (a_2 \,\&\, c_2)) = (1 - 2(\sqrt{.9} - .9)) \cong 1$$
$$pr(a_2 \,\&\, c_1) = (\sqrt{.9} - .9) >! (1 - [.9 + 2(\sqrt{.9} - .9)]) = pr(a_2 \,\&\, c_2)$$
$$pr(c_2/a_2) = (1 - \sqrt{.9}) \cong 0$$

For two theoretically interesting types of dilemma of the present sort, we have *first* a dilemma in which I am nearly certain that I am *rational,* on quite independent grounds nearly certain that *you* are rational, entirely confident that in the case it would be rational to maximize *expected utility,* and entirely confident that in the case confessing would be utility-maximizing for you and for me, as it *would* be. For a *second* type of dilemma of the present sort, we add to the general specifications for this sort (which include, I recall, that I am nearly certain that I will confess and, on quite independent grounds, nearly certain that you too will confess) the further specifications that I am nearly certain that I am rational, on quite independent grounds nearly certain that you are rational, *and* entirely confident that in the case it would be rational to maximize *news value.* In this second type of dilemma I will be nearly certain, indeed I am to be entirely confident, that confessing would maximize *news value,* for you and for me, as it *would* in this type of case. In this type of case, I am nearly certain that we will both confess and that I will get *five* years. And, given the independence of my opinions about you and me, in this type of case *if* I were to learn for sure that I was *not* going to confess, I would *remain* nearly certain that you were going to confess, and so I would be nearly certain that I was going to get *ten* years, which is worse. Bad news! *News* that I was not going to confess would be *bad* news.[7]

In dilemmas of the two types just described, I am nearly certain that we will do the same thing, nearly certain that we are both rational, and nearly certain that we will both do the rational thing. But even so, since your actions are by hypothesis *probabilistically* independent of mine, confessing is for me both utility-maximizing *and* news value maximizing. These Prisoner's Dilemmas are *not* Newcomb's Problems.[8]

A KIND OF PRISONER'S DILEMMA THAT IS A NEWCOMB'S PROBLEM.

Let me be nearly certain that we are "psychological twins" and that we will act alike, and let this near certainty of mine be independent of my opinions concerning what I will do and what you will do so that not only is it the case that I am nearly certain that we will do the same thing,

$$pr((a_1 \& c_1) \lor (a_2 \& c_2)) \cong 1,$$

but, as (3n) would have it, also the case that my possible acts would both be for me near certain signs that you were acting similarly:

$$pr(c_1/a_1) \cong 1$$

and

$$pr(c_2/a_2) \cong 1.$$

Perhaps, for example, I am nearly certain that we are identical *biological* twins, that throughout our lives we have been constant companions, and that we have always thought and acted alike when in situations as similar as our present ones seem to be. Perhaps, as a consequence of these convictions I am nearly certain that we will act alike in the present case.

In this kind of case, news of my action, whatever that news was, would for me be excellent evidence that you were acting similarly. My opinions concerning our actions, whatever these opinions are, do *not* in the present kind of case rest on quite independent grounds. On the contrary there will be near maximal *dependence* of these opinions one on the other. In this kind of dilemma I am nearly certain that you will do what I will do; *and,* whatever I *did,* I would *remain* nearly certain that you would do what I was doing. Dilemmas of the present kind satisfy condition (3n). We now stipulate that they satisfy condition (4). Such dilemmas are *logically* possible. For a numerical illustration, let probabilities and news values include:

$$pr(a_1 \& a_2) = 0 \qquad pr(a_2 \& c_1) = 0$$
$$pr(c_1 \& c_2) = 0 \qquad pr(a_2 \& c_2) = .1$$
$$pr(a_1 \& c_1) = .9 \qquad \textit{No}\,(a_1 \& c_1) = -5$$
$$pr(a_1 \& c_2) = 0 \qquad \textit{No}\,(a_2 \& c_2) = -1.$$

Given these probabilities and values, (i) and (ii),

$$pr(c_1/\,a_1) = 1 = pr(c_2/\,a_2);$$

(iii),

$$pr(c_2/a_1) = 0 = pr(c_1/a_2);$$

and (iv),

$$pr(c_1/a_1) \; \mathcal{N}_0 \, (a_1 \; \& \; c_1) + pr(c_2/a_1) \; \mathcal{N}_0 \, (a_1 \; \& \; c_2) = -5 < -1 =$$
$$pr(c_1/a_2) \; \mathcal{N}_0 \, (a_2 \; \& \; c_1) + pr(c_2/a_2) \; \mathcal{N}_0 \, (a_2 \; \& \; c_2).$$

A Prisoner's Dilemma can be of the present sort[9] even if I am nearly certain that we are both rational, quite certain that it would be rational to maximize *expected utility,* and quite certain that confessing would do that. For it is consistent with these conditions that news that I was *not* confessing should be excellent evidence that I was not being rational, *and* that you were *similarly* deficient and would thus *also* not be confessing. And a dilemma can be of the present sort even if I am nearly certain that we are both rational, quite certain that it would be rational to maximize *news value,* and nearly certain that we are not going to confess. For, again, surprising news concerning my action — in *this* type of dilemma that I am or will be *confessing* — could be excellent evidence that you too are or will be confessing. It could be excellent evidence not only that I am not doing the rational thing as I see it, but that you too are not doing the rational thing.

Finally, a dilemma can be of the present sort if, though I do not yet have any strong views concerning what we will do, I am confident that we will behave rationally because, uncritically and without putting this idea into so many words, I take for granted that, in simple situations such as the present one seems to be, most people do behave rationally. However, though a dilemma can be Newcomb-like in this way, it is very unlikely that a dilemma should be Newcomb-like in this way "just before" the perceived time of *action.* One supposes that by then I *would* have strong views concerning what *I* will do. Furthermore, it is very *likely* that any dilemma that was Newcomb-like in *this* way at some early stage of my deliberations would, by the perceived time of action, devolve into a *non*-Newcomb-like dilemma. For it is likely that by then I would have *views* regarding what it would be rational to do, views that were probabilistically independent, or largely so, of propositions concerning my own possible actions. It is likely that by then I would be confident of some particular action that it was the rational thing for me to do and that I was going to do it. But it would be strange indeed if, prominent among my reasons for thinking that this action was the rational thing for me to do, was the for-me-near-certain fact that I was going to do it. And so it is likely that by *then,* by the perceived time of action, I would have views regarding what *you* were going to do, since I would presumably still be taking for granted that you were going to do the rational thing — views that were themselves *independent* of my views concerning what I was going to do. It is thus likely, incidentally, that *news value* maximizers — at least sufficiently *sophisticated,* self-conscious and reflective news value maximizers — who were in a Prisoner's Dilemma that was Newcomb-like in the present way *early on* would in the *end,* or in the *event, not* cooperate.[10]

In dilemmas of the present sort, of which I have commented on three types (the third of which I have said is unlikely as a "moment-of-choice-Dilemma"), your actions are, in terms of my probabilities, probabilistically dependent on mine. In these dilemmas, while *confessing* would maximize *expected utility, not* confessing would maximize *news value.* Such dilemmas are logically possible, and news value maximizers who were, at their moments of choice, in such dilemmas would cooperate. Dilemmas of *this* sort *are* Newcomb's Problems.[11]

CONCLUSIONS

Some logically possible Prisoner's Dilemmas are Newcomb's Problems, and *some* are *not.* The character of a particular Prisoner's Dilemma will depend on the *grounds* participants have for their opinions concerning one another's actions. Participants in problems broadly like the Prisoner's Dilemmas may be nearly certain that they will act alike. And they may be nearly certain that they are rational and are utility maximizers, or that they are rational and are news value maximizers. But either way they still may or may *not* be in side-by-side Newcomb's Problems. Whether or not they *are* will in large part depend on what *makes* them nearly certain that they will act alike, on how they *come by* these opinions, and, in short, on whether or not each prisoner's opinions regarding his own action and the action of the other are epistemically *dependent* or *independent,* and if dependent to what extent.[12]

Not every Prisoner's Dilemma is a Newcomb's Problem. But some are. Some *logically possible* Prisoner's Dilemmas are Newcomb's Problems. But I am not sure whether or not many *real-life, moment-of-choice* Prisoner's Dilemmas are Newcomb's Problems or whether or not *any important* ones are. Whether or not any important real interaction problems that, like the Prisoner's Dilemma, feature dominance/optimality confrontations, also, like Newcomb's Problem, feature moment-of-choice utility maximization/ news value maximization confrontations, is a hard partly empirical question on which I do not have a confident opinion. Given my uncertainty here, I take some comfort in the belief that nothing important to the theory of rational agency turns on the answer to this question.[13]

NOTES

* Some of the ideas that follow took form in a conversation with David Gauthier, but even so, and whether or not this is fair, I accept full responsibility for those

ideas that are wrong, and for infelicities in the expression of any that are right. I have, I hope, profited from comments made by Leslie Burkholder and Richmond Campbell made on early versions of this paper.
1. Gibbard and Harper (1978), p. 157 in this volume.
2. Lewis (1979), p. 251 in this volume.
3. The title of his paper notwithstanding, it is plain that Lewis does not think that *every* Prisoner's Dilemma is a Newcomb Problem. But Lewis does observe that "Prisoner's Dilemmas are deplorably common in real life," and clearly implies that *many* Prisoner's Dilemmas, many *real-life* Prisoner's Dilemmas are Newcomb's Problems (Lewis (1979); p. 254 in this volume). Whether or not many real-life Prisoner's Dilemmas are Newcomb problems is, at least in Jeffrey's view, an issue of importance to theory. For reasons that I hope will be clear, I think that it is not *obvious* (though it may be true) that *any* real-life Prisoner's Dilemmas are "in the end" Newcomb problems.
4. I set out a theory of causal-decision matrices, expected utility and probability of causal conditional matrices, in Sobel (forthcoming).
5. This simple theory is for the agent who does not believe in objective chances, the agent for whom, for any propositions p and q, $(p \,\square\!\!\rightarrow q) \vee (p \,\square\!\!\rightarrow \sim q)$. When this agent is certain that actions a and $\sim a$ are open (and so causally possible), he is certain that a circumstance c is causally independent of a if, and only if, he is certain that

$$((a \,\square\!\!\rightarrow c) \leftrightarrow c) \ \& \ ((\sim a \,\square\!\!\rightarrow c) \leftrightarrow c)$$

and so only if, for him,

$$pr(a \,\square\!\!\rightarrow c) = pr(c)$$

6. See Jeffrey (1965), pp. 11–12, Jeffrey (1981b), pp. 484–85, and Jeffrey (1983), p. 15.
7. In a dilemma of this second type, I am nearly certain (1) that we will confess and (2) that we are both rational, and entirely confident (3) that it would be rational to maximize news value in the case and (4) that my confessing would maximize news value in the case. But how could I *come* by such opinions? Using "i" for me and "y" for you, I could *begin* being nearly certain that I was rational (2i), and entirely confident that it would be rational to maximize news value in the case (3). I might then "learn" through what I considered to be highly reliable channels that you were going to confess (1y), and on reflection I might then realize that my confessing would maximize news value (4), as it would, decide to confess, and become thereby nearly certain that I was going to confess (1i). I might *then* "learn" through the same channels that you were rational (2y). Indeed, I might "learn" through these channels that you have in similar ways come into the same opinions, and that in all ways relevant to what I take to be our present situation we are "epistemically indistinguishable." That is *one* way in which I could come to be in a dilemma of this second type, one way in which we could be in side-by-side dilemmas of this type. Probably, there are many other ways. Since the near-certainties and total-confidences (1) through (4) are consistent with the axioms of probability, one supposes there must be ways whereby they can come to co-exist, though perhaps not (imprecise notion) many ways.
8. For other dilemmas that are not Newcomb's Problems start with the stipulation that the agent is nearly certain that he will *not* confess and, "on quite independent grounds," nearly certain that the other agent will also not confess.

9. Nozick's "identical twin Prisoner's Dilemma" is of the present sort (Nozick (1969), pp.107–33 in this volume). Nozick's case, in contrast with the cases I sketch in the text, does not include assumptions concerning prisoners' views regarding their rationality.

10. "One might attempt to develop a theory of the *Sophisticated Rational Decision Maker* wherein sophistication is characterized stringently enough in terms of self-knowledge and causal reasoning so that for [sophisticated] decision makers the two paradigms [for deliberation, causal and evidential] are in approximate agreement" (Skyrms (1982), p. 698). See Sobel (forthcoming), n. 7.

11. Gauthier has held that (utility) maximizers who expected to find themselves in Prisoner's Dilemmas would have reason to "revise their conception of rationality" so that when interacting with like-minded agents they would of their own rational accords not confess. The revision that he has thought would recommend itself would be to a form of practical thinking that he calls "constrained utility-maximization." We now see that another revision could recommend itself at least for anticipated Newcomb-like Prisoner's Dilemmas. Utility maximizers who expected to find themselves in such situations would have a reason to revise their "ways of practical thinking" (their ways of "translating" beliefs and preferences into actions, with and *without* explicit thought and calculation), so that when interacting with like-minded agents in such situations they thought and, most importantly, *acted* as news value maximizers. Whether or not agents are *capable* of such mind-bending self-administered psychic surgery, how they would do it when and if they are capable of it, under what conditions if any utility maximizers would have sufficient *reasons* for revising their ways of practical thinking, what would be the exact forms of their revised conceptions of rationality, and what all this implies for the true nature of rationality, if such there be, as distinct from various conceptions thereof, are very hard further questions. See Gauthier (1975) and Sobel (1975) for a few superficial remarks on these matters.

12. Roughly stated, problems I count as Prisoner's Dilemmas, Levi counts as "versions of Newcomb's Problem" — see Levi (1975), especially pp. 162 and 164 — and my reasons for holding that not every Prisoner's Dilemma is a Newcomb Problem are like his for holding that not every "version of Newcomb's Problem" (in his sense) is a "Newcomb problem" (in my sense). Conceding terminology to Levi, every occurrence in the present paper of "Newcomb's *Problem*" and its cognates could be replaced by an occurrence of a cognate of 'Newcomb's *Paradox*' (occurrences in the present note excepted of course).

13. Jeffrey thinks that Newcomb's Problem is "a prisoner's dilemma for space cadets," a problem too artificial to mandate radical revisions in an otherwise satisfactory theory of rational decisions. But he is convinced that radical revisions *are* made necessary by Prisoner's Dilemmas, "the prisoners in which are paradox enow." (Jeffrey (1983), p. 25). I think that Newcomb's Problem, despite its artificiality, demonstrates the need for radical revisions in Jeffrey's logic of decision and that there may not be enough real-life Newcomb-like Prisoner's Dilemmas, or indeed enough real-life Newcomb-like problems of *any* sort, to convince *Jeffrey* that radical revisions in his theory are justified. Our differences include a difference on a methodological issue the full character of which is not clear to me.

V

COOPERATION IN REPEATED AND MANY-PERSON PRISONER'S DILEMMAS

17

The Insoluble Problem
of the Social Contract*

DAVID BRAYBROOKE

*La vertu est d'autant plus nécessaire
que l'État est moins fort.* — RENAN

The traditional problem of the social contract defies solution. Agents with
the motivations traditionally assumed would not in the circumstances traditionally assumed voluntarily arrive at a contract or voluntarily keep it up, as
we can now understand, more clearly than our illustrious predecessors, by
treating the problem in terms not available to them: the terms of Prisoner's
Dilemma and of the theory of public goods.

TWO FORMS OF THE CONTRACT

Of the several different forms of social contract distinguishable in traditional writings, I shall treat two: a first form according to which the contracting agents give mutual undertakings to do what is necessary to establish
an organized society living under laws protecting the interests of every
member; and a second form according to which the contracting agents give
mutual undertakings to assign authority to a certain identified or identi-

From *Dialogue* 15(1976): 3-37. Reprinted by permission.

fiable person or persons and to respect its exercise by that person or persons thereafter.

In general, the obstacles to having a contract of the one form are the obstacles to having a contract of the other. I shall therefore sometimes speak of "the contract," when what I say applies equally to either form or to the two conflated. When, however, as in Hobbes's case, both forms appear in sequence and it is important to resist any tendency to conflate them, I shall continually remark on the distinction.[1] There, as it will turn out, some obstacles would not arise so strongly for the second form if the first form could be obtained in spite of them. It cannot, but conflation makes this fact hard to see.[2]

Both forms of contract involve undertakings given by every agent present on the scene of the contract, and given in expectation of benefits contingent on the undertakings. I presuppose any of various ways of circumscribing the population that has an opportunity of joining in the contract; living within the same geographically isolated territory would be one such way, belonging to a distinctive linguistic community might be another. I assume that however circumscribed, the agents literally assemble at one place to give their undertakings. In both forms of contract, the undertakings are given in the form of promises, by each agent to every other, specifically by one public utterance or gesture before all the rest. The undertakings of all agents, given simultaneously, establish the institution in question — the society, as yet without a sovereign; the sovereign, perhaps a condition *sine qua non* for the continuance of the society.[3] Finally, each agent is motivated, in giving his undertaking, by the sum of (net) benefits that he expects to receive from the institution during its entire duration.

I shall take as the basic point of departure for my discussion of the contract Hume's criticism of the traditional doctrines that inasmuch as they presuppose a social and moral institution of promising they can consistently neither ascribe the beginnings of social institutions and organized social life to a social contract, entered into at some definite time, nor claim such a contract to be the foundation, in history or by rational reconstruction, of ethics.[4] To this criticism, one might add a comment drawn from Marxism, to the effect that the individualistic motivations ascribed to the contracting agents reflect the ideology and peculiar historical circumstances of the ascendant bourgeoisie, hence a very late development in a history of class-divided societies long organized on some principle of division or other.[5] Simmel gives even more general grounds for considering the individualism of the agents a late development: According to him, the sense of individual personality increases with the complexity of social organization. The specialized skill that an individual acquires and practises as part of a complex division of labor contributes to his sense of difference; but, beyond this contribution, Simmel (1955) finds the foundation for individuality in the assortment of groups with which any given person can freely affiliate. The more groups which a person actually joins, the more likely the assortment is to be unique, as is the combination of interests induced in each person so affiliated as a consequence of the multiple memberships. Seen in the light of these considerations, the problem of the social contract arises from postulating outside of society (of the society to be organized) a highly self-conscious individuality of personality that could itself only be produced by a society not merely formed and persisting but highly developed, indeed, specifically developed along the lines of a *Gesellschaft,* a society of multiple optional associations.

To merit attention in view of these considerations, the state of nature must be conceived of as arrived at by first postulating a highly developed society and then supposing it utterly dissolved by breakdown; or by postulating a number of such societies and "exporting" members of them to a new continent or to a desert island. The basic problem that is left is a problem about hypothetical reconstruction. It is a problem that may be gone into for different reasons: as an exercise in sociological theory, a field on this topic open still to philosophical adventures; or as an exercise, generally presupposing success of some sort in the sociological one, in clarifying the interrelationships of some themes in ethics. Were present society to break down, would the survivors, acting as rational agents, reconstitute it by entering into a social contract? Would they reconstruct any organized society by such means?

In this paper I shall concentrate on reconstructing, not necessarily the particular society that existed before the breakdown, but at least a society of some sort. This question is the primary problem. I shall aim to show that if the problem is set up, in respect to circumstances and motivations, in the traditional way, it is impossible to answer the question affirmatively. To be sure of arriving at a contract, and of having it kept up, one must change the problem, either by assuming different circumstances or by assuming different motivations.

I shall begin by considering circumstances that differ by affording agents a certain degree of natural protection against one another. In these circumstances, a society of sorts can be reconstructed on the basis of a convention more elementary than promising and capable of arising between pairs of agents without any contract between them, much less a general contract covering all agents together. The circumstances in which this possibility exists contrast significantly with the circumstances assumed in the traditional problem of the social contract. I shall go on to show that in those circumstances, with the traditional assumptions about motivation, no organized society reconstructed on the basis of a social contract will emerge. Then I shall consider some examples of the sorts of changes that might be introduced in the assumptions about motivation to obtain a solution. They will, of course, be question-begging assumptions, since the solution that they produce will be the solution to a different problem.

I shall not discuss (by any means) all the sorts of assumptions about motivation that might work in this connection. Some assumptions that impute to agents much less moral feeling than the ones that I do discuss would work, too: for example, Gauthier's assumption in (1974) and (1975) that the agents are prepared to cooperate with each other so long and only so long as each obtains from social cooperation a net gain over there being no social cooperation at all. (In effect, this assumption modifies the conception of rationality, whereas I shall leave rationality alone but make special assumptions about the benefits that the agents derive from cooperating or not cooperating.)

There are also many other ways, besides the one that I am about to discuss, of varying the circumstances so that the traditional problem disappears in favor of one that escapes at least its peculiar difficulties. One way, which is especially vivid and at the moment could hardly be better known, is taken by Rawls (1971). He assumes that the agents arrive at the scene of their deliberations at no cost to themselves and (in effect) that they can stay there, equally without cost, as long as they or Rawls, severally or jointly, please. Fateful consequences hang upon what they agree after deliberation to do, but they face no costs in reaching agreement; and they know that what they agree to will be put into effect for them at the same time as they descend from the original position to the real world. Rawls also modifies the assumptions about motivation. So little is left, on his approach, of the traditional problem that one might well wonder whether his is a problem about a social contract at all. One of the benefits of working through the traditional problem, taking it literally, is that one can establish afterwards just what elements, important or unimportant, of the traditional problem remain in these variants. The issues left behind — begged — may still be fundamental.

A SOCIETY OF SORTS RECONSTRUCTED THROUGH CONVENTION

Traditionally, the agents imagined to exist in the state of nature have been supposed to be selfish. It accords sufficiently well with tradition to suppose that they are *non tuistic* — possibly quite benevolent with respect to the households, families, or orphanages that they may have in their charge, but nevertheless determined to extract as much as possible from the other agents, and limited by no rules in doing so unless some efficacy already attaches to natural law. (Locke assumes some such efficacy; on the other hand, he makes so much allowance for the inconveniences of the state of nature, including the frequency of competition and war, as to give agents much the same grounds for seeking a social contract as Hobbes assumes.[6]) The individualism ascribed to the agents, as I have already pointed out, presupposes as much as the institution of promising characters and ideas which they could only have acquired in organized societies. Let us imagine, nevertheless, circumstances in which such agents could reconstruct an organized society without resorting to promises. We can get far enough with this reconstruction to give at least some support to Hume's notion that social institutions could originate as conventions, entered into from self-interest alone, without the use of the specific convention of promising, and prior to their acquiring any moral value. Among them, indeed, according to Hume, figures the most basic social convention of all, the convention of respecting one another's property in means of livelihood, to which the artificial virtue of justice is annexed once the social benefits of the convention have been appreciated from a disinterested point of view.[7]

Let us imagine circumstances like these: After the breakdown of the society or societies to which they formerly belonged, N and M move into adjoining farms, deserted by the people who owned them before the breakdown. No one, as N and M appropriately conceive, owns the farms now, because the conventions of ownership have broken down with the society: no agent can now count on any other to respect the conventions. Nevertheless, the boundaries—natural in part, in part artificial—respected by the former owners are still visible; and N and M each assume that, were conventions of ownership to be restored, his claim to own the farm that he occupies up to the old boundaries, together with everything normally found within those boundaries, would strike the other as more plausible than any other, and as acceptable. I shall use the possessive case as having, at any rate initially, no more force than these parallel assumptions by N and M warrant.

Every so often, let us suppose, N and M have opportunities to seize goods from each other's farm, whether by crossing over and picking the other's apples or asparagus or by failing to return the other's stray sheep or chickens. For a while, they each make full use of the opportunities. One morning, however, N comes to the boundary of M's farm, next to M's asparagus patch; both agents are in full view of each other, but M is just too far away from the asparagus patch to prevent N from getting away with the asparagus. N stares at the patch, basket in hand, then turning the basket upside down as a way of calling M's attention to the fact that the basket is empty, N turns away and goes off leaving the opportunity to take the asparagus unused.

M may not reciprocate when his next opportunity to take advantage of N occurs. There may be a number of false starts on either side. But let us imagine that in time, a gesture of forbearance like N's regarding the asparagus on the one side leads to a reciprocal action on the other. Later the same day, for example, M ostentatiously collars one of N's sheep, which has wandered onto M's land, and returns it to N. Again, I assume that M can get away with keeping the sheep. N and M are so equally matched physically that either can deter or prevent the other from taking advantage of him in his immediate presence; and their movable possessions are normally in the immediate presence of each agent if they are not beyond the reach of the other. Yet every so often, for a limited time only, each does turn by turn get the jump on the other; and they do so, let us assume, in perfect alternation, with more for each to gain (in his own eyes) than to lose when his turn comes.

Why should M reciprocate? M's motives (in regard to N) are *non tuistic;* but, like N he is at least rational enough to learn which courses of action are more, rather than less, advantageous from his point of view and adopt them after learning to identify them; he might have been so rational as to anticipate the results of such a learning process without having to go through it. If N is as rational as $M,$ they can learn, if they do not foresee from the beginning, when it will be for each more advantageous to act steadily in reciprocation than to act otherwise. Moreover, it will be more advantageous for each to do so, given the circumstances already assumed and some easily conceded technical conditions. First, neither agent must know when the series will end; otherwise it will be rational for one agent not to reciprocate on the last round; and then the motive for reciprocation will be undermined right back to the beginning.[8] Second, the values that the agents place upon the stakes must not be such that they would each gain more by taking turns as victims than by avoiding being victims at all; though if this condition fails, a symmetrical cooperative arrangement of another kind may be forthcoming.[9]

In making up his mind (in advance, or deliberating at the time) whether to engage in forebearance or restitution in any given round, each agent considers, first, that he can expect to be compensated by the other agent's action in this round or the next; and, second, that in the whole series of rounds he is as likely to be compensated on more occasions (one more) as he is to reciprocate on more. If the series lasts a long time, the fact that he might turn out to compensate more often than to be compensated would be negligible, since the value of what he lost on that one unreciprocated occasion, followed (let us say) by the death of the other agent, would be only a negligible proportion of the value of his gains or losses over the whole series.

The assumptions about matching physical strength and deterrence in each other's immediate presence rule out the possibility of one agent's being offered an opportunity to kill the other agent and thereafter seize all his possessions. The assumptions do not quite rule out an opportunity to gain more from taking advantage of the other agent on some one occasion than could be gained from reciprocation over the whole series of opportunities that the agents have turn by turn. If neither agent knows when such an opportunity might be presented one or the other, however, both agents would have grounds for keeping up the convention meanwhile; and if such an opportunity never came, the convention would be kept up as long as both survived.[10]

What stands in the way of extending the convention to embrace other people? I think the chief difficulty, which comes up as soon as even a third agent is brought in, lies in removing (at least substantially removing) any uncertainty that an agent who departs from the convention will be identified by the agent or agents who suffer the loss entailed. One might imagine a number of ways of removing such uncertainty, reflecting more or less accurately the features of real situations that keep it within limits. I shall remove it by boldly assuming that no agent can cross the boundary of another's farm without being detected and that the livestock on each farm are so placed as to let any given animal wander over the boundary only of one other farm. It may help to think of the farms as strung out along a long narrow peninsula like Digby Neck, Nova Scotia, with each farm straddling the whole width of the peninsula.

With this assumption in force, two phases in the extension of the convention may be distinguished. In the first, suppose there is no travelling: if the agents move at all, it is only far enough to trespass on an immediately neighbouring farm. Then extension over a multitude is quite straight-forward, barring occasions of extraordinary temptation. Every agent acts in accordance with the convention with each of his neighbors. No agent can treat the convention as something to which his contribution is superfluous. The convention, with its benefits, will not in fact continue to embrace any agent who does not contribute to it in a way entirely perceptible to the other agents who are his neighbors.

In the second phase, some travelling may be allowed for. Suppose it is known that every agent must at least once a year obtain, as his only source of Vitamin C, a supply of rose-hips from the southern end of the peninsula. If he could not safely leave his farm unguarded (with at least two neighbors in a position to victimize him while he is away), perhaps he will have to arrange to move south one day with all the rest. Or perhaps agents without farms will appear to act as specialized traders. Farmers on their way might combine to rob them (what we at least would call "robbing them"), but would be deterred by the loss of future supplies. At any rate, there would be some travelling, compatible with the convention and indeed illustrating it. If there were other perishable commodities that the farmers needed regularly and that required to be fetched from a distance, there might be quite a bit of travelling, whether by the farmers themselves or by a sizeable group of traders.

A society of sorts would thus emerge under these conditions. To move farther toward the complications of societies in the real world one would perhaps have to introduce, later than Lévi-Strauss (1949) himself would call for, the exchange of marriage-partners between family households; or, alternatively if not simultaneously, some effects of fellow-feeling, extending to the endorsement by moral sentiment of the convention discussed; and perhaps a division of labor as well. Hume may have been too ready to believe that the convention would emerge without the help of moral sentiment in circumstances more complicated than those of the society just described. Yet, bare skeleton though it may be, it is a society with intelligible arrangements that go some way toward justifying his conception of the convention's originating before it becomes a moral virtue to abide by it. The society described originates, with the convention on which it depends, from the rational pursuit by its members of their own interests, without any of them being prepared to make the least sacrifice in respect to these interests in order to promote the interests of the other parties to the convention.

Does the society described redeem the idea of a social contract? I do not think that it restores full credit for the idea; it depends for its origin on specially favorable conditions that the idea of a social contract has no right, in traditional discussions, to assume. Even so those conditions do not extend to making a convention, or a contract in lieu of a convention, superfluous. Some of the rival ideas—basic alternatives to the idea of having society originate (reoriginate) in a contract—would. If, for example, N and M and the other agents found themselves distinguished by what might be called "a strong division of labor," so that for any of them to survive, each had to do a job complementary to the jobs done by the others, the only job, moreover, that he was fitted by skill and strength to do, then they would certainly cooperate.[11] However, as Durkheim, who championed the division of labor (without insisting upon the strong sense just defined) as a more realistic basis for solidarity than anything contributed by the idea of a social contract, would have argued, cooperation in these circumstances would have no need of a convention or a contract (1902, Chapter 7).

By contrast, the circumstances actually assumed on Digby Neck may be regarded as a special case of the circumstances in which the idea of a social contract might be useful. If the institution of promising were available for the purpose, the agent might find it convenient, and certainly unobjectionable, to anticipate his acts of forbearance and restitution by promising to perform them on all subsequent occasions. Thus the society would be freely endorsed by everyone concerned, and endorsed by entering into a form of contract (a contract of the first form).

THE SOCIAL CONTRACT AS AN ELUSIVE PUBLIC GOOD

Only a society of sorts came about in the Digby Neck example; and though it came about as a result of *non tuistic* motivations conformable to traditional assumptions respecting arrival at a contract or a convention, it came about only because of circumstances specially favorable in a number of ways not assumed in traditional treatments. First, the agents were vulnerable only to a limited degree; they could not lose their lives to other agents; they could not even lose their property in their immediate presence. It is true, I did not rule out the possibility that an agent might lose all of his movable possessions in one fell swoop; if this possibility had looked like being realized very frequently, to make sure hypothetically of the emergence of the society illustrated I would have ruled out vulnerability in this respect too. Second, failures to reciprocate made a perceptible difference to the welfare of one or another of the two parties in the original pairs. Both the agent who profited from the failure and the agent who suffered would regard its impact as substantial. Third, failures to reciprocate were assignable, indeed assignable with certainty. When an agent suffered from such a failure, he knew precisely from whose action the damage proceeded. The pair-by-pair linkage through which the basic convention was repeated and extended, and the provisions for travelling, were both designed to preserve assignability. Fourth, for each member of each pair of agents, the opportunities to benefit and reciprocate alternated perfectly with each agent in turn standing to gain more than he lost. This assumption was perhaps stronger than necessary. It might have sufficed to assume that each agent believed (on reasonable grounds) that during the lifetimes of the pair he would stand to gain and lose equally often with more to gain (in his own eyes) than to lose over the whole series.

None of these favorable conditions obtain in the circumstances traditionally assumed in treating the social contract. The traditional contract does not have the advantage of being generated by pairwise multiplication. It is to be arrived at, as I pointed out in outlining its main features, by simultaneous undertakings by each agent to all the others covering in each case the agent's whole future lifetime. In the absence of the favorable conditions mentioned, it could not be arrived at in any case by first establishing a network of pairwise conventions or pairwise contracts. The absence of the favorable conditions prevents either pairwise conventions or pairwise contracts from emerging.

Traditionally, as Hobbes makes emphatically clear, the agents are vulnerable to the extent of having their lives at stake, and continually so, as well as their means of livelihood. Moreover, the agents, precarious and frightening as their situation may be in the state of nature, will be even worse off under a social contract that they abide by while others — agents in positions to prey upon them — do not: for, while they abide by the contract, they renounce opportunities to take advantage of other agents and lay aside (perhaps out of reach) the means of self-defense which they had in the state of nature. (It is this feature of the traditional problem that gives it the form in two-person cases of Prisoner's Dilemma.)

The other conditions are not (so far as I know) traditionally discussed. In the absence, however, of specific assumptions about the very special circumstances in which they would exist, one must contemplate the possibility of any agent's being able, in the absence of the efficient government hoped for from the contract, to get away with manifold depredations without his victims or anyone else assigning him the blame. In the large-number case, moreover, even violations that victims will surely feel (like being killed) may go unperceived as well as unassigned in the view of agents not so victimized. The difference between a system in which they have zero chance of being killed by another agent and a system in which the chance is very, very small may seem negligible (as far below the chances of death by natural accident, for example). The violations that tempt agents away from the contract need not be so drastic however. When the violations of the contract consist simply in withholding one's contribution to the joint enterprise (attending a political assembly; voting in an election; doing one's share of soldiering or of repairing the dikes) — the effects of the violation by any one agent may be so diffused that neither he nor anyone else will perceive a distinct impact from it. Finally, not every agent can assure himself of gaining more than he loses over his whole future lifetime by abiding by the contract while the other agents do likewise: Statistically, one may expect some to lose fairly steadily in the rounds of reciprocation, while others will find themselves in positions to gain by exploiting clusters of tempting opportunities to violate the contract.

The last condition is compatible with the emergence of a substantially effective contract, given reasonable luck with the frequencies involved. The other conditions make it impossible for any contract at all to emerge unless (keeping the circumstances constant) the agents' motivations deviate in a question-begging way from those traditionally assumed.

Some of the features of the traditional problem that direct us to this conclusion, though not all, can be seen in small-number cases, even in cases involving two agents. The problem takes the form of Prisoner's Dilemma without iteration (since the agents are to commit themselves, once and for all and simultaneously, to obtaining the contract and abiding by it, whichever of the two forms is in view). I shall repeat Luce and Raiffa's illustrative matrix:[12]

$$M$$

	b_1	b_2
	a_1 (9,9)	(0,10)
N		
	a_2 (10,0)	(1,1)

If N adopts strategy a_1, he commits himself to the contract; so does M, if he adopts strategy b_1. I shall assume throughout that all values associated with a given strategy appear in the cells, including those that given a distinction between "procedures" and "outcomes" would be assigned to procedures. The stakes, for Locke's milder agents, might not always be so vital as the stakes for Hobbes's fiercer ones; but the relative values of the cells for Locke's agents might have the same orderings.

Hobbes himself may be taken to rule out having the two agents arrive at the second form of contract by designating themselves (together) as the governing authority. For their professions of commitment will be mere words unless they have to fear, not just each other, as they do in the state of nature, but the sword, wielded by an authority that in power effectively transcends the powers which they have themselves.[13] In fact, rational agents, mindful of their symmetrical positions and of each other's rationality, will never arrive at the point even of professing commitment to the contract, in either form. To be sure, each agent will benefit from the contract, should the contract come into being — from the first form, at least as a step toward the second; from the second, as a means of rescuing them from the miseries of mutual aggression. However, each agent (as both know) stands to gain even greater benefits if he acts contrary to the contract while the other agent abides by the contract. A contract will not emerge. The agents' caution will deprive them of a solution that both would prefer; yet they cannot, on rational grounds, help but be cautious.

In the two-agent case, there can be no resort to a Hobbesian solution of assigning the enforcement of a contract of the second form to an agent who might otherwise be a party to the contract himself. Supposing (as Hobbes does suppose) that the agents are equally resourceful in the state of nature, why should either have less to fear from utterly subjecting himself to the other than from entering into a contract which the other would be free to violate?

Suppose there are three agents. Then two of the agents might, as part of a contract between them, confer on the third the authority to enforce the contract. But what would be the attractions to either of the contracting agents of entering into such an arrangement? As everyone concerned would recognize, identifying the particular persons to whom the damage could be brought home, such an arrangement would be tantamount to giving the authority — the sovereign — the power, on the pretext of enforcement, to join either contracting agent in a coalition that will unmercifully exploit the other. Would not both agents expect to do as well for themselves, if not better, by taking their chances with coalitions in the state of nature? If coalitions are to be formed, each agent has then a chance of forming one with every other (including the agent who would otherwise be the sovereign). One may doubt, however, whether any coalitions enduring long enough to engage sustained enterprises of aggression will be formed, since such coalitions would depend themselves on the emergence of firm contracts. Moreover, if such coalitions were formed the contracts involved would tend to vanish over time in favor again of a two-agent case of Prisoner's Dilemma. Several agents might combine to kill one or more agents left out of the combination, and seize their goods; but then several of those remaining would find it to their advantage (if they could coordinate, perhaps by some arbitrary signal) to combine against others remaining; and so on.

The mutually aggressive posture of *non tuistic* agents is not the essential obstacle to the contract. As Sobel has shown with his Farmer's Dilemma, in which the agents are so benevolent (though arrogantly determined to disregard the preferences of others) as to be entirely motivated by the benefits conferred on each other, an analogue of Prisoner's Dilemma will put the agents so much at crosspurposes as to prevent them from establishing the contract solution.[14] They need not even be at crosspurposes. As Sobel has shown with his Hunter's Dilemma, it may suffice for them to be facing a problem of coordination, the contract solution to which is for both the most desired outcome.[15] What prevents them from giving effect to that solution, the essential obstacle in all these cases, is that they cannot rely on each other; to make sure of avoiding a result even worse from their several points of view, they must each take precautions that lead away from the contract solution.

One can imagine achieving the desired coordination by imposing coercion from outside. This is Sobel's remedy for the dilemmas. As he would agree, however, resorting to such a remedy does not solve the contract problem, because it does not purport to solve the problem by means of a contract. It also leaves open the question of how to arrange for coercion, itself an essential part of the problem.

As Sobel recognizes, there are other ways of dealing with the problem, which equally imply abandoning hope of arriving at a solution of the problem as originally posed. One can, for example, tamper in other ways with the assumptions about motivation. Suppose that even without an enforcing sovereign, the agents, contrary to Hobbes's assumptions, keep promises that they make face-to-face and that each agent, knowing this fact about the others, can therefore rely upon them to do so. Since we are frankly assuming that the agents are, from their experience of organized social life in other societies, familiar with the institution of promising, there is nothing anomalous in invoking this familiarity; it does not even change the problem. It is the mutually known trustworthiness that we now suppose to accompany the familiarity which is anomalous. Since by being trustworthy and being known to be trustworthy, they achieve more of what they are aiming at than otherwise, should we not conceive that it is more rational for them to be these things? Yet this modified conception of rationality, as Sobel points out, if it is to give a different result from rationality without trustworthiness, must require the agents to disregard at least in part the incentives laid out for them (supposedly comprehensively) in the matrix.[16] If either agent can assume that the other will in fact be trustworthy, then he himself has more incentive to violate the contract than to keep it; but both agents can, as they both know, reason in this way; therefore, the original problem returns, unless both agents stand by their promises (and know they will) regardless. Obviously it is question-begging to assume that such conduct will occur; moreover, the mere assumption does not reach far enough to give the conduct any footing in the agents' motivations, which supposedly remain as pictured in the original matrix.

Again one must firmly distinguish between, on the one hand, everybody's acting cooperatively with everybody else, to everyone's benefit, and, on the other hand, anybody's having a compelling personal incentive to act cooperatively. Unless the matrix is changed, the compelling personal incentive runs in the other direction, against cooperative action. The agent may recognize that the benefits of everybody's acting cooperatively exceed for him and everybody else the benefits of nobody's so acting. He may recognize further that only the scheme of everybody's acting cooperatively would have a reasonable claim to everybody's assent, were there some device for eliciting this assent and giving it effect. Nevertheless, he will do better for himself if he acts independently, as the matrix, unchanged, continues to show: spectacularly better if the other agents should, unaccountably, act cooperatively for their part; at least better than he would do otherwise, if the others act independently, too.

Should not the matrix be changed, however? The dilemma disappears if the values in the cells change so that the contract outcome becomes an equilibrium solution as well as an optimum, with relative figures like the following, for example:

$$M$$

	b_1	b_2
a_1	(9,9)	(0,8)
a_2	(8,0)	(1,1)

N

The allusion to the promises being made "face-to-face" suggests that the cells in which one agent, by keeping his promise, opens himself up to exploitation by the other agent, who does not, should in fact be modified in the direction illustrated so as to take into account the shame which the other agent would feel about his treachery, given the reaction, face-to-face, of the victim. Again, the suggestion is question-begging, now even more strikingly so: How did the dilemma start up if the agents already had such fine conscientious feelings about their promises?

Moreover, even though I think that the suggestion is nonetheless well taken in the sense that the only way out of the problem is to make some such change in the matrix, shifting attention to a different and easier problem, I want to make it clear at this point that the suggestion does not in fact do away with the problem in all cases. It does not do away with the problem in the leading case. When the social contract is to emerge from the actions of a large number of people—Hobbes's "multitude"—face-to-face trustworthiness does not suffice for its emergence.

One can generalize all the features of Prisoner's Dilemma to the large-number case; and deploy there, with equal efficacy, the arguments that show the problem is insoluble, understood with those features.[17] However, with the change in numbers, remedies that—breaking with tradition—might work in the small-number case cease to work. Moreover, the insuperable obstacle to the emergence of the social contract in the large-number case can be most vividly formulated and hence most easily appreciated by shifting to another perspective—the perspective of a general argument about the supply of public goods. The argument is essentially due to Mancur Olson, Jr.[18] A public good, of which the social contract, at least in the large-number case, is an example, is a good in joint supply, such that the marginal cost of supplying it, once in existence, to any additional consumer, is zero. It is also a good such that no member of the public can be excluded from consuming it; nor can any member of the public reject it—everyone in the public consumes it in full whether or not he is perversely inclined to do without it. (Other examples, besides the social contract, include lighthouses; weather forecasting; the army, under civilian control, of one's own country; a disciplined police force.)[19]

Suppose now that, given the multitude who are to be embraced in the contract, the contribution which any one agent will make to establishing the contract will be negligible, so that it will make by itself no difference to the emergence or non-emergence of the contract in full strength, and also will go unperceived, so that even if there is anyone who cares whether the given agent contributes, the contribution or its absence will not be noticed. (Olson's own chief presentation of the argument goes somewhat astray by neglecting joint supply and by failing to distinguish and to insist on both features of the present supposition.)

It does not matter how little the contribution costs any given agent. The cost may amount to no more than the cost of using his voice to signify his undertaking to the rest of the multitude, the sound of his voice being drowned out by the sound of the others' (should the others speak). We can, however, assume more significant costs: the costs of journeying to join the assembled multitude; the costs of staying there, in boredom and discomfort; for *non tuistic* agents, the costs of foregoing chances to improve their personal fortunes while other agents are away at the place of meeting. The costs would then be significant. We may still consistently assume that the contribution of any one agent would be negligible and imperceptible. The agents may keep track of the movements of other agents in their own vicinity; but they may regard even their joint contribution as negligible and imperceptible. If enough people go to the meeting place for a contract to be instituted, there will be so many that in all probability no one there will be able to remark the absence of any particular agent, or of any group from a particular vicinity.

If every agent understands the position with respect to his own contribution, no agent will have any incentive to make it. The contract in either form will emerge, or fail to emerge, regardless of his action. If it emerges, his contribution will have been superfluous; if it does not emerge, made in vain. In both cases, any effort or sacrifice on his part would have been idle — effort and sacrifice thrown away.[20]

(Compare the situation on Digby Neck: there perceptibility alone, and its connection with reprisals by his neighbors, blocks Olson's argument; and though idealized there, it corresponds to a real factor bearing on actions to obtain public goods. If agents form a network and their actions are perceptible to their neighbors, there may be enough social pressure to bring about actions each of which, by itself, might otherwise have to be reckoned as not worth doing. One would still have to account for the — question-begging — pressure. On Digby Neck, of course, an agent's neighbors have vital interests of their own at stake in observing his actions and responding in kind; so the social pressure is explained, as it cannot always be explained, or counted on, in the situations that Olson has in mind.)

Hobbes treats arriving at a contract of the first form as a step toward arriving at a contract of the second form, which is perfectly natural, even if one distinguishes between the two forms more firmly than Hobbes does. But Hobbes does not keep in mind the difference between the two steps; he does not see that each has its own difficulties. In fact, the difficulties arising for the first step, once it is singled out for attention, can be seen to be insuperable on his own assumptions. The first step requires agents to come to the meeting-place and once there wait through a discussion period of some length (after perhaps waiting for the arrival of other agents before the discussion begins). Only when the discussion period ends will the sovereign have been identified and invested with power; and it is quite illegitimate to imagine that the sovereign can be called upon to enforce the first form of contract, on which the discussion depends, while the discussion is going on. If the discussion period, in inception or continuation, requires of the agents the least cost or effort, it will not begin. If by accident it does begin, it will not continue—the agents will slip away one by one to engage in other pursuits. The discussion itself, with the first form of contract on which it depends, is a public good, which agents with the assumed motivations would have no rational incentive to assist into being or to keep in being by making the necessary contributions. Besides running the two forms of contract together in his mind, and failing to distinguish their separate difficulties, Hobbes may have thought the costs of the discussion negligible to the vanishing point. Suppose the agents are already assembled, perhaps by accident, and tentatively agreed upon whom to designate as sovereign, so that the discussion period endures only an instant. But at best this view of the matter is plausible only for the small-number case.

In the large-number case as well as in the small-number case, fear that the other agents will at most only pretend to enter into the contract leads agents with the traditionally assumed motivations to renounce the project of obtaining a contract at the beginning. Suppose this fear, which leads to the mediocre result of Prisoner's Dilemma, can be assumed away. No agent need fear more for his life from being duped into a pretended contract than from conducting his own defense in the state of nature. Would the fact that a contract of the second form, once in being, reduces the grounds for fearing violent death, in Hobbes's eyes the most powerful of grounds, lead agents to accept the costs of contributing to the public good of having a contract? It might, if the alternatives were obtaining a reduction in the chances of a violent death as against not obtaining this reduction. These are not, however, the alternatives that the agent faces respecting the first form of contract, the essential first step toward obtaining a contract of the second form. The alternatives that he faces are having the reduction with or without his contribution as against not having the reduction with or without his contribution. The reduction in the chances of a violent death will come about or not come about whatever he does.

Hobbes's scheme for generating the contract thus fails, in the large-number case, in its first step, beyond hope, as we shall see in a moment, of remedying by assuming either benevolent feelings, which may not work even in the small-number case, or face-to-face trustworthiness. Let me digress for a moment to comment on the situation that would exist if by some miracle the discussion period does begin and continue to within an instant of designating the sovereign. Even then, strictly speaking, the agents have no incentive to bear the costs that they must individually bear to bring the second form of contract into being. Trifling through those costs may be—

merely the cost for each of raising his voice, perhaps — they must still appear in each individual case a waste of effort. Hobbes and others might well protest at this point that it is unrealistic to think that agents will balk at such trifles. I agree; I am ready to concede, moreover, that there may be no grounds for ascribing to Hobbes or other classical theorists of the social contract a view of rationality according to which agents will be so finely motivated as to take trifles into account. So I would not insist upon Olson's argument at this particular junction; but I would call attention to the fact that waived with the argument is the strict universality of the principle that rational agents do not bear costs which they can recognize to be unnecessary.

The project will still not end with a contract of the second form unless the fears associated with Prisoner's Dilemma vanish in this connection too. Suppose by a second miracle they are repressed for a moment and the sovereign is established. Then, if the sovereign is perfectly efficient, individual agents must expect to be detected and punished when they violate the contract to take advantage of anyone else; so they each have an additional incentive to abide by the contract once it has been established. Here, one may perhaps grant, the fear of death will restrain them. What, however, will Hobbes have proved? He appears, once we get (with the help of a couple of miracles) this far, to have changed the subject. He has shown that an effective sovereign can, with the threat of force, keep men in order; but he has not shown that rational *non tuistic* agents will voluntarily agree either to establish such a sovereign or to keep it in being. They keep it in being by acting rationally on their fear of coercion; not by anything like continued adherence to a voluntary continued contract.

Moreover, sovereigns in the real world are far from being perfectly efficient (as Hobbes himself well knew: consider his example of the man who locks up his goods when at home and arms himself when he travels though in a settled kingdom).[21] Insofar as they are not, agents will be from time to time in positions to violate the contract without much risk of being detected. Will they be too fearful of death or other penalties to run small risks? Realism about people's utility-functions suggests that, with no abatement of their rationality, they will not be; in fact people take greater rather than lesser risks of death continually. They would, for example, do very little travelling if they did not; they would not even cross streets so often. Thus in the large-number case, even if somehow a government does emerge from the project of obtaining a contract, rational agents will not voluntarily abide by it to the extent of refraining from victimizing each other or even to the extent of bearing each his share of the costs of keeping the government up; and insofar as the government is inefficient rational agents cannot expect each other to abide by the contract voluntarily or involuntarily.

CHANGING THE PROBLEM BY CHANGING THE ASSUMPTIONS ABOUT MOTIVATION

The traditional problem of the social contract is insoluble; if one wants to pose a soluble problem about the rational reconstruction of organized society, one must change the problem. The change may move far away from the traditional problem (to assuming, in effect, that the traditional problem has somehow been solved by some standing commitment to social cooperation; or even further, to assuming, besides such a commitment, circumstances less literally urgent or dangerous). Or the change may stop relatively close by. The problem that I imagined arising on Digby Neck differs substantially in respect to the circumstances in which reconstruction is to be sought; perhaps it does not differ so much as to relinquish all claim to closely resembling the traditional problem. Differences between the traditional problem and soluble problems — and hence the character of the traditional problem — can also be illuminated by moving around the neighborhood on the opposite side — the side on which the assumptions about motivation differ. Instead of changing the circumstances, leaving the motivations as traditionally assumed, as was done on Digby Neck, let us leave the circumstances as traditionally assumed, and change the motivations. What changes in the assumptions about motivation will lead to a social contract?

Waiving miracles and returning to the problem of getting the project underway by (say) obtaining a contract of the first form, endowing the agents with benevolent or altruistic feelings might seem to help matters. If the agents are endowed with such feelings, the problem is changed in this respect: No agent need any longer fear being killed or robbed by another. Here perhaps one might want to say that Locke's tendency to set up the problem in a different way, assuming milder agents who may even like one another, has been fully realized; but in the large-number case the problem, even when transformed to this degree, remains insoluble. Failures to contribute whose effect is diffused — like the effect of any one agent's not attending Hobbes's discussion period — will occur in accordance with Olson's argument, as would similar violations of an existing contract were one to exist. To apply an insight of Gordon Tullock's (1971), even an agent who is attracted to the project of a contract by the benefits it will confer upon others will be acting contrary to prevailing assumptions about rationality if he gives up anything in support of the project. For what he gives up will be thrown away: if the benefits to others that the contract offers are realized, they will be realized without his contribution; if they are not, he cannot even console himself with the thought that his effort or sacrifice was a laudable attempt. No, they were, either way, quite wasted; the agent would have done better to save his strength and other resources for benevolent uses not connected with the contract.

Could Olson's argument be evaded by having each agent, benevolent or not, assume on a probabilistic basis a share of the effort required to bring the contract into being?[22]. Suppose that if only a fraction of the whole population of agents made each a rather small contribution a contract of the first form would be established. (The same argument applies to arriving directly from the state of nature at a contract of the second form.) Could not then every agent fix for himself a definite probability of making such a contribution? The higher the probability, the more nearly certain the emergence of the contract would be; but whatever the probability, there would seem to be sufficient incentive for the agent to act in accordance with it so long as his expectation of gain from the contract exceeds his expectation of cost in making the contribution.

There are several things wrong with this suggestion, unfortunately. The higher the probability in question, the less needed will be a contribution of any given size from any single individual agent; his position will take on the features that Olson assumes. But how is the probability to be fixed, or the size of the contribution? Even if the aggregate of contributions needed were fixed, the proportion of contributors and hence the size of each individual contribution required remains variable, along with the probability of making the contribution and the approximation desired to certainty of success. These are matters with arbitrary elements that can be settled only by an organized society with a capacity for legislation.

Moreover, it is a mistake to suppose that the aggregate of contributions needed can be fixed. If it could be, every agent could undertake an equal share with a probability equal to one; but then Olson's assumption that each agent's contribution taken by itself is negligible is violated — should any agent withhold his share, the contract will fail. One might say, "So much the worse for Olson's assumptions," were it not for the fact that realism is on Olson's side. Having or not having a contract — having or not having an organized society — is a matter affected by degree vagueness: there is no exact minimum of contributions that make the difference between having a contract and not having one. Hence every agent is always in the position of being able to assume that his own contribution, which would be just one more pebble on the heap, would not by itself make a difference.

Benevolence will not suffice to produce a social contract. It will not suffice to keep one up either. What would? What ways of begging the question respecting motivations might succeed? I shall from this point on abstract from the distinction between the two forms, since the arguments will apply equally well to either (or to both, conflated). I shall also speak indifferently of arriving at the contract and of keeping it up, on the grounds that rational agents will no more be able to arrive at a contract which they know will not be kept up than they will be able to keep up a contract which they cannot arrive at.

Let us try begging the question by assuming trustworthiness (without assuming benevolence).

Face-to-face trustworthiness will go at most only part of the way. If the multitude is very large, the number of other agents with whom any given agent can deal on a face-to-face basis will be a negligible proportion of the whole number. He, with the agents that he trusts, will not suffice, any more than he would by himself, to keep the contract going. If the contract is continually observed by the rest of the multitude, he and the agents that he trusts will make only a negligible contribution by observing it themselves. So far Olson's argument seems to apply. Moreover, on the point of getting away with violating the contract unperceived, will not the agent be able to do so with respect to the rest of the multitude? His face-to-face trustworthiness would only inhibit him from violating the contract with any of the small circle of agents with whom he deals on a face-to-face basis.

Here, however, Olson's argument suffers a set-back. For if the net-work of face-to-face acquaintance extends continuously through the whole population of agents, so, as we move from agent to agent, will the scope of inhibitions. Hence the contract will be kept up across the network.

In other respects, however, the contract will lapse. For no agent will be inhibited by face-to-face trustworthiness from violating the contractual relation with agents who do not belong to his own circle of acquaintances. There will be, for every single agent, a great number of such agents, indeed, almost the whole multitude; and by Olson's argument, returning in strength, it will be waste effort for any single agent to keep up the contract with respect to them (and in a Hobbesian perspective, unsafe or at least imprudent).

To have the contract kept up by every agent with respect to every other — to have even a reasonable violation-minimizing approximation of this ideal — trustworthiness must reach beyond face-to-face acquaintances. Agents must understand that in entering the contract they are making a promise to everyone else; and they must be in this respect trustworthy in relation to everyone else, and known to be so. Once again, to escape the contract problem the problem has had to be changed and the question begged (though, one might remember, still not so much begged as it would be if one had some intention of tracing the origin or justification of moral rules and virtues to the contract). Is it realistic to assume that so much confidence can be put in men's promises?

Another way of arriving at the contract would rely, not on inflexible attachment to promises, but on attachment to the No Suckers Rule. By "the No Suckers Rule," I mean the moral rule that one is not to let other people do all the work of bringing about benefits which one will share in and to the production of which one is in a position to make what I shall call an "additionally sufficient contribution," namely a contribution that, added to the contributions demanded by the same rule from other people on the scene, will suffice or more than suffice to produce the benefits in question. If the total contributions forthcoming more than suffice, the Rule would be improved upon as to efficiency by specifying smaller contributions; in the absence of efficient specifications, the Rule leaves it up to individual agents to make additionally sufficient contributions in amounts that leave their consciences at rest.

If the No Suckers Rule is to operate against Olson's argument, it must be understood as requiring contributions made as a matter of principle, even when there are rational grounds for any single agent to consider his contribution, taken by itself, to be redundant. He may himself recognize its redundancy, taken by itself, and claim no more for the contribution, taken by itself, than that it constitutes a symbolic gesture, which he would be too uncomfortable in his own mind to omit, whether or not other people will witness it and appreciate the symbolism. A set of agents, all of whom are sufficiently attached to the Rule to make the contributions required by a social contract (and who know each other to be so attached), would each be able to make his contribution in confidence that the others would do so, too. A contract would emerge and persist.

Of course, assuming attachment to the No Suckers Rule is question-begging, too. Is it any more realistic? I do not know whether it is more realistic than an assumption of widespread trustworthiness; but I might point out that it is perhaps realistic enough to explain the fact that most people living under democratic governments take the trouble to vote in elections, an actual phenomenon as hard to explain in the face of Olson's argument as the hypothetical emergence and continuation of a social contract. Moreover, might one not claim enough realism either for attachment to the Rule or attachment to promising so that they are convincingly realistic if they are combined in one assumption? Where one kind of attachment is, though present, too weak to do the job, the other may guarantee the missing part of the motivation; and vice versa.

Besides assuming that such attachments can be counted upon, they must, of course, be given a footing in the agents' motivations. I have indicated how to do so for the No Suckers Rule. An equally straightforward brazen approach may be taken in the case of the rule about keeping promises. Just as one may assume that the agents significantly discount the expected benefits of any action when the action violates the No Suckers Rule, one may also assume that they do so when, through infidelity to some particular promise, the action violates the rule about keeping promises. One can, if one wishes, extend the assumption to having the agents revise upward their expectations of benefits when the benefits are accompanied by a heartwarming sense of having kept the faith and done one's share. In the two-person case, if the discounts and revisions upward change the relative values of the matrix sufficiently for every agent, the form of Prisoner's Dilemma will disappear and the contract cell will become the equilibrium solution. In the large-number case, viewed either in the perspective of Prisoner's Dilemma or in the perspective of the public goods argument, the value of abiding by the rules ascends high enough to overshadow any value to be gained from using the resources so committed otherwise.

Would it be excessive optimism to suppose that such values exist for every agent, given some real population of live agents? Perhaps so: at least a few agents in the population may, sometime or other in their lives, find themselves in positions such that their opportunities to gain by violating the contract are too great to be offset by their attachment to promising and to the No Suckers Rule, even though those attachments may be quite strong. If such agents and opportunities are few, however, each of the other agents may be able to reckon that his personal chances of having to suffer depredations on this account through encountering such agents at times propitious to them are small; and the contract would evidently survive.

It is true that in various real populations strong attachments to the requisite rules may not be widespread. On the other hand, their prevalence, if it were a fact, would hardly be inexplicable. Do not people in our society internalize the rule of keeping promises and the No Suckers Rule in childhood, from infancy and nursery school on? It is even easy to get them to do so: children love to help; and they do not start out mistrustful — the difficulties children would have about keeping up a social contract have more to do with impulse and shortness of attention-span than with absence of goodwill.

Moreover, one could plausibly treat the discussion phase of arriving at the contract as tending to intensify the attachments required to establish the contract and keep it in being.[23] I take it that this is one way of developing a point about the inconsistency of entering into an agreement to act "interdependently" and then using, to decide on one's actions, criteria which ignore this interdependence. "To do so is in itself to violate the agreement," one might say. "It is, indeed, to show that one has not *really* entered it." Suppose, in the discussion phase, the agents develop trust in one another as they simultaneously explore the possibility of establishing a contract and discover each other to have some attachments of the sort that favor establishing one and keeping it up. Would it not be schizophrenic for an agent to take part in a discussion phase of this kind, on these terms, and then switch back to acting without regard for the other agents? On the contrary, such a discussion phase would surely reinforce his other-regarding attachments; and if the impressions gathered in the discussion should fade in time, they could be periodically renewed by going through something like the discussion phase as a community exercise. (In fact this happens, in civics classes, public ceremonies, and many other connections).

Were the agents to have the motivations in question and have them in sufficient strength, they would escape from the problem and enjoy the benefits of a social contract. These might still be important benefits in spite of the question-begging involved in the assigned motivations. For in the absence of the mutual undertakings establishing the contract, the agents might, treating each other at crosspurposes, fail to obtain the benefits of cooperation even though cooperation could be arranged for.

Would they still be rational agents, with the motivations in question assigned to them? There are two points to make in answer to this question.

First, although the theory of rational choice owes some of its most striking successes in application to narrow assumptions about motivation, the theory is ready to accept any motivations whatever (except perhaps a will to be inconsistent in preferences). Agents will rationally enter into and keep up a social contract if, and only if, they have certain motivations that are not entailed by being rational. Yet being rational does not entail selfish or *non tuistic* motivations rather than unselfish or tuistic motivations, nor does it entail motivations opposed to other-regarding rules rather than motivations attached to them.

Second, without the motivations in question (or others that might work to the same effect), rationality confines agents to inferior results. Someone who cared for the human race, if he could not count upon people acquiring such motivations through socialization, would do well to preclude the freedom to be rational without them, and implant instincts supporting the social contract. How much regard and respect should we have for rationality when it is not associated with suitable motivations? I think, strictly limited respect. Rationality by itself does not suffice to promote people's interests, whatever these interests may be.

Of course, it has been recognized from ancient times that the advice to be rational is incomplete if the people concerned are not willing to waive questions about basic tastes. The surprising discovery that recognizing the insolubility of the problem of the social contract opens to view is that the advice to be rational is incomplete even when questions about basic tastes have been waived — incomplete in a special way. Waiving those questions, one might still consider the advice to be rational complete, when addressed to a single person who is to live in isolation (a rare case) or (perhaps all too common a case) to a single person who is to live in the midst of others of whom he knows no more than that they are rational and *non tuistic.*

The advice is incomplete advice and bad advice, however, when it is addressed to a group of people, taking into account the relations, fruitful or otherwise, which they might have with each other. Complete advice, good advice to a group of people, whatever their interests may be, consists in advising them to be not only rational in the pursuit of those interests, but to accord as well very thoroughgoing respect to rules (like keeping promises and not playing other people for suckers) that coordinate their pursuits.

APPENDIX[24]

The convention-establishing agents N and M adapt their actions to the intentions which they learn to ascribe to one another. It would be ironic indeed if the pattern of cooperation to which they advance should turn out to be something that they would not have adopted had they been fully rational and informed of each other's rationality to begin with. Yet this suggestion has cropped up; and since Luce and Raiffa give only general assurances that rational agents will arrive at cooperative solutions in iterated Prisoner's Dilemma with sequences of finite but unknown length it may be helpful to spell out how such a solution may be arrived at in an iteration of our game resembling Prisoner's Dilemma. Let the stakes for N (Row) and M (Column) be represented by Luce and Raiffa's matrix for Prisoner's Dilemma:

$$M$$

	b_1	b_2
a_1	(9,9)	(0,10)
a_2	(10,0)	(1,1)

N moves first in any round. (So the rounds will have first an a move, second a b move, e.g., a_{13} b_{13}; but I shall also consider pairings that overlap rounds, for example, b_{13} a_{14}.) If he omits to pick M's asparagus, M makes a gain (in his eyes) of 9 as compared with what would have happened otherwise, the loss of the asparagus. If M reciprocates by returning M's sheep, N gains (in N's eyes) 9. On the other hand, if M does not reciprocate, he gains both the asparagus (9) plus the sheep (1), while N loses out altogether (0). If N picked the asparagus, while M kept the sheep, each would gain at the other's expense, but each would also lose one of his own possessions, which he might specially prize, because he had budgeted for its use. If (1,1) seems to value having the other agent's goods too little, it may of course be imagined larger. It seems reasonable, however, to assume that each agent orders having his own plus the other agent's goods about having just his own and this in turn above having only the other's, while he puts at the bottom having neither.

The possible sequence of moves, with each agent's move illustrating one of the two strategies open to him, may be exhaustively partitioned as follows:

(I) (Pairs matching throughout, cooperative)
  a_{11} b_{11} a_{12} b_{12} a_{13} b_{13} ... a_{1n} b_{1n}

(II) (Pairs matching throughout, noncooperative)

$a_{21} b_{21} a_{22} b_{22} a_{23} b_{23} \ldots a_{2n} b_{2n}$

(III) (Sequences in which Row scores one or more *coups* against Column, but not vice versa)

$\ldots b_{1j} a_{2j+1} \ldots$

(IV) (Sequences in which Column scores one or more *coups* against Row, but not vice versa)

$\ldots a_{1j} b_{2j} \ldots$

(V) (Sequences in which *coups* are scored on both sides)

$\ldots b_{1j} a_{2j+1} \ldots a_{1r} b_{2r}$

(VI) (Mixed sequences without *coups*)

$\ldots b_{2j} a_{1j+1} \ldots V \ldots a_{2r} b_{1r} \ldots$

I do not count an instance of $b_{2j} a_{1j+1}$ or $a_{2r} b_{1r}$ as a *coup*, because though one agent gains at the expense of the other from the pair of moves, the gain does not go to the agent moving second in the pair; the agent moving second does not take advantage of the agent moving first — on the contrary, he omits to compensate himself for the non-cooperative action of the other.

Which sequences of moves will emerge from the actions of agents perfectly rational and fully informed from the beginning? The value of a sequence for either agent is given by the quantity

$$x \cdot u_{(a_1, b_1)} + y \cdot u_{(a_1, b_2)} + z \cdot u_{(a_2, b_1)} + t \cdot u_{(a_2, b_2)}$$

where $x + y + z + t = n$. Row will wish to maximize z; failing z, x; failing x or z, t; and to minimize y. Column will wish to maximize y; failing y, x; failing x or y, t; and to minimize z. Consider the quantities

$$Q_1 = u_{1(a_2, b_1)} + u_{1(a_1, b_2)} \text{ and } Q_2 = u_{2(a_1, b_2)} + u_{2(a_2, b_1)}.$$

These give the values for 1 (*N* or Row) and 2 (*M* or Column), respectively, of a pair of pairs in which the two agents take advantage of each other turn by turn.

Suppose that

$$Q_1 < 2 \cdot u_{1(a_1, b_1)} \text{ and } Q_2 < 2 \cdot u_{2(a_1, b_1)};$$

in other words, the agents do better for themselves by cooperating over any pairs than by taking turns as victim and exploiter. Nevertheless, each agent could conceivably do even better for himself if he could score some coups against the other. The other agent, however, has nothing to gain by conceding coups in the hope of obtaining some himself — by assumption, if they split coups evenly over the whole sequence each would do worse than by adhering to the cooperative solution. The other agent may therefore be expected, in his own interest, to do whatever he can to minimize the number of coups carried out against him. What can he do? It would be sufficiently effective (and perhaps optimal in deterrence because of its simplicity) to adopt the policy of reverting consistently after any coup scored by the first agent to his second, non-cooperative strategy, for the rest of the sequence. A more refined policy, which would be equally effective with fully rational agents, would be simply to follow the non-cooperative strategy for a number of rounds, long enough to wipe out the special gains from the coup.

In either case, with both agents adopting an effective policy of retaliation, neither agent will have any incentive to carry out a coup against the other. Hence Row must accept that z will have to set at zero; and Column, that y will have to be. They have each then to maximize the quantity.

$$x \cdot u_{1(a_1, b_1)} + t \cdot u_{1(a_2, b_2)};$$

but for both this is done by setting x as high as possible relatively to t, which implies acting as in the one sequence falling in the first partition, where $x = n$ and $t = 0$. In effect, in a consolidated matrix the northeast and southwest cells drop out and the preponderant value of the northwest cell determines the issue.

A cooperative solution of another kind emerges, outside the bounds of Prisoner's Dilemma strictly defined and of analogies to it, if Q_1 and Q_2 do not conform to the supposition above. Again enforcing cooperative alternation by each adopting a policy of retaliation, the two agents take turns as victim and exploiter; or else the two sorts of cooperative solutions prove equally attractive, and the agents choose between them by resort to some device of chance.

In effect, I have assumed in the above argument that the probability of a given agent's surviving to make in turn his next move changes only negligibly over the whole sequence. If it should fall very drastically at any point in the sequence the cooperative solution might be jeopardized on grounds like those arising in the case of iteration for a known number of times. However, I think the assumption of negligible change is not especially implausible: In their eighties, N and M may still have very nearly the same expectation of seeing each other on the next of two given days as they did in their twenties — so long at least as they both continue in good health.

NOTES

* The present paper is a revised version of a paper entitled, "The Social Contract Returns, This Time as an Elusive Public Good," Copyright, 1974, The American

Political Science Association, and presented at its 1974 meeting in Chicago. That paper in turn was a revision of one of two papers that I contributed in June 1974 to the Institute on Moral and Social Philosophy held in Toronto by the Canadian Philosophical Association following its annual meeting. I am grateful to David Gauthier and J. Howard Sobel, who took part in the Institute with me, for their comments. Indeed I must thank Gauthier in particular for stimulation at every stage, early and late, that the paper has passed through. I am grateful to Gerald C. MacCallum and James F. Reynolds, too, who were the commentators in Chicago; and to various other people, including Max Black and Virginia Held, besides those who took part from the floor in the discussions in Toronto and Chicago. My Dalhousie colleague William R. Mathie kindly helped keep me in mind of some of the chief features of Hobbes's doctrine.

1. Hobbes, though in fact he has a use for one version of the first form, argues nevertheless that only the second form can be effective. For him the first form appears in sequence with the second form; and he tends to run the two forms together in his mind, thinking of them as involving one formula, which first displays a blank or placeholder where the names of the person or persons who are to be the sovereign are to be filled in, but which in the end exhibits, in place of the blank or placeholder, the names filled in. Hobbes, *Leviathan:* see the formula of covenant given at the beginning of Chap. 18 with the formula given in the antepenultimate paragraph of Chap. 17. Moreover, Hobbes thinks of agreement to having the formula filled in as contemplated (for example, by majority vote) as committing the agents to accepting the formula filled in. Actually, a separate agreement is required (since the initial agreement, if it is obtained at all, continues only at the pleasure of the parties); and the two steps present separate (though analogous) problems.

2. The second form of contract is of course not to be confused with a form of contract between agents who become subjects and an agent who becomes sovereign over them. Hobbes, followed (for very different reasons) by Rousseau, denies that such a contract makes sense. *Leviathan,* Chap. 18, fourth paragraph; see *Du contrat social,* Livre I, Chap. 7. If the contract is conceived of as purporting to confer unrestricted power on the sovereign — which unrestricted power Hobbes and Rousseau wish (again for very different reasons) to ascribe to the sovereign — I for one would not dispute the point. Like Hume, however, I think there is no reason for thinking that such a contract must purport to confer unrestricted power; and good grounds for thinking that it makes perfect sense if it does not. Hume, "Of the Original Contract," fifth paragraph (1777). I need not pursue the issue here.

3. In insisting upon having the agents literally assemble at one place and give simultaneous undertakings, I am forcing a point that the traditional discussions do not settle. Hobbes's words, for example, might possibly bear other interpretations, according to which the undertakings succeed one another in various ways; and he does not require that all the circumscribed agents literally assemble. See especially *Leviathan,* Chap. 18, fifth paragraph. My interpretation however, not only respects best the consideration, prominent in Hobbes's mind, that all the other assembled agents must reciprocate; it is more favorable to his argument. Any arrangement for giving the undertakings consecutively would increase the costs and risks of having a contract, as would having the agents dispersed rather than assembled.

4. Hume, ibid.; and his *Treatise of Human Nature,* Book 3, Section 7.

5. See Marx's brief discussion of Rousseau's "contrat social" in the *Grundrisse,* General Introduction. A more extended critique could easily be elaborated along

the lines that I have sketched by transposing the points made by such a Marxist writer as Althusser in criticising individualism in economic theory. See *passim* Althusser and Balibar (1968).

6. Locke, *Second Treatise of Government,* Chap 3, at the end; Chap. 9, at the beginning.
7. Hume, *Treatise,* Book 3, Section 2.
8. As J. Howard Sobel, elaborating a point made by Luce and Raiffa (1957), pp. 98–99, shows in (1972), pp. 148–177.
9. See (after reading the next footnote) Appendix to this paper.
10. To review the motivational question in more technical terms: Each pair of alternating opportunities to forbear and to be compensated can be looked upon as constituting a game similar to Prisoner's Dilemma. ("Similar" only, because the agents move in turn, rather than simultaneously.) Over the whole series of opportunites, moreover, one agent would gain most if the other agent abided by the convention while he steadily violated it. However, this option is not available over the series as a whole. In a curiously mixed discussion, cited by Sobel, which fails to come to decisive grips with what rational motivation exactly means in such circumstances, Luce and Raiffa do allow for the agents to achieve some of the benefits of cooperation through learning to practice "collusion" even in a game with a known finite number of pairs of stages; and allow that a fully cooperative solution may emerge if the agents do not know when the series will end. (For further discussion, see Appendix.)
11. The assumption is stronger than one that shapes a version of a dilemma called "Hunter's Dilemma" by Sobel and discussed by him in this version, (1972), pp. 168–169. There the agents fail to cooperate even though both would do somewhat better if they accepted a division of labour. Under a strong division of labour, none of the agents has an acceptable option outside the one form of cooperation.
12. Luce and Raiffa (1957), p. 95, at top. I have multiplied all the figures by 10.
13. *Leviathan,* Chap. 17, second paragraph.
14. The matrix for Farmer's Dilemma looks the same as the matrix for Prisoner's Dilemma, but the figures bear a different interpretation in this sense: each agent values the cells in accordance with the benefits that they confer in his eyes upon the other agent, that is, each agent is motivated to act exactly contrary to Shaw's maxim, "Do not do unto others what you would have them do unto you; their tastes may be different." Sobel (1972), pp. 154–159.
15. The matrix for Hunter's Dilemma, filled out for comparison with the illustration of Prisoner's Dilemma, has a form that can be illustrated as follows:

$$M$$

	b_1	b_2
a_1	(2,2)	(3,3)
a_2	(3,3)	(1,1)

N

It is best for both that one hunts while the other returns to tend the campfire, and it does not matter which agent does either task; what both wish to avoid as the worst outcome is the one in which both go on hunting (a_2, b_2) and the fire goes out for want of tending. Sobel, (1972), at pp. 159–60. Sobel argues that no strategy is tenable for either agent. With different assumptions, one might argue that they will both end up going back to tend the fire (a_1, b_1).

16. Sobel (1972), p. 159, note; p. 164.

17. There are a number of ways of generalizing Prisoner's Dilemma to the n-person case. One can generalize it to all games in which the equilibrium result (the dominant choice for everyone) differs from what (with suitable measures of redistribution at least) would be the optimum result. Schelling (1973) discusses the variety of situations that then have to be considered. Schelling, in exploring this variety, is chiefly interested in such questions as what proportion of agents must make cooperative choices for the optimum to result and how the total payoff at the optimum is divided (before redistribution) between cooperative agents and non-cooperative ones. He leaves unsettled, as a problem of "organization," the question how players are to be assigned to making cooperative and non-cooperative choices. This problem is central for my purposes and remains central under any relevant generalization. It takes the form of demanding that the optimum (or any gains from cooperation less than the optimum) result from the agents' assigning themselves to cooperative or non-cooperative roles. Over the whole range of situations that can plausibly be associated with the traditional problem of the social contract (situations that are instances of what Schelling calls "uniform multi-person prisoner's dilemma"), the incentive for self-assignment to a cooperative role is, for every agent acting individually, missing. It is no less missing when (as one must realistically allow) the benefits of cooperation — a social contract; a government — can be substantially realized when substantially less than the whole number of agents act cooperatively. Moreover, the problem of getting a majority to enter into the contract and keep it up, if only a majority are required to make it effective, is the same sort of problem, on a smaller scale, as the problem of getting everyone to enter.

18. Olson (1965). See especially the Introduction and the opening passages of Chapter 1.

19. Ironically, the concept of a public good has often been used to give a purported explanation of the origin or rational foundation of government. Admittedly, government is a public good; but it does not follow that rational agents will cooperate in producing it. For a discussion of the general fallacy, see again Olson, ibid.; for a discussion concentrating on its use in purported explanations of the existence of governments, Aranson (1974).

20. Hardin (1971) has shown that, formally, the circumstances and motivations assumed by Olson's argument, can be looked upon precisely as constituting an n-person Prisoner's Dilemma. It seems to me, in fact, that the only formal feature contributed by Olson's assumptions is limiting the difference between the payoff to a given agent when he does not contribute (though everyone else does) and his net payoff when he contributes (along with everyone else) to just the cost of his contribution. Yet the two perspectives are intuitively — shall I say, phenomenologically? — very different. I think most of this difference, perhaps all, may be attributed to the fact that in the Prisoner's Dilemma perspective one is inclined (misled to a degree by the anecdote that gave the dilemma its name) to stress the agents' fears of being doublecrossed, while in the perspective of Olson's argument about public goods one is inclined to stress the idleness, from any agent's point of view, of making any contribution.

21. *Leviathan,* Chap. 13.

22. This suggestion came up during the discussion in Toronto.

23. A hopeful speculation commonly raised by commentators on Prisoner's Di-

lemma. There is some favorable experimental evidence. See Rapoport and Orwant (1964), pp. 296–297.

24. This appendix echoes and responds to a discussion at the CPA Institute, and especially to points made by Gauthier and Sobel. I have also had very useful concrete help respecting it from fellow-members of the Aspen/Cornell colloquium
on rational choice, especially from Bernard Grofman, who has done extensive
original work on iterated Prisoner's Dilemma.

18

Utility Maximizers
In Iterated Prisoner's Dilemmas*

JORDAN HOWARD SOBEL

Maximizers in isolated Prisoner's Dilemmas are doomed to frustration. But
in Braybrooke's view maximizers might do better in a series, securing
Pareto-optimal arrangements if not from the very beginning, at least eventually. Given certain favorable special conditions, it can be shown according to Braybrooke and shown even without question-begging motivational
or value assumptions, that in a series of dilemmas maximizers could manage
to communicate a readiness to reciprocate, generate thereby expectations of
reciprocation, and so give rise to optimizing reciprocations which, in due
course, would reinforce expectations, the net result of all this being an in-
creasingly stable practice to mutual benefit. In this way neighbours could
learn to be good neighbours: they could learn to respect each other's property, to engage in reciprocal assistance, and perhaps even to make and
keep promises covering a range of activities. So maximizers are, Braybrooke holds, capable of a society of sorts. Out of the ashes they might
build something. But even under favorable conditions they could not build
much and most conditions would defeat them almost entirely, for many-

From *Dialogue* 15 (1976): 38–53. Reprinted by permission.

person dilemmas whether isolated or in series would be quite beyond them, question-begging motivational assumptions aside. In settings at all like those in which we live, utility maximization assuming only 'traditional' motivation is self-defeating without remedy, and most certainly not an adequate basis for social life.[1] The probable *inference* from this, Braybrooke has suggested, is that maximization is inadequate as a conception of individual rationality:[2] for surely truly rational agents would be if not perfectly well designed at least better designed for communal living than utility maximizers would be assuming only "traditional," non-question-begging values or motivation. Or, if this inference is denied and maximization is not challenged as a conception of rationality, we can conclude instead, Braybrooke has more recently suggested (p. 299, this volume), that the advice, "Be rational," is incomplete, and when addressed to groups should be supplemented by, "And be somewhat 'untraditional' in your values; respect at least some rules that would make coordination and cooperation possible even in many-person interaction problems."

In my view the case against utility maximization given only "traditional" values is at once stronger and weaker than Braybrooke maintains. It is stronger in that barring question-begging "untraditional" motivational assumptions maximizers would not optimize in iterated, any more than in isolated, two-person Prisoner's Dilemmas. Barring "untraditional" values, that a situation will or may come up again cannot matter to hyperrational maximizers in ways they could invariably exploit: they would know each other and their situations too well to learn from experience in past situations what actions to expect in a current situation. And the case against utility maximization given only "traditional" values is weaker in that the inference from its admitted inadequacy as a basis for society to its inadequacy as a principle of individual rationality is a non sequitur. Nor is the recommendation, recently put in place of this inference, of "untraditional" coordination-and cooperation-enabling values well-founded. These points are developed in turn below.

THE DEFEAT OF UTILITY MAXIMIZERS IN ITERATED PRISONER'S DILEMMAS

We consider two series: first one of definite, known length; then one of indefinite, unknown length. Regarding each the issue will be the performance that would be forthcoming from *hyperrational* maximizers, unerring maximizers who know they are unerring, know the utility structures of their situations, know they know these things, and so on: maximizers about whom it is an important fact that they expect of each other nothing more nor less than maximization.[3]

Let the matrix for an isolated dilemma be:

308   *Paradoxes of Rationality and Cooperation*

$$B$$

	b_1	b_2
a_1	2 / **2**	1 / **4**
a_2	4 / **1**	3 / **3**

A

Row's utility for an outcome (for example, for the outcome associated with his employment of a_1 while B employs b_1) is given in bold-face type in the lower felt corner of the cell for the outcome (in the example, Row's utility is 2). Column's utilities are given in light-face type in the upper right corners. Assume, following Braybrooke, that each dilemma in the series to be considered involves ordered, non-simultaneous moves. For simplicity, let A always make the first move. (In following Braybrooke we depart, of course, from the tradition in which the Prisoner's Dilemma is a game in normal form, moves being taken "simultaneously.") The *moves* open in each round of the series are for A, a_1 and a_2, and for B, b_1 and b_2, but each player has, we suppose, in each round a choice between many *strategies* each of which determines, perhaps conditionally on the history of the series, a move in the round in hand. Included among strategies open to A are four categorical strategies on the model of,

   α_1: a_1 regardless of moves or strategies in previous rounds if there have been previous rounds

In addition to these categorical stategies, we assume that our hyperrational maximizers can somehow employ various conditional strategies in which a move in a round is made conditional on moves or strategies made or chosen in earlier rounds if any. Here are two examples:

   α_3: a_2 if either b_2 in each previous round or this is the first round; otherwise a_1

   α_4: a_2 if either both b_2 in each previous round and not a_2 in the ten just previous rounds or this is the first round; otherwise a_1

Each dilemma in the series considered is thus an $n \times n$ game, where n, the number of strategies open to each player, is vastly greater than 2. But how are we to understand the choice in a round of a strategy, as distinct from the execution in a round of a move? We assume the players do both things, we eschew the artificiality of slips of paper upon which strategies are submitted to an umpire who then makes the move. How then is the choice of a strategy, as distinct from a move, to be understood? Perhaps as the execution of a move *with a certain intention or plan in mind,* or *conceived under a certain description or rule (or maxim).* However, it is well to emphasize that the choice of a strategy is only for the round in hand: a player remains free in subsequent rounds to choose the same strategy again or a different one; choice of a strategy in a round entails no commitment to, and is not tantamount to, choosing it in all subsequent rounds or even in the next round (barring certain "untraditional" values). (Strategy choices in rounds of a series are quite different from strategy choices in the *super-game* for the series in which each player chooses *once* for *all* rounds, making moves in rounds conditional, perhaps, on moves in earlier rounds. See Luce and Raiffa (1957), pp. 99–102. The relevance of the super-game, and what hyperrational maximizers would do in it, to the *series* of games and what such maximizers would do in *it* is not clear.)

We assume that in each round in a series the history of the series before this round, not only the moves made but the strategies used, is common knowledge. We assume this, though it is, I think, hard to see how what strategies have been used could be common knowledge among hyperrational maximizers with "traditional" values. *Other* agents could *tell* each other what they were doing, what their intentions and plans were, but it will be plain from what follows that, with Hodgson, I doubt that hyperrational traditional maximizers would be capable of that kind of communication. We of course suppose throughout that no rules for truthtelling, promise-keeping, or the like are *enforced*. We suppose throughout that our maximizers are in *this* sense in a state of nature. So we assume, despite difficulties, complete knowledge of the history of the series. And we *allow* expectations for a round to be affected by such historical knowledge: more precisely we do not assume that they are *not* so affected, though it is an open secret that I will *argue* that they are not. But we *do* assume, though this assumption will be suspended once, that *utilities* in the $n \times n$ matrix for a round are not affected by strategies employed or moves made in earlier rounds except in so far as these strategies and moves affect probabilities, not values, of consequences of strategy pairs in the round. We assume, for example, that our players do not in the present place value on "*consistency*" with their past performances (though this assumption is suspended once); and that they do not value *reciprocation,* doing unto others what others have done unto one. Indeed, for definiteness and though this detail is not exploited in the arguments to come, we assume that utilities in the $n \times n$ matrix for a round in series to be considered here are a function of the utilities in the 2×2 matrix for the isolated dilemma according to the following rule: The entry for A in cell (α_i, β_j) of the matrix for round r is

$$(2p^1 + \ldots + 2p^k + \ldots) + (4q^1 + \ldots + 4q^k + \ldots) +$$
$$(1r^1 + \ldots + 1r^k + \ldots) + (3s^1 + \ldots + 3s^k + \ldots)$$

wherein p^k is *how likely* the pair (a_1, b_1)'s occurring in exactly k rounds including and subsequent to round r *would be made by* the use of strategies α_i and β_j in round r (given the history of the series before round r);[4] q^k, s^k, and t^k are related similarly to the pairs (a_1, b_2), (a_2, b_1), and (a_2, b_2) respectively. Of course, whether or not strategy choices in round r can, without affecting values of possible consequences and in this way utility matrices for future rounds, influence moves in subsequent rounds in the hyperrational community, is the *issue* that concerns me. If and when there is no such influence, p^k, for example, is simply the (unconditional) probability of the pair (a_1, b_1)'s occurring in exactly k rounds including and subsequent to round r. The entry of B in cell (α_i, β_j) is determined similarly: more precisely, interchange the constants "1" and "4" in the displayed sum.

For series of *definite* length we consider a series of length 3 and assume that this length is common knowledge and that it is common knowledge from the beginning and throughout the series that in each round it is common knowledge which round is then current and thus how many rounds remain. It is clear that this series resolves into the moves a_1 and b_1 in each round, and that any series of definite known length resolves similarly for hyperrational maximizers. Consider first the last round. Strategically it might as well be isolated and will resolve into a_1 and b_1. In the last round the series has no future that might somehow be affected by strategy choices or moves made. And the past of the series is then irrelevant. The history of the series to this round will not, we assume, affect the utility matrix for this round. And even if the history of the series could generate expectations regarding strategies of the other party in this round this history would not thereby be relevant, since expectations are in the last round plainly irrelevant. Neither would then need to know what the other had done, or was going to do, in this the last round, since each would have dominant strategies all pairs of which would yield a_1 and b_1. The last round might as well be isolated and will resolve into a_1 and b_1. And this will be obvious in the second, or next to last, round. It will be known then that there are no future rounds for which possible effects need to be taken into account: it will be known that, in the relevant sense, the next to the last round has no future, that strategically it might as well be last. So this round too will resolve as if isolated. And so will the first round.

So much for series of definite lengths. In them each dilemma resolves for hyperrational maximizers as if isolated. (What "intelligent players" would do depends on what such players are like. Identifying several we might experiment, though results of such experiments would of course be irrelevant to our problems, unless we had reason to think that "intelligent players," at least some "intelligent players," were hyperrational maximizers. In fact, however, it seems likely that this ideal is only approached, never realized, in actual communities. See Luce and Raiffa (1957), p. 101.) *Indefinite* series, and this is the sort in which Braybrooke is interested, may work differently.

At any rate, the argument used for the definite case does not apply. It was crucial to that argument that ideal maximizers would know when they were in the last round, the next to the last round, and so on.

To fix the discussion we consider a series which is indefinite under the following rule: there is a probability p such that at each round the probability of another round is p. There are, of course, other, more realistic rules. One could allow p to decrease as the series progresses. But the simpler specification serves present purposes and if anything makes reaching the conclusion I seek more difficult than more realistic rules would.

What will hyperrational maximizers do in such series? The answer is that they will do just what they do in isolated dilemmas, the reason being that the *chance* that there are dilemmas to come can, for hyperrational maximizers, make no more difference than can the known fact that there are a certain number more to come. (And would it not be strange if this were not so, if, in particular, hyperrational maximizers who knew only that there was a chance of more dilemmas would not only behave differently, but would do *better* than hyperrational maximizers who knew the facts?)

Dilemmas to come could make a difference for hyperrational maximizers only if, when involved in a series, such maximizers could through their strategy choices in early rounds *teach* each other what to expect in later rounds. If this were possible, then choices would not only resolve the round in hand but might generate expectations of similar choices in future rounds which expectations could, in due course, affect choices in these future rounds. Players, through present choices, might be able to control the conduct of future rounds, affecting each other's expectations, each other's actions, and even their own future actions: they might in effect set precedents for themselves, making reasonable, by doing similar actions now, future actions which would otherwise have been unreasonable. That is how the fact or chance of future dilemmas might be thought to make a difference. And so it might for many agents, even for many maximizers; but not for hyperrational maximizers. Given the thoroughness of their knowledge of one another and their situations, and the way in which they would form expectations regarding one another's actions, assuming only "traditional" values, the processes described cannot work for them. As long as they are and remain hyperrational and "traditional" they know each other too well to *teach* each other what to expect or to set for themselves effective *precedents*.

Members of hyperrational communities of maximizers expect from each other at a given time choices that are reasonable, that is, maximizing. But then, assuming "traditional" values, hyperrational maximizers can in situations that are possible for them,[5] invariably form expectations concerning each other's conduct and do so without regard to past performances in like situations.[6] Consider the *first* or earliest situation of some kind. What is done, the strategy that is used, the random choice among strategies that is made, since reasonable in maximizing terms is for our maximizers expectable, and expectable, clearly, without regard to *this* situation's past, for in the relevant sense the *first* situation of some strategic kind *has no past*. But then expectations of repetitions of the performance in this situation in analogous subsequent situations must be similarly formulable without regard to *their* pasts: what made the response reasonable and expectable in the first case *necessarily* attaches to it in every subsequent analogous case with regard to which *hyperrational* maximizers might form expectations partly on the basis of responses in earlier cases. So reasonable past performances can make no difference to present expectations. *They* can be ignored. And of course *unreasonable* past performances either have no place in our scheme or can be contemplated only by assuming that our presently ideal hyperrational maximizers may have once been other than ideal hyperrational maximizers. But even if unreasonable, that is, not maximizing, past performances are entertained by us in this way, it is plain that hyperrational maximizers would ignore them as quite irrelevant to present expectations. Therefore hyperrational "traditional" maximizers would know what to expect of each other without regard to the past.

This conclusion can be put somewhat differently: hyperrational maximizers would not learn what to expect of each other from experience or by induction. They would, we can assume, reason inductively about natural events, but they would form expectations regarding each other's *actions* in a different way. They know each other and the structures of their situations so well that the only inductive projection they *might* make are projections that could for them *serve no purpose*. Hyperrational maximizers *might* project each other's responses in a type of case to future cases quite like the base case in all respects that bear on what utility maximizers ought to do. Hyperrational maximizers would not project to *other* cases, cases *not* on all fours strategically with the base case: they would realize that what was done in the base case by one of their own was no evidence at all for what to expect in relevantly, that is, strategically, *different* cases. But they might project to cases strategically quite like the base case, though such projections would be idle since what made certain responses reasonable in the base case would make like responses in these future cases reasonable and to be expected *without projection*. Hyperrational maximizers, to return to an earlier form of words, would, supposing still only "traditional values," know what to expect of each other without regard to the past. But then, and this is the really pertinent result, through present choices they could not generate or make a difference to future expectations. They could not *teach* or set *precedents*.[7] At least this is so barring certain motivational assumptions, quite bizarre on a "traditional" view but quite human. Consideration of one such assumption may serve to clarify and reinforce my position.

Suppose that *A* places a premium on "consistency," on doing again whatever he has done before whether or not it was uniquely reasonable, or reasonable at all, in the first place. (Doing again under what circumstances? Let us say: doing again in situations that would have, if isolated, the same matrix as the initial situation would have if it were isolated.) He is not a creature of habit. Rather he is a man with a sense for what might be termed "personal traditions." Given a premium on constancy, A can, by what he does in early rounds, affect his utilities for possible outcomes of interaction in later rounds: he does with his actions what certain other maximizers (for example, *truthful* maximizers,[8] maximizers who value saying and having themselves said truths, and *trustworthy* maximizers, maximizers who value doing what they have promised to do) can do with words. Indeed, if the premium on "consistency" is great enough, A can by employing a strategy *commit* himself to it: by employing it he can, the premium being great enough, render it *dominant* evermore. So he might, for example, commit himself to α_3. Suppose he did. B, knowing that A was committed to α_3, would, if the fixed chance p of a next trial is great enough, have no choice but to respond with a strategy that yielded b_2. Or A might commit himself to α_4 in which case again, if the numbers are right, B would have no choice but to respond with a strategy that yielded b_2. (I have supposed only that A has the passion for "consistency." Were it shared and the dilemmas constituted of simultaneous choices, I suspect that neither could know what to do and that the series, for reasons of a sort explained elsewhere, would not resolve. (See note 5, above.) I suspect that the same is true of some of the super-games considered by Luce and Raiffa (1957), p. 102.)

So a hyperrational maximizer, if possessed of a certain quite human even if "untraditional" motivation, could through his actions "teach" other hyperrational maximizers what to expect of him: his actions themselves could give them good reasons for expecting certain actions from him. But hyperrational maximizers who lacked his passion would lack his teaching, and precedent-setting, capacities as well. It is true that they too would be consistent, choosing always as they have chosen, but this would be due not to concern for constancy, but to the obvious fact that what is reasonable and maximizing in a case is so in every *repetition* of it. *Hyperrational maximizers can through choices in a round in a series of interaction problems affect* EXPECTATIONS *in future rounds* ONLY BY *affecting the* UTILITY MATRICES *for these future rounds by affecting* VALUES *of consequences of possible strategy n-tuples in these rounds.* For example choices in early rounds in a series of dilemmas might affect expectations in later rounds, if the entry in a cell of the $n \times n$ matrix for this later round were determined by a formula like the one displayed above, and players could, through their early choices, affect the *constants* in this formula. It is only in such ways that hyperrational maximizers can teach by doing, or set effective precedents for themselves. But then *"traditional"* maximizers cannot, in general, teach or set precedents. (Utilities for later rounds can, even supposing only "traditional" values, be functions of outcomes of, and so choices in, earlier rounds, but not in ways that make possible, as do certain "untraditional" values, the controlled manipulation, through one's choices, of future expectations. In the absence of such values, utilities for outcomes of interaction in later rounds will generally depend, not on an *individual's* choices in previous rounds but on outcomes of, and pay-offs in, previous rounds, that is (in two-person interactions) on *pairs* of choices in previous rounds.) So the presence or absence, chance great or small, of future rounds can make no difference for hyperrational "traditional" maximizers. Dilemmas in a series, whether of definite or indefinite length, will defeat such maximizers in just the way in which all should agree that isolated dilemmas will defeat them.

THE SIGNIFICANCE OF THIS DEFEAT

Hyperrational utility maximizers who possess only "traditional" values will not optimize in Prisoner's Dilemmas whether or not they (the maximizers) are repeating offenders. More generally, to their disappointment and frustration, they will often fail to sustain what would be mutually beneficial social arrangements. On the general point Braybrooke and I agree, though I give maximization even lower marks here than he does. But what *follows* from this? Here we disagree. Braybrooke has suggested that what follows is that maximization is an inadequate conception of individual rationality, that individual rationality is either something more or something else. But clearly there is a gulf between premise and conclusion. There is suppressed, I think, the assumption that *truly* rational and well-informed agents would do as well by their several and collective interests as any agents could, with their interests in their circumstances. But then, while it would be nice if this principle of harmony were true, it is at least not yet available as a premise for criticizing conceptions of rationality. Given the complexity of interaction problems, and the current state of theories about them, we must, I think, allow that reason may *not* conquer all. Utility maximizers are sure that reason alone has its limits, and even their opponents should allow that so far as anyone now knows this is a *possibility*.

Utility maximizations may be inadequate as a conception of individual rationality. Perhaps there is more to individual rationality than preferences for outcomes that are representable by a utility function and actions in accordance with these preferences where actions are (as if) viewed as "gambles" on possible outcomes. Rationality may for example impose additional constraints on an agent's ends taken either singly or as a system. And perhaps, moving in the other direction, utility maximization is not even always *part* of practical rationality: perhaps, for example, a rational agent would sometimes, when possessed of only weakly based assessments of probabilities, refuse to choose amongst his actions as if they were "gambles" on possible outcomes. Utility maximization may be, in any number of ways, inadequate as a conception, or total theory, of individual rationality. I do not dispute this. *All* I claim is that the issue, whether or not and if so how utility maximization is inadequate as a conception of individual rationality cannot presently be settled by showing how it is inadequate in what, on the face of it, is a quite different and possibly unrelated way, namely, as a basis for communal life.

Braybrooke no longer, in "The Insoluble Problem of the Social Contract," presses the inference here criticized, but instead without questioning the adequacy of maximization as a conception of rationality, he suggests that the inadequacy for social living of maximization given only "traditional" values shows the need for and, in a sense, the wisdom of "untraditional" values. *Complete advice,* we are told, to a *group* of people – advice addressed to them as a group that they are to take, if at all, only collectively – would include not only the admonition to be rational but the direction *to respect* rules, respect for which would enable members of the group to coordinate and cooperate in pursuit of their various ends. Complete collective advice, we are told, would include the recommendation of certain "untraditional" motives or values.

What about this most recent conclusion of Braybrooke's? I think that it is still objectionable, though in ways different from the old conclusion. Complete advice to persons in groups includes, he tell us, the admonition that they respect certain rules and respect them evidently, in the first place or to begin with, *not* for what some would perceive to be their intrinsic merits, but for certain *ulterior* reasons: no *intrinsic* merits are suggested by Braybrooke. A group of persons who do not already respect such rules is to harken to some set of them in the first place it seems for the good that can flow from the group's respecting them. Now I suppose that this sort of thing is possible, and that, as persons can make themselves *believe* things for ulterior (non-evidential) reasons, so persons for ulterior reasons can make themselves *respect* things. Such self-manipulation, though not easy, is in various measures for some persons sometimes possible. But I would always hesitate to recommend it and would in every case hope for other better means to the ends that it would serve perhaps only precariously, if it were general through the community. It would always be more decent, and often it would be safer, to do without such double-dealing. But what alternatives are there, assuming only "traditional" values? One simple-minded alternative to manufacturing *respect* for certain rules, one alternative that sometimes is available, would be arranging for the *enforcement* of these rules. Of course, the project entails at least some ways, already established, of coordination and cooperation, but then this does not after all distinguish it from the project of *collective* self-manipulation. How is that to be accomplished in a social vacuum? Each self-manipulator-to-be might require assurance that others were "with him." ("But what remedies *would* be available to hyperrational "traditional" maximizers in a *social* vacuum?" Possibly none. From which might follow the collective advice, "By all means stay *out* of that condition!" That advice would at least be addressed only to groups that might have the means to take it.)

My criticisms of the collective advice Braybrooke advocates, and of the unqualified character of his advocacy, are that this advice would not always work, that even when it worked it would not always be the best advice possible, and finally that even when it was the best advice it could entail substantial costs and risks which Braybrooke does not mention. (Compare with remarks in my (1975), p. 685.) I resist the temptation to discuss further and in a general way, advice addressed to groups or, as I have termed it, "collective advice" and to discuss especially what is involved in a group's *taking* such advice.

And I also resist a greater temptation to elaborate upon the *intrinsic* merits of rules which would enable persons to coordinate and cooperate. Most persons on reflection would in fact, discover considerable intrinsic merit in some such rules, and perceive as grotesque and disfiguring a restriction to "traditional," purely forward-looking, values, that is, an *indifference,* for purposes of present decisions, to the past, to even one's own personal past. Elaborating on this theme, however, would be a different story from the present one, a different kind of story—important, and if well told capable of honestly and openly changing people's minds, but having nothing to do with the *social* limitations of "traditional," purely forward-looking, values assuming maximization (to reverse the order this once), which this paper has been concerned with.

NOTES

* A revised and expanded version of comments made on a paper presented by David Braybrooke to the Institute on Moral and Social Philosophy sponsored by the Canadian Philosophical Association in Toronto, June 3–5, 1974. "The Insoluble Problem of the Social Contract," reprinted from *Dialogue*, is a revised version of that paper.

1. The tradition in question is that of Hobbesian state-of-nature analysis, in which traditional values are always, though generally without explicit notice, assumed to be exclusively forward-looking: in this tradition it is axiomatic that proper or *rational* values are for states of affairs without regard to their pasts. The motto in this tradition for proper values could be: What is done is done. Thus the seventh Law of Nature is, *"That in Revenges* (that is, retribution of Evil for Evil.) *Men look not at the greatnesse of the evill past, but the greatnesse of the good to follow."* Thomas Hobbes, *Leviathan* (New York and London, 1950), p.

126. This law could hardly appeal to men who place a *value* on retribution of evils done, and a value that varies with the greatness of that evil. But then such values are *contrary to reason,* and, equivalently, the seventh law of nature is, though Hobbes does not in *Leviathan* insist on this point, already unconditionally binding in nature. Far from being a help, however, this is a part of the problem in nature: more precisely, the *general* exclusion of backward-looking values is an important part of the problem, or at any rate my reconstruction of the problem, in nature. Regarding the supposed irrationality of backward-looking revenge, and the special status (pointed out to me many years ago by W. D. Falk) of the seventh law, consider that this law is not only somehow "consequent to the next before it, that commandeth Pardon, upon security of the Future time," but

> *Besides,* Revenge without respect to the Example, and profit to come, is triumph, or glorying in the hurt of another, tending to no end; (for the End is always somewhat to come;) and glorying to no end, is vainglory, and contrary to reason; and to hurt without reason, tendeth to the introduction of Warre; which is against the law of Nature, and is commonly stiled by the name *Cruelty.* (pp. 126–27).

Cruelty is contrary to reason whether or not one has sufficient security that others will not be cruel: that is, cruelty is contrary to reason even in nature. (Consider Thomas Hobbes, *De Cive or the Citizen* (New York, 1949), p. 56: the note to Part I, Chapter 3, paragraph 27.) And, by implication, *all* rational values are exclusively forward-looking, "for the End is always somewhat to come."

And so lines from *Leviathan* are a footnote to this paper which is, of course, but a footnote to that great work. I owe thanks to Willa Freeman Sobel for many helpful suggestions and discussions concerning in particular, but not only, the idea of forward-looking values.

2. The suggestion, not repeated in "The Insoluble Problem of the Social Contract," is made in the following words in the paper that was presented in Toronto (See note*, above.) and also in (1974), a revised version of that paper:

How much regard and respect should we have for rationality when it is not associated with suitable motivations? I think, strictly limited respect. Perhaps we could take the line that rationality by itself has no indefeasible claim to respect. Perhaps, however, we would do better to hold that since rationality, conceived minimally as operating without motivations which eliminate the problem, leads to self-defeat in Prisoner's Dilemmas and the contract problem for the "multitude" (also in Sobel's variants), rationality so conceived is an inadequate conception of rationality. Ironically, the minimal conception has attracted many thinkers because it seemed both hard-headed and ethically neutral.... Yet it will not work, even in its own terms: it is, as the chief merit of studying the contract problems may be to tell us, collectively self-defeating in its own terms, which cannot be charged against conceptions more ancient, and wiser.

3. I discuss the hyperrational community in greater detail in Sobel (1972), pp. 149–53.

4. The awkwardness of the formula, how likely ψ would be made by ϕ is deliberate. This formula is not supposed to express the conditional probability of ψ given ϕ, but is intended to express the result of adjusting the (unconditional) probability of ψ by the likely *influence,* if any, of ϕ on ψ. The lesson, I hold, of Newcomb's

Problem is that some such measure is to take the place of conditional probabilities in expected utility calculations. But more of this in another place.

5. The qualification is necessary. Not every situation possible for agents is possible for hyperrational maximizers. Arguments in support of this proposition, and examples of situations that are not possible for hyperrational maximizers, can be found in my (1972) and (1975).

6. Note that the argument being constructed for series of two-person Prisoner's Dilemmas of indefinite, unknown lengths is actually completely general. Its conclusion covers *all* series, whether of definite known or indefinite under some rule and unknown length, of *all* kinds of interaction structures. The conclusion that hyperrational maximizers cannot teach or set precedents, barring "untraditional" motivational assumptions, covers, for example, not only series of structures in which dominant strategies are not jointly Pareto-optimal, but also series of coordination problems in which no strategies are dominant and in which therefore there might at first appear to be more scope for teaching and precedents.

7. For an excellent discussion, with which I am in substantial disagreement, of teaching effects in a hyperrational community of maximizers, see Gibbard, (1971), pp. 156–75. Gibbard writes, "Perhaps Hodgson is saying it is irrational to rely on induction from past acts of promise-keeping, but I see no reason why it should be irrational" (p. 170). My claim is of course not that among hyperrational maximizers induction from past acts is irrational, but that it is always *unnecessary*. The heart of the matter, if I am right, is that the only projections hyperrational maximizers could make from one another's past acts would be unneeded projections to cases *quite* like the base cases.

8. See Lewis (1972), pp. 17–9. Assume that "you" and "I" are hyperrational maximizers. (So "you" and "I" are not you and I.) Let them be in a coordination problem such that it is in the interest of each to push red if and only if the other pushes red: let (R, R) be for each one of the two best equilibria. "You" has said, "I pushed red." Can "I" believe him? An affirmative answer, Lewis assures us, is consistent with what has so far been assumed, since it is consistent with their hyperrationality that "you" and "I" should be, and know each other to be, truthful in the extensional sense of saying only true things (when it is best to instill true beliefs). Lewis does not say that 'you' and 'I' might, consistent with their hyperrationality, know each other to be truthful in my sense (truthful in the sense of valuing saying truths), but of course they might be, and know each other to be, truthful in this sense. And supposing that they are truthful in my sense would provide one explanation of why they are extensionally truthful, and one explanation of how they *know,* presumably even without experience and at the very *beginning* of their relationship, that they are extensionally truthful. One way of explaining this would be to say that they are by their *values* truthful. Is there *another* way, given that they, "you" and "I," are hyperrational maximizers?

"But as a matter of fact we know we are extensionally truthful. You and I know this." How else could we talk? This is 'knowledge that [we] do in fact possess' (Lewis. p. 19). So why not inquire *realistically* into how we know? Perhaps that would reveal 'another way.'" Perhaps. But since we are not "you" and "I," since we are not hyperrational maximizers, it is just as likely that an empirical investigation would only confuse the issue.

Consider Mackie's discussion of coordination in (1973). Regarding a symmetrical situation with two best equilibria—the structure could be

	2	1
2	**1**	
	1	2
1	**2**	

he asks. "How do we solve this apparently insoluble problem?" In practice, Mackie observes, "one person happens to move . . . before the other . . . [who] then adapts his own movement to fit in with that of the first" (p. 293). That seems right; often, at any rate, we negotiate such situations in the way Mackie describes. But *hyperrational* maximizers never just happen to move, they need reasons. And there are situations possible for hyperrational maximizers in which each must move without prior observational knowledge of the other's move. (That is true even of us.) Mackie holds, incidentally, that coordination problems possessed of unique best equilibria, for example,

	2	1
2	**1**	
	1	3
1	**3**	

resolve without the participants' monitoring each other's moves, but he does not say *how* such situations resolve supposing "each is aiming simply at maximizing utility" (p. 291). For reasons not spelled out he holds that it is obvious that hyperrational maximizers would do well in these situations, so he does not say *how* they would manage or even how *we* manage in such situations. I discuss, in (1975) pp. 681–2, note 3, a way that does *not* work for hyperrational maximizers, and maintain that no way does work for *them*.

19

The Emergence of Cooperation among Egoists*

ROBERT AXELROD

Under what conditions will cooperation emerge in a world of egoists without central authority? This question has played an important role in a variety of domains including political philosophy, international politics, and economic and social exchange. This article provides new results which show more completely than was previously possible the conditions under which cooperation will emerge. The results are more complete in two ways. First, *all* possible strategies are taken into account, not simply some arbitrarily selected subset. Second, not only are equilibrium conditions established, but also a mechanism is specified which can move a population from noncooperative to cooperative equilibrium.

The situation to be analyzed is the one in which narrow self-maximization behavior by each person leads to a poor outcome for all. This is the famous Prisoner's Dilemma game. Two individuals can each either cooperate or defect. No matter what the other does, defection yields a higher payoff than cooperation. But if both defect, both do worse than if both cooperated. Figure 1 shows the payoff matrix with sample utility numbers attached to

	Cooperate	Defect
Cooperate	$R = 3$, $R = 3$	$S = 0$, $T = 5$
Defect	$T = 5$, $S = 0$	$P = 1$, $P = 1$

$T > R > P > S$
$R > (S + T)/2$

Note: The payoffs to the row choosers are listed first.

FIGURE 1

From *American Political Science Review* 75, no.2 (1981): 306–18. Reprinted by permission.

the payoffs. If the other player cooperates, there is a choice between cooperation which yields R (the reward for mutual cooperation) or defection which yields T (the temptation to defect). By assumption, $T > R$, so it pays to defect if the other player cooperates. On the other hand, if the other player defects, there is a choice between cooperation which yields S (the sucker's payoff), or defection which yields P (the punishment for mutual defection). By assumption, $P > S$, so it pays to defect if the other player defects. Thus no matter what the other player does, it pays to defect. But if both defect, both get P rather than the R they could both have got if both had cooperated. But R is assumed to be greater than P. Hence the dilemma. Individual rationality leads to a worse outcome for both than is possible.

To insure that an even chance of exploitation or being exploited is not as good an outcome as mutual cooperation, a final inequality is added in the standard definition of the Prisoner's Dilemma. This is just $R > (T + S)/2$.

Thus two egoists playing the game once will both choose their dominant choice, defection, and get a payoff, P, which is worse for both than the R they could have got if they had both cooperated. If the game is played a known finite number of times, the players still have no incentive to cooperate. This is certainly true on the last move since there is no future to influence. On the next-to-last move they will also have no incentive to cooperate since they can anticipate mutual defection on the last move. This line of reasoning implies that the game will unravel all the way back to mutual defection on the first move of any sequence of plays which is of known finite length (Luce and Raiffa, 1957, pp. 94–102). This reasoning does not apply if the players will interact an indefinite number of times. With an indefinite number of interactions, cooperation can emerge. This article will explore the precise conditions necessary for this to happen.

The importance of this problem is indicated by a brief explanation of the role it has played in a variety of fields.

1. *Political Philosophy.* Hobbes regarded the state of nature as equivalent to what we now call a two-person Prisoner's Dilemma, and he built his justification for the state upon the purported impossibility of sustained cooperation in such a situation (Taylor, 1976, pp. 98–116). A demonstration that mutual cooperation could emerge among rational egoists playing the iterated Prisoner's Dilemma would provide a powerful argument that the role of the state should not be as universal as some have argued.

2. *International Politics.* Today nations interact without central control, and therefore the conclusions about the requirements for the emergence of cooperation have empirical relevance to many central issues of international politics. Examples include many varieties of the security dilemma (Jervis, 1978) such as arms competition and its obverse, disarmament (Rapoport, 1960); alliance competition (Snyder, 1971); and communal conflict in Cyprus (Lumsden, 1973). The selection of the American response to the Soviet invasion of Afghanistan in 1979 illustrates the problem of choosing

an effective strategy in the context of a continuing relationship. Had the United States been perceived as continuing business as usual, the Soviet Union might have been encouraged to try other forms of non-cooperative behavior later. On the other hand, any substantial lessening of U.S. cooperation risked some form of retaliation which could then set off counter-retaliation, setting up a pattern of mutual defection that could be difficult to get out of. Much of the domestic debate over foreign policy is over problems of just this type.

3. *Economic and social exchange.* Our everyday lives contain many exchanges whose terms are not enforced by any central authority. Even in economic changes, business ethics are maintained by the knowledge that future interactions are likely to be affected by the outcome of the current exchange.

4. *International political economy.* Multinational corporations can play off host governments to lessen their tax burdens in the absence of coordinated fiscal policies between the affected governments. Thus the commodity exporting country and the commodity importing country are in an iterated Prisoner's Dilemma with each other, whether they fully appreciate it or not (Laver, 1977).

In the literatures of these areas, there has been a convergence on the nature of the problem to be analyzed. All agree that the two-person Prisoner's Dilemma captures an important part of the strategic interaction. All agree that what makes the emergence of cooperation possible is the possibility that interaction will continue. The tools of the analysis have been surprisingly similar, with game theory serving to structure the enterprise.

As a paradigm case of the emergence of cooperation, consider the development of the norms of a legislative body, such as the United States Senate. Each senator has an incentive to appear effective for his or her constituents even at the expense of conflicting with other senators who are trying to appear effective for *their* constituents. But this is hardly a zero-sum game since there are many opportunities for mutually rewarding activities between two senators. One of the consequences is that an elaborate set of norms, or folkways, have emerged in the Senate. Among the most important of these is the norm of reciprocity, a folkway which involves helping out a colleague and getting repaid in kind. It includes vote trading, but it extends to so that many types of mutually rewarding behavior that "it is not an exaggeration to say that reciprocity is a way of life in the Senate" (Matthews, 1960, p. 100; see also Mayhew, 1975).

Washington was not always like this. Early observers saw the members of the Washington community as quite unscrupulous, unreliable, and characterized by "falsehood, deceit, treachery" (Smith, 1906, p. 190). But by now the practice of reciprocity is well established. Even the significant changes in the Senate over the last two decades toward more decentralization, more openness, and more equal distribution of power have come without abating the folkway of reciprocity (Ornstein, Peabody and Rhode, 1977). I will show that we do *not* need to assume that senators are more honest, more generous, or more public-spirited than in earlier years to explain how cooperation based on reciprocity has emerged and proven stable. The emergence of cooperation can be explained as a consequence of senators pursuing their own interests.

The approach taken here is to investigate how individuals pursuing their own interests will act, and then see what effects this will have for the system as a whole. Put another way, the approach is to make some assumptions about micro-motives, and then deduce consequences for macro-behavior (Schelling, 1978). Thinking about the paradigm case of a legislature is a convenience, but the same style of reasoning can apply to the emergence of cooperation between individuals in many other political settings, or even to relations between nations. While investigating the conditions which foster the emergence of cooperation, one should bear in mind that cooperation is not always socially desirable. There are times when public policy is best served by the prevention of cooperation—as in the need for regulatory action to prevent collusion between oligopolistic business enterprises.

The basic situation I will analyze involves pairwise interactions.[1] I assume that the player can recognize another player and remember how the two of them have interacted so far. This allows the history of the particular interaction to be taken into account by a player's strategy.

A variety of ways to resolve the dilemma of the Prisoner's Dilemma have been developed. Each involves allowing some additional activity which alters the strategic interaction in such a way as to fundamentally change the nature of the problem. The original problem remains, however, because there are many situations in which these remedies are not available. I wish to consider the problem in its fundamental form.

1. There is no mechanism available to the players to make enforceable threats or commitments (Schelling, 1960). Since the players cannot make commitments, they must take into account all possible strategies which might be used by the other player, and they have all possible strategies available to themselves.

2. There is no way to be sure what the other player will do on a given move. This eliminates the possibility of metagame analysis (Howard, 1971) which allows such options as "make the same choice as the other player is about to make." It also eliminates the possibility of reliable reputations such as might be based on watching the other player interact with third parties.

3. There is no way to change the other player's utilities. The utilities already include whatever consideration each player has for the interests of the other (Taylor, 1976, pp. 69–83).

Under these conditions, words not backed by actions are so cheap as to be meaningless. The players can communicate with each other only through the sequence of their own behavior. This is the problem of the iterated Prisoner's Dilemma in its fundamental form.

Two things remain to be specified: how the payoff of a particular move relates to the payoff in a whole sequence, and the precise meaning of a strategy. A natural way to aggregate payoffs over time is to assume that later payoffs are worth less than the earlier ones, and that this relationship is expressed as a constant discount per move (Shubik, 1959, 1970). Thus the next payoff is worth only a fraction, w, of the same payoff this move. A whole string of mutual defections would then have a "present value" of $P + wP + w^2P + w^3P \ldots = P/(1 - w)$. The discount parameter, w, can be given either of two interpretations. The standard economic interpretation is that later consumption is not valued as much as earlier consumption. An alternative interpretation is that future moves may not actually occur, since the interaction between a pair of players has only a certain probability of continuing for another move. In either interpretation, or a combination of the two, w is strictly between zero and one. The smaller w is, the less important later moves are relative to earlier ones.

For a concrete example, suppose one player is following the policy of always defecting, and the other player is following the policy of *TIT FOR TAT*. *TIT FOR TAT* is the policy of cooperating on the first move and then doing whatever the other player did on the previous move. This means that *TIT FOR TAT* will defect once for each defection by the other player. When the other player is using *TIT FOR TAT*, a player who always defects will get T on the first move, and P on all the subsequent moves. The payoff to someone using *ALL D* when playing with someone using *TIT FOR TAT* is thus:

$$V(\text{ALL } D| \ TFT) = T + wP + w^2P + w^3P \ldots$$
$$= T + wP(1 + w + w^2 \ldots)$$
$$= T + wP/(1 - w).$$

Both *ALL D* and *TIT FOR TAT* are strategies. In general, a *strategy* (or decision rule) is a function from the history of the game so far into a probability of cooperation on the next move. Strategies can be stochastic, as in the example of a rule which is entirely random with equal probabilities of cooperation and defection on each move. A strategy can also be quite sophisticated in its use of the pattern of outcomes in the game so far to determine what to do next. It may, for example, use Bayesian techniques to estimate the parameters of some model it might have of the other player's rule. Or it may be some complex combination of other strategies. But a strategy must rely solely on the information available through this one sequence of interactions with the particular player.

The first question one is tempted to ask is, "What is the best strategy?"

This a good question, but unfortunately there is no best rule independent of the environment which it might have to face. The reason is that what works best when the other player is unconditionally cooperative will not in general work well when the other player is conditionally cooperative, and vice versa. To prove this, I will introduce the concept of a *nice* strategy, namely, one which will never be the first to defect.

Theorem 1. If the discount parameter, w, *is sufficiently high, there is no best strategy independent of the strategy used by the other player.*

Proof. Suppose A is a strategy which is best regardless of the strategy used by the other player. This means that for any strategies A' and B, $V(A|B) \geq (A'|B)$. Consider separately the cases where A is nice and A is not nice. If A is nice, let $A' = ALL\ D$, and let $B = ALL\ C$. Then $V(A|B) = R/(1-w)$ which is less than $V(A'|B) = T/(1-w)$. On the other hand, if A is not nice, let $A' = ALL\ C$, and let B be the strategy of cooperating until the other player defects and then always defects. Eventually A will be the first to defect, say, on move n. The value of n is irrelevant for the comparison to follow, so assume that $n = 1$. To give A the maximum advantage, assume that A always defects after its first defection. Then $V(A|B) = T + wP/(1-w)$. But $V(A'|B) = R/(1-w) = R + wR/(1-w)$. Thus $V(A|B) < V(A'|B)$ whenever $w > (T-R)/(T-P)$. Thus the immediate advantage gained by the defection of A will eventually be more than compensated for by the long-term disadvantage of B's unending defection, assuming that w is sufficiently large. Thus, if w is sufficiently large, there is no one best strategy.

In the paradigm case of a legislature, this theorem says that if there is a large enough chance that a member of Congress will interact *again* with another member of Congress, then there is no one best strategy to use independently of the strategy being used by the other person. It would be best to be cooperative with someone who will reciprocate that cooperation in the future, but not with someone whose future behavior will not be very much affected by this interaction (see, for example, Hinckley, 1972). The very possibility of achieving stable mutual cooperation depends upon there being a good chance of a continuing interaction, as measured by the magnitude of w. Empirically, the chance of two members of Congress having a continuing interaction has increased dramatically as the biennial turnover rates in Congress have fallen from about 40 per cent in the first 40 years of the Republic to about 20 per cent or less in recent years (Young, 1966, pp. 87–90; Jones, 1977, p. 254; Patterson, 1978, pp. 143–44). That the increasing institutionalization of Congress has had its effects on the development of congressional norms has been widely accepted (Polsby, 1968, esp. n. 68). We now see how the diminished turnover rate (which is one aspect of institutionalization) can allow the development of reciprocity (which is one important part of congressional folkways).

But saying that a continuing chance of interaction is necessary for the development of cooperation is not the same as saying that it is sufficient. The demonstration that there is not a single best strategy still leaves open the question of what patterns of behavior can be expected to emerge when there actually is a sufficiently high probability of continuing interaction between two people.

THE TOURNAMENT APPROACH

Just because there is no single best decision rule does not mean analysis is hopeless. For example, progress can be made on the question of which strategy does best in an environment of players who are using strategies designed to do well. To explore this question, I conducted a tournament of strategies submitted by game theorists in economics, psychology, sociology, political science and mathematics (Axelrod, 1980a). Announcing the payoff matrix shown in Figure 1, and a game length of two hundred moves, I ran the fourteen entries and *RANDOM* against each other in a round robin tournament. The result was that the highest average score was attained by the simplest of all the strategies submitted, *TIT FOR TAT*.

I then circulated the report of the results and solicited entries for a second round. This time I received sixty-two entries from six countries.[2] Most of the contestants were computer hobbyists, but there were also professors of evolutionary biology, physics, and computer science, as well as the five disciplines represented in the first round. *TIT FOR TAT* was again submitted by the winner of the first round, Anatol Rapoport of the Institute for Advanced Study (Vienna). And it won again. An analysis of the three million choices which were made in the second round shows that *TIT FOR TAT* was a very robust rule because it was nice, provocable into a retaliation by a defection of the other, and yet forgiving after it took its one retaliation (Axelrod, 1980b).

THE ECOLOGICAL APPROACH

To see if *TIT FOR TAT* would do well in a whole series of simulated tournaments, I calculated what would happen if each of the strategies in the second round were submitted to a hypothetical next round in proportion to its success in the previous round. This process was then repeated to generate the time path of the distribution of strategies. The results showed that as the less-successful rules were displaced, *TIT FOR TAT* continued to do well with the rules which initially scored near the top. In the long run, *TIT FOR TAT* displaced all the other rules and went to what biologists call fixation (Axelrod, 1980b).

This is an ecological approach because it takes as given the varieties which are present and investigates how they do over time when interacting with each other. It provides further evidence of the robust nature of the success of *TIT FOR TAT.*

THE EVOLUTIONARY APPROACH

A much more general approach would be to allow all possible decision rules to be considered, and to ask what are the characteristics of the decision rules which are stable in the long run. An evolutionary approach recently introduced by biologists offers a key concept which makes such an analysis tractable (Maynard Smith, 1974, 1978). This approach imagines the existence of a whole population of individuals employing a certain strategy, *B,* and a single mutant individual employing another strategy, *A.* Strategy *A* is said to *invade* strategy *B* if $V(A|B) > V(B|B)$ where $V(A|B)$ is the expected payoff an *A* gets when playing a *B,* and $V(B|B)$ is the expected payoff a *B* gets when playing another *B.* Since the *B*'s are interacting virtually entirely with other *B*'s, the concept of invasion is equivalent to the single mutant individual being able to do better than the population average. This leads directly to the key concept of the evolutionary approach. A strategy is *collectively stable* if no strategy can invade it.[3].

The biological motivation for this approach is based on the interpretation of the payoffs in terms of fitness (survival and fecundity). All mutations are possible, and if any could invade a given population it would have had the chance to do so. Thus only a collectively stable strategy is expected to be able to maintain itself in the long-run equilibrium as the strategy used by all.[4] Collectively stable strategies are important because they are the only ones which an entire population can maintain in the long run if mutations are introduced one at a time.

The political motivation for this approach is based on the assumption that all strategies are possible, and that if there were a strategy which would benefit an individual, someone is sure to try it. Thus only a collectively stable strategy can maintain itself as the strategy used by all — provided that the individuals who are trying out novel strategies do not interact too much with one another.[5] As we shall see later, if they do interact in clusters, then new and very important developments become possible.

A difficulty in the use of this concept of collective stability is that it can be very hard actually to determine which strategies have it and which do not. In most biological applications, including both the Prisoner's Dilemma and other types of interactions, this difficulty has been dealt with in one of two ways. One method has been to restrict the analysis to situations where the strategies take some particularly simple form such as in one-parameter models of sex-ratios (Hamilton, 1967). The other method has been to re-strict the strategies themselves to a relatively narrow set so that some illus-trative results could be attained (Maynard Smith and Price, 1973; Maynard Smith, 1978).

The difficulty of dealing with all possible strategies was also faced by Michael Taylor (1976), a political scientist who sought a deeper understand-ing of the issues raised by Hobbes and Hume concerning whether people in a state of nature would be expected to cooperate with each other. He too employed the method of using a narrow set of strategies to attain some il-lustrative results. Taylor restricted himself to the investigation of four par-ticular strategies (including *ALL D, ALL C, TIT FOR TAT,* and the rule "cooperate until the other defects, and then always defect"), and one set of strategies which retaliates in progressively increasing numbers of defections for each defection by the other. He successfully developed the equilibrium conditions when these are the only rules which are possible.[6].

Before running the computer tournament, I believed that it was impos-sible to make very much progress if all possible strategies were permitted to enter the analysis. However, once I had attained sufficient experience with a wide variety of specific decision rules, and with the analysis of what hap-pened when these rules interacted, I was able to formulate and answer some important questions about what would happen if all possible strategies were taken into account.

The remainder of this article will be devoted to answering the following specific questions about the emergence of cooperation in the iterated Pris-oner's Dilemma:

    (1) Under what conditions is *TIT FOR TAT* collectively stable?

    (2) What are the necessary and sufficient conditions for any strategy to be collectively stable?

    (3) If virtually everyone is following a strategy of unconditional defec-tion, when can cooperation emerge from a small cluster of new-comers who introduce cooperation based on reciprocity?

TIT FOR TAT AS A COLLECTIVELY STABLE STRATEGY

TIT FOR TAT cooperates on the first move, and then does whatever the other player did on the previous move. This means that any rule which starts off with a defection will get T, the highest possible payoff, on the first move when playing *TIT FOR TAT*. Consequently, *TIT FOR TAT* can only avoid being invadable by such a rule if the game is likely to last long enough for the retaliation to counteract the temptation to defect. In fact, no rule can invade *TIT FOR TAT* if the discount parameter, w, is sufficiently large. This is the heart of the formal result contained in the following theorem.

Readers who wish to skip the proofs can do so without loss of continuity.

Theorem 2. TIT FOR TAT *is a collectively stable strategy if and only if* w $\geq$ max $((T-R)/(T-P), (T-R)/(R-S))$. *An alternative formulation of the same result is that* TIT FOR TAT *is a collectively stable strategy if and only if it is invadable neither by* ALL D *nor the strategy which alternates defection and cooperation.*

Proof. First we prove that the two formulations of the theorem are equivalent, and then we prove both implications of the second formulation. To say that *ALL D* cannot invade *TIT FOR TAT* means that $V(ALL\ D|TFT) \leq V(TFT|TFT)$. As shown earlier, $V(ALL\ D|TFT) = T + wP/(1-w)$. Since *TFT* always cooperates with its twin, $V(TFT|TFT) = R + wR + w^2 R \ldots = R/(1-w)$. Thus *ALL D* cannot invade *TIT FOR TAT* when $T + wP/(1-w) \leq R/(1-w)$, or $T(1-w) + wP \leq R$, or $T - R \leq w(T-P)$ or $w \geq ((T-R)/(T-P))$. Similarly, to say that alternation of *D* and *C* cannot invade *TIT FOR TAT* means that $(T + wS)/(1-w^2) \leq R/(1-w)$, or $((T-R)/(R-S)) \leq w$. Thus $w \geq ((T-R)/(T-P))$ and $w \geq ((T-R)/(R-S))$ is equivalent to saying that *TIT FOR TAT* is invadable by neither ALL D nor the strategy which alternates defection and cooperation. This shows that the two formulations are equivalent.

Now we prove both of the implications of the second formulation. One implication is established by the simple observation that if *TIT FOR TAT* is a collectively stable strategy, then no rule can invade, and hence neither can the two specified rules. The other implication to be proved is that if neither *ALL D* nor Alternation of *D* and *C* can invade *TIT FOR TAT,* then no strategy can.

TIT FOR TAT has only two states, depending on what the other player did the previous move (on the first move it assumes, in effect, that the other player has just cooperated). Thus if *A* is interacting with *TIT FOR TAT,* the best which any strategy, *A,* can do after choosing *C* is to choose *C* or *D.* Similarly, the best *A* can do after choosing *D* is to choose *C* or *D.* This leaves four possibilities for the best *A* can do with *TIT FOR TAT:* repeated sequences of *CC, CD, DC,* or *DD.* The first does the same as *TIT FOR TAT* with another *TIT FOR TAT.* The second cannot do better than both the first and the third. This implies if the third and fourth possibilities cannot invade *TIT FOR TAT,* than no strategy can. These two are equivalent, respectively, to Alternation of *D* and *C,* and *ALL D.* Thus if neither of these two can invade *TIT FOR TAT,* no rule can, and *TIT FOR TAT* is a collectively stable strategy.

The significance of this theorem is that it demonstrates that if everyone in a population is cooperating with everyone else because each is using the *TIT FOR TAT* strategy, no one can do better using any other strategy *provided* the discount parameter is high enough. For example, using the numerical values of the payoff parameters given in Figure 1, *TIT FOR TAT* is uninvadable when the discount parameter, w, is greater than 2/3. If w falls below this critical value, and everyone else is using *TIT FOR TAT*, it will pay to defect on alternative moves. For w less than 1/2, *ALL D* can also invade.

One specific implication is that if the other player is unlikely to be around much longer because of apparent weakness, then the perceived value of w falls and the reciprocity of *TIT FOR TAT* is no longer stable. We have Caesar's explanation of why Pompey's allies stopped cooperating with him. "They regarded his [Pompey's] prospects as hopeless and acted according to the common rule by which a man's friends become his enemies in adversity" (trans. by Warner, 1960, p. 328). Another example is the business institution of the factor who buys a client's accounts receivable. This is done at a very substantial discount when the firm is in trouble because

> once a manufacturer begins to go under, even his best customers begin refusing payment for merchandise, claiming defects in quality, failure to meet specifications, tardy delivery, or what-have-you. The great enforcer of morality in commerce is the continuing relationship, the belief that one will have to do business again with this customer, or this supplier, and when a failing company loses this automatic enforcer, not even a strong-arm factor is likely to find a substitute (Mayer, 1974, p. 280).

Similarly, any member of Congress who is perceived as likely to be defeated in the next election may have some difficulty doing legislative business with colleagues on the usual basis of trust and good credit.[7]

There are many other examples of the importance of long-term interaction for the stability of cooperation in the iterated Prisoner's Dilemma. It is easy to maintain the norms of reciprocity in a stable small town or ethnic neighborhood. Conversely, a visiting professor is likely to receive poor treatment by other faculty members compared to the way these same people treat their regular colleagues.

Another consequence of the previous theorem is that if one wants to prevent rather than promote cooperation, one should keep the same individuals from interacting too regularly with each other. Consider the practice of the government selecting two aerospace companies for competitive development contracts. Since firms specialize to some degree in either air force or in navy planes, there is a tendency for firms with the same specialties to be frequently paired in the final competition (Art, 1968). To make tacit collusion between companies more difficult, the government should seek methods of compensating for the specialization. Pairs of companies which shared a specialization would then expect to interact less often in the final competitions. This would cause the later interactions between them to be worth relatively less than before, reducing the value of w. If w is sufficiently low, reciprocal cooperation in the form of tacit collusion ceases to be a stable policy.

Knowing when *TIT FOR TAT* cannot be invaded is valuable, but it is only a part of the story. Other strategies may be, and in fact are, also collectively stable. This suggests the question of what a strategy has to do to be collectively stable. In other words, what policies, if adopted by everyone, will prevent any one individual from benefiting by a departure from the common strategy?

THE CHARACTERIZATION OF COLLECTIVELY STABLE STRATEGIES

The characterization of all collectively stable strategies is based on the idea that invasion can be prevented if the rule can make the potential invader worse off than if it had just followed the common strategy. Rule B can prevent invasion by rule A if B can be sure that no matter what A does later, B will hold A's total score low enough. This leads to the following useful definition: B has a *secure position* over A on move n if no matter what A does from move n onwards, $V(A|B) \leq V(B|B)$, assuming that B defects from move n onwards. Let $V_n (A|B)$ represent A's discounted cumulative score in the moves before move n. Then another way of saying that B has a secure position over A on move n is that

$$V_n(A|B) + w^{n-1}P/(1-w) \leq V(B|B),$$

since the best A can do from move n onwards if B defects is get P each time. Moving the second term to the right side of the inequality gives the helpful result that B has a secure position over A on move n if $V_n(A|B)$ is small enough, namely if

$$V_n (A|B) \leq V(B|B) - w^{n-1}P/(1-w). \tag{1}$$

The theorem which follows embodies the advice that if you want to employ a collectively stable strategy, you should only cooperate when you can afford an exploitation by the other side and still retain your secure position.

Theorem 3. The Characterization Theorem. B *is a collectively stable strategy if and only if* B *defects on move* n *whenever the other player's cumulative score so far is too great, specifically when* $V_n(A|B) > V(B|B) - w^{n-1}(T + wP/(1-w))$.

Proof. First it will be shown that a strategy B which defects as required will always have a secure position over any A, and therefore will have $V(A|B) \leq V(B|B)$ which in turn makes B a collectively stable strategy. The proof works by induction. For B to have a secure position on move 1 means that $V(A|ALL\ D) \leq V(ALL\ D|ALL\ D)$ according to the definition of secure position applied to $n = 1$. Since this is true for all A, B has a secure position on move 1. If B has a secure position over A on move n, it has a secure position on move $n + 1$. This is shown in two parts.

First, if B defects on move n, A gets at most P, so

$$V_{n+1}(A|B) \leq V_n(A|B) + w^{n-1}P.$$

Using Equation (1) gives:

$$V_{n+1}(A|B) \leq V(B|B) - w^{n-1}P/(1-w) + w^{n-1}P$$

$$V_{n+1}(A|B) \leq V(B|B) - w^n P|(1-w).$$

Second, B will only cooperate on move n when

$$V_n(A|B) \leq V(B|B) - w^{n-1}(T + wP/(1-w)).$$

Since A can get at most T on move n, we have

$$V_{n+1}(A|B) \leq V(B|B) - w^{n-1}(T + wP/(1-w)) + w^{n-1}T$$

$$V_{n+1}(A|B) \leq V(B|B) - w^n P/(1-w).$$

Therefore, B always has a secure position over A, and consequently B is a collectively stable strategy.

The second part of the proof operates by contradiction. Suppose that B is a collectively stable strategy and there is an A and an n such that B does not defect on move n when

$$V_n(A|B) > V(B|B) - w^{n-1}(T + wP/(1-w)),$$

that is, when

$$V_n(A|B) + w^{n-1}(T + wP/(1-w)) > V(B|B). \qquad (2)$$

Define A' as the same as A on the first $n-1$ moves, and D thereafter. A' gets T on move n (since B cooperated then), and at least P thereafter. So,

$$V(A'|B) \geq V_n(A|B) + w^{n-1}(T + wP/(1-w)).$$

Combined with (2) this gives $V(A'|B) > V(B|B)$. Hence A' invades B, contrary to the assumption that B is a collectively stable strategy. Therefore, if B is a collectively stable strategy, it must defect when required.

Figure 2 illustrates the use of this theorem. The dotted line shows the value which must not be exceeded by any A if B is to be a collectively stable strategy. This value is just $V(B|B)$, the expected payoff attained by a player using B when virtually all the other players are using B as well. The solid curve represents the critical value of A's cumulative payoff so far. The theorem simply says that B is a collectively stable strategy if and only if it defects whenever the other player's cumulative value so far in the game is above this line. By doing so, B is able to prevent the other player from eventually getting a total expected value of more than rule B gets when playing another rule B.

The characterization theorem is "policy-relevant" in the abstract sense that it specifies what a strategy, B, has to do at any point in time as a function of the previous history of the interaction in order for B to be a collectively stable strategy.[8] It is a complete characterization because this requirement is both a necessary and a sufficient condition for strategy B to be collectively stable.

Two additional consequences about collectively stable strategies can be seen from Figure 2. First, as long as the other player has not accumulated too great a score, a strategy has the flexibility to either cooperate or defect and still be collectively stable. This flexibility explains why there are typically many strategies which are collectively stable. The second consequence

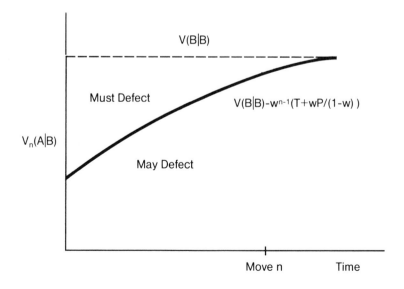

FIGURE 2

is that a nice rule (one which will never defect first) has the most flexibility since it has the highest possible score when playing an identical rule. Put another way, nice rules can afford to be more generous than other rules with potential invaders because nice rules do so well with each other.

The flexibility of a nice rule is not unlimited, however, as shown by the following theorem. In fact, a nice rule must be *provoked* by the very first defection of the other player, that is, on some later move the rule must have a finite chance of retaliating with a defection of its own.

Theorem 4. For a nice strategy to be collectively stable, it must be provoked by the first defection of the other player.

Proof. If a nice strategy were not provoked by a defection on move n, then it would not be collectively stable because it could be invaded by a rule which defected only on move n.

Besides provocability, there is another requirement for a nice rule to be collectively stable. This requirement is that the discount parameter w, be sufficiently large. This is a generalization of the second theorem, which showed that for *TIT FOR TAT* to be collectively stable, w has to be large enough. The idea extends beyond just nice rules to any rule which might be the first to cooperate.

Theorem 5. Any rule, B, *which may be the first to cooperate is collectively stable only when* w *is sufficiently large.*

Proof. If B cooperates on the first move, $V(ALL\ D|B) \geq T + wP(1 - w)$. But for any B, $R/(1 - w) \geq V(B|B)$ since R is the best B can do with another B by the assumptions that $R > P$ and $R > (S + T)/2$. Therefore $V(ALL\ D|B) > V(B|B)$ is so whenever $T + wP/(1 - w) > R/(1 - w)$. This implies that $ALL\ D$ invades a B which cooperates on the first move whenever $w < ((T - R)/(T - P))$. If B has a positive chance of cooperating on the first move, then the gain of $V(ALL\ D|B)$ over $V_1(B|B)$ can only be nullified if w is sufficiently large. Likewise, if B will not be the first to cooperate until move n, $V_n(ALL\ D|B) = V_n(B|B)$ and the gain of $V_{n+1}(ALL\ D|B)$ over $V_{n+1}(B|B)$ can only be nullified if w is sufficiently large.

There is one strategy which is *always* collectively stable, that is regardless of the value of w or the payoff parameters T, R, P, and S. This is *ALL D*, the rule which defects no matter what.

Theorem 6. ALL D is always collectively stable.

Proof. ALL D is always collectively stable because it always defects and hence it defects whenever required by the condition of the characterization theorem.

This is an important theorem because of its implications for the evolution of cooperation. If we imagine a system starting with individuals who cannot be enticed to cooperate, the collective stability of *ALL D* implies that no single individual can hope to do any better than just to go along and be uncooperative as well. A world of "meanies" can resist invasion by anyone using any other strategy—provided that the newcomers arrive one at a time.

The problem, of course, is that a single newcomer in such a mean world has no one who will reciprocate any cooperation. If the newcomers arrive in small clusters, however, they will have a chance to thrive. The next section shows how this can happen.

THE IMPLICATIONS OF CLUSTERING

To consider arrival in clusters rather than singly, we need to broaden the idea of "invasion" to invasion by a cluster.[9] As before, we will suppose that strategy *B* is being used by virtually everyone. But now suppose that a small group of individuals using strategy *A* arrives and interacts with both the other *A*'s and the native *B*'s. To be specific, suppose that the proportion of the interactions by someone using strategy *A* with another individual using strategy *A* is *p*. Assuming that the *A*'s are rare relative to the *B*'s, virtually all the interactions of *B*'s are with other *B*'s. Then the average score of someone using *A* is $pV(A|A) + (1-p)V(A|B)$ and the average score of someone using *B* is $V(B|B)$. Therefore, a p-*cluster of* A *invades* B if $pV(A|A) + (1-p)V(A|B) > V(B|B)$, where *p* is the proportion of the interactions by a player using strategy *A* with another such player. Solving for *p*, this means that invasion is possible if the newcomers interact enough with each other, namely when

$$p > \frac{V(B|B) - V(A|B)}{V(A|A) - V(A|B)}. \qquad (3)$$

Notice that this assumes that pairing in the interactions is not random. With random pairing, an *A* would rarely meet another *A*. Instead, the clustering concept treats the case in which the *A*'s are a trivial part of the environment of the *B*'s, but a nontrivial part of the environment of the other *A*'s.

The striking thing is just how easy invasion of *ALL D* by clusters can be. Specifically, the value of *p* which is required for invasion by *TIT FOR TAT* of a world of *ALL D*'s is surprisingly low. For example, suppose the payoff values are those of Figure 1, and that *w* = .9, which corresponds to a 10 per cent chance two interacting players will never meet again. Let *A* be *TIT FOR TAT* and *B* be *ALL D*. Then $V(B|B) = P/(1-w) = 10$; $V(A|B) = S + wP/(1-w) = 9$; and $V(A|A) = R/(1-w) = 30$. Plugging these numbers into Equation (3) shows that a *p*-cluster of *TIT FOR TAT* invades *ALL D* when $p > 1/21$. Thus if the newcomers using *TIT FOR TAT* have any more than about 5 per cent of their interactions with others using *TIT FOR*

TAT, they can thrive in a world in which everyone else refuses ever to co-operate.

In this way, a world of meanies can be invaded by a cluster of *TIT FOR TAT*—and rather easily at that. To illustrate this point, suppose a business school teacher taught a class to give cooperative behavior a chance, and to reciprocate cooperation from other firms. If the students did, and if they did not disperse too widely (so that a sufficient proportion of their interactions were with others from the same class), then the students would find that their lessons paid off.

When the interactions are expected to be of longer duration (or the time discount factor is not as great), then even less clustering is necessary. For example, if the median game length is two hundred moves (corresponding to $w = .99654$) and the payoff parameters are as given in Figure 1, even one interaction out of a thousand with a like-minded follower of *TIT FOR TAT* is enough for the strategy to invade a world of *ALL D'S*. Even when the median game length is only two moves ($w = .5$), anything over a fifth of the interactions by the *TIT FOR TAT* players with like-minded types is sufficient for invasion to succeed and cooperation to emerge.

The next result shows which strategies are the most efficient at invading *ALL D* with the least amount of clustering. These are the strategies which are best able to discriminate between themselves and *ALL D*. A strategy is *maximally discriminating* if it will eventually cooperate even if the other has never cooperated yet, and once it cooperates it will never cooperate again with *ALL D* but will always cooperate with another player using the same strategy.

Theorem 7. The strategies which can invade ALL D *in a cluster with the smallest value of* p *are those which are maximally discriminating, such as* TIT FOR TAT.

Proof. To be able to invade *ALL D,* a rule must have a positive chance of cooperating first. Stochastic cooperation is not as good as deterministic cooperation with another player using the same rule since stochastic cooperation yields equal probability of S and T, and $(S + T)/2 < R$ in the Prisoner's Dilemma. Therefore, a strategy which can invade with the smallest p must cooperate first on some move, n, even if the other player has never cooperated yet. Employing Equation (3) shows that the rules which invade $B = ALL\ D$ with the lowest value of p are those which have the lowest value of p^*, where $p^* = (V(B|B) - V(A|B))/(V(A|A) - V(A|B))$. The value of p^* is minimized when $V(A|A)$ and $V(A|B)$ are maximized (subject to the constraint that A cooperates for the first time on move n) since $V(A|A) > V(B|B) > V(A|B)$. $V(A|A)$ and $V(A|B)$ are maximized subject to this constraint if, and only if, A is a maximally discriminating rule. (Incidentally, it does not matter for the minimal value of p just when A starts to cooperate.) *TIT FOR TAT* is such a strategy because it always cooperates for $n = 1$, it cooperates only once with *ALL D,* and it always cooperates with another *TIT FOR TAT.*

The final theorem demonstrates that nice rules (those which never defect first) are actually better able than other rules to protect themselves from invasion by a cluster.

Theorem 8. If a nice strategy cannot be invaded by a single individual, it cannot be invaded by any cluster of individuals either.

Proof. For a cluster of rule A to invade a population of rule B, there must be a $p \leq 1$ such that $pV(A|A) + (1-p)V(A|B) > V(B|B)$. But if B is nice, then $V(A|A) \leq V(B|B)$. This is so because $V(B|B) = R/(1-w)$ which is the largest value attainable when the other player is using the same strategy. It is the largest value since $R > (S+T)/2$. Since $V(A|A) \leq V(B|B)$, A can invade as a cluster only if $V(A|B) > V(B|B)$. But that is equivalent to A invading as an individual.

This shows that nice rules do not have the structural weakness displayed in *ALL D*. *ALL D* can withstand invasion by any strategy, as long as the players using other strategies come one at a time. But if they come in clusters (even in rather small clusters), *ALL D* can be invaded. With nice rules, the situation is different. If a nice rule can resist invasion by other rules coming one at a time, then it can resist invasion by clusters, no matter how large. So nice rules can protect themselves in a way that *ALL D* cannot.[10]

In the illustrative case of the Senate, Theorem 8 demonstrates that once cooperation based on reciprocity has become established, it can remain stable even if a cluster of newcomers does not respect this senatorial folkway. And Theorem 6 has shown that without clustering (or some comparable mechanism) the original pattern of mutual "treachery" could not have been overcome. Perhaps these critical early clusters were based on the boardinghouse arrangements in the capital during the Jeffersonian era (Young, 1966). Or perhaps the state delegations and state party delegations were more critical (Bogue and Marlaire, 1975). But now that the pattern of reciprocity is established, Theorems 2 and 5 show that it is collectively stable, as long as the biennial turnover rate is not too great.

Thus cooperation can emerge even in a world of unconditional defection. The development cannot take place if it is tried only by scattered individuals who have no chance to interact with each other. But cooperation can emerge from small clusters of individuals, as long as these individuals have even a small proportion of their interactions with each other. Moreover, if nice strategies (those which are never the first to defect) eventually come to be adopted by virtually everyone, then those individuals can afford to be generous in dealing with any others. The population of nice rules can also protect themselves against clusters of individuals using any other strategy just as well as they can protect themselves against single individuals. But for a nice strategy to be stable in the collective sense, it must be provocable. So mutual cooperation can emerge in a world of egoists without central control, by starting with a cluster of individuals who rely on reciprocity.

For a fuller treatment of these themes see Robert Axelrod, *The Evolution of Cooperation* (1984).

NOTES

*I would like to thank John Chamberlin, Michael Cohen, Bernard Grofman, William Hamilton, John Kingdon, Larry Mohr, John Padgett and Reinhard Selten for their help, and the Institute of Public Policy Studies for its financial support.

1. A single player may be interacting with many others, but the player is interacting with them one at a time. The situations which involve more than pairwise interaction can be modeled with the more complex n-person Prisoner's Dilemma (Olson, 1965; G. Hardin, 1968; R. Hardin, 1971; Schelling, 1973). The principal application is to the provision of collective goods. It is possible that the results from pairwise interactions will help suggest how to undertake a deeper analysis of the n-person case as well, but that must wait. For a parallel treatment of the two-person and n-person cases, see Taylor (1976, pp. 29–62).
2. In the second round, the length of the games was uncertain, with an expected median length of two hundred moves. This was achieved by setting the probability that a given move would not be the last one at $w = .99654$. As in the first round, each pair was matched in five games. See Axelrod (1980b) for a complete description.
3. Those familiar with the concepts of game theory will recognize this as a strategy being in Nash equilibrium with itself. My definitions of invasion and collective stability are slightly different from Maynard Smith's (1974) definitions of invasion and evolutionary stability. His definition of invasion allows $V(A|B) = V(B|B)$ provided that $V(B|A) > V(A|A)$. I have used the new definitions to simplify the proofs and to highlight the difference between the effect of a single mutant and the effect of a small number of mutants. Any rule which is evolutionarily stable is also collectively stable. For a nice rule, the definitions are equivalent. All theorems in the text remain true if "evolutionary stability" is substituted for "collective stability" with the exception of Theorem 3, where the characterization is necessary but no longer sufficient.
4. For the application of the results of this article to biological contexts, see Axelrod and Hamilton (1981). For the development in biology of the concepts of reciprocity and stable strategy, see Hamilton (1964), Trivers (1971), Maynard Smith (1974), and Dawkins (1976).
5. Collective stability can also be interpreted in terms of a commitment by one player, rather than the stability of a whole population. Suppose player Y is committed to using strategy B. Then player X can do no better than use this same strategy B if and only if strategy B is collectively stable.
6. For the comparable equilibrium conditions when all possible strategies are allowed, see below, Theorems 2 through 6. For related results on the potential stability of cooperative behavior, see Luce and Raiffa (1957, p. 102), Kurz (1977) and Hirshleifer (1978).

7. A countervailing consideration is that a legislator in electoral trouble may receive help from friendly colleagues who wish to increase the chances of reelection of someone who has proven in the past to be cooperative, trustworthy, and effective. Two current examples are Morris Udall and Thomas Foley. (I wish to thank an anonymous reviewer for this point.)
8. To be precise, $V(B|B)$ must also be specified in advance. For example, if B is never the first to defect, $V(B|B) = R(1 - w)$.
9. For related concepts from biology, see Wilson (1979) and Axelrod and Hamilton (1981).
10. This property is possessed by population mixes of nice rules as well. If no single individual can invade a population of nice rules, no cluster can either.

20

Individual Sanctions, Collective Benefits

RUSSELL HARDIN

Our experience from daily life is that people are often, even generally, quite cooperative. But this experience is of face-to-face interactions, typically even dyadic interactions. Being cooperative face-to-face is different from being cooperative en masse in a fundamentally important way. Being cooperative in small number, especially dyadic interactions is commonly—but not always—rational in the narrow sense that it serves one's self-interest. Being cooperative in large number interactions to provide collective benefits typically is not rational in this narrow sense.

One of the most vexing problems in social theory is how to achieve voluntary cooperation in collectively beneficial projects when cooperation involves individual costs. It has long been recognized that cooperation in dyadic contexts can be effectively motivated by simple self-interest. The argument for cooperation carries in iterated dyadic interactions and in dyadic interactions that may be embedded in a larger network of dyadic interactions. The argument may be generalized to cover small number interactions but it clearly breaks down for very large number interactions, or collective actions, that are not merely aggregations of dyadic interactions (Hardin 1982a, chaps. 10–12.).

Numerous efforts have been made to overcome this apparent failure of rational self-interest in motivating collective action. I wish to consider three classes of arguments for rational cooperation and to show that they all fail. In general, they fail because they cannot ground cooperation in individual sanctions based in denial of relevant collective benefits to noncooperators. It is precisely such sanctions that motivate cooperation in dyadic interactions. I will then argue that a purely genetic derivation that makes sense for motivating cooperation in dyadic interactions will likewise fail to generalize to large-number collective actions. Finally, I will argue that cooperativeness in collective actions can sometimes be motivated by self-interest if there are relevant associated interactions between dyadic pairs in the larger group but even here the conclusion is weak.

DYADIC EXCHANGE

First let us lay out the problem at the dyadic level and then turn to the group level. A potential simple two-party exchange has the payoff structure of the Prisoner's Dilemma (Hardin 1982b). As represented in game 1, I may yield X to you in exchange for your yielding Y to me. We should make an exchange if I would rather have Y and you would rather have X. Suppose I value X at 1 unit of money and you value it at 2 units, while you value Y at 1 unit and I value it at 2 units. With these valuations, the possible payoffs to each of us are those represented in game 1 if you are the Column player and I am the Row player.

		Column	
		Yield Y	Keep Y
	Yield X	2,2	0,3
Row			
	Keep X	3,0	1,1

Game 1: Simple Exchange

That there are gains to be made from trade in an interaction means that there is an outcome which is Pareto-superior to the status quo, which is to say that at least one party is better off after the trade and none is worse off. In our simple exchange game, both parties are better off if they reciprocally yield their holdings than if they both keep their holdings. We may say that the outcome at the upper left, in which the players trade, is *strongly* Pareto-superior to the outcome at the lower right, in which there is no trade. The great interest in the Prisoner's Dilemma derives from the fact that, although it has the strongly Pareto-superior outcome in which both players cooperate, we generally expect players in single-play Prisoner's Dilemmas not to cooperate, which would mean not to exchange in the present context. The reason for noncooperation is that each of us has a *dominant strategy* of not cooperating. If we cannot make our choices contingent on each other's, each of us is better off not cooperating no matter what the other does. Moreover, the mutual non-cooperation outcome is an *equilibrium* for the game because neither of us has an interest in unilaterally switching strategies to cooperation.

Against the Prisoner's Dilemma structure of simple exchange, we are accustomed to thinking that mutually beneficial exchanges will be made. In simple economic contexts, the reason for success is that the parties yield their holdings to one another simultaneously. Unless you turn over Y to me on the spot, I will not turn over X to you. Hence, our moves are contingent on each other. When exchange has this character, we may call it *discrete*. It is discrete in time and it may well be discrete from other relationships between us: we may never deal with one another again. With the qualification discussed below, exchange in a market is often discrete in this sense.

There is another way to insure against the noncooperative outcome in the simple exchange Prisoner's Dilemma. This is to be involved in an ongoing relationship involving future exchanges so that, de facto, we are involved in an iterated Prisoner's Dilemma. In an iterated Prisoner's Dilemma, cooperation in this play may be justified in order to secure the cooperation of the other player in future plays of the game. If you know that my cooperation on the next play is contingent on your cooperation this play, you may clearly suffer a net loss if you do not cooperate this play (Luce and Raiffa 1957, pp. 97–102; Shubik 1959, pp. 224–25; Taylor 1976; Hardin 1982a, chap. 9). Hence, we may commonly expect exchange to be consummated outside market contexts. Indeed, we may even expect to see it consummated in contexts in which one party must yield X long before the other yields Y. What gives each party the incentive to carry through with yielding holdings at each relevant moment is the ongoing relationship between them, a relationship which may be enormously beneficial to both if maintained over the long run even though neither party will ever be at great risk of being taken for a very expensive ride at any given moment. Hence, we may refer in these contexts to *relational exchange* (Macneil 1980).

Suppose our encounter were governed by no relational aspects whatsoever and that we were purely self-interested in our motives. I have X and you have Y. When we part, who has what is likely to be determined by physical prowess or apparent prowess. I may seize *Y* and run; you may raise your fist and demand *X*. If purely discrete encounters are governed by prowess, it is of little concern — in determining the outcome — whether mutually beneficial exchanges would be possible. Hence, discrete exchange seems inherently almost impossible if prowess matters.

Nevertheless we may usefully differentiate exchanges into more or less relatively discrete and relatively relational as ideal types. Market exchange is itself not strictly discrete because what makes it workable is a set of institutions to enforce rules of exchange. In this sense, in a market exchange you and I rely on ongoing relationships which one or both of us have with relevant social institutions. Given the background of *institutional sanctions,* such as those under law and those available to organizations, you and I can enter into nearly discrete exchange with one another without fear that prowess will play a determining role in our encounter. Still, we can do so only if our exchange of holdings is simultaneous or if, to use an old-fashioned legal term which Macneil has brought back to favor, we can "presentiate," that is, make present, all of the future aspects of our exchange by, say, entering into an institutionally sanctioned contract that binds one or both of us to action in the future. "Presentiation is . . . a recognition that the course of the future is bound by present events, *and* that by those events the future has for many purposes been brought effectively into the present" (Macneil 1974, p. 589, his emphasis).

It is commonly understood that cooperation in an iterated Prisoner's Dilemma may be insured without institutional sanctions. Or, perhaps better, we should say that in spontaneous relationships, as opposed to those governed by contractual agreement and sanctions, institutional sanctions may be important only in defining boundaries on what general classes of behavior may be expected. Hence, the sanctions with which we need to be concerned within those boundaries are *relational sanctions,* that is, sanctions which are invoked by one party against another by the withdrawal of the first party from further exchanges. Such sanctions are powerful motivators in dyadic relationships, and as I will note below, they can also be used to enforce cooperation in collective action under relevant circumstances.

These two categories do not exhaust the realm of possible sanctions. Perhaps most obviously, there may be moral sanctions. Of greater concern in the present context of self-interested behavior, there may also be sanctions inherent in damage to one's reputation from not following through on the delivery of a promised good or a threatened harm. The damage includes effects on one's reputation from dealing with third parties. In this case, it is the possible withdrawal *by others* from future exchanges with oneself that may compel one to deliver. We may lump this incentive with relational sanctions which are specific to a particular ongoing relationship without confusion in what follows.

GROUP-LEVEL INTERACTIONS AND RATIONAL CHOICE

There are at least three classes of group-level problems of interest here:
(1) Collective action;
(2) Cooperation in a wide network of dyadic exchanges; and
(3) Generalized altruism.
The first of these is generally governed by the logic of collective action, according to which cooperation typically is not narrowly rational. The second is nothing more than a generalization of the single dyadic exchange relationship, discussed above, in which cooperation typically is rational. The third cannot sensibly be seen as narrowly rational although it has been argued by some that it is. The three classes are often run together in discussion despite the fact that the structures of incentives in the three are radically different.

Taylor (1976) supposes that rational, contingent choosing can solve the large-number dilemma. Axelrod shows that cooperative strategies are evolutionarily stable in his sense for dyadic interactions. He notes, "It is possible that the results from pairwise interactions will help suggest how to undertake a deeper analysis of the n-person case as well, but that must wait" (Axelrod 1984, p. 216). Elster (1979, pp. 63–65) assimilates the large-number to the dyadic problem and supposes that the "instant rationality" that would prescribe not cooperating can best be overcome by prior habituation to altruistic action. One habituates oneself because one forsees the interest one has in having the relevant habits. One also foresees that one will not act well if left to rational calculation in each relevant moment.

Taylor, Axelrod, and Elster consider the dyadic problem and wish to relate it to the problem of collective action. Axelrod's analysis does not generalize beyond the dyadic problem except to cooperation in a wide network of dyadic interactions. Taylor's analysis is compatible with this generalization, although he does not carry it through. But he does generalize his results to small-number collective actions and even to very large-number collective actions, although it is implausible that this latter extension would succeed. Elster runs the collective action and dyadic problems together and resolves them with a quasi-rational argument for generalized altruism.

ANARCHY AND COOPERATION

Taylor generalizes the arguments for cooperation in an iterated 2-person Prisoner's Dilemma to *n*-person collective actions in the following way. Suppose you are in an *n*-person iterated Prisoner's Dilemma in which *n* is greater than 2. It will clearly be rational for you to cooperate on the condition that *all others cooperate if, and only if, you do and all defect otherwise*. This is directly analogous to the standard argument for the self-interested rationality of cooperation in an iterated dyadic Prisoner's Dilemma discussed above. To make the argument go, we merely have to assume that all others act as one. But it is not necessary that *all* others act as one so long as *enough* others do. Taylor's claim is that we can suppose enough others often will act in this contingent way to make n-Prisoner's Dilemmas cooperatively resolvable. They will act as one because it is in their interest to have their Prisoner's Dilemma resolved.

In many classes of n-Prisoner's Dilemma interactions, it will be in my interest to cooperate if I am faced with a large enough subgroup who make their cooperation contingent on mine. This follows because it will commonly be true that some subgroup of less than n members that includes me could provide the larger group's collective benefit in such a way that each member of the subgroup receives a net benefit. (One can easily devise analytical examples for which this claim is not true, but for practical cases of serious interest it is likely to be true.) Call a minimal such subgroup a k-subgroup (Hardin 1982a, p. 41). A k-subgroup, K, can provide its larger group's collective benefit in a way that benefits every member of K; but if any member of K drops out, the resultant k-1 subgroup cannot provide the larger group's benefit without a net loss to at least one of the remaining members of K. Hence, there is some force to Taylor's argument, since if k-1 members of a relevant k-subgroup approach me with an offer of contingent cooperation, it is, in a limited sense, rational of me to cooperate. It is rational only in a limited sense for the reason that I might retort to my k-1 colleagues that you are also available as their final member and that I do not care to join them when you could do so.

Taylor's argument does not depend on assuming that the subgroup of contingent cooperators is one short of being a k-subgroup. Indeed, the device of such contingent cooperating is likely to be of real interest only if the cooperators number much more than k, since in many collective actions the members of a k-subgroup would receive only marginal net benefits after putting up the entire costs of providing their larger group's benefits. Taylor's resolution therefore typically becomes attractive only if it can be used to increase the number of cooperators well beyond k. Suppose then that a subgroup of contingent cooperators numbering far more than k approaches me. What is it rational for me to do in response to this group's contingent offer of cooperation if only I also cooperate? Unfortunately for this group, its threat not to cooperate if I do not is far less credible than my counterthreat simply not to cooperate and to call its bluff. If the group did indeed carry out its threat, it would thereby make its own members significantly worse off by denying them the net benefits of their own cooperation, benefits they could receive without my cooperation. The only reason for me to cooperate would be that I seriously believed their group threat. They, however, have reason to cooperate irrespective of what I do.

In either case, whether the contingent cooperators who approach me number k-1 or more than that, we face a difficult bargaining problem. The question whether I should rationally cooperate with the contingent cooperators is sadly ill-determined. The answer, if it is to become better determined, must turn on considerations other than those inherent in the payoffs of our specific collective action interaction. For example, the subgroup of contingent cooperators might contract with some third party to have to pay a large penalty should it not follow through on its threat not to cooperate if I do not. Of course, I might do the equivalent on my side to secure my own threat not to cooperate no matter what the subgroup did. We are in Schelling's world of analytically indeterminate outcomes, a world in which Taylor's resolution of our problem cannot finally be compelling. This is not to say that some actual groups may not actually resolve their collective action problems in Taylor's fashion, but only to say that we have little reason to assert that their failing to do so would be proof of their members' individual irrationality. (See further Hardin 1982a, pp. 153–54.)

Another way to see the inherent difficulty in Taylor's resolution is to note that the resolution assumes itself. Our original n-Prisoner's Dilemma is an iterated collective action problem. It would be odd to resolve this problem by stipulating that, no matter what n is, the iterated collective action problem for n-1 is resolvable and then deducing from the resolution of the $(n$-1)-person problem that the larger n-person problem is resolvable. This is effectively the resolution that Taylor offers.

THE EVOLUTION OF COOPERATION

Axelrod (1984) explains widespread habits of cooperation in the usual way as instances of rational play in iterated Prisoner's Dilemmas. He adds to this a test by simulation of the long-run "robustness" of various strategies in playing iterated Prisoner's Dilemmas with large numbers of essentially anonymous others where each of these Prisoner's Dilemmas is played with only one other person. His simulation shows that against a large number of various alternative strategies the very simple Tit-for-Tat strategy yields the best outcome. In Tit-for-Tat one cooperates on the first move of the iterated game and thereafter one cooperates on each move if the other cooperated on the previous move and defects otherwise. This strategy is proved, under certain minimal assumptions, to be "initially viable" and "collectively stable" in the following respects. A cluster of players using it benefits from continuing to use it even in a larger community of others who use alternative strategies; and the others, if they wish to improve their outcomes, will have to convert to Tit-for-Tat.

This is a clever and impressive result. But note that the fundamental assumption from which it follows is that cooperation in a 2-person iterated Prisoner's Dilemma is rational if the other person will cooperate only in return for one's own cooperation. Can we generalize this assumption to cover *n*-person interactions where *n* is large? We can, but the generalization is hollow in precisely the way that Taylor's result for *n*-Prisoner's Dilemma is hollow.

On this analysis, standard variants of iterated Prisoner's Dilemmas can be cooperatively resolved by contract by convention: the tacit contract to cooperate is achieved by convention rather than by agreement (Hardin 1982a, chap.10). How widespread a contract by convention is likely to be in a population depends inversely on the size of the typical group involved in the Prisoner's Dilemma interaction (p. 218). Truth-telling and promise-keeping are largely at issue in dyadic relationships, and contract-by-convention regulation of these is very widespread. It would be contrary to most individuals' interests not generally to tell the truth and keep promises in many societies. To build up a similar contract by convention to regulate cooperation in large-number collective actions is far more difficult. It might not be impossible, because we might successfully sanction uncooperative members of our large group by excluding them from dyadic exchange relations with us. But, if they could not be excluded from the collective benefits of group effort, we could not sanction them effectively by refusing to supply the collective benefit without simultaneously harming ourselves, as argued in the discussion of Taylor's thesis above.

Axelrod's footnote hope "that the results from pairwise interactions will help suggest how to undertake a deeper analysis of the *n*-person case as well" (Axelrod 1984, p. 216) is likely to be forlorn for the simple reason that it is directly demonstrable that cooperation in such cases is typically contrary to one's interests, the more so the larger *n* is. If *n* is small enough and the potential gains from cooperation are large enough, people may successfully cooperate. But if a few people defect and thereby gain higher payoffs for themselves, the cooperators may face a hard choice. They may continue to cooperate because cooperation yields them a net positive payoff. Or they may choose to defect until the defectors begin to cooperate as well. The latter choice entails even lower payoffs at first while all defect in the hope of inducing unanimous cooperation for much higher payoffs in the longer run. But the ploy may fail because the defectors may hold out. In our iterated 2-Prisoner's Dilemma, if you are defecting I can improve my payoff even in the immediate term by defecting as well. Since cooperating while you defect cannot benefit me, you cannot credibly expect me to do so. But in the *n*-person case, if *k* for the group is less than *n*, defectors who number *n* − *k* or fewer might credibly expect *k* or more others to continue to cooperate because it would be in their interest to do so. In sum we must conclude that cooperative behavior in very small — especially dyadic — Prisoner's Dilemmas may generalize to cover a large population of self-interested people among whom ongoing relationships are commonplace, but that the argument which yields this result does not generalize to large-number Prisoner's Dilemmas or collective actions.

Axelrod cites cases that might seem to be large-number rather than dyadic interactions. For example, he discusses the managed futility of trench warfare during World War I (Axelrod 1984, pp. 73–87). The front-line troops in the trenches achieved tacit understanding not to harm one another even while each side barraged the other with artillery and rifle fire. Despite the vast numbers of men involved in this cooperative effort to avoid the ostensible purpose of the warfare, the relationship was essentially dyadic. If anyone on either side violated the peaceable arrangement, the whole side was presumably accountable. Had the arrangement literally required the separate tacit agreement between each person on one side with every person on the other, it would have been impossible.

Note that evolutionary stability is achievable for only certain kinds of exchanges: those that can be repeated over and over or broken up into piecemeal parts to be spread out over time *and* that involve predictably commensurate exchange values. Certain fundamentally important dyadic exchanges cannot easily be treated this way despite their having a long time horizon. For example, consider the problem of marital fidelity. The larger community will determine what values are credible—in particular it will determine the credible range of expected values for both marital fidelity and the romantic involvements of the unfaithful, since these are not a priori commensurate values.

If the evidence of community experience is that the value of extramarital involvements very often trumps that of marital fidelity it may be very difficult for any individual to establish credibility for valuing fidelity over license. As a result, anyone entering a new marriage must realistically discount its future value rather heavily. Hence, the present value of the full expected run of marriages in a licentious community will tend to be lower than that of marriages in a stable community. Hence, even modest values put on attractions of the moment may trump the relatively low expected value of a marriage. Cooperativeness in commitment to a faithful marriage may therefore break down in general as the rate of infidelity goes up. The potentially faithful remnant will appreciate all too well the Old Puritan's complaint: "I am sure of no one but thee and me—and sometimes I'm not so sure of thee."

Note that here the failure does not result from a principled, subjective discounting of future benefits and costs. Rather, the discounting is objectively determined by low expectations of receiving certain future benefits. It is not that those benefits are discounted just because they would be in the future but that their likelihood of being received is significantly lower in the future than in the present.

THE GRAND PATH

Elster (1979, p. 63) introduces his argument for preferring altruism to rational calculation with a wonderful passage from Descartes's letter to Princess Elizabeth in January 1646:

> The reason that makes me believe that those who do nothing save for their own utility ought also, if they wish to be prudent, work, as do others, for the good of others, and try to please everyone as much as they can, is that one ordinarily sees it occur that those who are deemed obliging and prompt to please also receive a quantity of good deeds from others, even from people who have never been obliged to them; and these things they would not receive did people believe them of another humor; and the pains they take to please other people are not so great as the conveniences that their friendship of those who know them proves to be. For others expect of us only those deeds we can render conveniently, nor do we expect more of them; but it often happens that deeds that cost others little profit us very much, and can even save our life. It is true that occasionally one wastes his toil in doing good and that, on the other hand, occasionally one gains in doing evil; but that cannot change the rule of prudence that relates only to things that happen most often. As for me, the maxim I have most often observed in all the conduct of my life has been to follow only the grand path, and to believe that the principle shrewdness is not to wish at all to use shrewdness. (Blom 1978, pp. 176–77.)

The first point to make about Descartes's argument is that he is very clearly asserting, in the sprawling first sentence, that relational sanctions should motivate any sensible person to be cooperative. I think it reasonable also to suppose he is essentially concerned with very small-number interactions, generally even with dyadic exchanges, iterated over long relationships. In addition to direct sanctions within a particular exchange relationship he notes the related sanction of reputation, which, again, we can assimilate to relational sanctions without confusion.

The second point to make is that Descartes seems very clearly to recognize difficulties in personal decision-making. In modern jargon, we suffer from limits to our knowledge, our ability to calculate the consequences and advantages of specific actions, and our time to make decisions. Hence, among other shortcuts, we should make relatively general decisions about classes of commonplace problems rather than leave each instance of the class up for decision as it occurs. It is shrewder to avoid minute applications of our shrewdness. Hence, although we may occasionally act cooperatively even when we might have benefitted from not cooperating, overall we will surely benefit from simply being cooperative.

Descartes's account is a remarkably modern, straightforwardly rational analysis of how to behave in certain circumstances. Elster, however, uses the passage from Descartes in an account of why it is better to let extra-rational motivations guide us in the relevant contexts. He says that Descartes is "arguing that it is rational in the long run to help others, even if irrational in the short run" (Elster 1979, pp. 64–65.) The only sense in which dyadic co-operation that is rational in the long run can be said to be irrational in the short run is the following hypothetical sense. It would be irrational *if* it were isolated from the long-run interaction. But the whole point of Descartes's argument is to suppose that the short-run cooperation is generally not isolated from the longer run of the interaction. In such a case, short-run cooperation is fully rational.

Elster goes on to argue that, faced with this general problem, one should sooner strive to change one's character to be altruistic than follow Descartes's prescription for being rationally self-interested. This is an empirical claim of the sort that one cannot refute on analytical grounds, but I think it is not compelling. There is some confusion in the ordinary language understanding of what motivates us to various actions — so much, indeed, that one may suspect that many people would think that acting cooperatively because it is in one's general interest to do so just is to have the "character from which help will flow 'sans violence, sans art, sans argument,'" as Pascal puts it (Elster 1979, p. 65). But I think it not at all difficult for most people to learn from childhood tutorials that being generally cooperative with those with whom one often deals is wise. Childhood tutorials in developing right character are not conspicuously either more commonplace or more effective than those in learning to act according to one's larger interest. Descartes's understanding seems to me to be descriptively superior to Pascal's, although one must suspect that there are occasional saintly types who do as Pascal recommends for reasons of genuine altruism.

The issue is not whether altruism is plausibly rational, of course, but whether cooperativeness is rational and whether much of what we might call altruism is merely rational cooperativeness. It would be foolish to suppose that there is no such thing as genuine, unreciprocated, and unrewarded altruism — surely there is. But note that there may be a real difference in the wider implications of acting from interest and acting from altruism when the "other" toward whom one is acting is a group rather than an individual. In Elster's argument, the point of motivating oneself in advance to behave in certain ways is generally to serve one's own interest by preventing akratic failures of will that would harm one's interest. Looking at the rewards of the moment, I might fail to cooperate with you now and thereby lose future benefits. Changing my character, with Elster and Pascal, or acting, with Descartes, from a general principle of cooperativeness would serve me better than my weak-willed calculations would. But my failure to cooperate in a large-number collective action is not likely to be merely the result of akrasia or weakness of will—it is most likely to be a genuinely self-serving action that makes me better off now and in the longer run. I may change my character to be altruistic or utilitarian enough to cooperate in large-number collective actions, but I cannot justify doing so on the grounds of my own interest.

As was true of Axelrod's analysis, it is also true of the arguments of Descartes on the one hand and of Elster and Pascal on the other that an understanding of dyadic iterated exchange relations does not yield us an analogous understanding of large-number iterated collective actions.

GROUP-LEVEL INTERACTIONS AND GENETIC EVOLUTION

It is important to note that Axelrod's so-called evolutionary model as discussed above is a strictly rational, not a genetic, model. Axelrod shows that the Tit-for-Tat strategy can become stably established even in a part of a larger community in which it is not generally followed. It becomes stable because people are rewarded for their dyadic cooperativeness, not because cooperators are more successful than others at passing on their genes. However, in work done with William D. Hamilton, Axelrod (1984, pp. 88–105) extends his analysis to biological evolution of cooperative traits that help to ensure survival even when specific acts of cooperation may well entail the risk of extinction for the individual cooperator. One might suppose that altruism in humans has evolved in this manner and that it would regulate cooperation not only in dyadic exchange relationships but also in large-number collective actions.

Consider the following sketchy argument. Almost all of an earlier, primitive generation's interactions might have been at the level of the extended family or small, interrelated tribe. Hence, generalized altruism might have been beneficial to group survival in general even while it was detrimental to any individual who happened into a relationship with an adversary tribe. What happens over the long run of evolutionary development is that those tribes which do evolve such a trait of altruism survive better than those which do not. Hence, selection at the level of the group produces a trait at the level of the individual. This remarkable result takes the sting out of the kin-selectionist prediction that I would lay down my life for two of my brothers or eight of my cousins. Why? Because it does not require that altruism be coded for genetic relationship. It can have been coded quite generally just because almost all actual relationships were, under the conditions of primitive social organization, between people who were genetically very closely related. If the trait were encoded for genetic relationship, it would, of course, yield a negligible motivation for me to act kindly toward someone from, say, the Sahel even if it yielded a very strong motivation for me to act kindly toward my son.

Generalization of the group-level evolution of the individual trait for altruism produces two problems, which should be kept analytically separate. First is the problem of our acting altruistically toward any and every other individual whom we might encounter. Second is the problem of our acting "altruistically" toward large groups as opposed to individuals.

Consider the first problem. Suppose we have inherited a trait for altruism from our tribal forebears. How would it motivate us in modern encounters with many strangers? Surely its working would be tempered by conflict with other genetically evolved traits such as, especially, that for seeking our own direct benefit. We could say that we are generally altruistic or cooperative but that our altruism is more likely to be overridden by our interest the less likely our altruism is to benefit us in return or the more likely it is to harm us. This result will be enhanced if our reason intervenes on the side of our interest. Hence, a genetically evolved trait for altruism need not have produced a society radically unlike those we actually know.

Elster (1979, p. 146) says, "Altruism, trust and solidarity are genuine phenomena that cannot be dissolved into ultra-subtle forms of self-interest." We may agree with him and still understand that quite unsubtle forms of self-interest can dominate altruistic motivations. Indeed, to see altruism as a genetically evolved trait on the sketch here is to see why it might be severely overridden by self-interest much of the time for the simple reason that a genetic explanation seems likely to yield a far stronger trait for self-interest than for altruism. Oddly, therefore, the genetic explanation of altruism may not lead us to embellish the rational account of dyadic cooperativeness by very much. That account might still be the one that dominates our understanding of social interaction at the dyadic level. Indeed, if our dealings with strangers seem to be radically less altruistic than our dealings with near associates, as they seem to be, we should sensibly conclude that it is rather a difference in interest than in altruism that motivates this difference in our dealings.

Now turn to the second problem above, the generalization of the genetic explanation of altruism from the dyadic to the large-number level, which is the problem that chiefly concerns us here. It would be a fallacy of composition to suppose without argument that the notion of altruism that fits dyadic and small-number interactions is the same as or has the properties of some notion of altruism that would apply to an individual's relationship to a large group. One might rather suppose that attitudes toward groups should simply be aggregations of attitudes toward individuals and that to speak of the "attitude toward a group" is merely a shorthand way of speaking of a relevant aggregation of attitudes toward the individuals in the group. This way of addressing our problem, however, reduces the motivation to be cooperative in a collective action to the motivation to be cooperative toward each of the other beneficiaries of the collective action. But this immediately suggests the following issue in the scope of the motivation of altruism.

Altruism might be provoked by anything from life-threatening conditions to minor conveniences. A genetic trait for dealing with the latter is unlikely to be selected at the level of the group as a guarantee for improved survival prospects. But my contribution to a collective action can seldom do more than add a little to the convenience of the lives of the other beneficiaries of my group's collective provision of some benefit. Hence it is unlikely that contributions to collective action can be seen as simply motivated by an unreasoning genetic trait for altruism.

This conclusion is only strengthened by the slightest realism in considering the role of reasoned calculation in contributing to collective actions. Clearly there are likely to be multifarious opportunities for beneficial collective action in any group. Which of these opportunities gets selected for action will determine whether my contribution to it will even make sense as an altruistic action toward each of my fellow group members. Hence, my supposedly altruistic actions cannot simply be instinctive — they must be mediated by active reason. But if they are mediated by reason they are unlikely to be analogous to altruistic actions in dyadic relationships. What Hume calls passion might be sufficient to move me to jump into the lake to rescue you as you flounder in the water; it will not be sufficient to move me to contribute a check or an hour's effort to our complex collective endeavor to elect a candidate or drain the mosquito infested marsh that abuts our property.

Oddly, in such contexts, passion might be sufficient to move me *not* to contribute because my general genetic instinct for securing my interests might be brought into play without any difficult prior reasoning about where my interests lie. Typically, if I am to behave altruistically toward all of the members of my group in a collective action problem, I will have to do so in the face of reasoned considerations about the problem and my interests. I may well behave altruistically, but my behavior cannot trivially be reduced to a genetic trait. Such behavior is likely in large part to be socially learned, not genetically inherited tout court.

In sum, the genetic explanation of cooperative behavior has the same problem that the rational explanation has. It can straightforwardly apply to dyadic or small-number interactions, but it cannot be simply generalized to apply to large-number Prisoner's Dilemmas or collective actions. If there is to be a genetic evolutionary explanation for altruism in collective action contexts, it will have to be more complicated than that for cooperativeness in dyadic relationships. One way we might proceed with such an explanation is to suppose that small acts of kindness, while they do not directly enhance survival prospects, do contribute to solidarity. Solidarity might then contribute to group survival. The crude quality of chauvinist urges might fit such a genetic explanation. But solidarity normally involves reinforcement through direct contact with group members, which generally means a small number of members in the group. Hence, it can work at large-group levels only through some kind of federated structure that allows relevant interactions to be at the small-group level. At that level, rational explanations of cooperativeness may be far more compelling than such indirect genetic explanations.

CONCLUDING REMARKS

In general it appears that the usual explanations for cooperativeness at the dyadic level do not readily translate into explanations for cooperativeness at the large-number level. Indeed, the self-interest explanation generally recommends against cooperativeness at the large-number level. Can cooperation in collective action then not be motivated? It can, in at least two ways: moral and rational. Morally, we can come through reason and intuition, perhaps based in sympathy, to count the interests of others along with our own when we act. For likely genetic reasons we can probably not expect people often to give anything approaching equal weight to the interests of others. Hence, moral explanations of behavior in most contexts will not generally override self-interest explanations or even, where they seem compelling, genetic explanations.

Self-interest might seem to rule out cooperation in collective action. However, all that has been shown above is that self-interest cannot work directly from the sanction of threatened defection by a group of cooperators in a collective action, as it can do for dyadic and very small-group iterated Prisoner's Dilemmas. But there are other bases for individual sanctions that can be used to motivate cooperation in collective actions. Most obviously, there is the possibility of being sanctioned by an outside agency, such as the state.

But even in purely voluntaristic contexts there may be sanctions available. In particular, members of a group that benefits from some collective provision can use withdrawal from dyadic exchange relations as a sanction against those who do not contribute to the group's collective action. Such withdrawal need not be irrational nor need it require moral motivation. One can use it at negligible loss to onself in those contexts in which there are alternative partners for the relevant kind of dyadic exchange. If all cooperating members of the group used this sanction against all non-cooperating members, the latter might suffer substantial losses while the former suffered only minor losses, so minor as to be outweighed by the prospect of converting the non-cooperators to cooperation. (Hardin, 1982a, pp. 195-97).

As with the genetic argument for solidarity above, this explanation of individual sanctioning for group benefit cannot easily generalize to very large groups unless the latter are organized federally to allow smaller-group interactions to govern the sanctioning of miscreants. It will also work best for collective actions that are iterated or ongoing so that the relevant learning can take place. Hence, again, we should not expect to see generalized cooperativeness in collective action but only specific cooperativeness in groups that have some history of interaction. Anomic cooperativeness in collective action, as well as in dyadic interaction, makes little sense on either genetic or rational models.

Biographical Notes

Contributors

ROBERT AXELROD is Professor of Political Science and Public Policy at the University of Michigan, Ann Arbor. His previous publications include *Conflict of Interest,* 1970, *Structure of Decision,* 1976, and *The Evolution of Cooperation,* 1984. His research interests cover several fields. In mathematical modeling he works with game theory and computer simulations. In international relations he is primarily interested in international security affairs and foreign policy formation. In cognitive processes he employs themes from limited rationality and artificial intelligence approaches. He is currently investigating the evolution of social and political norms.

DAVID BRAYBROOKE is Professor of Philosophy as well as of Political Science at Dalhousie University and has been active in both subjects. His books include *A Strategy of Decision* (with C.E. Lindblom), 1963; *Three Tests for Democracy,* 1968; *Traffic Congestion Goes Through the Issue Machine,* 1974; two works on the philosophy of social science, one published 1965, the other forthcoming; *Ethics in the World of Business,* 1983; and a forthcoming treatise on the concept of needs.

LAWRENCE H. DAVIS is an Associate Professor of Philosophy at the University of Missouri–St. Louis. He is the author of *Theory of Action,* in the Prentice-Hall *Foundations of Philosophy* series 1979, and a number of papers in action theory, philosophy of mind, and ethics. Currently he is doing research in philosophy of religion.

ELLERY EELLS is an Assistant Professor of Philosophy at the University of Wisconsin–Madison. His research interests include philosophy of science, the philosophical foundations of decision theory and probability theory, probabilistic causality, and inductive logic. He is author of *Rational Decision and Causality,* 1982, and several articles on decision theory, foundations of probability theory, and probabilistic causality.

DAVID GAUTHIER is Professor of Philosophy at the University of Pittsburgh. He is the author of *Practical Reasoning,* 1966, *The Logic of Leviathan,* 1969, and the forthcoming *Morals by Agreement,* as well as numerous articles. His principal research interest is in contractarian moral and political theory, from both systematic and historical perspectives. In his work he endeavours to combine the insights of Thomas Hobbes with the concepts of the theory of games.

ALLAN GIBBARD is Professor of Philosophy in the Department of Philosophy at the University of Michigan, Ann Arbor. He has written on a variety of subjects, chiefly in moral philosophy and the theory of social choice.

RUSSELL HARDIN is Professor of Political Science and Philosophy and Chair of the Committee on Public Policy Studies at the University of Chicago. He is the editor of *Ethics: An International Journal of Social, Political and Legal Theory* and the author of *Collective Action,* 1982. His current research is in the ethics and strategy of nuclear weapons policy and in rational choice and ethics. He is completing a book manuscript on "Morality Within the Limits of Reason."

WILLIAM L. HARPER is Professor of Philosophy at the University of Western Ontario. He is co-editor of *Ifs,* 1981. His research lies primarily in decision theory and the theory of rational belief change.

TERENCE HORGAN received his Ph.D. from the University of Michigan in 1974 and is now an Associate Professor of Philosophy at Memphis State University. Working primarily in metaphysics and the philosophy of mind, he has published numerous articles, among them: "The Case Against Events," *Philosophical Review,* 1978; "Action Theory Without Actions," *Mind,* 1981; "Supervenience and Microphysics," *Pacific Philosophical Quarterly,* 1982; and "Science Nominalized," *Philosophy of Science,* 1984. His primary current research interests include applying the concept of supervenience within metaphysics and philosophy of mind, and applying non-standard logico-grammatical devices as a means of defending a minimalist ontology.

FRANK JACKSON, who has held appointments at La Trobe University, the University of Adelaide, and SUNY at Buffalo, is currently Professor of Philosophy at Monash University. He is the author of *Perception,* 1977, and of articles on a number of topics, concentrating on the philosophy of mind, action and value, conditionals, and confirmation.

ISAAC LEVI is Professor of Philosophy at Columbia University. He is the author of *Gambling with Truth,* 1973, and *The Enterprise of Knowledge,* 1980. He has written many papers, a selection of which was recently collected in *Revisions and Decisions,* 1984. He is on the editorial board of *The Journal of Philosophy.* His work, together with the contributions of H. E. Kyburg, was the subject of a book edited by R. Bogdan in the *Profiles* series.

DAVID LEWIS teaches philosophy at Princeton University. He is the author of *Convention: A Philosophical Study,* 1969; *Counterfactuals,* 1973; *Philosophical Papers,* Vol. I, 1983, Vol. II, forthcoming; and *On the Plurality of Worlds,* forthcoming. His research interests fall principally in metaphysics, semantics, and philosophy of science.

EDWARD F. McCLENNEN, is an Associate Professor of Philosophy at Washington University, St. Louis. He is co-editor of a two-volume collection of papers, *Foundations and Applications of Decision Theory,* 1978, and author of numerous articles on topics in social ethics, decision theory, and game theory. He served in 1983–84 as Director of a Council for Philosophical Studies Institute on Public Choice Theory. He is currently working on a book on the foundations of decision and game theory, as well as a set of lectures on the history of ethical theory.

ROBERT NOZICK, Professor of Philosophy at Harvard University, has written on a wide range of topics. His major works are *Anarchy, State and Utopia,* 1974, which won a National Book Award, and *Philosophical Explanations,* 1981, which won the Ralph Waldo Emerson Award of Phi Beta Kappa. His current projects are writing his next book, *The Best Things in Life,* and making a series of televised discussions for The Public Broadcasting System.

ROBERT PARGETTER is at present Senior Lecturer, Department of Philosophy, La Trobe University and has written articles on laws, possible worlds, confirmation, other minds, and the problem of evil.

JORDAN HOWARD SOBEL is Professor of Philosophy at University of Toronto, and has held appointments at Wayne State University, Princeton University and UCLA. His principal fields of research are decision theory, ethics, and logic. Among his publications, "Utilitarianisms: Simple and General" and "The Need for Coercion" are particularly well-known.

JOHN WATKINS is Professor of Philosophy at the London School of Economics. Formerly President of the British Society for the Philosophy of Science (1972–5) and co-editor of *The British Journal for the Philosophy of Science,* 1974–9, he is author of *Hobbes's System of Ideas,* 1965, second edition 1973, and of *Freiheit und Entscheidung,* 1978, and of numerous articles in the fields of political philosophy, social philosophy, philosophy of social sciences, decision theory, human freedom, metaphysics, confirmation theory and epistemology. His main work, *Science and Scepticism,* is being published by Princeton University Press.

Editors

RICHMOND CAMPBELL is Professor of Philosophy at Dalhousie University where he has taught since 1968. He is the author of *Self-Love and Self-Respect: A Philosophical Study of Egoism,* 1979, and articles on ethics, epistemology, philosophy of science, and philosophy of mind. His most recent papers are "Novel Confirmation" with T. Vinci, *British Journal for the Philosophy of Science,* 1984, and "Sociobiology and the Possibility of Ethical Naturalism" in *Morality, Reason, and Truth,* edited by D. Copp and D. Zimmerman, 1985.

LANNING SOWDEN is currently a research fellow at the University of Melbourne. His recent work has been on decision theory and ethics.

Bibliography of Works Cited

Editors' note: For readers who want to explore some of the non-philosophical literature that bears on the issues addressed in this volume, we offer some brief advice. A good, non-technical introduction to game theory, with references to the political, economic, and psychological literature, may be found in Morton D. Davis (1973). A mathematical treatment of game theory and its applications across disciplines appears in Jones (1980). Game theory had its origin in work by a mathematician and an economist. The pioneering foundational text is von Neumann and Morgenstern (1944, 1947, 1953). An economist who has contributed significantly in showing the power of game theory as an analytical tool is Schelling (1960, 1973, 1978, and 1984). For examples of very recent work by economists in utility and risk theory, see Machina (1983) and the references there, and the collection edited by Stigum and Wenstop (1983). Readers who are especially interested in the use of game theory in political and social analysis should look at Howard (1971), Brams (1975a and 1976), and Ullmann-Margalit (1977), as well as the works in political and social theory cited in the essays above, such as Taylor (1976), Elster (1979) and Axelrod (1984). A general introduction to social and political applications is provided by Barry and Hardin (1982). That work is a useful collection of essays dealing with the implications of individual actions and preferences for determining social choices and includes commentary on Kenneth Arrow's Impossibility Theorem and the significance of the voting paradoxes. Many analytical and experimental studies have been done by psychologists on the applications of game theory, particularly on the Prisoner's Dilemma. See the classic studies of Luce and Raiffa (1957) and Rapoport (1960, with Chammah, 1965, and 1966). An overview and references to surveys of the early experimental studies of the Prisoner's Dilemma are provided in Rapoport (1974). Finally, for an example of a psychological study that has broad ramifications for decision theory and is currently much discussed in the literature, the reader should see Tversky and Kahneman (1981). The works mentioned in this note give, of course, only a very small sample from the enormous literature on game and decision theory that has appeared in the last fifty years. Applications of game theory have been extended to many disciplines, even to theology. (See Brams, 1983, for a discussion of the game-theoretic implications of omniscience, for example, in relation to Newcomb's Problem, omnipotence, immortality, and incomprehensibility.) The bibliography below contains the references suggested above and those cited in the essays.

Adams, E. (1976). *The Logic of Conditionals.* Boston: Reidel.

———, and R. Rosenkrantz (1980). "Applying the Jeffrey Decision Model to Rational Betting and Information Acquisition." *Theory and Decision* 12: 1–20.

Allais, M., and O. Hagen, eds. (1979). *Expected Utility and the Allais Paradox.* Dordrecht: Reidel.

Althusser, L., and E. Balibar (1968). *Lire le Capital.* Paris: Maspero.

Aranson, P.H. (1974). "Public Goods, Prisoners' Dilemmas, and the Theory of the State." Delivered at the 1974 Annual Meeting of the American Political Science Association (available now in the microfilmed proceedings: to be published).

Art, R.J. (1969). *The TFX Decision: McNamara and the Military.* Boston: Little, Brown.

Axelrod, R. (1980a). "Effective Choice in the Prisoner's Dilemma." *Journal of Conflict Resolution* 24: 3–25.

——— (1980b). "More Effective Choice in the Prisoner's Dilemma." *Journal of Conflict Resolution* 24: 379–403.

——— and W.D. Hamilton (1981a). "The Evolution of Cooperation." *Science* 211: 1390–96.

——— (1981b). "The Emergence of Cooperation Among Egoists." *American Political Science Review* 75: 306–318. Reprinted in this volume: 320–39.

——— (1984). *The Evolution of Cooperation.* New York: Basic Books.

Bar-Hillel, M., and A. Margalit (1972). "Newcomb's Paradox Revisited." *British Journal for the Philosophy of Science* 23: 295–304.

Barry, B.F., and R. Hardin, eds. (1982). *Rational Man and Irrational Society?* Beverly Hills: Sage.

Black, M. (1978). "The 'Prisoner's Dilemma' and the Limits of Rationality." *International Studies in Philosophy* 10: 7–22.

Blom, J.L. (1978). *Descartes: His Moral Philosophy and Psychology.* New York: New York University Press.

Bogue, A.G., and M.P. Marlaire (1975). "Of Mess and Men: The Boardinghouse and Congressional Voting, 1821–1842." *American Journal of Political Science* 19: 207–30.

Bolker, E.D. (1967). "A Simultaneous Axiomatization of Utility and Subjective Probability." *Philosophy of Science* 34: 330–40.

Brams, S.J. (1975a). *Game Theory and Politics.* New York: Macmillan.

———(1975b). "Newcomb's Problem and Prisoner's Dilemma." *Journal of Conflict Resolution* 19: 596–612.

———(1976). *Paradoxes in Politics.* New York: Macmillan.

———(1983). *Superior Beings; If They Exist How Would We Know?* New York: Springer-Verlag.

Brandt, R. (1959). *Ethical Theory.* New Jersey: Prentice Hall.

Braybrooke, D. (1974). "The Social Contract Returns, This Time as an Elusive Public Good." Presented to the American Political Science Association at its meeting in Chicago, 29 August–2 September, 1974.

———(1976). "The Insoluble Problem of the Social Contract." *Dialogue* 15: 3–37. Reprinted in this volume: 277–306.

Cargile, J. (1975). "Newcomb's Paradox." *British Journal for the Philosophy of Science* 26: 234–39.

Cartwright, N. (1979). "Causal Laws and Effective Strategies." *Nous* 4: 419–37.

Davis, L. H. (1977). "Prisoners, Paradox, and Rationality." *American Philo-sophical Quarterly* 14: 319–27. Reprinted in this volume: 45–59.

———(1985). "Is the Symmetry Argument Valid?" This volume 255–63.

Davis, M. (1970, 1973). *Game Theory: A Nontechnical Introduction.* New York: Basic Books.

Dawkins, R. (1976). *The Selfish Gene.* New York: Oxford University Press.

Domotor, Z. (1978). "Axiomatizing the Logic of Decision." In C. A. Hooker, J. J. Leach, and E. F. McClennen, eds., *Foundations and Applications of Decision Theory* 1: 227–31. Dordrecht: Reidel

Darwall, S. L. (1983). *Impartial Reason.* Ithaca, NY: Cornell University Press.

Durkheim (1902). *De la division du travail social.* Paris: Alcan.

Eells, E. (1981). "Causality, Utility, and Decision." *Synthese* 48: 295–329.

———(1982). *Rational Decision and Causality.* Cambridge and New York: Cambridge University Press.

———, and E. Sober (1983). "Probabilistic Causality and the Question of Trans-itivity." *Philosophy of Science* 50: 35–57.

———(1984a). "Newcomb's Many Solutions," *Theory and Decision* 16: 59–105.

———(1984b). "Metatickles and the Dynamics of Deliberation." *Theory and De-cision* 17: 71–95.

———(1985a). "Causation, Decision, and Newcomb's Paradox." This volume: 183–213.

———(1985b). "Reply to Jackson and Pargetter." This volume: 219–23.

———(1985c). "Causal Decision Theory." *Proceedings of the 1984 Biennial Meeting of the Philosophy of Science Association,* Vol. 2, forthcoming.

———(1985d). "Levi's 'The Wrong Box'." *Journal of Philosophy* 82: 91–104.

———, and E. Sober (forthcoming). "Common Causes and Decision Theory." *Philosophy of Science.*

Ellsberg, D. (1961). "Risk, Ambiguity, and the Savage Axioms." *Quarterly Jour-nal of Economics* 75: 643–69.

Elster, J. (1978). *Logic and Society: Contradictions and Possible Worlds.* New York: Wiley.

———(1979). *Ulysses and the Sirens.* Cambridge: Cambridge University Press.

———(1982). "Sour Grapes — Utilitarianism and the Genesis of Wants," in Amartya Sen and Ben Williams, eds., *Utilitarianism and Beyond.* Cambridge: Cambridge University Press.

Fine, K. (1975). Critical Review of D. Lewis's *Counterfactuals. Mind* 84: 451–58.

Fisher, R. A. (1959a). *Statistical Methods and Scientific Inference.* 2nd revised edition. NewYork: Hafner.

———(1959b). *Smoking: The Cancer Controversy, Some Attempts to Assess the Controversy.* Edinburgh: Oliver and Boyd.

———(1974). *Collected Papers.* J. H. Bennett, ed. Adelaide: University of Ade-laide.

Gauthier, D. (1974). "Rational Cooperation." *Nous* 8: 53–65.

———(1975). "Reason and Maximization." *Canadian Journal of Philosophy* 4: 411–33.

———(1984). "Deterrence, Maximization, and Rationality." *Ethics* 94: 474–95.

———(1985a). *Morals by Agreement.* Oxford: Clarendon Press. Forthcoming.

———(1985b). "Maximization Constrained: The Rationality of Cooperation."

Sections 2 and 3 (abridged) of Chapter 6 in *Morals by Agreement*. Reprinted in this volume 75–93.

————(1985c). "Bargaining, and Justice." *Social Philosophy and Policy*. Forthcoming.

Gibbard, A. (1971). "Utilitarianism and Coordination." Unpublished Doctoral Dissertation. Harvard University.

————, and Harper, W. L. (1978). "Counterfactuals and Two Kinds of Expected Utility." In C. A. Hooker, J. J. Leach, and E. F. McClennen, eds., *Foundations and Applications of Decision Theory* 1: 125–62. Dordrecht: Reidel. Reprinted (abridged) in this volume: 133–58.

————(1979). "Decision Matrices and Instrumental Expected Utility." Paper presented to a conference at the University of Pittsburg.

Gillespie, N. (forthcoming). "The Dynamics of Deliberation in Complex Cases."

Grofman, B. (1975). "A Comment on 'Newcomb's Problem and the Prisoner's Dilemma'." Manuscript.

Hamilton, W. D. (1964). "The Genetical Theory of Social Behavior (I and II)." *Journal of Theoretical Biology* 7: 1–16, 17–32.

————(1967). "Extraordinary Sex Ratios." *Science* 156: 477–88.

Hammond, P. (1976). "Changing Tastes and Coherent Dynamic Choice." *Review of Economic Studies*. 43: 159–73.

————(1982a). "Utilitarianism, Uncertainty, and Information." In A. Sen and B. Williams, eds., *Utilitarianism and Beyond*. Cambridge: Cambridge University Press.

————(1982b). "Consequentialism and Rationality in Dynamic Choice Under Uncertainty." *Economics Technical Report No. 387*. Institute for Mathematical Studies in the Social Sciences, Stanford University.

Hardin, G. (1968). "The Tragedy of the Commons." *Science* 162: 1243–48.

Hardin, R. (1971). "Collective Action as an Agreeable *n*-Prisoner's Dilemma." *Behavioral Science* 16: 472–81.

————(1982a). *Collective Action*. Baltimore, MD.: Johns Hopkins University Press for Resources for the Future.

————(1982b). "Exchange Theory on Strategic Bases." *Social Science Information* 21: 251–72.

————(1985). "Individual Sanctions, Collective Benefits." This volume: 339–54.

Harper, W. L., R. Stalnaker, and G. Pearce, eds. (1981). *Ifs*. Dordrecht: Reidel.

Harsanyi, J. C. (1961). "On the Rationality Postulates Underlying the Theory of Cooperative Games." *Journal of Conflict Resolution* 5: 179–96.

————(1962). "Rationality Postulates for Bargaining Solutions in Cooperative and Non Cooperative Games." *Management Science* 9: 141–53.

Hinckley, B. (1972). "Coalitions in Congress: Size and Ideological Distance." *Midwest Journal of Political Science* 26: 197–207.

Hirshleifer, J. (1978). "Natural Economy versus Political Economy."*Journal of Social and Biological Structures* 1: 319–37.

Hobbes, Thomas (1642). *De Cive* or *the Citizen*.

———— (1651). *Leviathan*.

Hooker, C. A., J. J. Leach, and E. F. McClennen, eds. (1978). *Foundations and Applications of Decision Theory*. Dordrecht: Reidel.

Horgan, T. (1979). "'Could', Possible Worlds, and Moral Responsibility." *Southern*

Journal of Philosophy 17: 345–58.

———(1981). "Counterfactuals and Newcomb's Problem." *Journal of Philosophy* 78: 331–56. Reprinted in this volume: 159–82.

———(1985). "Newcomb's Problem: A Stalemate." This volume 223–34.

Howard, N. (1971). *Paradoxes of Rationality: Theory of Metagames and Political Behavior.* Cambridge, MA: MIT Press.

Hubin, D., and G. Ross (forthcoming). "Newcomb's Perfect Predictor." *Nous.*

Hume, David (1739–40). *A Treatise of Human Nature.*

———(1751). *An Enquiry Concerning the Principles of Morals.*

———(1777). "Of the Original Contract." *Essays and Treatises on Several Subjects.* London: Cadell.

Jackson, F., and R. Pargetter (1983, 1985). "Where the Tickle Defense Goes Wrong." *Australasian Journal of Philosophy* 61 (1983): 295–99. Reprinted in this volume with postscript: 214–19.

Jeffrey, R. C. (1965). *The Logic of Decision.* New York: McGraw-Hill.

———(1977). "Axiomatizing the Logic of Decision." In C. A. Hooker, J. J. Leach, and E. F. McClennen, eds., *Foundations and Applications of Decision Theory* 1: 227–31. Dordrecht: Reidel.

———(1981a). "Choice, Chance and Credence." In G. H. von Wright and G. Floistad, eds., *Philosophy of Language/Philosophical Logic.* The Hague: Nijhoff.

———(1981b). "The Logic of Decision Defended." *Synthese* 48: 473–92.

———(1983). *The Logic of Decision.* 2nd edition. Chicago and London: University of Chicago Press.

Jervis, R. (1978). "Cooperation under the Security Dilemma." *World Politics* 30: 167–214.

Jones, A. J. (1980). *Game Theory: Mathematical Models of Conflict.* New York: Wiley.

Jones, C. O. (1977). "Will Reform Change Congress?" In Lawrence C. Dodd and Bruce I. Oppenheimer, eds., *Congress Reconsidered.* New York: Praeger.

Korner, S., ed. (1974). *Practical Reason.* Oxford: Blackwell.

Kurz, M. (1977). "Altruistic Equilibrium." In B. Balassa and R. Nelson eds., *Economic Progress, Private Values, and Public Policy.* Amsterdam: North Holland.

Kyburg, H. (1974). *Logical Foundations of Statistical Inference.* Dordrecht: Reidel.

———(1980). "Acts and Conditional Probability." *Theory and Decision* 12: 149–71.

Laver, M. (1977). "Intergovernmental Policy on Multinational Corporations, A Simple Model of Tax Bargaining." *European Journal of Political Research* 5: 363–80.

Levi, I. (1974). "On Indeterminate Probabilities." *Journal of Philosophy.* 71: 391–418.

———(1975). "Newcomb's Many Problems." *Theory and Decision* 6: 161–75.

———(1980). *The Enterprise of Knowledge.* Cambridge, MA: MIT Press.

———(1982). "A Note on Newcombmania." *Journal of Philosophy* 79: 337–82.

———(1983). "The Wrong Box." *Journal of Philosophy.* 80: 534–42.

———(1985a). "Epicycles." *Journal of Philosophy* 82: 104–6.

———(1985b). "Common Causes, Smoking, and Lung Cancer." This volume: 234–47.

Lévi-Strauss, C. (1949). *Les structures elementaires de la parente.* Paris: P.U.F.

Lewis, D. (1972). "Utilitarianism and Truthfulness." *Australasian Journal of Philosophy* 50: 17–19.

———(1973a). *Counterfactuals.* Cambridge, MA: Harvard University Press.

———(1973b). "Causation." *Journal of Philosophy* 70: 556–67.

———(1976a). "The Paradoxes of Time Travel." *American Philosophical Quarterly* 13: 145–52.

———(1976b). "Probabilities of Conditionals and Conditional Probabilities." *Philosophical Review* 85: 297–315.

———(1979a). "Prisoners' Dilemma Is a Newcomb Problem." *Philosophy and Public Affairs* 8: 235–40. Reprinted in this volume: 251–55.

———(1979b). "Counterfactual Dependence and Time's Arrow." *Nous* 13: 455–76.

———(1981). "Causal Decision Theory." *Australasian Journal of Philosophy* 59: 5–30.

———(1983). "Levi against U-Maximization." *Journal of Philosophy* 80: 531–34.

Locke, John (1690). *Second Treatise of Government.*

Luce, R. D., and H. Raiffa (1957). *Games and Decisions.* New York: Wiley.

Lumsden, M. (1973). "The Cyprus Conflict as a Prisoner's Dilemma." *Journal of Conflict Resolution* 17: 7–32.

Machina, M. (1983). "The Economic Theory of Individual Behaviour Toward Risk: Theory, Evidence, and New Directions." *Economics Technical Report No. 433.* Institute for Mathematical Studies in the Social Sciences. Stanford University.

Mackie, J. L. (1973). "The Disutility of Act-Utilitarianism." *Philosophical Quarterly* 23: 289–300.

———(1977). "Newcomb's Paradox and the Direction of Causation." *Canadian Philosophical Review* 7: 213–225.

McClennen, E. (1983). "Sure Thing Doubts." In B. Stigum and F. Wenstop, eds., *Foundations of Utility and Risk Theory with Applications.* Dordrecht: Reidel.

———(1985). "Prisoner's Dilemma and Resolute Choice." This volume: 94–104.

MacLean, D., ed. (1984). *The Security Gamble: Deterrence Dilemmas in the Nuclear Age.* Totowa, NJ: Roman and Allanheld.

Macneil, I. R. (1974). "Restatement (Second) of Contracts and Presentations." *Virginia Law Review* 60: 589–610.

———(1980). *The New Social Contract.* New Haven, CT: Yale University Press.

Matthews, D. R. (1960). *U.S. Senators and Their World.* Chapel Hill: University of North Carolina Press.

Maugham, S. (1934). *Sheppey.* New York: Doubleday.

Mayer, M. (1974). *The Bankers.* New York: Ballantine.

Mayhew, D. R. (1975). *Congress: The Electoral Connection.* New Haven, CT: Yale University Press.

Maynard Smith, J., and R. Price (1973). "The Logic of Animal Conflict." *Nature* 246: 15–18.

———(1974). "The Theory of Games and the Evolution of Animal Conflict." *Journal of Theoretical Biology* 47: 209–21.

———(1978). "The Evolution of Behavior." *Scientific American* 239: 176–92.

Nagel, T. (1970). *The Possibility of Altruism.* Oxford: Oxford University Press.

Nash, J.F. (1951). "Non-cooperative Games." *Annals of Mathematics* 54: 286–95.
Nozick, R. (1963). "The Normative Theory of Individual Choice." Unpublished Doctoral Dissertation. Princeton University.
———(1969). "Newcomb's Problem and Two Principles of Choice." In Nicholas Rescher, ed., *Essays in Honor of Carl G. Hempel*. Dordrecht: Reidel. Reprinted (abridged) in this volume: 107–33.
O'Hara, J. (1934). *Appointment in Samarra*. NY: Random House.
Olin, D. (1976). "Newcomb's Problem: Further Investigations." *American Philosophical Quarterly* 13: 129–33.
———(1978). "Newcomb's Problem, Dominance, and Expected Utility." In C. A. Hooker, J. J. Leach, and E. F. McClennen, eds., *Foundations and Applications of Decision Theory* 1: 227–31. Dordrecht: Reidel.
Olson, M., Jr. (1965). *The Logic of Collective Action*. Cambridge, MA: Harvard University Press.
Ornstein, N., R. L. Peabody, and D. W. Rhode (1977). "The Changing Senate: From the 1950s to the 1970s." In L. C. Dodd and B. I. Oppenheimer, eds., *Congress Reconsidered*. New York: Praeger.
Parfit, D. (1984). "The Self-Interest Theory." In *Reasons and Persons*. Oxford: Clarendon Press.
Patterson, S. (1978). "The Semi-Sovereign Congress." In A. King (ed.), *The New American Political System*. Washington, DC: American Enterprise Institute.
Polsby, N. (1968). "The Institutionalization of the U.S. House of Representatives." *American Political Science Review* 62: 144–68.
Raiffa, H. (1968). *Decision Analysis*. Reading, MA: Addison-Wesley.
Rapoport, A. (1960). *Fights, Games, and Debates*. Ann Arbor: University of Michigan.
———, and C. Orwant (1964). "Experimental Games: A Review." In M. Shubik, ed., *Game Theory and Related Approaches to Social Behavior*. New York: Wiley.
———, and A. M. Chammah (1965). *Prisoner's Dilemma — A Study in Conflict and Cooperation*. Ann Arbor: University of Michigan.
———(1966). *Two-Person Game Theory*. Ann Arbor: Michigan University.
———(1974). "Prisoner's Dilemma — Recollections and Observations." In Rapoport, ed., *Game Theory as a Theory of Conflict Resolution*, pp. 18–34. Dordrecht: Reidel.
———(1975). "Comment on Brams's Discussion of Newcomb's Paradox." *Journal of Conflict Resolution* 19: 4.
Rawls, J. (1971). *A Theory of Justice*. Cambridge, MA: Harvard University.
Rousseau, Jean-Jacques (1762). *Du contrat social*.
Savage, L. J. (1954, 1972). *The Foundations of Statistics*. New York: Dover.
Schelling, T. C. (1960). *The Strategy of Conflict*. Cambridge, MA: Harvard University Press.
———(1973). "Hockey Helmets, Concealed Weapons, and Daylight Savings: A Study of Binary Choices with Externalities." *Journal of Conflict Resolution* 17: 381–428.
———(1978). "Micromotives and Macrobehavior." In T. Schelling, ed., *Micromotives and Microbehavior*. New York: Norton. pp. 9–43.

————(1984). *Choice and Consequence.* Cambridge, MA: Harvard University Press.

Schlesinger (1974). "The Unpredictability of Free Choices." *British Journal for the Philosophy of Science* 25: 209–21.

Segerberg, K. (1979). "Epistemic Considerations in Game Theory." *Theory and Decision* 11: 363–73.

Sen, A. (1974a). "Choice, Orderings and Morality." In S. Korner, ed., *Practical Reason.* Oxford: Blackwell.

————(1974b). "Reply to Comments." In S. Korner, ed., *Practical Reason.* Oxford: Blackwell.

Shubik, M. (1959). *Strategy and Market Structure: Competition, Oligopoly, and the Theory of Games.* New York: Wiley.

————, ed. (1964). *Game Theory and Related Approaches to Social Behavior.* New York: Wiley.

————(1970). "Game Theory, Behavior, and the Paradox of the Prisoner's Dilemma: Three Solutions." *Journal of Conflict Resolution* 14: 181–94.

Simmel, G. (1955). "The Web of Group-Afflictions." R. Bendix, trans., *Conflict: The Web of Group Afflictions.* Glencoe, IL: The Free Press. *Philosophie des Geldes* 5th ed., Berlin: Duncker & Humblot, 1930.

Skyrms, B. (1980a). *Causal Necessity: A Pragmatic Investigation of the Necessity of Laws.* New Haven, CT: Yale University.

————(1980b). "The Role of Causal Factors in Rational Decision." *Causal Necessity.* New Haven, CT: Yale University.

————(1982). "Causal Decision Theory." *Journal of Philosophy* 79: 695–711.

Smith, M. B. (1906). *The First Forty Years of Washington Society.* New York: Scribner's.

Snyder, G. H. (1971). "'Prisoner's Dilemma' and 'Chicken' Models in International Politics." *International Studies Quarterly* 15: 66–103.

Sobel, J. H. (1970). "Utilitarianisms: Simple and General." *Inquiry* 13: 394–449.

————(1972). "The Need for Coercion." In J. R. Pennock and J. W. Chapman, eds., *Coercion: Nomos XIV.* Chicago and New York: Aldine & Atherton.

————(1975). "Interaction Problems for Utility Maximizers." *Canadian Journal of Philosophy* 4: 677–88.

————(1976). "Utility Maximizers in Iterated Prisoner's Dilemmas." *Dialogue* 15: 38–53. Reprinted in this volume: 306–19.

————(1978). *Chance, Choice and Action: Newcomb's Problem Resolved.* Manuscript.

————(1985). "Not Every Prisoner's Dilemma Is a Newcomb Problem." This volume: 263–74.

————(forthcoming). "Circumstances and Dominance Arguments in a Causal Decision Theory." *Synthese.*

Sowden, L. (1984). "The Inadequacy of Bayesian Decision Theory." *Philosophical Studies* 45: 293–313.

Stalnaker, R. (1968). "A Theory of Conditionals." In *Studies in Logical Theory.* American Philosophical Quarterly Monograph Series, No. 2.

————, and R. Thomason (1970). "A Semantic Analysis of Conditional Logic." *Theoria* 36: 23–42.

————(1972/1981). A letter to David Lewis in W. L. Harper, R. Stalnaker, and G. Pearce, eds. *Ifs*. Dordrecht: Reidel.

Stern, C. (1981). "Lewis's Counterfactual Analysis of Causation." *Synthese* 48: 333–45.

Taylor, M. (1976). *Anarchy and Cooperation*. New York: Wiley.

Thaler, R. H., and H. M. Shefrin (1981). "An Economic Theory of Self Control." *Journal of Political Economy* 89: 392–406.

Trivers, R. L. (1971). "The Evolution of Reciprocal Altruism." *Quarterly Review of Biology* 46: 35–57.

Tversky, A., and D. Kahneman (1981). "The Framing of Decisions and the Psychology of Choice." *Science* 211: 453–58.

Tullock, G. (1971). "The Paradox of Revolution." *Public Choice* 11: 89–99.

Ullman-Margalit, E. (1977). *The Emergence of Norms*. Oxford: Clarendon Press.

Von Neumann, J., and O. Morgenstern (1944, 1947, 1953). *Theory of Games and Economic Behavior*. Princeton: Princeton University.

Warner, R., (trans.) (1960). *War Commentaries of Caesar*. New York: New American Library.

Watkins, J. (1970). "Imperfect Rationality." In R. Borger and F. Cioffi, eds., *Explanation in the Behavioural Sciences*. Cambridge: Cambridge University Press.

————(1974). "Comment: Self-Interest and Morality." In S. Korner, ed., *Practical Reason*. Oxford: Blackwell.

————(1985). "Second Thoughts on Self-Interest and Morality." This volume: 59–74.

Wilson, D. S. (1979). *Natural Selection of Populations and Communities*. Menlo Park, CA: Benjamin/Cummings.

Yaari, Menahem E. (1977). "Endogenous Changes in Tastes: A Philosophical Study," *Erkenntnis* 11: 157–96.

Young, J. S. (1966). *The Washington Community, 1800–1828*. New York: Harcourt, Brace & World.